Classic Horror Films
and the Literature
That Inspired Them

ALSO BY RON BACKER

Mystery Movie Series of 1930s Hollywood
(McFarland, 2012)

Mystery Movie Series of 1940s Hollywood
(McFarland, 2010)

Classic Horror Films and the Literature That Inspired Them

Ron Backer

McFarland & Company, Inc., Publishers
Jefferson, North Carolina

LIBRARY OF CONGRESS CATALOGUING-IN-PUBLICATION DATA

Backer, Ron, 1951–
　　Classic horror films and the literature that inspired them / Ron Backer.
　　　　p.　cm.
　　Includes bibliographical references and index.

　　ISBN 978-0-7864-9896-3 (softcover : acid free paper) ∞
　　ISBN 978-1-4766-2021-3 (ebook)

　　1. Horror films—History and criticism.　2. Horror tales—Film adaptations.　3. Horror tales, American—19th century—History and criticism.　4. Horror tales, English—19th century—History and criticism.　5. Horror tales, American—20th century—History and criticism.　6. Horror tales, English—20th century—History and criticism.　I. Title.

PN1995.9.H6B23 2015
791.43'6164—dc23   2015012072

BRITISH LIBRARY CATALOGUING DATA ARE AVAILABLE

© 2015 Ron Backer. All rights reserved

No part of this book may be reproduced or transmitted in any form or by any means, electronic or mechanical, including photocopying or recording, or by any information storage and retrieval system, without permission in writing from the publisher.

On the cover: poster art from *Bride of Frankenstein*, 1935 (Universal Pictures/Photofest)

Printed in the United States of America

McFarland & Company, Inc., Publishers
　Box 611, Jefferson, North Carolina 28640

For my father

Table of Contents

Introduction	1
1. *Frankenstein* by Mary Shelley	3
2. "The Tell-Tale Heart" by Edgar Allan Poe	27
3. "The Queen of Spades" by Alexander Pushkin	36
4. *The Strange Case of Dr. Jekyll and Mr. Hyde* by Robert Louis Stevenson	43
5. *Dracula* and "Dracula's Guest" by Bram Stoker	62
6. *The Phantom of the Opera* by Gaston Leroux	89
7. *The Magician* by W. Somerset Maugham	103
8. "The Fall of the House of Usher" by Edgar Allan Poe	109
9. "Spurs" by Tod Robbins	120
10. *The Island of Dr. Moreau* by H.G. Wells	126
11. *The Invisible Man* by H.G. Wells	137
12. "The Black Cat," "Morella" and "The Facts in the Case of M. Valdemar" by Edgar Allan Poe	145
13. *Black Moon* by Clements Ripley	156
14. "The Raven" by Edgar Allan Poe	162
15. *The Hands of Orlac* by Maurice Renard	169
16. *Burn Witch Burn!* by Abraham Merritt	176
17. "The Devil and Daniel Webster" by Stephen Vincent Benét	186
18. *The Edge of Running Water* by William Sloane	192
19. *The Undying Monster* by Jessie Douglas Kerruish	200

20. *Uneasy Freehold* by Dorothy Macardle	207
21. "The Body Snatcher" by Robert Louis Stevenson	214
22. *The Picture of Dorian Gray* by Oscar Wilde	221
23. "Casting the Runes" by M.R. James	228
24. *Carmilla* by Sheridan Le Fanu	234
25. *The Werewolf of Paris* by Guy Endore	244
26. *The Turn of the Screw* by Henry James	251
27. *Conjure Wife* by Fritz Leiber	257
28. "The Birds" by Daphne du Maurier	263
29. "The Case of Charles Dexter Ward" by H.P. Lovecraft	271
30. *The Haunting of Hill House* by Shirley Jackson	278
31. "The Family of the Vourdalak" by Aleksei Tolstoy	287
32. "The Masque of the Red Death" by Edgar Allan Poe	296
33. "The Viy" by Nikolai Gogol	302
34. *Rosemary's Baby* by Ira Levin	308
35. *The Devil Rides Out* by Dennis Wheatley	314
36. "Don't Look Now" by Daphne du Maurier	321
37. *The Exorcist* by William Peter Blatty	326
38. *Ritual* by David Pinner	333
39. *Carrie* by Stephen King	340
40. *The Shining* by Stephen King	348
Bibliography	355
Index	357

Introduction

As far back as I can remember, I have been an avid horror film fan and an avid reader of just about every type of literature. Nevertheless, I seldom read any horror novels or short stories, except, of course, for Mary Shelley's *Frankenstein* and Bram Stoker's *Dracula*. (I read those two classics when I was young and, like many others, I was disappointed in the former and thrilled by the latter.) Thus, when I conceived of the idea of writing a book about horror films and the literature that inspired them, I was surprised to learn how many classic horror films were based on works of literature. Who knew?

Most of the novels and short stories that are covered in this book were first-time reads for me, including some well-known classics of the literature of horror, such as Robert Louis Stevenson's *Dr. Jekyll and Mr. Hyde*, Oscar Wilde's *The Picture of Dorian Gray* and Shirley Jackson's *The Haunting of Hill House*. What a delight to read quality stories such as these for the first time! How did I ever miss them all these years? In addition, I read some obscure works of horror which turned out to be surprisingly entertaining, such as "The Queen of Spades" by Alexander Pushkin, *Burn Witch Burn!* by Abraham Merritt and *The Edge of Running Water* by William Sloane. Is there anything more exhilarating than picking up a book or a short story with little expectation of reading something good, and then being blown away by how marvelous the story is? I also took the opportunity to re-read *Frankenstein* and *Dracula*, finally appreciating the quality of the former while still being thrilled by the latter.

As I was writing this book, I was never entirely certain in my own mind as to whether the book was primarily about literature or primarily about film. I finally concluded that the book was equally about both. After reading the short stories and novels from which they were adapted, I acquired a better understanding and appreciation of the horror films I love. After viewing the horror films that were inspired by them, I also came to better appreciate some excellent works of literature. There is a true symbiotic relationship in experiencing the same tale of horror in two different forms of art.

This book is not a catalogue of the similarities and differences between works of literature and the films based upon them. If that were all this book aimed to do, several charts would have been sufficient. Rather, I have tried to characterize, criticize and analyze the interrelationships between the two forms of art to better appreciate them both. It is my hope that other avid horror film fans will take the time to read some of the literature that inspired many of the classic horror films. I believe they will be pleasantly surprised by those reading experiences, just as I was.

The scope of this book is clearly set forth in its title. This book is about horror films and horror literature, not about old dark houses, serial killers, insanity or imagined events. To qualify for inclusion in this book, there must be something of the supernatural, monstrous or the mystic in the narrative, i.e., something that is not found in real life. Unfortunately, horror abounds in real life, but for this book I am talking about the realm of imagination only.

In all, there are 43 works of literature addressed in this book, including novels, short stories, novellas and even a poem, resulting in a discussion of 62 movies in the category of horror films. Whether one reads the literature first and then views the film, or if it one reverses that order, there is much enjoyment, and even horror, to be found in these classics of the genre.

CHAPTER 1

Frankenstein by Mary Shelley

The beginnings of *Frankenstein* were conceived in the summer of 1816, when Mary Godwin (Shelley) and Percy Shelley, along with Percy's physician, John Polidori, visited Switzerland. There they became the neighbors of George Gordon Byron, better known as Lord Byron. Byron was a well-known romantic poet of his day, as was Percy Shelley. It was a rainy summer and the incessant rain kept the group indoors for many days. One night they read a volume of ghost stories and at Lord Byron's suggestion, each of them agreed to write his or her own horror story. Several days later, Mary dreamed the story of a man who created life, which she eventually turned into her novel, *Frankenstein*. ("The Vampyre" [1819] by John Polidori, another famous horror story of its day, can also trace its beginnings to that same night.)

Mary Shelley's novel was first published in 1818, when Mary was only 20 years old. Almost 200 years since its publication, *Frankenstein* by Mary Shelley is still one of the most significant literary influences on the cinema of horror.

Background

Mary Shelley was born on August 30, 1797, in London, England. She passed away on February 1, 1851, at the age of 53. Although now almost completely forgotten, Mary wrote books both before and after *Frankenstein*, mostly fiction, but two of which were stories of her travels. (Mary's interest in travel can be seen in her most famous novel, which, at times, seems like a travelogue.) She also wrote short stories and other nonfiction. In 1831, Mary revised *Frankenstein* somewhat for inclusion in Bentley's Standard Novels, a popular series of inexpensively published books. Mary also wrote a new introduction to the novel, in which she detailed the story of the genesis of the famous work on that rainy night in 1816. The 1831 edition of *Frankenstein* is the edition of the book that is most widely read today.

The Literature

Those people who come to the novel *Frankenstein* after viewing the 1931 film version or one of the many remakes, and that is the order in which most people will currently become acquainted with the novel, will be disappointed by the lack of a significant horror element to the narrative. *Frankenstein* is primarily a philosophical novel. It is also a tale of personal triumph, defeat, revenge and ultimate tragedy on the part of Dr. Frankenstein and a tale of birth, maturation, character change, revenge and ultimate tragedy on the part of the monster.

The novel starts out with a framing story in a series of letters written by Captain Robert Walton to his sister back in England. Walton is leading a seafaring expedition to the frozen north but his ship has become stuck in ice. One day Walton sees from a distance a creature of gigantic stature riding a sledge team and then later a man half dead on another team. The latter person, Victor Frankenstein, is brought on board Walton's ship and after some revival of his health, relates a strange tale to Walton about his creation of a living being with a hideous face, the creature's attempts to interact with society, the murderous activities of the creature including the killing of Victor's wife Elizabeth and Victor's pursuit of the monster across Europe and now to the Arctic Circle. After relating the story of the monster to Walton, Victor, still weak from the pursuit and the agony of his life, passes away. The monster comes on board the ship, sees that he has finally ended Victor's life, and tells Walton that he intends to die also. As the narrative ends, the creature disappears into the distance and the darkness.

A brief synopsis of a novel tends to highlight the plot and disregard the style of the writing and the many scenes from the book that are not directly relevant to the main plot. Thus, the above summary of *Frankenstein* seems to imply that the book has a strong central plot which emphasizes its elements of horror. That is not, in fact, the case. Shelley writes in the style of her era, employing unfamiliar words, inserting literary references into the novel that may escape even the most knowledgeable of readers and writing in long and complex sentences. Much of the novel is spent with the internal thoughts of the characters and the anguish they are suffering, rather than on action sequences. Between the important plot moments, Shelley digresses with details of trips taken by the characters, family histories and literary allusions. The horror elements of *Frankenstein* are seemingly deliberately downplayed by Shelley, especially for those who come to the novel after the films.

The reader learns little about how Victor amassed the materials for his creature, other than a brief mention of visits to the charnel houses, dissecting rooms and slaughter houses. Victor gives no explanation as to how he created the creature and there is no significant laboratory scene showing how Victor breathed life into his creation. Victor merely says, in Chapter V, "It was on a dreary night of November that I beheld the accomplishment of my toils. With an anxiety that almost amounted to agony, I collected the instruments of life around me, that I might infuse a spark of being into the lifeless thing that lay at my feet." That is just about all that Shelley writes of the conception of Victor's living being. Even the later killings by the monster are not described in detail; they are usually related in retrospect.

Thus, a reader who is expecting to read a shocking and horrific story of the creation of a hideous monster and its murderous rampages will be sorely disappointed. However, that expectation comes from the horror films about Frankenstein's monster and not from any realistic prospects about the book itself. The initial power of the novel comes, in part, from the idea of creating a hideous monster and challenging God about life itself, but the novel's staying power comes mainly from the issues raised by Shelley in her work and the manner in which Shelley handles them.

In the almost 200 years since Mary Shelley's novel was first published, literary critics and academicians have ascribed many themes to the book, including parental responsibility, homosexuality, incest, feminism and loss of identity. Nevertheless, for the more literal of readers, such as your author, there appear to be two primary themes in the book.

One relates to the subtitle or alternate title of the novel, *The Modern Prometheus*. Even though Prometheus is never mentioned in the novel, Mary Shelley's intent is clear. In Greek mythology, Prometheus was a god who stole the secret of fire from Zeus and gave it to mankind. Zeus then punished Prometheus for his defiance by having him tied to a rock. Each day, a great eagle ate Prometheus' liver, a very painful experience, and each night the liver grew back, only to be eaten again the next day by the eagle. By analogy, Victor Frankenstein discovered (or stole) the secret of life from the Creator, something man should never have done. Victor is punished for his sins by the deaths of those closest to him, including his wife Elizabeth, his best friend Henry Clerval and his younger brother William, before Victor himself perishes. (There is another version of the Prometheus legend which has Prometheus creating man out of clay, a story which could also apply to the alternate title of Mary Shelley's novel, but since that use by Shelley of Prometheus in the title would be descriptive, rather than thematic, the better known version of the Prometheus story will be discussed herein.)

However, even with the subtitle *The Modern Prometheus*, the theme of science-gone-mad is rarely addressed in the novel. In Chapter IV, as Victor is relating his story to Captain Walton, he states, "Learn from me, if not by my precepts, at least by my example, how dangerous is the acquirement of knowledge, and how much happier that man is who believes his native town to be the world, than he who aspires to become greater than his nature will allow." In that same chapter, Victor's hubris shows through, directly challenging God by stating that he hopes he can create a new species that would bless him "as its creator and source."

These types of comments by Victor, however, are few and far between in the novel, and there are no discussions or debates in the story about the ethical and religious limits of scientific research. In addition, while Victor clearly suffers significant mental torment and the very real loss of his companions in the story as a result of his experiments with the beginning of life, the engine of that destruction is the very real Frankenstein monster, not God or fate or karma. Additionally, in wreaking his havoc on Frankenstein, the monster states that he is seeking revenge more than punishment, as for example, in Chapter XVII, when Victor initially refuses to create a mate for the monster. The creature responds that if Victor does not do so, "I will revenge my injuries; if I cannot inspire love, I will cause fear; and chiefly towards you my arch-enemy, because my creator, do I swear inextinguishable hatred." Thus, Victor is punished, not for discovering the secret of life but rather, for mistreating his creation, thus undercutting the theme of the modern Prometheus.

In the prologue to the film *The Bride of Frankenstein* (1935), a fictional Mary Shelley says, in response to a comment that her book will never be published because it is too shocking, "The publishers did not see that my purpose was to write a moral lesson—the punishment that befell a mortal man who dared to emulate God." In fact, though, while that is a theme of the book, in the context of the entire work, it is a minor theme.

The more important theme of *Frankenstein*, which is also explored from time to time in the movie versions, is man's inhumanity to someone different from him and the effect of that display of inhumanity on the innocent victim. If the reader believes the monster's story of his early life, the creature was born or created as a blank slate, with the capacity to be a loving, feeling and positive reflection of mankind. The novel spends much time going through the monster's awakening to his existence as a child (although a rather large one) through his maturation process, as he transforms into a thinking and feeling adult creature. The key scenes here are the months which the creature spends learning about life while occupying the hovel outside the cottage of Felix, Agatha and their father. The creature is impressed with their beauty and kindness and feels affection for them. He even cuts wood for them at night, to relieve them of some of their burdens. If the creature can just introduce himself to his friends and they accept him, the creature could become a part of the brotherhood of man.

However, man is not willing to accept this kind, compassionate and articulate creature, simply because of his grotesque appearance. This sends the creature over the edge, becoming the vengeful and murderous demon that people expect him to be. As the creature tells Captain Walton in the last chapter (Walton letter of September 12), "My heart was fashioned to be susceptible of love and sympathy ... [but was] wrenched by misery to vice and hatred."

In his solitude and abandonment, the creature has become a monster, not one created by Victor but one created by mankind in general. This is a theme worthy of such a famous novel, can be analogized to aspects of modern society and is one that lingers with the reader even after the book has been laid down. It is also a theme that is addressed upon occasion in the Frankenstein movies, particularly in *Bride of Frankenstein* (1935).

While downplaying its horror elements, *Frankenstein* is always compelling, as it tees up a debate between Victor and the monster over their respective treatments of each other. Even though Shelley has created a vicious killing machine in the monster, it is hard not to have sympathy for his plight, once again showing the dichotomy in the story. While *Frankenstein* is not primarily a horror story, the novel's tale of revenge, including the threats of the monster against Victor Frankenstein, create a compelling tale of suspense, among the philosophical musings. Near the end of the story, the roles reverse and it is Victor who is seeking revenge against his creature, stalking him all over the European continent before almost finding him in the frozen North. However, Victor has, indeed, created a Frankenstein monster and it is the creature, in the end, who achieves the final act of revenge.

Whether *Frankenstein* is a horror story or a mystery, a romance or a philosophical novel, after almost 200 years since its first publication, the book is still being read and not just because of its influence on subsequent horror films. That influence, however, cannot be ignored, as Mary Shelley's *Frankenstein* along with Bram Stoker's *Dracula* are the two works of literature that have been the most influential on the cinema of horror.

The Films

Frankenstein (1910)

Frankenstein first made it to the cinema in 1910, in a short film of slightly more than 12 minutes in length. Filmed at the Edison Studios in the Bronx in

New York City, the movie was thought lost for many years. Indeed, the only part of the film that seemed to survive was a publicity still from an Edison catalog showing Charles Ogle playing the monster. However, a fairly good copy of the short was finally located in a private collection and the film played to the general public, for the first time in over eight decades, in 1993. The movie is now often referred to as *Edison's Frankenstein.*

One would not expect that a short, silent movie would follow the novel very closely and it does not. Indeed, the first title card reads, "A Liberal Adaptation From Mrs. Shelley's Famous Story For Edison Production." In looking at the short film from the perspective of 100 years later, while the story and the production are primitive, indicative of the year in which the film was produced, the creation scene is actually quite impressive, with the creature coming together as its basic elements meld into one form in a fiery cauldron, seemingly resulting more from magic than science. (Although there is little in the novel about the creation of the monster, *Edison's Frankenstein* appears to be closest to Mary Shelley's description than any other film adaptation.) The monster eventually interrupts Dr. Frankenstein and his bride on their wedding night, an incident familiar to fans of the 1931 film. At the end, the creature is "overcome by love and disappears," as the title card reads, into Frankenstein's mirror.

Edison's Frankenstein was not a financial success. Thereafter, there were at least two other silent film versions of the novel and other silent films took some inspiration from Mary Shelley's novel. However, with the success of *Dracula* (1931), Universal Studios decided to adapt another famous horror novel to the screen and *Frankenstein* was the obvious choice.

Frankenstein (1931)

According to the credits, *Frankenstein* (1931) is from the novel by Mrs. Percy B. Shelley, a most unusual manner in which to refer to Mary Wollstonecraft Shelley. However, despite the credit. most of the well-remembered scenes from the film do not come from the novel, such as the early scenes of grave robbing, the stealing of a brain from the University, the stunning creation sequence, the attempt by Dr. Waldman to destroy the monster and the ultimate destruction of the creature in the fire at the windmill. Victor Frankenstein's first name has been inexplicably changed to Henry and the Henry (Clerval) of the novel has now become Victor (Moritz). Henry's bride-to-be, Elizabeth, is still an important character, but most of the rest of the characters are new, including the laboratory assistant Fritz, Henry's father Baron Frankenstein, and Henry's medical schoolteacher Dr. Waldman (although the name, but not the character, is the same as the novel's M. Waldman, Victor's chemistry professor at the university).

Dr. Frankenstein (Colin Clive), on the left, and his assistant, Fritz (Dwight Frye), look at a potential source of a brain for the creature in *Frankenstein* (1931). Unfortunately, the cadaver's neck is broken and its brain is useless.

The horror aspects of the story are emphasized in the film, particularly in the early quest for bodies and brains and the terrific laboratory scene for the creation of the monster. For the most part, these incidents were skipped over in Mary Shelley's novel. Perhaps most importantly, there is the face of the film monster, an iconic image of popular culture. With his flat top, sunken cheeks, bulging forehead and stitches and scars, along with the electrodes in his neck, the monster is the epitome of horror.

Fortunately, no attempt was made to replicate Mary Shelley's description of her own creation. She wrote, in Chapter V,

> His yellow skin scarcely covered the work of muscles and arteries beneath; his hair was of a lustrous black, and flowing; his teeth of a pearly whiteness; but these luxuriances only formed a more horrid contrast with his watery eyes, that seemed almost of the same colour as the dun white sockets in which they were set, his shriveled complexion and straight black lips.

Despite the fact that characters in the novel react with horror to the features of the monster throughout the book, Shelley's description of Victor's handiwork makes the creature seem not all that bad. For the film, however, Jack Pierce's makeup for the monster, developed on the face of Boris Karloff, is the personification of horror, shocking for its time and even shocking today, for those whose visions of the monster come only from television shows, cartoons and even advertising. Karloff's face is the perfect foundation for Pierce's handiwork and no one who played the monster later, even employing the same makeup (including Karloff), was ever so terrifying as Karloff in this first film.

In the novel, Shelley writes that Victor Frankenstein, as a result of the difficulty with working with small body parts, decided to make his creature a being of giant stature, eight feet in height and proportionately large. Similarly, the movie monster is tall and imposing, the one aspect of the creature carried over into the film. However, Shelley's creation can run so fast that he descends down a mountain "with greater speed than the flight of an eagle" (Chapter XVII) and rows across the waters "with an arrowy swiftness" (Chapter XX). The movie monster seldom runs; his walking sometimes seems more like lumbering. Indeed, as sequel followed sequel at Universal Studios, the monster seemed to lumber more and more.

Frankenstein moves along at a quick pace, consuming only about 70 minutes of screen time. There are no interludes of travel around Europe, personal anguish, criminal arrests and trials or the framing story of Captain Walton. The only detour to the main story comes from the scenes with Henry's father, Baron Frankenstein, whose moments in the film are played for a lighter tone so as to provide a contrast to the mood of the rest of the feature. The dissimilarity between novel and film in mood, point of view, setting and plot is stark.

That is not to say that the film eschewed all aspects of Mary Shelley's novel. Obviously, the core plot of a doctor who intends to create life in the nature of man but instead creates a monster comes from Mary Shelley's tome. In addition, some of the significant scenes in the film are clearly inspired by some aspects of the novel. Who can forget the moment when the monster discovers little Maria playing at the side of the lake with her flowers? Because she is young and only wants a friend, she is not afraid of the monster. In the novel, after all who see his face have disdained the creature, the creature sees a beautiful child coming toward him and has a thought. "Suddenly, as I gazed on him, an idea seized me, that this little creature was unprejudiced, and had lived too short a time to have imbibed a horror of deformity. If, therefore, I could seize him, and educate him as my companion and friend, I should not be so desolate in this peopled earth" (Chapter XVI). Unfortunately, that child, who turns out to be Victor's brother, is also afraid of the creature, causing the monster to kill the young boy. Thus, similar scenes are handled differently in the novel and the film.

In the book, after Victor destroys the mate he started to create for the creature, the monster makes a chilling threat: "Are you to be happy while I grovel in the intensity of my wretchedness? ...[R]emember, I shall be with you on your wedding-night" (Chapter XX). Victor takes that statement as a threat to his own well-being but after the wedding is completed and Victor and Elizabeth leave on their honeymoon, the creature kills Elizabeth. In terms of suspense and intrigue, this may be the highlight of the novel, as the unseen monster stalks Henry and his wife on their night of bliss.

In the movie, the monster also attacks Elizabeth on her wedding night, but before the marriage ceremony is performed. When Elizabeth's screams shatter the calm of the wedding house, the monster escapes, leaving Elizabeth shaken but unharmed. Here, because 1930s filmmakers tended not to have unhappy endings to their movies, even ones that were horror films, the Elizabeth of the movie must escape unscathed, even though the Elizabeth of the novel is brutally murdered. In at least this one instance, the novel is more effective than the film in its horror and shock value.

In the introduction to *Frankenstein*, actor Edward Van Sloan speaks directly to the audience, describing the upcoming film as follows: "We are about to unfold the story of Frankenstein, a man of science, who sought to create a man after his own image, without reckoning upon God." And, in fact, this modern Prometheus theme is considered somewhat in the movie, just as it is a minor theme in the novel. In the celebrated creation scene, after the hand and arm of the monster move, Henry Frankenstein famously says, in this once censored line, "In the name of God. Now I know what it feels like to be God." Thus, Henry Frankenstein is explicitly attempting to steal the secret of life from God, much as Prometheus stole the secret of fire from Zeus.

Dr. Waldman is the figure of rational science in the film, never dreaming to try to discover the unknown, as Henry desires. Waldman is always attempting to have Frankenstein end his experiments and destroy his creation, which Waldman sees only as a monster and nothing else. Thus, there is some implied debate about the role and limits of science in society but it is hardly fleshed out in the film. Since, at the end of the feature and unlike the book, the creature does not cause the death of Dr. Frankenstein, the modern Prometheus aspects of the tale are undercut.

As to the theme of man's inhumanity to deformity and the effects on the victim, that is undercut by the placement of a criminal brain into the creature's body and the fact that the monster's murderous demeanor is caused more by the torture done by Fritz than by his own deformity. The one scene that begins to

The Frankenstein monster (Boris Karloff) attacks Elizabeth (Mae Clarke) on her wedding night in *Frankenstein* (1931).

explore the issue of the monster's true character, the encounter with Maria at the lake, while memorable and effective, is so short in duration and is so out of place with the rest of the film (even in its setting, which is just about the only scene shot outdoors in the film) that it is not sufficient to address this important theme from the book. That would have to wait until the sequel, *Bride of Frankenstein* (1935).

With the publication of *Frankenstein*, Mary Shelley brought a new expression into the English language—a Frankenstein monster, i.e., a creation or discovery that brings about the creator's ruin. At the end of the novel, Victor Frankenstein dies as a result of his long struggles with the monster, although not at the direct hand of the monster. At the end of the film, Henry was also supposed to die at the hand of the monster, this time by being thrown out of the windmill, to his apparent death. However, at the last instance, a short epilogue was added, with Henry clearly surviving and presumably then marrying Elizabeth and living happily thereafter. For horror fans who have only seen this version of the novel, the meaning of the expression "Frankenstein monster" must seem incomprehensible.

Bride of Frankenstein (1935)

Bride of Frankenstein was one of the first horror film sequels ever made. While Mary Shelley never wrote a sequel to her novel, she left the ending of her book ambiguous enough that she could have written a sequel had she ever decided to do so. After the death of Victor Frankenstein, the creature states, "But soon I shall die.... Soon these burning miseries will be extinct." Then, as the narrator, Captain Walton, writes, the creature jumped off the boat into the nearby ice-raft and he "was soon borne away by the waves and lost in darkness and distance" (Chapter XXIV, Walton letter of September 12). If Shelley were writing in the modern era, there would be no doubt that two or three sequels would be forthcoming.

The film credits to *Bride of Frankenstein* state, "Suggested by the original story written in 1816 by Mary Wollstonecraft Shelley." At least they finally used the correct name of the author. In fact, *Bride of Frankenstein* was more than suggested by Mary Shelley's story; a number of the script ideas were clearly inspired by the novel.

The film opens with an introductory vignette, much as the novel opens with the expository letters of Captain Walton. In this case, though, director James Whale creates a fictional sequel to a real event—the night when Mary Shelley first conceived of her novel of human creation. Here, once again, Mary is in the company of Percy Shelley and Lord Byron, on a ghostly night "when the air itself is filled with monsters." Mary surprises her lover and friend with news that the creature never died in the windmill (using the ending of the prior film and not the novel) and announces that there is more of the story left to tell.

This opening sequence to *Bride of Frankenstein* is often overlooked by horror film fans who are anxious to proceed to the true beginning of the feature, but there is much to admire in this introductory scene. The setting is in a dark castle high on a hill; there is a storm of wind and lightning outside. Inside, Mary and the others are talking in a room with the highest of ceilings, as a delicate minuet plays in the background. It is, as Mary says, "a perfect night for mystery and horror," presumably just like the night that the real Mary Shelley purportedly first conceived of her famous novel.

However, the opening is more than just a mood setter for the film to come. In a clever bit of casting, Elsa Lanchester, who plays Mary Shelley, will later play the monster's mate in the surprising conclusion to the film. Much as God has

A lobby card for *The Bride of Frankenstein* (1935).

created man in his own image, Mary has created the female creature in her own image. In the novel, Victor does not get far enough along in his creation of the female being for Mary Shelley to give a description of her, but it would not have been surprising to the reader if that creature had resembled the real Mary Shelley.

In addition, by placing Elsa Lanchester in the dual role, the filmmakers have tied the opening of the film into its conclusion, making the film into one that Mary Shelley may just have related to Percy Shelley and Lord Byron on that stormy night. There is also continuity with the original *Frankenstein* (1931), the plot of which Lord Byron summarizes at the beginning of the film, as the initial revelation of the respective faces of the creature and his mate in each film is accomplished by a series of shots, each one bringing the viewer closer to the head, finally ending in an extreme close-up of the creature, and Henry exclaiming some variation of "Alive, alive" as each of his creations moves.

Of course, the main story of *Bride of Frankenstein* does not come from the novel. In Shelley's book, there is no escape by the creature from the watery grave below the windmill, no Dr. Pretorius to convince Henry to create a mate for his monster, no creation scene for the mate and no final destruction of Frankenstein's laboratory. Nevertheless, much of the film has its roots in the novel.

At one point in the monster's wanderings in the book, he sees a young girl fall from the side of a cliff, into a rapid stream. The monster jumps in and rescues her, dragging her to the shore. The creature's reward is a rifle bullet in the shoulder from a friend of the girl's. There is a similar scene in *Bride of Frankenstein* when a pretty young shepherdess, on seeing the creature, falls off a cliff into a pool of water, to be rescued by the monster. Despite the creature's heroics, the girl's screams draw two hunters, who shoot at the creature.

One of the most memorable scenes in the film is the monster arriving at the blind hermit's hut and being welcomed as a friend. The creature is so overcome by the kindness of the stranger that a tear comes from his eye and drips down his cheek. With this one small moment, the creature is no longer a monster but has become a man. (This also ties into the tear in the monster's eyes at the end of the film as he takes one last look at his intended before blowing up the Frankenstein laboratory.)

The creature's growth as a person then continues at the hermit's hut, as he learns to speak a few words and even put some ideas together, such as "Alone bad, friend good." Although hardly as erudite as Mary Shelley's creature, the movie monster is stating one of the prime ideas from the novel, which leads into the idea of creating a mate for the monster in both the novel and the movie. The moments in the hermit's hut and the later creation of the mate and her reaction to the creature are the key scenes in the film, raising *Bride of Frankenstein* above the limits of the usual horror film and into the upper echelons of cinema classics.

This scene in the blind hermit's hut is clearly inspired by the time that Mary Shelley's monster spends in the hovel outside the cottage of Felix and Agatha and their father, De Lacey. The father, who is blind, plays the guitar just as the film blind man plays the violin. The creature of the novel learns to speak by overhearing the lessons given to the foreigner, Safie, at the blind man's cottage. The monster of the film learns to speak by the direct lessons from the hermit. In the book, the creature hopes to introduce himself into society by becoming a friend of De Lacey's, who cannot see his face. Whatever small progress he makes is terminated by the return of the children and their reaction to the hideousness of the monster. In the film, it is two hunters who disrupt the idyllic setting of the hermit's hut and eliminate the creature's few days of happiness.

The sequence in the blind hermit's hut is the most explicit evocation of the novel's theme of man's inhumanity to those who are different, showing that the monster, when treated with kindness and friendship, had the capacity to become more like a man than a monster. It works in conjunction with the scene with Maria in the first film and the creature's later attempt to establish some rapport with the mate that Frankenstein creates for him. (The insertion of an abnormal brain into the monster's cranium is conveniently forgotten in *Bride of Frankenstein*.) The monster of the novel talks incessantly about his character and how it was adversely affected by the reactions of those who meet him. The two Universal films make the same point, without talk, but by example.

Indeed, the idea of having the monster talk in *Bride of Frankenstein* clearly comes from the novel. The creature of the book learns to speak and, for that matter to read, while listening to the lessons that the blind man gives to Safie. De Lacey is such a good teacher that the monster eventually reads books like *Paradise Lost* by John Milton and *Plutarch's Lives*. As he relates the story of his life to Victor Frankenstein, his dialogue is laced with words such as benevolence, patriarchal, omnipotent and augmented. Perhaps there is another unspoken theme to Mary Shelley's novel—the benefits of home schooling. While the creature of *Bride of Frankenstein* never comes close to the level of speech of the monster of the novel, he is at least able to convey his understanding of good and bad and the need for a mate.

The theme of the modern Prometheus is barely touched on in this sequel, essentially limited to an early discussion between Henry and Elizabeth after Henry recovers from his injuries at the hands of the monster. He says, "I've been cursed for delving into the mysteries of life.... I dreamed of being the first to give to the world the secret that God is so jealous of." This is a fairly explicit reference to the analogy of Prometheus. In this debate, it is Elizabeth who assumes the position of Dr. Waldman from the first film, trying to convince her fiancé that his experiments with the creation of life amount to blasphemy.

Of course, the idea of a bride for the monster comes from the novel, where the creature blackmails Victor into starting to create one for him, partly by threatening the well being of Elizabeth. In the film, it is Dr. Pretorius and the creature who together blackmail Frankenstein into creating the mate, by kidnapping and threatening Elizabeth. The clear difference between the two works is that Victor Frankenstein never completes his creation of the mate for the monster in the novel while Henry Frankenstein does create a bride for the monster and one that shows that Henry's skills have improved since the time of the first film.

The ending of *Bride of Frankenstein* is a stunner, not just in its fabulous laboratory scene (for this viewer, the best one ever put on film), but also for its surprise ending. Only a handful of horror films end with a surprise, a few exceptions being *The Mummy* (1932), with the heroine being saved by the god Isis after her protectors are rendered powerless, *The Ghost of Frankenstein* (1942), with Ygor's brain not being a proper blood-type match for the monster, causing it to become blind, and, of course, *Bride of Frankenstein* (1935), with the female creature, instead of embracing the monster, rejecting the monster because of its horrid features.

While that surprise ending, of course, does not come from the novel, Mary Shelley actually suggested it in her book. Once Victor begins the creation process for his female creature, he starts to have self-doubts, worrying that he might be creating another murderous and wretched creature to terrorize the world. Or, he worries, he might be creating a new race of devils that could make the condition of man precarious on the earth. Or, he theorizes, "she also might turn with disgust from him to the superior beauty of man; she might quit him, and he be again alone, exasperated by the fresh provocation of being deserted by one of his own species" (Chapter XX).

The latter, of course, is what occurs in *Bride of Frankenstein*, a surprise ending perhaps suggested by Mary Shelley herself. However, whatever the source of the idea, the ending of the movie is a triumph, as the mate shrieks in horror at the sight and touch of the monster, deftly bringing together the two themes of the book and the movies—the practical limits of science and the effects of man's inhumanity to an apparent monster. The creature says, "She hate me, like others." He is exasperated, as Shelley wrote, by the rejection by his own species. He goes on a rampage, destroying the laboratory and all who are in it, except for Henry Frankenstein and his wife Elizabeth.

Because Henry Frankenstein survives once again, the meaning of the term "Frankenstein monster" has once again been undercut for a semi-happy ending

In *Bride of Frankenstein* (1935), the bride (Elsa Lanchester) stands, with the assistance of Dr. Frankenstein (Colin Clive) as the monster (Boris Karloff) and Dr. Pretorius (Ernest Thesiger) look on.

to the feature. But that does not take away from the exceptional film that went before, surprisingly based on much of Mary Shelley's original novel written over a century before.

The Curse of Frankenstein (1957)

Much as *Frankenstein* (1931), along with *Dracula* (1931), started the first cinema horror cycle of the early 1930s, and *Son of Frankenstein* (1939) started the second horror film cycle of the 1940s, *The Curse of Frankenstein* (1957) inaugurated the third, and probably last, horror film cycle of the movies, one that stretched into the mid–1960s. The film was made at Hammer Studios in England, quickly making Hammer the most preeminent name in film horror since Universal Studios gave up the title near the end of World War II.

According to the credits, *The Curse of Frankenstein* is "[b]ased on the classic story by Mary W. Shelley." And, much like the novel, the main story is told by Victor Frankenstein in flashback, although not to Captain Walton. Instead, he tells his tale to a priest, just before Victor is about to be executed for his crimes. However, unlike the book, there is no verbal narration over the scenes then shown, so it as if Victor Frankenstein is not actually relating the tale.

The script of the film by Jimmy Sangster strays far from the original source material. Here, at a young age, Baron Victor Frankenstein learns the study of science from his tutor, Paul Krempe, leading to Victor's interest in creating a living being. After bringing a dead animal back to life, Frankenstein starts in on the work for which he was born—giving life to an inanimate creature.

The form of the creature is put together from the body of a hanged criminal (with Frankenstein cutting the face off because it has been mutilated from the pecking of birds), the hands of a famous sculptor, eyes bought at a charnel house and the brain of a distinguished elderly scholar, Professor Bernstein. However, because Frankenstein had to kill Bernstein in order to take his brain, Krempe, who has been questioning Victor's methods for quite some time, gets into a major fight with Victor, resulting in the brain being damaged. The creature is nevertheless given life, at which time it instantly attacks Frankenstein. Krempe kills the creature with a shotgun wound to the face, but Frankenstein later gives life to his creature once again. Later, when the monster appears to be after Elizabeth, Frankenstein douses it in fire, causing it to fall into a vat of acid. The framing story returns, and as the film ends, Victor is being led to his execution at a guillotine.

As can be seen from this plot summary, there is little of Mary Shelley in *The Curse of Frankenstein* except, paradoxically, for some small matters. There is a reference in the novel to Victor Frankenstein visiting a charnel house to obtain some of his materials, so Victor's stop in the movie at the charnel house (a vault or tomb where human skeletons are stored) comes from the book. When the monster wanders off, he does discover a blind man but he dispatches him with no regrets. The climax of the story related by Frankenstein takes place on the eve of the wedding night of Victor and Elizabeth, just as a major event in the novel occurs on the wedding night of the young couple. Other than that, *The Curse of Frankenstein* has a completely original script.

In particular, neither of Mary Shelley's themes from the novel carries over into the film. While Paul Krempe has major disputes with Frankenstein about his experiments, they really relate to his mutilation and unauthorized appropriation of dead bodies or their body parts (and, of course, the deliberate killing of Professor Bernstein). There are no discussions about Frankenstein invading the exclusive provinces of God, and Frankenstein is punished at the end of the film for the killings that his monster did, not for daring to challenge God. As

Dr. Frankenstein (Peter Cushing), right, with the help of his assistant, Paul Krempe (Robert Urquhart), attempts to revive the dead puppy in the tank, as a prelude to more significant work, in *The Curse of Frankenstein* (1957).

to the theme of man's inhumanity to creature, since the creature attempts to strangle Victor Frankenstein the first instance he sees him, that theme remains unaddressed in this film. (Indeed, since Victor uses a damaged brain in this film, just as Henry used a criminal brain in the 1931 film, the creature never stands a chance.) There are no conflicting emotions from the viewer toward the creature; the monster is a killer, pure and simple.

The Karloff make-up for the monster was under copyright by Universal Studios, so Hammer had to go in a different direction in *The Curse of Frankenstein*. Its creature has a gnarled and scarred face, with what seems to be one watery eye and one natural eye. He even has a full head of natural hair, at least at the beginning. Christopher Lee plays the monster and his make-up more resembles the creature from the novel than that of Karloff's, but only in the sense that the creature has a head of normal size and shape. However, as noted above in the discussion of *Frankenstein* (1931), Mary Shelley was somewhat reticent in describing the hideousness of her creature in the novel. Therefore, any make-up artist creating the face of the monster for a Frankenstein horror film has somewhat free rein. What clearly did not carry over from the novel is the incredible size of the creature; Hammer's monster is normal in height and bulk. Nevertheless, while Lee's make-up is effective, it is instantly forgettable, as Karloff's never is.

For those familiar with the novel and the prior films, there is one paradoxical moment early in the film when Paul Krempe first views the face of the monster, before it is brought to life. Paul comments on the gruesomeness of the face. Victor Frankenstein replies, "I admit he isn't a particularly good looking specimen at present, but don't forget, one's facial character is built up by what is behind it—in the brain. A benevolent mind and the face assumes the patterns of benevolence; an evil mind and an evil face."

Interestingly, this is the exact opposite of the lesson from the novel (and the prior films), where a potentially kind creature becomes a murderer because of the public's reaction to its face. Clearly this Victor Frankenstein never read Mary Shelley's novel and therefore never learned from it. If he had, perhaps his ensuing problems would not have occurred.

Frankenstein by Mary Shelley is hardly an easy film to adapt to the cinema. The book has few scenes of real horror and the story line rambles all over Europe, even to the Arctic Circle. In *The Curse of Frankenstein*, Hammer took the core concept of Mary Shelley's and adapted it into a story all its own and one that deliberately did not mimic the prior films from Universal. The film is innovative in its use of color and was one of the first, if not the first horror film, to imbue the genre with a sexuality, both in the attire of the women and Victor's rolls in the hay with the maid Justine (a name from the novel) to its emphasis on violence, epitomized by the creature simply killing the blind man, rather than attempting to interact with him. In that moment with the blind man, it is as if the Hammer filmmakers were thumbing their noses at prior incarnations of the story, essentially announcing that this is a horror film only, with no time for a morality play.

And as a horror film, *The Curse of Frankenstein* is a great success. While most people justifiably admire the manner in which the face of the monster is first unveiled in the 1931 film, note also how cleverly it is done in this film. Here, Victor believes his experiment has failed and leaves his laboratory in an attempt to locate Paul for some assistance. In the meantime, the monster comes to life with Victor unaware. When Victor then opens the lab door, expecting to see the shell of his being lying where he left him, the monster is already standing, but with the bandages around his head. As the camera moves in for a medium shot, the creature yanks the bandages off his head. The camera then moves in for a tight close-up of the gruesome monster's face, with the whole scene being a sudden shock for the audience.

There are also moments of great danger in the film, such as at the end when the monster stalks Elizabeth across the high balconies of the Frankenstein mansion. There is the fiery demise of the creature, as he is doused in fire and falls into the acid bath. There is the framing story of Frankenstein in prison and his apparent guillotining at the end of the film.

The Curse of Frankenstein is a first class production, as the few prior horror films of the 1950s seldom were. The film brought new life to the horror genre and it is easy to see why it started a new wave of horror, first in the British cinema and then, in the early 1960s, the American cinema.

Mary Shelley's Frankenstein (1994)

Mary Shelley's Frankenstein purports to be a faithful adaptation of the famous novel and in order to establish its bona fides, it starts with a voice over narration from Mary Shelley herself, which comes almost word for word from her introduction to the 1831 edition of the book. She talks about a story that "would speak to the mysterious fears of our nature and awaken thrilling horror." There is then an introductory crawl which sets the time of the story at the beginning of the nineteenth century, a time when interest in scientific advances and the "lust for knowledge had never been greater." The viewer assumes that the film is referring to Victor Frankenstein, but instead it is a reference to Captain Robert Walton, an explorer who is obsessed with reaching the North Pole. Thus the film establishes one of the interesting mirror images from the novel—Walton and Frankenstein both seeking out the unknown at risk to themselves and others.

Mary Shelley's Frankenstein is the first Frankenstein film to use the framing story of Walton meeting Victor Frankenstein after Walton's ship becomes stuck in the ice. The story then moves to the flashback of Victor's life, similar to the manner in which the novel handles the narrative.

The main story of the film does follow Mary Shelley's novel closer than prior film adaptations, including Victor's move to medical school at Ingolstadt, his philosophical dispute with one of his professors, the creation of the monster, Victor's disgust at the creature's abnormality, the monster learning about life in the hovel outside the blind man's cottage and his later acts of revenge against Victor's family. However, there are still many changes from the original plot, large and small. In the film and unlike in the novel, Victor first meets Henry Clerval at medical school in Ingolstadt; there Dr. Waldman had already done experiments with creating life and Victor builds on his research; the brain for the creature is that of Dr. Waldman who was untimely killed by a man to whom Waldman was attempting to give a vaccination; and the creation occurs during a cholera epidemic in the area.

The most significant change relates to the bride for the monster. Victor responds to the creature's threats and starts to create one, and then suddenly and inexplicably (in the film version) ends his experiment. The monster therefore kills Elizabeth on her wedding night, as threatened. Victor grabs the limp body of his new creation, sans heart, and recreates his own bride of Frankenstein using the equipment he had luckily just gathered together to create a bride for the monster. The semi-hideous female, facial scars and stitches all, is then torn between the affections of Victor and the creature and as a result of that and the realization of her own repulsive face, commits suicide by dousing herself in fire. Nothing like that ever takes place in Mary Shelley's novel.

Much like the novel, Victor creates his living being in his student apartment, but the apartment in the film appears to be the largest apartment any student has ever rented anywhere and at any time in the entire history of the world. The creation sequence of *Mary Shelley's Frankenstein* is particularly weak, mainly because it is so confusing. The camera moves in and out, employing different shots with no substantive effect on the viewer. Victor jumps and climbs around the equipment for no apparent reason. Sometimes there seem to be borrowings from *Frankenstein* (1931) with electrical current buzzing around the apartment and the creature being lofted into the air. At other times, Victor seems to be using a combination of amniotic fluid and acupuncture to bring life to the slab on the table. The score is completely inappropriate, being in the nature of thriller music rather than music that provides a foreboding or awe-inspiring backdrop. During the entire process, Victor is stripped to the waist for no appreciable reason.

Victor's reaction to his creature is also confusing. Why does he immediately shun it? (Mary Shelley's book is also somewhat murky on this issue.) Does the creature die on that first day and then come back to life on its own? In both this scene and the creation scene, the director goes for style over exposition, making the film hard to follow. With so much attention given to technique, the filmmakers essentially forget to stun the audience with the face of the monster, which is partially disclosed at the end of the creation scene almost as an oversight, thereby missing a potentially great moment, which was beautifully done in *Frankenstein* (1931) and *The Curse of Frankenstein* (1957). In fact, the first clear view of the creature's face does not come until he is off in the woods on his own. The creature's face is also nothing special, highlighted by several very large stitches and scars. There is no doubt that the creature is being played by actor Robert De Niro. The makeup on the creature is another missed opportunity.

Neither the modern Prometheus theme nor the theme of man's inhumanity to others is addressed in the film. There is a moment in the feature that almost addresses the latter issue, when the creature finally comes into the blind man's cottage to meet him, but since the scene is so brief, it has little thematic effect. The creature in *Mary Shelley's Frankenstein* is a killing machine only, with few vestiges of humanity. Indeed, the whole section of the film where the monster goes off on his own and eventually meets the blind man's family does not work because the thoughts of the creature are never conveyed to the audience. Mary Shelley's novel, which is told from the viewpoint of the creature at this point in the story, is much more effective in this regard.

There is, however, an interesting and different theme put forth in the film, which is only a subtext of the book. When the creature and Victor finally meet, the creature questions his own identity, assuming he even has one. Is he a mixture of the body parts that comprise his structure or are they just "raw materials," as Victor suggests? The creature can speak, read, play a musical instrument and kill, not from learning those skills, but from attributes contained somewhere in his inner being. Does he also have a soul, just as Victor does, or are his attributes just trace memories of the brain, as Victor suggests? The creature justifiably asks whether Victor ever considered the consequences for his creature if he were brought to life without a past or an identity.

These are all very interesting questions from the film monster. They are also addressed, however slightly, in Mary Shelley's original work, such as when the creature says to Victor, "But where were my friends and relations? No father had watched my infant days, no mother had blessed me with smiles and caresses; or if they had, all my past was now a blot, a blind vacancy in which I distinguished nothing" (Chapter XIII). Similar to the novel, this theme of lack of identity is simply mentioned briefly in the film and then forgotten, until cleverly brought up again at the end, when the creature refers to the dead Victor Frankenstein as his father.

Despite the many changes from the novel, *Mary Shelley's Frankenstein* comes surprisingly close to the storyline of the original novel. The acting is top notch, particularly Kenneth Branagh as a more youthful Victor Frankenstein than is usually portrayed on the screen. Branagh does overact from time to time, but that is a tradition for actors portraying a Frankenstein, including Colin Clive in the 1931 original and Basil Rathbone in *Son of Frankenstein* (1939). Another plus is the substantial location shooting, particularly for those scenes set in mountains and the frozen north.

Yet for all of that, *Mary Shelley's Frankenstein* has no soul, with little sympathy or understanding conveyed for either Victor Frankenstein or his monster. The direction shows bravura skills but the camera work seems to be employed solely to demonstrate the skill of the director. It adds little to the mood of the tale or the effectiveness of the story. There is more skill shown by both James Whale and Terrence Fisher in their unveilings of the monster's face in *Frankenstein* (1931) and *Curse of Frankenstein* (1957), respectively, than in all of *Mary Shelley's Frankenstein*. In many respects, the film's big budget seems to be wasted.

Mary Shelley's Frankenstein, though an innovative experiment in bringing a difficult novel to the screen, is ultimately a failure. It does not successfully recreate the ideas of the novel or the horror of the prior film adaptations. Nevertheless, for those interested in the Frankenstein saga and, in particular, Mary Shelley's book, the film has some value.

Other Adaptations

There have been many other versions of the story of Frankenstein's monster, both in film and on television. After *Bride of Frankenstein*, Universal produced six more films that included the character of the monster. However, the theme of the modern Prometheus is all but forgotten in these films except, perhaps accidentally, in the sense that the sins of Henry Frankenstein are visited on his two sons (*Son of Frankenstein* [1939] and *The Ghost of Frankenstein* [1942]) and a granddaughter (*Frankenstein Meets the Wolf Man* [1943]). Nevertheless, other than in *The Ghost of Frankenstein*, Henry's offspring are alive and well at the end of the film.

Also, the monster gradually becomes a killing machine in these films, showing little of the humanity it exhibits in the original film and its sequel, except, perhaps, in the creature's interaction with young children in *Son of Frankenstein* and *The Ghost of Frankenstein*. It is difficult to find much of Mary Shelley in these films, although the first three pictures after *Bride of Frankenstein* are highly entertaining.

Hammer Studios continued to make Frankenstein movies after *The Curse of Frankenstein* (1957), with Victor Frankenstein returning over and over again, instead of his monster. There is little of Mary Shelley in these Hammer film sequels, although in *Frankenstein Created Woman* (1967), the Dr. Frankenstein of the Hammer films finally accomplishes Mary Shelley's original idea of creating a female creature and a quite attractive one, at that.

The end of the original cycle of Frankenstein films came with *Abbot and Costello Meet Frankenstein* (1948) where the monster, even though the role is played straight, becomes a comic foil for the comedy duo. This occurs again in *Young Frankenstein*, Mel Brooke's loving spoof, which was released in 1974, although there the monster does do some mugging for the cameras. Then there is *The Munsters*, a television show that aired on CBS from 1964 to 1966. The head of the Munster family is the affable Herman Munster, played by Fred

Gwynne, wearing a version of the original Frankenstein makeup from the early Universal Frankenstein movies.

The two movie comedy versions of the legendary monster are favorites among horror film fans and even the television show has its moments. But, what would Mary Shelley think if she learned that when she bid her "hideous progeny" to "go forth and prosper," as she wrote in the introduction to the version of her book published in 1831, that many people would only know her monster as a figure of comedy, rather than one of tragedy, as she originally intended?

CHAPTER 2

"The Tell-Tale Heart" by Edgar Allan Poe

In *An Illustrated History of the Horror Film*, Carlos Clarens wrote, referring to *The Avenging Conscience* (1914), that as might be expected by those familiar with film history, D.W. Griffith directed the first masterpiece of screen horror. Griffith, of course, was the innovative American director of many silent film classics, including *Birth of a Nation* (1915) and *Intolerance* (1916). He is not generally known as a director of horror films, although he did dabble around the fringes of the field upon occasion. What Clarens could also have written is that as might be expected by those familiar with the history of horror literature, that "first masterpiece of screen horror" incorporated works by Edgar Allan Poe, the renowned American writer of many classic horror short stories.

Background

Edgar Allan Poe, the second of three children of traveling stage actors, was born in Boston, Massachusetts, on January 19, 1809. Both of Edgar's parents died within three years of his birth. Thereafter, John and Frances Allan, a wealthy couple from Richmond, Virginia, took Edgar in, and in 1812, the Allans had Edgar christened as Edgar Allan Poe.

Poe's first book of poetry, *Tamerlane and Other Poems*, was published when Poe was only 18. Thereafter, Poe wrote other books of poetry, edited various literary magazines and contributed short stories, most containing horror content, to newspapers and other periodicals. His greatest success was the poem "The Raven," published in 1845 in New York in *The Evening Mirror* and *The American Weekly*. Thereafter, "The Raven" was republished in other newspapers and periodicals, cementing Poe's fame among both the educated classes and the masses.

Poe's short stories and poems were the inspiration for numerous films, several of which are discussed in this book. Poe died on October 7, 1849, at the age of 40.

The Literature

"The Tell-Tale Heart" is the story of the killing of a defenseless old man, related in a stream of consciousness manner by an unnamed narrator. Why did the narrator kill the old man? He loved the old man, the old man never did him any wrong and the narrator had no desire to steal anything from him. The sole cause of the homicide was an eye of the old-timer. "One of his eyes resembled that of a vulture—a pale blue eye, with a film over it." Whenever the narrator saw the eye, his "blood ran cold."

As the narrator is about to kill the old man, he begins to hear the beating of the frightened man's heart, growing louder and louder until the narrator believes that everyone can hear it. Nevertheless, he still kills the old man. The next day, when the police arrive to investigate, the narrator is totally calm and allows the police to search the entire house. The police officers are satisfied, particularly because of the narrator's easygoing manner. The police then decide to sit in the bedchamber to chat and while there, the narrator once again hears the "hellish tattoo" of the dead man's heart, growing louder and louder and louder. Finally, the pressure is too much and the narrator shrieks out his confession, telling the police, in the last line of the story, to tear up the planks of the floor where the body has been buried, believing they will discover the beating of the old man's hideous heart.

As was often the case in a story by Edgar Allan Poe, there is much ambiguity in "The Tell-Tale Heart." There is never any explanation of the relationship between the old man and the narrator. It is not clear to whom the narrator is telling his story; it could be an attorney, a psychiatrist, a judge or someone completely unknown. It is not even clear that the sounds the narrator keeps hearing are imaginary, as there is a mention in the story of "death watches in the wall" of the old man's bedroom, which could be a reference to deathwatch beetles which sometimes create sounds which are similar to a heartbeat.

These ambiguities are intentional on Poe's part, contributing to the effectiveness of Poe's tale of paranoia and, despite the narrator's belief, of madness. It does not matter what the relationship is between the narrator and the old man, since the narrator kills the old man for a non-reason, namely, his eye. It does not matter to whom the narrator is telling his story, since "The Tell-Tale Heart" is a complete monologue of madness without interruption by a representative of the world of the sane. Even if deathwatch beetles initially caused some of the sounds of beating, the narrator overreacts to the sounds. He irrationally believes that the beating keeps getting louder and louder. He crazily believes that the sounds are caused by the old man's non-beating heart.

The narrator's purpose in recounting his misdeed is to prove that he is not mad, but by the time the very short story concludes, the reader has no doubt that the narrator is insane. The narrator incorrectly associates sanity with calmness. He cannot be mad because he relates his tale with composure. He cannot be mad because he patiently waited eight days before killing the old man. He cannot be mad because he treats the police officers with ease when they come to investigate. Poe has created a type of killer that is all too common today—composed and sane on the outside yet seething with hate and madness on the inside, a monster of everyday life.

Similar to Captain Queeg in Herman Wouk's *The Caine Mutiny*, the narrator unintentionally reveals his madness in a monologue in which he is trying to convince everyone that he is sane. In Poe's storytelling, though, it is not just madness and paranoia that is revealed. It is also guilt and a randomness of violence, related within the context of a heart beating after death, making Poe's tale one of horror, not of the rational. Even when the details of the story are gone from the reader's mind, the sounds of the beating heart remain, as vivid as Poe described them in his story.

The Films

The Avenging Conscience or "Thou Shalt Not Kill" (1914)

The Avenging Conscience incorporates elements of several tales and poems written by Edgar Allan Poe, particularly "The Tell-Tale Heart" and "Annabel Lee," although the film is not strictly a horror film. *The Avenging Conscience* is actually a strange blend of Victorian morality play, old-fashioned melodrama and perfect crime mystery, with a little bit of horror thrown in. It is not really an adaptation of any particular writing by Edgar Allan Poe but, instead, is an unusual mixture of several of Poe's story ideas and themes.

A young man, whose mother died in childbirth, has been raised by his uncle to adulthood. The uncle expects the young man to commit to the family business but instead, he has fallen in love with a pretty young girl whom he calls "Annabel," the name apparently inspired by the literature of Poe that the nephew constantly reads. The nephew introduces his girlfriend to the uncle, who accuses Annabel of being a woman of common repute. That causes the young lovers to split. The nephew then decides that he can only turn his life around by killing his uncle, which he accomplishes by choking the uncle to death. The nephew then entombs the uncle's body behind the fireplace, carefully replacing all of the bricks so that no one can see that anything has changed. However, the nephew's avenging conscience overwhelms him. He constantly sees images of his uncle walking and being choked. He believes he hears the beating of his uncle's heart. The nephew finally confesses his crime to a detective and then, in his grief, tries to hang himself. His sweetheart Annabel then commits suicide by jumping off a cliff near the sea.

In Poe's "The Tell-Tale Heart," it is the element of sound that provides most of the impact on the reader. The beating of the old man's heart after death provides the primary atmosphere of horror that the story evokes. Thus, it was the height of arrogance for D.W. Griffith to attempt to adapt, at least in part, such a story for the silent cinema, where the most important facet of the story could not be duplicated. Paradoxically, though, it is the moments in the film when the nephew believes that his uncle's heart is still beating that are the most effective.

When a detective comes to question the nephew about the whereabouts of his uncle, the interview occurs in the room in which the killing took place and in which the uncle's body is now entombed behind the fireplace. During the discussion, the pendulum of a clock is steadily beating and the detective constantly taps his pencil on the table, both creating sounds like the beats of a heart. (Unfortunately, it does take a title card to connect the sound of the tapping pencil to the beat of a heart.) The nephew becomes nervous, as shown by his clasped hands that cannot seem to remain still and by the nephew interrupting the detective's hand movements, trying to stop the detective from tapping his pencil. The detective then starts tapping with his foot, another heartbeat-like sound. With the chirping of an owl, a vision of small creatures and a return of the uncle's ghost-like image, it is all too much for the nephew and he confesses to the murder.

This scene is a masterpiece of the silent cinema, illustrating that in the right hands, silent movies could create an abundance of sounds. Although substantively different than the ending of Poe's short story, Griffith nevertheless successfully recreates the mood and horror of the tale, with nary a sound actually being heard by the viewer.

Unfortunately, most of the rest of *The Avenging Conscience* does not work as well. Although somewhat disguised by the melodramatic artifices of the narrative, the uncle's interference in the nephew's love affair is an unconvincing motivation for the killing of the uncle. Thus, the screenwriters have failed in their requisite task of creating an interesting beginning to the story of the tell-tale heart, to complement Poe's exciting climax to the tale. Indeed, the motivations of all of the characters are confusing; they are only believable in the context of the melodramatic nature of the film.

In addition, there is just too much moralizing in the film, as foretold by the subtitle of the film, "Thou Shalt Not Kill." The religious references are heavy handed, including the incorporation of images of Christ and Moses. The happy ending of the film, that all that has gone before was a dream, undercuts most of the horror elements of the movie. (Of course, it was not all that unusual for a fantasy film of the time period to turn out to be a dream or the ravings of an insane person. See, for example, *The Cabinet of Dr. Caligari* [1920].) The idyllic love of the nephew and the sweetheart is symbolized at the end of the film, with shots of the mythological Pan, some children and several creatures of the fields and forests juxtaposed with shots of the young lovers, a cringe-worthy scene.

The relationship of *The Avenging Conscience* to "The Tell-Tale Heart" is obvious. In addition, bits of other Poe stories and poems can be seen in the film. The most significant one is the six-stanza poem "Annabel Lee," which was first published in 1849, shortly after the death of Edgar Allan Poe. It was the last complete poem that Poe wrote. "Annabel Lee" is about a deep love torn asunder by the sudden death of the title character when she drowns in a storm near the sea. Her lover, however, never forgets her and every night he returns to the edge of the sea to, in his words, "lie down by the side / Of my darling."

In *The Avenging Conscience*, by naming the sweetheart "Annabel," featuring young lovers who are torn apart and ending with Annabel's death by the sea, there is a tenuous relationship to the poem "Annabel Lee." Also, some of the lines of that poem are quoted in the titles.

In addition to the obvious inspirations from "The Tell-Tale Heart" and "Annabel Lee," the entombing of the body in a wall comes from the short story "The Black Cat," published in 1843. The little creatures that the nephew sees in his ramblings are inspired by the ghouls in the poem "The Bells," which was published in 1849, after Poe's death. In the poem, the ghouls roll, dance and yell, but they are neither man nor woman, neither brute nor human. Also, the titles often quote other writings of Poe's, including lines from "To One in Paradise," a poem published in 1834.

One of the small joys of watching *The Avenging Conscience* is to try to unearth as many references to Poe's works as possible, much like watching the 1940s Sherlock Holmes movies from Universal to see what scraps of Arthur Conan Doyle can be found in each film. The only other reason to watch the movie is for its historical importance because, while *The Avenging Conscience* is usually considered the first great horror film, its horror elements are significantly muted. The film is noteworthy for its historical significance and for one great scene, not as a compelling viewing experience for a modern fancier of horror films. *The Avenging Conscience* is neither a great film nor a great horror film.

The Tell-Tale Heart (1960)

The Tell-Tale Heart (1960) was not directed by a famous director such as D.W. Griffith or Jean Epstein. There were no famous horror film stars in the cast such as Vincent Price or Christopher Lee. The film was not shot in color, as were most of the horror films of its era. The film was overshadowed at the time by the series of Poe adaptations done by director Roger Corman. As a result, *The Tell-Tale Heart* (1960) is a true forgotten horror. Nevertheless, and despite the film's virtual anonymity, those who finally have a chance to see the film will be pleasantly surprised.

The protagonist is Edgar Marsh, the town librarian, who walks with a limp and is inexperienced around women. One day, a very attractive young lady, Betty Clare, moves into an apartment across the way from Edgar's house. Edgar finally gets up all of his courage and invites her out on a series of dates. Edgar falls in love with Betty, not realizing that the affection is not returned and that Betty treats him more with pity than fondness. While out to dinner one night, Edgar, oblivious to his situation with Betty, introduces Betty to his best friend, the debonair Carl Loomis. The two immediately fall in love. When Edgar accidentally discovers the betrayal, he brutally attacks and kills Carl and places the body beneath the floorboards of his study. The climax of the story comes straight from Poe, as the beating of Carl's heart drives Edgar mad. He confesses his crime to the police.

Poe's story "The Tell-Tale Heart" provides a terrific ending for any mystery or horror film. The challenge to the screenwriters is to create the beginning and middle of the story. In this 1960 version of Poe's story, the screenwriters concocted a love triangle between Edgar, Carl and Betty, and while that may not be the most innovative of background stories for Poe's climax, it suffices for this film, particularly because the screenplay takes the time to allow the audience to get to know and understand the principal characters. Edgar's potential mental instability is established early on in the film, by his inability to even communicate with a woman who approaches him in a bar, the drugs he takes and his private collection of dirty pictures. There is some nuance in the characterization of Carl, as he does all in his power not to fall in love with Betty, because he knows it will hurt his good friend Edgar. Adrienne Corri is a knockout as Betty Clare, disguising some of the slow parts of the film.

The production of *The Tell-Tale Heart* belies its B-movie status. Numerous extras fill scenes, whether on the streets or in bars and restaurants. The direction of the film has some style. The time period of the story seems to be the era of Poe himself, with horse drawn carriages and gas lighting. Period films are more expensive to make than movies set in contemporary times, yet the production of this film does not seem to stint on the period recreations. Since it sometimes seems as if Poe wrote in black and white, not color, the black and white photography is a plus.

The key scenes in *The Tell-Tale Heart* occur, as expected, when Edgar hears the beating heart. On the first occasion, Edgar, who has fallen asleep in his chair, starts to dream of images of Carl and his killing. Edgar suddenly awakes and for the first time he hears the tympanic rhythm of the beating heart. There is a pan down the empty steps of the house to the outside of the study where Carl's body has been placed, leaving no doubt as to the source of the sounds. The problems continue the next night. Edgar cannot sleep because the many sounds of the house, such as the swinging clock pendulum, the dripping of the water from the bath faucet, and later, the sound of dripping when there is no water dripping, keep him awake. In addition, there are the sounds of the crackling of a swinging light fixture, noises of insects, a rolling chess piece and the metronome on the piano. Throughout, the beating of the heart dominates the other sounds.

The use of sound in these scenes is exceptional, as all of the sounds, not just the thumping of Carl's heart, seem to be driving Edgar crazy. The payoff for these scenes occurs when Edgar looks under the piano, where Carl's remains have been placed under the floorboards. The floorboards themselves are pulsating, as if Carl's beating heart (which is then as loud as it has ever been heard in the film) is pushing the wood up and down, a true moment of horror, unexpected by any reader of Poe.

However, the filmmakers did not end the horror there. Edgar cuts open the body and pulls Carl's heart out; it is still visibly and aurally beating. Edgar then drives far away from the city and buries the heart in the woods, yet later in the film, the heart, still underground in the woods, starts to beat again. When Edgar returns to his apartment, he once again hears the beating heart. He checks Carl's hidden body under the floorboards. Carl's chest still appears to be beating even though the heart had been previously removed from Carl's body. The telltale heart of this film version is both gruesome and horrific, adding a visual element to Poe's story of the sounds of madness.

As good as this film is, there are several unsatisfactory parts. A passing shot, which indicates that Edgar lives on Rue Morgue, seems gratuitous. The framing story of the narrative as a dream of Edgar Alan Poe's is disappointing, just as the dream ending in *The Avenging Conscience* was. Once Poe awakes from his dream, he looks out the window and sees a young woman moving into an apartment across the way, perhaps making the film into a never-ending story (i.e., dreams within dreams), stealing the finish of *Dead of Night* (1945).

These are minor points, as *The Tell-Tale Heart* (1960) is a fine adaptation of Poe's famous short story. With a well-known director, the clever use of sounds in *The Tell-Tale Heart* would have garnered much renown. In a better-known film, the gruesome scenes with the beating heart would have acquired much notoriety. For fans of the genre, they are all standout moments, making *The Tell-Tale Heart* a forgotten gem of a horror film.

Other Adaptations

"The Tell-Tale Heart" has been adapted for the screen on many occasions. The first official adaptation was a 1928 short titled "The Telltale Heart." Run-

Betty Clare (Adrienne Corri) calls the police to investigate her suspicion that Edgar Marsh (Laurence Payne), far left, has murdered her lover, Carl Loomis, in *The Tell-Tale Heart* (1960). The policemen are played by John Martin, left, and John Scott.

ning about 24 minutes, it was apparently shot in an expressionistic style, similar to the two versions of Poe's "The Fall of the House of Usher" also released in that same year.

The first sound version of "The Tell-Tale Heart" was released in England in 1934, under the name, *The Tell-Tale Heart*. However, when it was released in America, the title was changed to *Bucket of Blood*. Thereafter, there have been many other adaptations of Poe's short story, including several for television.

Chapter 3

"The Queen of Spades" by Alexander Pushkin

Even though "The Queen of Spades" was first published in 1834, the story actually evokes memories of *The Twilight Zone*, a television series that was first on the air about 125 years later. Just like the best episodes in Rod Serling's famous show about the dimension of imagination, Alexander Pushkin's tale is simple and straightforward, has just a hint of the supernatural, ends with a surprising plot twist and leaves several questions unanswered.

Background

Alexander Pushkin was born in Moscow, Russia, in 1799. In 1823 he started writing his most famous work, *Eugene Onegin*, a novel in verse that was first published in its entirety in 1833. Like several of his other works, including "The Queen of Spades," a short story first published anonymously in 1834, *Eugene Onegin* was eventually adapted into an opera. Pushkin also wrote historical works, short stories and plays. Pushkin, who has been called Russia's greatest poet, died in 1837.

The Literature

"The Queen of Spades" concerns Hermann, a Russian military officer who desires to learn the secret of the cards, i.e., how to select three correct cards in three successive games of faro and make a large fortune. The only person who knows the secret is Countess Anna Fedotovna who, about 60 years before, won a significant amount of money by winning three straight games of faro by employing the trick. Hermann tricks Lizaveta Ivanovna, the pretty young companion of the Countess, into believing that Hermann has fallen in love with her, resulting in Lizaveta finally inviting Hermann to come over to the house late one night when the Countess is asleep. Hermann then sneaks into the room of the elderly Countess and threatens her with a gun, resulting in her death by a heart attack. Afterwards, Hermann finally obtains the secret from the ghost of the Countess. Hermann proceeds to a card game in Moscow and starts to win money by playing three, seven and ace on successive nights. Unfortunately, on the third night, the unexpected happens. Hermann loses all his winnings and more, ending up in an insane asylum for the rest of his life.

Part of the appeal of Pushkin's story is the manner in which he misdirects the reader. Most of the story appears to be a simple Gothic romance, with time spent detailing the Countess' ill treatment of her companion, Lizaveta, and then concluding with what appears to be Lizaveta's rescue from her life of drudgery by Hermann, her handsome Prince Charming. Pushkin succeeds in this misdirection partly by his cleverness, relying on most readers' interest in a love story with a happy ending, and partly by some cheating, by writing that Hermann's daily letters to Lizaveta were written by Hermann "under the inspiration of passion" (Part III), a statement which turns out to be false. Thus, it is a surprise to the reader to find that Hermann is only using Lizaveta to gain entrance into the presence of the Countess.

As part of his misdirection, Pushkin throws out other ideas, such as Hermann possibly being the natural child of the Countess (Part V) or Hermann thinking he must become the lover of the elderly Countess in order to learn her secret (Part II). Pushkin never follows through on those thoughts, making it difficult for the reader to determine what is real and what is supposition. All the while, the story goes back and forth in time, adding to both the confusion and the interest of the narrative.

Once the death of the Countess occurs, "The Queen of Spades" finally becomes a tale of the supernatural. There is the wink by the dead Countess at Hermann when he kneels beside her coffin and the ghostly visit of the Countess to Hermann on the night of her funeral. When the ghost of the Countess divulges the secret of the cards to Hermann, she tells him that she has come to him against her wishes because she was ordered to do so, another statement that is never explained in the story. At the conclusion of the story, the queen of spades figure on the card smiles ironically and winks at Hermann, just as the Countess did in her coffin. These are all eerie moments, indeed.

Or are they? Pushkin's story can be read simply as a tale of the psychological, with Hermann imagining all that happens after the Countess dies, caused by his guilt over his accidental contribution to the death of the Countess. After all, nothing of the supernatural occurs before the Countess passes away. Hermann's imaginings could have also been aggravated by his sudden turn to heavy drinking. Both the success and failure of Hermann at the card game can simply be deemed to be the luck of the cards, not a series of events controlled by the ghost of the Countess.

Is "The Queen of Spades" a tale of the supernatural or a tale of a mind slowly going insane? It is impossible to say. That is only one of the questions that Alexander Pushkin leaves unanswered in his engrossing tale of Hermann and the secret of the three lucky cards.

The Films

The Queen of Spades/Pikovaya dama (1916)

This 1916 Russian film is an extremely faithful adaptation of Alexander Pushkin's short story "The Queen of Spades." Just about every scene in the film is based on a moment from the story. Many of the title cards and some of the dialogue come from the short story, not necessarily word for word but surely inspired by Pushkin's language. Given that the Pushkin story is always engrossing, it is surprising that the film is so disappointing. However, there is a lesson to be learned in that anomaly, as basic as that lesson is—print is a different medium than film and what works in print will not necessarily work in film.

Pikovaya dama is generally shot in a straightforward manner and although it is not done exactly in the manner of a stage play, there are usually few camera cuts or unusual angles employed, adding to the boring nature of the feature. Also, the camera is usually stationary and there are minimal close-ups, keeping the audience at a distance from the characters and preventing the audience from truly becoming involved in the tale. The elaborate sets, period costumes and multiple extras are essentially wasted in this movie. This 1916 film is clearly not from the innovative period of Russian filmmaking, as exemplified by Sergei Eisenstein's *Battleship Potemkin* (1925).

Interestingly, the only time the filmmakers divert from Pushkin's story is one of the few times they display some creativity and imagination. This occurs in the scene in which the Countess retires to her bedchamber, unaware that Hermann is about to accost her. The Countess dreams of one of the assignations in her bedroom from her younger days, which contrasts nicely with Hermann entering the room to confront the old woman. Finally, there is some style in the storytelling.

Most of the time, however, *Pikovaya dama* is a movie of missed opportunities. One of the important scenes from Pushkin's story that is skipped in the film (at least in the print viewed) is the incident at the funeral, when the dead Countess seems to wink at Hermann. The omission of this incident undercuts the supernatural nature of the tale. The film does show the moment where the dead Countess mysteriously appears at Hermann's side to tell him the secret of the cards, but she simply appears and then disappears, with no style in the telling and no atmosphere in the setting, once again undercutting the mystical side of the tale.

If *Pikovaya dama* is not a tale of the supernatural, is it a tale of madness? Perhaps, but unfortunately that aspect of the story is not well-developed either. Hermann may seem driven during the story, surely interested in wealth to the exclusion of everything else, but his madness does not manifest itself until after Hermann plays the third card and loses all of his winnings. Up until that point, *Pikovaya dama* seems more like a costume drama than a story of either the mind or the supernatural. While the film precisely replicates Pushkin's story line, it does not replicate the atmosphere or mood of the story nor the story's deliberate ambiguity, characteristics that have made the story into a classic.

The film comes alive after Hermann plays the third card. Once he realizes that he has played the queen of spades instead of the ace, he sees the visage of the Countess in the card, an incident that comes from Pushkin's story. While the special effect employed is basic, that moment is well-handled. Indeed, it is one of the few paranormal scenes in the feature.

Hermann then runs out of the card room. He is next shown sitting on a couch, with a cutout figure of a woman to the side of him, framed and hanging on the wall. As Hermann in his madness continuously repeats the sequence of the cards to himself, the cutout dissolves into a large playing card with a single spade on it. Suddenly Hermann is sitting outside by a wall, entangled in what seem to be vines or a spider's web and then just as suddenly he is back in the room again, with the cutout on the wall back in place. Hermann is next shown in his hospital bed at an asylum playing cards, as the three, seven and ace float by, while an image of the Countess watches over him. Although inter-titles are employed in these scenes, they are unnecessary as Hermann's insanity is shown completely by the visuals. These last scenes of *Pikovaya dama* are the most inventive and engrossing moments in the film, showing the potential the production had, if only the same amount of creativity were used in the remainder of the feature.

The 1949 British version of "The Queen of Spades" is, to a large degree, also faithful to the short story, but the latter film contains just enough embellishments to the story line and exhibits such a masterful and stylish rendering of atmosphere and horror that a classic film was created from Pushkin's same source material. Even considering the difference of 30 years between the two films and the advanced techniques and equipment that were available in 1949, the 1916 version pales in comparison to its sound remake. *Pikovaya dama* demonstrates that just being faithful to a film's source material, as wonderful as that material may be, is not enough to create a good film.

The Queen of Spades (1949)

Anatole de Grunwald, who was born in Russia although he grew up in England and did most of his film work in his adopted country, produced this sound version of Alexander Pushkin's famous short story. The film *The Queen of Spades* is set in Russia but has an all–British cast, and as fine as that cast is, the film does have the feel of a screen adaptation of a classic English novel set in the mansions and taverns of London. If it were not for the strange Russian names of the characters and the mention of vodka from time to time, no viewer would realize that the film is actually taking place in 19th century St. Petersburg. However, the setting of the tale is not one of the film's critical aspects and that nitpick aside, *The Queen of Spades* is one of the best British films of the supernatural, in the same class as the much more famous *Dead of Night*, released just four years earlier.

Given that *The Queen of Spades* runs over 90 minutes and is based upon a short story, it is surprising how close an adaptation the film version is, with very few scenes added to extend the film's running time to that of a full length feature. There is no obvious padding in the movie, with the only significant detours from the main story line arising from the scenes in a gypsy tavern and a dance by one of the gypsy girls. The principal difference in the main plot between the two versions comes in flashback scenes early in the film where Hermann learns, by reading a book titled *The Strange Secrets of the Count de Saint Germain*, how the Countess acquires the secret of the three winning cards. According to the book, the Countess learns the trick from the mysterious Count de Saint Germain, a man who keeps a strange collection of wax figures that contain the souls of those who had fallen under his evil influence. Once she obtains the secret knowledge, the Countess then goes to church to pray before a painting of the Virgin Mary and Jesus but the faces of those figures then disappear into blackness. However, with the secret of the cards, the Countess wins a substantial amount of money at faro, but as the book about St. Germain states, "The horrors of her visit to Saint Germain left a mark on her soul for the rest of her life."

In addition to this backstory being somewhat different from Pushkin's tale, it clearly establishes *The Queen of Spades* as a tale of the supernatural. With the wizard-like creature at the bookstore where Hermann finds the book about St.

Germain, the wax figures of the Count's victims, the scene in church where the faces of Mary and Jesus turn black and the secret of the three winning cards, there can be no ambiguity or misdirection. *The Queen of Spades* is a story of the unreal and nothing else. Or so it seems.

At the end of the film, however, much like Pushkin's short story, the film version seems to revert to a tale of the psychological and of insanity. There are many manifestations of Hermann's real-world madness. After the surprising death of the Countess, Hermann goes to Lizaveta's room but he is in such a state of shock that he is unable to carry on a conversation with Lizaveta, ignoring what she says and talking to himself. After the funeral of the Countess, Hermann retires to his abode and starts to drink to excess. Just before the Countess returns to him to divulge the secret of the cards, Hermann is sleeping so perhaps all that occurs after is only a bad dream. Later, when Hermann goes to propose to Lizaveta, at the direction of the ghost, and Lizaveta rejects him, Hermann completely loses it, talking maniacally and spouting to Lizaveta that later that night he will become wealthy, people will then grovel at his feet and then he will stomp on them. Hermann's madness is accentuated by the lighting of the scene that emphasizes the depraved look on his face. Just as in the short story, when Hermann loses at the card game, he goes mad, repeating over and over the sequence of the cards, as he is hauled off to the asylum. Thus, *The Queen of Spades* commences with a story that is firmly rooted in the supernatural but ends with a tale that could be one of mysticism or could be one of madness. The film is actually more of an enigma than Pushkin's short story.

Much of the impact of *The Queen of Spades* arises from its direction, cinematography and its mise-en-scéne. The key moment in the film is when the dead Countess comes to Hermann's apartment to finally reveal the secret of the three cards. Much of the atmosphere is created by sounds, first the tapping that awakens Hermann, then the squeaking and banging of the door, the shuffling of someone walking and then the loud roar of the wind. The only visual manifestation of the arrival of the countess is the wind, which blows the curtains, knocks down lamps and bottles and swirls paper and debris throughout the room. The scene is shot in light and shade, indirectly lit from radiance through the windows and a swinging light in the room, with Hermann often being shown in shadows and dark. The payoff to the scene is not the physical appearance of the Countess but rather, the sound of her echoing voice only. It is one of the eeriest ghost scenes in all of film history, even with no ghost ever being shown.

Other scenes in the film also display the same style of filmmaking with, for example, the effectiveness of the scenes related to the Countess' death accentuated by the tick tock of a clock in the mansion and the bells on a fast moving sleigh outside, and the flashback scene at the Count's palace heightened by the neighing of some horses which sound like screams. The ghostlike quality of the death of the Countess is aided by the snow falling on the exterior of the mansion. Contrasting light and shadow are employed throughout the movie, particularly in shots involving Hermann. The clever decision to forgo the image of the ghost of the Countess when she reappears to Hermann is matched by the decision not to show the queen of spades of the cards smiling or winking at Hermann at the end of the card game, as it apparently did in the short story, for that undoubtedly would have seemed quite silly on the screen, destroying the atmosphere of the film.

Of course, all is not perfect with the film. In addition to employing a totally non–Russian cast, the musical score by Georges Auric is jarring at times, upon occasion being overly dramatic. The reader actually learns more about Lizaveta and her character in the few paragraphs Pushkin devotes to her in his short story than the viewer does in watching the entire film. There is also a serious gap in the narrative. Even though the viewer is told that the Countess sold her soul for the secret of the cards, no grave consequences of that decision are ever shown. In fact, even after selling her soul, the Countess lives to a very old age and is quite wealthy at the time of her death, still retaining her important status among the elite of St. Petersburg. In other words, after embellishing Pushkin's explanation as to how the Countess obtained the secret of the three cards, the film never follows through on that story line, simply disregarding that part of the tale when it becomes inconvenient to the main plot of the film.

However, *The Queen of Spades* does capitalize on Pushkin's happy ending, providing Lizaveta with a fallback Prince Charming in the person of Andrei, who authentically chases Lizaveta throughout the movie and is also the person who beats Hermann at his game of cards, making the downfall of Hermann doubly satisfying. Thus a film about the supernatural, madness, gambling and the selling of souls ends on a happy note, a satisfactory conclusion for the viewer after all of the horror that has gone before.

Other Adaptations

There have been many other film versions of Pushkin's "The Queen of Spades," including several from France and Russia. In addition, an opera based upon "The Queen of Spades," composed by Peter Ilyich Tchaikovsky, premiered in St. Petersburg, Russia, in 1890. Titled *Pikovaya dama* in Russian, the opera has been performed many times since. It is still probably the most famous adaptation of Pushkin's short story about Hermann and the secret of the three winning cards.

Chapter 4

The Strange Case of Dr. Jekyll and Mr. Hyde by Robert Louis Stevenson

Robert Louis Stevenson's famous novella may be the most filmed work of all time. There were numerous silent versions, including three made in 1920 alone. In the early sound era, there was a famous 1932 production starring Frederic March, a 1941 production starring Spencer Tracy and then a Hammer production in 1960. Thereafter, there have been numerous television and film remakes.

This is all somewhat surprising because *The Strange Case of Dr. Jekyll and Mr. Hyde* runs less than 100 pages and is actually more of a mystery than a horror story. Nevertheless, the short work has been the inspiration for at least as many horror films as either *Frankenstein* or *Dracula*, two of the most famous print horror works of their day.

Background

Robert Louis Stevenson was born in Edinburgh, Scotland, in 1850, the only child of Thomas and Margaret Balfour Stevenson. After studying engineering and the law at Edinburgh University, he turned to writing, making his early mark as an essayist and later as a novelist, in works such as *Treasure Island* (1883), *Dr. Jekyll and Mr. Hyde* (1886) and *Kidnapped* (1886). Suffering from ill health throughout most of his life, Stevenson passed away in 1894 at the age of 44.

The Literature

The Strange Case of Dr. Jekyll and Mr. Hyde begins as a mystery as Gabriel John Utterson, a prominent London attorney and a long-time friend of Dr. Jekyll's, investigates the reason for the disappearances of the good Dr. Jekyll and his seemingly strange relationship with the evil Mr. Hyde. Utterson finally discovers the secret of his friend by reading two documents he discovers after the death of Mr. Hyde and the apparent disappearance of Dr. Jekyll. One is a writing from Dr. Hastie Lanyon, a former friend and colleague of Dr. Jekyll's, who writes of the day he saw Hyde instantly change into Dr. Jekyll. The metamorphosis shakes Lanyon to his roots, causing him the deadliest of terrors. The second document is the story of Jekyll and Hyde written by the hand of Dr. Jekyll which relates the story of his experiments in splitting the good and evil nature in one person, resulting in the creation of the evil Mr. Hyde and what turned out to be the eventual deaths of both personas.

The first part of *The Strange Case of Dr. Jekyll and Mr. Hyde* works very well as a mystery, as the strange occurrences revolving around Mr. Hyde are parceled out bit by bit in Utterson's chronicle, with the reader not really sure what is actually transpiring with Dr. Jekyll. There are, however, several good clues to what has happened, including the smallish Hyde wearing the larger clothes of Dr. Jekyll's and the similarity in the handwriting of the two. There are therefore enough clues for the reader to solve the case but only if he is willing to suspend his disbelief just a little. However, as good a mystery as *Jekyll and Hyde* may be, if the novella were only a mystery, it would be long forgotten today. The story has enthralled millions, even to this day, because of its horror components.

The horror elements of the Jekyll and Hyde story are almost all self-contained within the writings of Lanyon and Jekyll. Lanyon describes the surprise and sudden metamorphosis of Hyde into Jekyll as if seeing a man restored from death. Jekyll describes the first painful transformation from Jekyll to Hyde as one of "a grinding in the bones, deadly nausea, and a horror of the spirit that cannot be exceeded at the hour of birth or death" ("Henry Jekyll's Full Statement of the Case"). The real shock of the tale comes, however, when Jekyll, suddenly and unexpectedly, turns into Hyde without drinking the potion. Jekyll realizes that he has lost control of his darker side; he is no longer able to prevent an evil creature from prowling the streets of London. This loss of control over evil is the aspect of Stevenson's novella that has inspired many horror films over many years, not the mystery elements that preceded it.

The Strange Case of Dr. Jekyll and Mr. Hyde incorporates several familiar components of horror novels and films, before they became commonplace.

Many horror stories have a transformation scene, such as a man turning into a werewolf or a vampire turning into a bat. Stevenson gives the reader many of those. Creatures of the night often plausibly deny their affliction. Early on, Jekyll similarly tells Utterson not to worry because "the moment I choose, I can be rid of Mr. Hyde" ("Dr. Jekyll Was Quite at Ease"). The reader later learns that Jekyll was already beginning to lose control of Hyde at the time the statement was made.

In emphasizing the mystery elements of the chronicle, an engrossing way of telling his tale, Robert Louis Stevenson was unfortunately de-emphasizing the thematic attributes of the material. These do come through at the end, however, in the Full Statement of the Case by Dr. Jekyll. Jekyll touches on the issues of addiction (as early on he is often unable to prevent himself from taking the potion to turn into Hyde and experience the undignified pleasures of Hyde's lifestyle), on the limits of science (as he worries about the long term effects of his drug but still takes it, risking the consequences) and the effects of a repressive society on nonconforming conduct (the past sins of Jekyll's life, although not described in the novella, but which have caused him significant guilt feelings, surely pale in comparison to the Mr. Hyde that Jekyll has inflicted on the city of London).

The primary theme of the novella, however, is the good and evil residing in one person and the ability of man to reconcile the two. Jekyll writes of the dichotomy in his life from an early age. On the one hand, he had an excellent nature, being honorable, industrious and fine. On the other, his more shameful tendencies often came to the fore, such as a certain impatient gaiety of disposition that upon occasion led to shameful pleasures. Jekyll frequently thought about these inconsistencies in his nature, realizing that he was neither good nor bad but rather, a combination of the two. He eventually wondered whether the two elements of personality could be separated, so that the unjust personality could go his own way, not limited by the goodness of his twin, and the just personality could go on to do good things, without fear of being exposed to disgrace by his opposite side. Dr. Jekyll thereafter devised a potion that turned him into the evil Dr. Hyde. However, even from the beginning, the evil Hyde seemed stronger than the good Dr. Jekyll. As time went on, Hyde became more evil than before, trampling a young girl on the street and clubbing a member of Parliament to death.

Stevenson warns that the evil side of an individual is the stronger of the two, with the good side always required to fight to remain on the side of the just and to avoid temptation. Although there are no Biblical references in the story, this theme of *Jekyll and Hyde* would make a good subject for a Sunday sermon. The weakness in Stevenson's work, though, is that since Jekyll is a true loner, he has no one to talk with in the story. As a result, there are no discussions of this theme of good fighting evil, or, for that matter, any of the other themes of the novelette. Thus, Stevenson can only raise the issue of the internal (and eternal) fight between good and evil that each of us faces; he is never able to truly explore the issue. There are some obvious missed opportunities in Stevenson's work.

Of course, few horror films are predisposed to address issues of intellectual dimensions, although, perhaps unwittingly, many actually do. Horror films are primarily about horror and presumably a work from the literature of horror is chosen by a filmmaker for its potential for terror and shock on the silver screen and not for the force of its ideas. Many filmmakers over many years obviously decided that Robert Louis Stevenson's tale of Dr. Jekyll's aspirations, misfortunes and eventual demise laid a solid foundation for a cinematic work of horror. In many cases the final products on the screen confirmed the wisdom of those decisions.

The Films

Dr. Jekyll and Mr. Hyde (1920)

The most well-regarded silent film adaptation of *Dr. Jekyll and Mr. Hyde* is the 1920 version starring John Barrymore. Screenwriter Clara S. Beranger cleverly eschews the mystery approach that Stevenson had assumed towards his material and always focuses the story on Dr. Jekyll and his alter ego, which is the same slant that all later films would take. The switch of emphasis works particularly well when there is a quality actor in the roles of Jekyll and Hyde and given that in the most important versions of the story, those actors are John Barrymore, Frederic March and Spencer Tracy, that high standard is easily met.

John Barrymore was still in his 30s and in good health when *Dr. Jekyll and Mr. Hyde* was made. He is a wonder in this film. Barrymore's Dr. Jekyll is tall, cultured and handsome, an excellent counterpoint to the stooped over and tortured-looking Mr. Hyde. The first metamorphosis from Jekyll into Hyde is the best in the film. When Jekyll swallows the mysterious potion, he is instantly wracked with pain, cries out in anguish, grabs his throat and experiences convulsions. A close-up of Jekyll's face then reveals the scraggly hair hanging down on both sides of his head, his eyes wide and his mouth pinched. With little makeup, the handsome Jekyll has been transformed into the repulsive Hyde. Unfortunately, there is then a disconcertingly ineffective (by today's standards) dissolve as Barrymore's fingers grow longer and misshapen, although those

In this publicity photograph of a scene near the conclusion of *Dr. Jekyll and Mr. Hyde* (1920), Mr. Hyde (John Barrymore) turns his attention to Millicent Carew (Martha Mansfield), the love interest of Dr. Jekyll.

strange fingers fit well with Hyde's slightly stooped posture throughout the movie. Later transformations into Hyde are not as clever as the first one, involving more unconvincing dissolves rather than Barrymore's consummate acing skills.

Robert Louis Stevenson provides almost no description of the evil Hyde, other than to say that he is pale and dwarfish. Neither of those characteristics is, thankfully, carried over into the film version, with a tall figure of a man surely much more terrifying than a creature of small stature. Stevenson writes in his novella, without ever describing why, that Hyde creates a feeling of disgust, loathing and fear in those who see him. The film version does the same with Hyde but through the visuals, which is exactly what a moving picture is supposed to do. In fact, when Hyde reappears later in the film, he is an even more disgusting figure, with the makeup enhanced to display a slanted, pointed head and a toothy, malevolent smile.

While Stevenson's novelette has no female characters of significance, the 1920 movie version takes a different approach. Clara S. Beranger developed the plot point (which would then become a convention of the Jekyll and Hyde of the cinema) of Jekyll interacting with both a respectable woman and disreputable woman, paralleling the good and evil nature of Dr. Jekyll himself. The good woman is Millicent Carew, the bland but virtuous woman who is in love with Dr. Jekyll. The attractive Martha Mansfield plays Millicent but the role is standard stuff and Mansfield is easily forgettable in the part. The exciting but immoral woman is Miss Gina, the Italian singer upon whom Jekyll is transfixed but with whom he is afraid to follow through on his desires. In the guise of Mr. Hyde, however, Jekyll has no such inhibitions. He is excited to have an affair with Gina, a figure of depravity from the world of saloons and stages. Nita Naldi, a quite buxom actress even by today's standards, plays Gina. Gina's role in the film is small but no one would ever describe Nita Naldi as forgettable.

There is another twinning of characters in the film, also paralleling the dual nature of Jekyll and Hyde. Dr. Richard Lanyon is the representative of good science, an individual almost as upstanding as Dr. Jekyll himself once was. His opposite is the wealthy Sir George Carew, Millicent's father. Carew admits to doing some wild things in his life. It is he who tempts Jekyll to experience life, including its seamier side, arguing that a man cannot "destroy the savage in him by denying its impulses." Carew takes Jekyll out on a night on the town, actually daring him to experience the immoral aspects of London life. At one point, Carew says to Jekyll, "The only way to get rid of a temptation is to yield to it," a direct quotation from *The Picture of Dorian Gray* by Oscar Wilde (Chapter II), another work which addresses the good and evil in one person's soul. (In this film version of Stevenson's story, the character of Sir George Carew is similar to, and quotes several times, Lord Henry Wotton from Oscar Wilde's novel.)

Unlike the Dr. Jekyll of the novel, the film version of the character is a true saint, referred to as a Saint Anthony by one character. The first title card for Dr. Jekyll describes him as an "idealist and philanthropist—by profession, a doctor of medicine." At his free clinic, Jekyll helps the seriously ill, from young people to the elderly. The Dr. Jekyll of the Stevenson's novelette wonders why the potion unleashed his totally evil side, not his very best side ("Henry Jekyll's Full Statement of the Case"). In this film version, it could not have gone any other way. Dr. Jekyll in this film is the epitome of all that is good in people.

Unlike Stevenson's Dr. Jekyll, Barrymore's Dr. Jekyll does not wonder or feel guilty about any misdeeds over his lifetime—he has none. Thus, a theme of the novella, the effect of a repressive society on the character of the individual, is not considered in the silent film version. Indeed, the main theme of Stevenson's work, the struggle between good and evil, is also not prominent in this film version. One reason for this oversight is that similar to the novel, there is no one with whom Jekyll can discuss his ideas and concerns. Additionally, unlike a reader of the written work, the film audience is seldom privy to Jekyll's inner thoughts. At one point, the filmmakers try to convey Jekyll's anguish from his loss of control of Hyde by a strange special effect in which a giant insect seems to take over Jekyll's body and turn him into Hyde. However, this scene is confusing and inconsistent with the style of the rest of the film. It simply does not work. Without dialogue, Jekyll's anguish and lack of control, the real horror elements of the novella, cannot be adequately conveyed to the viewer.

Dr. Jekyll and Mr. Hyde cleverly imports the two brutal acts that were related by Gabriel John Utterson in Stevenson's novella. Hyde runs into a young child and starts to step on him before a mob intervenes. The scene in the film is somewhat mild; the description of the incident in the novelette is far more repulsive. Later, Hyde clubs Sir George Carew to death and here the film mirrors the written work in the ferociousness of the act. The movie scene also works well because Hyde has a motive to kill Carew. Hyde must kill Carew because Carew has witnessed one of Jekyll's unexpected transformations into Hyde.

Several of the titles in the film are overwrought, a characteristic of many silent films. One card states, "As Hyde plunged deeper into vice, his trail was soon strewn with victims of his depravity." However, the footage subsequent only shows him ending his relationship with Gina. Thereafter a title reads, "For some time Dr. Jekyll renounced the dark indulgences of Hyde—until in an hour of weakness the demon, long caged burst forth more malignant than before." The following footage depicts Hyde in a low class bar, possibly dealing with prostitutes, but showing little else. In these scenes, *Dr. Jekyll and Mr. Hyde* is using the text to convey the story, rather than the visuals, undercutting whatever depravity or malignancy Hyde supposedly has.

The ending of the film is clever, expanding on the finish of the novelette to create a very cinematic conclusion. Jekyll, hiding in his laboratory, sends Poole to locate certain drugs that Jekyll needs for his potion. Poole realizes that Jekyll is in dire condition and sends for Dr. Lanyon and Millicent Carew. Unbeknownst to everyone, Jekyll has turned into Hyde behind closed doors and when Millicent enters, she is at great risk. A full screen close-up of Hyde, evil exuding from his face, enhances the tension. Hyde touches Millicent with those long, strange fingers and tries to embrace her, a shuddering moment, before he drops to the floor, dead from the poison he has just taken. It is an excellent scene.

When Dr. Lanyon comes into the laboratory, he sees Hyde's dead body and then in awe, sees it transform back into Jekyll. Then, so that Millicent will never know the truth about Dr. Jekyll, he tells her, "Hyde has killed—Dr. Jekyll." While Lanyon believes he is lying for a good purpose, he is unknowingly telling the truth, for it is Mr. Hyde who killed Dr. Jekyll and all of the goodness in him. It is rare to find a film in which evil triumphs over good, but that is, in fact, the story of Jekyll and Hyde. So, in its last title, this silent movie version of the tale, whether accidentally or not, ties back to the theme of Stevenson's work—that good must always be vigilant so that evil does not defeat the worthy in all of us.

Dr. Jekyll and Mr. Hyde (1920) is an excellent film. After all these years, it compares very favorably with the famous sound versions to follow.

Dr. Jekyll and Mr. Hyde (1932)

An in-vogue term for describing a certain group of Hollywood films from the early 1930s is "pre–Code." The pre–Code era in Hollywood was the approximate five-year period beginning in 1929, when sound films first dominated the market, until mid–1934, when a strict production code was self-imposed by Hollywood. Pre–Code films were sexier, more adult and less strict about good triumphing over evil than post–Code films. A prime example of a pre–Code movie is the 1932 version of *Dr. Jekyll and Mr. Hyde*, a film which emphasizes the sensuality and sexuality implied in Robert Louis Stevenson's novella as no other film adaptation before or since has ever done quite so effectively.

In this adaptation, Dr. Jekyll is a famous doctor and scientist who lectures the medical community on the good and evil in man while at the same time operating a charity clinic which provides medical care for the poor. Jekyll is engaged to Muriel Carew but her strict father, General Carew, refuses to accelerate the wedding date, requiring Jekyll and Muriel to wait another eight months for their nuptials. Frustrated, Jekyll returns to his experiments on dual personality, devises his fateful potion and upon turning into Hyde, seeks out Ivy Pierson, a seductive music hall performer he once met as Dr. Jekyll. Hyde intimidates Pierson and takes her as his mistress, but over time turns to beating and whipping her. Eventually, Hyde, jealous of Ivy going to talk to Jekyll, chokes Ivy to death. Hyde is pursued, trapped in Dr. Jekyll's lab and then shot to death. As the film ends, Mr. Hyde, in death, transforms back into Dr. Jekyll.

The first characteristic of the 1932 version of Stevenson's novella that everyone notices is the direction of the film. Rouben Mamoulian's approach to the film is stylistic in the extreme, and generally Mamoulian's direction is a decided plus for *Dr. Jekyll and Mr. Hyde*. Mamoulian uses a split screen, often on a diagonal divide, to tie scenes together but also to compare and contrast what is going on in the two scenes. He often inserts a separate inanimate object in a shot, usually a candle or a candelabrum, turning a bland two-shot into an interesting three-shot. His camera frequently lingers on a flower, statuary or other object of art either while an event is occurring or immediately thereafter, once again never allowing his visuals to become boring. Mamoulian's work is aided by the film's impressive sets with the high ceilings, particularly Dr. Jekyll's spacious laboratory, filled with lab equipment in one area and wooden walkways and stairs in others.

On some occasions, however, Mamoulian's stylistic approach does not work. For example, when Muriel and Jekyll profess their love for each other, there are extreme close-ups of each of their eyes, for no reason of significance or effectiveness for the scene. As another example, in the opening sequence of the movie, Dr. Jekyll proceeds from his house to a lecture hall in a complete point-of-view shot reminiscent of the directorial style of *Lady in the Lake* (1947). There is no purpose to this style of direction, except to show the skill of the craftsman.

The one important moment in the opening point-of-view sequence is the quick surprise of seeing the handsome face of Dr. Jekyll suddenly appear in the mirror. In fact, mirrors are a continuing motif of the film, with Jekyll viewing his first transformation into Hyde through his laboratory mirror (the Jekyll of the novelette originally had no mirrors in his lab) to a happy Ivy suddenly shocked by the appearance of Hyde in her apartment mirror, realizing quite quickly that her life is in jeopardy. The motif of mirrors subtlety raises the questions as to which manifestation of Jekyll is the real Jekyll, the good doctor or the wicked Hyde, and which is just a likeness created by the potion.

The highlight of most Jekyll and Hyde films is the first transformation sequence and the 1932 feature does not disappoint. Mamoulian delays Jekyll's drinking of the potion to the last possible instance, first with a shot of a skeleton, the writing of a note to Muriel and then a close-up of the glass before Jekyll downs the potion while looking into a mirror. Instantly Jekyll is wracked with pain. He grabs his throat, his mouth appears bigger, his face becomes shadowy and seems to change shape, and then after a montage of earlier scenes from the film, Hyde re-appears in the mirror, with almost no resemblance to Jekyll. The transformation scene is re-done several times throughout the film, and each time it is a feat of cinema magic, accomplished by March's performance, color filters gradually exposing Hyde's makeup and hidden jump cuts.

Frederic March is shown in a publicity photograph for his dual role in *Dr. Jekyll and Mr. Hyde* (1932). On the left is Dr. Jekyll and on the right is Mr. Hyde.

Frederic March's Hyde is a true figure of horror. His face is ape-like in quality, with its hairy top sitting on a misshapen head, large, crooked teeth that he cannot fully contain within his wide mouth, slightly swelled features and a flat nose. March dominates the film when he is in the guise of Hyde, betraying none of the characteristics of the good Dr. Jekyll. Marsh's movements are often ape-like in manner, as he swings or jumps from place to place to avoid capture. Robert Louis Stevenson was somewhat reticent in his description of Hyde in the novella but March's Hyde does display some of the dwarfish characteristics of Stevenson's Hyde, a rare occurrence in film versions of the story.

The Dr. Jekyll of the 1932 film version is much closer to the good doctor of the novella rather than to the character portrayed by John Barrymore in the silent film. While March's Jekyll does have his charity clinic for the poor, where he treats all of his patients with dignity, he is still a complex mixture of good and evil, The montage inserted into the first transformation scene shows Jekyll's dispute with General Carew over the timing of the marriage to Muriel and his threat of strangling Carew, and his not-too-difficult seduction by Ivy Pierson which Lanyon calls disgusting.

Thus, because of the complexity of Jekyll's character, the 1932 feature sets the foundation for a sophisticated discussion of the good and evil in one person. Surprisingly, that discussion never actually occurs. Jekyll hardly addresses the issue when he explains his ideas to others, the story is so bare in detail that Jekyll's inner struggles hardly come to the forefront, and once Hyde appears, he becomes such an overwhelming personality that, for a time, it seems that Jekyll has disappeared from the chronicle. As a partial replacement for this significant topic from the novella, *Dr. Jekyll and Mr. Hyde* substitutes the cliché of science-gone-mad, as when Lanyon tells Jekyll early in the film, "There are bounds beyond which one should not go," and Jekyll concludes late in the film, "I have gone further than Man should go." However, while science is the basis for Dr. Jekyll's experiments, the method by which he splits the human psyche into two is never explained and *Jekyll and Hyde*, in its many manifestations, is always a work of horror, not a work of science fiction. Thus, the science-gone-mad theme is jarringly out-of-place in this movie.

The true theme of the film and the one that makes *Dr. Jekyll and Mr. Hyde* (1932) a true pre–Code production is its emphasis on regressive societal attitudes toward sex and their effect on individual conduct. This theme is only implied in Stevenson's novelette and not necessarily with regard to sexual activities. In the film, Jekyll is in love with Muriel but due to the conventions of the society in which they live, their nuptials have been postponed to far into the future and they are left with a few chaste kisses, a waltz and a chance to talk alone for only a few seconds. This contrasts with the day when Jekyll spots a young woman being beaten on the street. He carries her up to her room and places her on her bed so that he can examine her. That woman, Ivy Pierson, exudes sensuality as she tries to seduce Jekyll, touching him suggestively, doing a striptease with her garters and stockings, baring her back and forcefully kissing him. The last lingering image of Ivy is the swinging of her shapely leg. This type of scene would be missing from films in just a few short years.

After Jekyll leaves Ivy's room, the image of Ivy with her swinging leg, imploring Jekyll to "Come back soon," is superimposed on the screen, as though Jekyll cannot get Ivy out of his mind. The same did not occur when Jekyll kissed Muriel. It is no coincidence that the first time Hyde goes out of the laboratory, it is not to commit acts of violence. Rather, once Jekyll learns that Muriel is leaving the country for a month and his desires are going to be frustrated once again, Hyde goes out in search of Ivy, the obvious vehicle of relief for his sexual drives which are inhibited by the society in which he dwells.

It is significant that the first time Jekyll turns into Hyde without taking the potion, it is when Jekyll is on his way to Muriel's to announce the date of their marriage. In a choice between the staid, upper class life with Muriel and the exciting and violent life with Ivy (one of male dominance, physical abuse and rape), Hyde's evil desires easily win out over Jekyll's commonplace life style choice. *Dr. Jekyll and Mr. Hyde* (1932) has a decided sexual element that is only hinted at in Stevenson's novella.

Only a few incidents from the novella are incorporated into the film. Near the end, Lanyon obtains the secret potion from Jekyll's laboratory and then is horrified as Hyde uses it to turn back into Jekyll, an incident that comes directly from Stevenson's work. Also, much like the novella, Hyde clubs General Carew to his death, but the background to the killing is totally different in the film than in the novella. These two scenes from the novella segue into the exciting conclusion of the film in which Hyde is chased all over London until he is caught and killed at Jekyll's laboratory. Stevenson's novella ended mildly; this film surely does not. The conclusion of *Dr. Jekyll and Mr. Hyde* (1932), which involves multiple transformations of Jekyll and Hyde and several acts of violence, is an exciting way to end a tale of split personality, sexual desire, societal restrictions and, of course, of horror. *Dr. Jekyll and Mr. Hyde* (1932) is probably the best screen version of Robert Louis Stevenson's tale.

Dr. Jekyll and Mr. Hyde (1941)

Whatever guidelines one might use to determine if a film is an A-production, *Dr. Jekyll and Mr. Hyde* (1941) clearly qualifies. The film was made at MGM, the premiere Hollywood studio at the time. It boasts three top Hollywood stars, Spencer Tracy, Ingrid Bergman and Lana Turner. The sets are magnificent and sometimes striking, with high ceilings and large, detailed interiors. Numerous extras fill scenes where necessary. The director is Victor Fleming, who previously directed *Gone With the Wind* (1939) and *The Wizard of Oz* (1939). In fact, the 1941 production of *Jekyll and Hyde* may be the most lavish horror film ever made.

Nevertheless, while *Dr. Jekyll and Mr. Hyde* (1941) is a fine film, it pales in comparison to the 1932 production starring Frederic March and, in fact, pales in comparison to many low budget horror films of the 1940s. Plainly, the horror genre does not require extravagant budgets to produce effective films.

For those who have seen the 1932 version of Robert Louis Stevenson's novella, a plot summary of the 1941 film is not really required. In fact, one difficulty with *Dr. Jekyll and Mr. Hyde* (1941) is that it is not really an adaptation of Robert Louis Stevenson's famous novella. Rather, it is a remake of the 1932 version and a close remake, at that. While the 1932 version incorporated some elements from the 1920 film version starring John Barrymore, the 1920 and 1932 versions were clearly different works. No one can say that about the 1932 and 1941 versions. It is therefore not clear why such a close remake of the 1932 version was made after less than a decade had gone by.

Another problem with the 1941 version is that it does not incorporate any of the themes of the Stevenson novella. The central issue of good and evil in one man is addressed at a dinner party early in the film and then forgotten. With a clergyman at the dinner table, there is an opportunity to discuss the religious aspects of Jekyll's theoretical dichotomy but that opportunity is squandered. The theme of the limits of scientific research is also ignored, except for one moment near the end of the film where Lanyon accuses Jekyll of committing the supreme blasphemy. However, this theme is glossed over earlier in the film and Lanyon and Jekyll barely address the subject at the end, so the topic is immaterial to this version of the story.

The most significant defect in the 1941 version, as contrasted with the 1932 version, is its superficial treatment of the effects of a regressive society on sexual yearnings, a result of the Hollywood Production Code, in full force in 1941. That treatment severely limits the frankness of the production, with only vague hints of anything sexual in the tale and nothing of an explicit nature. Thus, when Ivy Peterson first meets Dr. Jekyll and attempts to seduce him, the scene plays more like an innocent flirtation between two adults than a moment of sexual temptation. All that is shown is Ivy asking Jekyll to examine her back, Ivy taking off her stockings and garter (but not as a sensual striptease) and then one good kiss between the two. As beautiful as Ingrid Bergman is, she exudes no sensuality because these scenes are chaste, in the extreme. It is hard to believe that Jekyll even remembers Ivy when he first turns into Hyde.

While there is no question that Ingrid Bergman was a more beautiful woman than Miriam Hopkins, Hopkins radiated sexuality in her first scenes with the Dr. Jekyll character in the 1932 version. Ingrid Bergman does not. Lana Turner is also beautiful as Bea Emery but much like Ingrid Bergman, conveys no hint of danger or desire. Since Bea and Ivy attract Dr. Jekyll in an equivalent manner, the underlying sexual tension of this version of the novella is missing, creating a huge void in the film. Clearly the term "pre–Code" does have some significance in evaluating films; it is not just an in-vogue term.

As a result, *Dr. Jekyll and Mr. Hyde* (1941) can be assessed only as a horror film, without regard to underlying themes. Unfortunately, the movie also comes up short in that regard. A usual highlight of a *Jekyll and Hyde* movie is the first transformation. Here, Jekyll takes the potion, falls to the floor and then there is a montage of his imaginings, such as leaves and flowers in a pond, images of Bea and Ivy, Jekyll whipping two horses which turn into Bea and Ivy (a rare sexual image for the film) and oozing mud. Scary this is not. Jekyll then rises from the floor to look at himself in a fogged up mirror, and in a clever moment, wipes the mirror several times, to allow his new image to come into better focus. However, there is no payoff to the scene, as Hyde looks a lot like Jekyll, although a little crazed, but then the first close-up of Jekyll in the church at the beginning of the film made Jekyll seem a little crazed also.

Hyde's makeup is very disappointing although, in a sense, it is very close to Robert Louis Stevenson's vision of Mr. Hyde. While Spencer Tracy's Hyde is not dwarfish, he does display an "impression of deformity without any nameable malformation' and "a displeasing smile," which is Stevenson's description from the novella (chapter titled "Search for Mr. Hyde"). The second transformation into Hyde is done with a similar montage scene and perhaps an even weaker payoff when Jekyll once again looks in the mirror at his new visage. For a horror film, these are critical missed opportunities because this Mr. Hyde is not the least bit scary.

To be fair, the later transformations from Jekyll into Hyde in the film are substantially better, with dissolves and blurs as the transformations are made onscreen. They are impressive bits of movie magic. Also, Hyde's makeup becomes more hideous as the movie goes forward, making Hyde more of a monster as the story proceeds. Nevertheless, first impressions are important, even in horror films, and *Dr. Jekyll and Mr. Hyde* (1941) cannot recover from the disappointing transformation scenes that occur early in the film. Other missed opportunities are the strangling of Ivy, hidden behind a couch with nary a scream or a choking sound from Ivy, and the caning of Sir Charles Emery, which occurs below the screen image, once again without much sound to enhance the violence. There are truly no scenes of great horror in this film.

Dr. Jekyll and Mr. Hyde (1941) has many positives. The acting is superb, with Spencer Tracy successfully conveying the difference between Jekyll and Hyde without the assistance of much makeup and Ingrid Bergman excellent as she plays against type as Ivy (although the Ivy of this film version is hardly a bad woman, just one who is down on her luck). Has Bergman ever looked more beautiful in films? Lana Turner is fine as Bea Emery, but Jekyll's betrothed has always been a thankless part in all of the screen versions that employ the character. Donald Crisp also stands out as Bea's stern father.

The direction of Victor Fleming's is excellent, employing unusual downward and upward camera angles, shots between people and through openings in furniture, sometimes having Jekyll/Hyde slip in and out of fog, Jekyll sometimes appearing as a walking shadow with his dark hat, cape and cane, and the use of mirror images for effect, although, once again, the use of mirrors comes from the 1932 version. At one point in the film, there is a stunning foreshadowing of the uncontrolled transformation of Jekyll into Hyde, as Jekyll walks down the street whistling Ivy's bar song, switches to waltz he had once danced with Bea and then uncontrollably segues back into the bar song, as the Hyde personality takes over. It is one of the most inventive moments in all of the *Jekyll and Hyde* films. Unfortunately, there are not enough of those moments in this film.

If one has never seen an earlier version of the story, *Dr. Jekyll and Mr. Hyde* (1941) is good enough, particularly because of its excellent production values. In the end, though, the movie is disappointing for horror film fans and

In *Dr. Jekyll and Mr. Hyde* (1941), Dr. Jekyll (Spencer Tracy), walking down the street, is unaware that he is about to involuntarily turn into Mr. Hyde.

for devotees of Stevenson's novella, as it has few horror elements and even less of Stevenson's thematic material. The 1941 film plays less as a horror film and more as another entry in MGM's series of films based on famous works of literature, such as *Anna Karenina* (1935), *The Good Earth* (1937) and *Pride and Prejudice* (1940), all very good films in their own right.

While *Dr. Jekyll and Mr. Hyde* (1941) is also good, it is hard to be enthusiastic about the feature as a horror film. "Good but bland" is a fair description of Dr. Jekyll but the phrase also accurately describes this film version. Perhaps the most stinging criticism of the 1941 film version is this—there have been much better film adaptations of Stevenson's novella, ones for which many viewers are, in fact, quite enthusiastic.

The Two Faces of Dr. Jekyll/House of Fright (1960)

Given the pedigree of the actors who had previously essayed the roles, one might expect that an actor of some stature would be chosen to play Jekyll and Hyde in this first British version of Robert Louis Stevenson's novella. Alas and alack, by 1960, horror films in general and *The Two Faces of Dr. Jekyll* in particular, had such limited status that the parts went to Paul Massie, an unknown actor then and, quite frankly, still a virtually unknown actor today. At least Christopher Lee, in the process of becoming a horror film icon at Hammer, has a supporting role in the film.

Based on the change in title, film audiences might expect that *The Two Faces of Dr. Jekyll* would be different than Robert Louis Stevenson's novella and the famous film versions that had come before it. In that regard, they are correct. In this incarnation, Dr. Jekyll is a scientist with a heavy beard and mustache and very deep voice who, when he injects himself with his serum, transforms into the clean-shaven and very handsome Edward Hyde instead of a creature of physical horror. However, there is still that unadulterated evil in Hyde, which results in him committing rape and murder. The film ends in a surprise, with the arrest of Dr. Jekyll for the crimes of Mr. Hyde's.

The Two Faces of Dr. Jekyll simply does not work. It is an unworthy successor to the three Jekyll and Hyde films previously discussed in this chapter. One of its most significant problems is that it is really not much of a horror film. There are no transformation scenes; there are simply cutaways and then a revelation of Mr. Hyde reappearing or, more often, Dr. Jekyll reappearing. As to indicia of Hyde's evil, Hyde beats a man in a bar, throws a beggar to the street, watches bare knuckle boxing, goes to low class bars and smokes at opium dens. At one point, Dr. Jekyll describes Mr. Hyde in his scientific notes by writing, "No degeneracy is low enough to satisfy him." Most viewers probably then think, "Please show me some degeneracy because I haven't seen much so far."

In fact, and unlike the novella and the prior film versions, Hyde is a handsome fellow, surely more so than Dr. Jekyll. As a result, Hyde is not frightening at all. He is more like Dorian Gray, with a handsome exterior and a hidden dark side. Even near the end of the film, when Hyde displays his most evil disposition by killing three people, the movie still plays more like a mystery than a horror film, with Hyde avenging the extramarital affair between Kitty and his best friend, Paul Allen, by raping Kitty and killing Paul and then cleverly trying to blame it on the purported suicide victim, Dr. Jekyll. This is simply not the stuff of horror films, or, perhaps more accurately, not the stuff of effective horror films.

In addition to Hyde being handsome, not gruesome, there is another interesting reversal of a concept from Stevenson's novella. In this film version, it is Jekyll who usually returns unexpectedly, to the chagrin of Hyde, not the reverse. While this is an intriguing variation on the story, it once again undercuts the horror elements because one of the significant aspects of the novella, carried over into prior film versions, is Jekyll's awareness of his increasing loss of control

The handsome Mr. Hyde (Paul Massie) first meets Maria (Norma Mala), the masked exotic dancer and snake charmer, in *The Two Faces of Dr. Jekyll/House of Fright* (1960). Hyde will eventually go on to kill Maria.

over his own mind and body when Hyde suddenly appears without Jekyll taking the potion. Unfortunately, this facet of the Stevenson novella, one of its true horrors, is missing from *The Two Faces of Dr. Jekyll*.

The Two Faces of Dr. Jekyll probably addresses the war between the good and evil inside a single man more directly than any other versions of the tale, with Dr. Jekyll constantly trying to take back his body from the evil Mr. Hyde but Hyde always seeming to have the upper hand. (This is somewhat reminiscent of the novella, with Stevenson suggesting that the evil side of man is often stronger than his good side.) There is a clever moment in the film when Jekyll has a debate with the reflection of Hyde in the mirror becoming, in essence, a debate between good and evil. In this scene, the film visualizes each man's internal struggle between his virtuous and dark sides. Here, the film works better than the novella, since Stevenson could only conjecture about and comment upon the subject in his novella.

Nevertheless, the problem with the film's attempt at addressing the theme of good and evil in man is that there are no virtuous characters in the film to contrast with the evil Mr. Hyde. Jekyll himself is an unworthy person, having neglected his home and spouse for many years in the name of science. His wife, Kitty, is a slut, having an affair with Paul Allen behind Jekyll's back. Allen is supposedly Jekyll's best friend but still gambles excessively and touches up Jekyll for "loans" while at the same time bedding Jekyll's wife. Even after Hyde meets some prostitutes at a bar and intends to leave with one, the pimp knocks Hyde over the head, Hyde's money is stolen and Hyde is left face down in the street, unconscious. It is difficult to satisfactorily address issues of good and evil when there are no good people in the film.

The Two Faces of Dr. Jekyll is from that time period when Hammer was remaking all of the horror classics, often taking many liberties with the source material. These Hammer films were always top notch productions and *The Two Faces of Dr. Jekyll* is no exception, with high production values including color and wide screen, period costumes and details, numerous extras where required, strikingly beautiful woman and excellent acting. All the same, the movie seems somewhat bland and, surprisingly, also comes up short in another trademark of Hammer, bringing sex to the horror film. In that regard, the 1960 version of Stevenson's novella pales in comparison to the 1932 version, which, after 80 years, still retains a sensual vitality that *The Two Faces of Dr. Jekyll* never had.

Other Adaptations

As noted above, there were many silent versions of *Dr. Jekyll and Mr. Hyde*, with the first one as early as 1910 and three versions in 1920 alone. However,

John Barrymore's version was so successful that there were no more silent versions and the two sound films starring Frederic March and Spencer Tracy put an end to sound versions for quite a while. However, after the Hammer version in 1960, there seems to have been almost non-stop adaptations of the novel in film and television. There has even been a successful musical version, titled *Jekyll and Hyde*, a play that opened on Broadway in 1997 and ran for 1,543 performances and numerous film variations on the story, such as *The Son of Dr. Jekyll* (1951) and *Daughter of Dr. Jekyll* (1957) and comedy versions, such as *Abbott and Costello Meet Dr. Jekyll and Mr. Hyde* (1953) and *The Nutty Professor* (1963), the latter being the only watchable Jerry Lewis feature. The concept has also been adapted for other types of horror films such as *Black Friday* (1940) and *House of Dracula* (1945), and, of course, the concept of good and evil residing in one individual is a part of the werewolf mythology. Robert Louis Stevenson would surely be surprised at how long lasting and flexible his short novel has become in the entertainment industry, even more than 100 years after its first publication.

CHAPTER 5

Dracula and "Dracula's Guest" by Bram Stoker

Although there are some references to vampires in poems of the 1700s, novels and short stories about vampires are a phenomenon of the 1800s, including "The Vampyre," a short story by John Polidori which first appeared in print in 1819, *Varney the Vampire: or, The Feast of Blood* by James Malcolm Rymer, first published beginning in 1845 in a series of cheap weekly pamphlets known as penny dreadfuls and *Carmilla*, an 1872 novella written by Sheridan Le Fanu and discussed in Chapter 24 of this book.

As a group, these works and others of the 19th century established many of the conventions of the vampire genre. Some were well known in their day. However, after the release of Bram Stoker's *Dracula* in 1897 and its adaptations into films and a play, these earlier stories became largely forgotten, with *Dracula* becoming the definitive work in the field, a distinction it still holds to this day, even with the plethora of vampire stories published in recent years.

Background

Abraham "Bram" Stoker was born in Dublin, Ireland, on November 8, 1847. After graduation from college, he became a civil servant at Dublin Castle, the seat of the British government in Ireland. While working there, Stoker started a career in writing, publishing theater reviews and short stories and then non-fiction works, including a two-volume biography of Henry Irving, a famous British stage actor.

Dracula (1897) was Stoker's fifth published novel. Stoker began making notes on the story as early as 1890 and spent many years researching topics relevant to his novel. Stoker's personal notes on *Dracula* indicate that he consulted 32 major reference novels on topics such as the occult, European folklore, stories of vampires, medicine, the devil and the Carpathians, with one of his important influences being Emily Gerard's 1885 essay "Transylvania Superstitions," a work about the folklore of Transylvania. *Dracula* received good reviews upon its publication, but the novel's true fame did not arise until it was adapted to the stage and the cinema, all of which occurred after Stoker's death in 1912. Stoker wrote other novels after the publication of *Dracula* but none achieved the renown of *Dracula*.

The Literature

Dracula by Bram Stoker

Despite the fact that it was first published over 100 years ago and exhibits some of the old-fashioned writing style of its era, *Dracula* is still an entertaining novel for the modern reader. Even for a horror film aficionado who has seen many different adaptations of the novel for the cinema, there are still many unexpected delights to be found in the written work.

Some of the most striking parts of the novel are contained in its early chapters which detail Jonathan Harker's trip to Castle Dracula in the Carpathians in Hungary and his terrifying experiences there. In addition to moments familiar to horror film fans, there are many other horrific scenes in this section of the novel, such as Dracula dispersing a pack of vicious wolves who are surrounding Harker's stagecoach, Dracula climbing head first down the outside wall of his castle, Dracula bringing a baby to his castle in a bag and throwing it to the castle's three female vampires for their nightly sustenance, Dracula's wolves later attacking the baby's mother and killing her and Harker trying to kill the undead Dracula when he is lying in his coffin during the day.

The story of Dracula's sea journey to England by boat named the *Demeter* comes next. This is a short part of the narrative but it is one of the most terrifying, as seamen on the ship keep disappearing for no discernible reason. Eventually there are reports of a stranger on board, who is tall, thin and pale, but no one can seem to find him. With only two people left on the ship, the mate learns something so ghastly about the stranger that rather than tangle with the unknown monster, he jumps off the boat to his death. All alone, the captain decides to tie his hands to the wheel of the ship and hope for survival.

One of the most fascinating sections of *Dracula* concerns the metamorphosis of Lucy Westrena from the beautiful young fiancée of Arthur Holmwood into the evil vampire who preys on young children, ending with the killing of

Lucy by means of a stake through the heart. When Dr. Van Helsing reads newspaper stories of young children with bite marks on their necks and a mysterious woman in the area, he has no doubt who the culprit is. After confirming his suspicions, Van Helsing brings Arthur, Dr. Seward and Quincey Morris to the outside of Lucy's tomb. Lucy is then on the prowl but when she returns to her tomb and observes the four, as Dr. Seward describes it, "she drew back with an angry snarl ... her eyes blazed with unholy light, and the face became wreathed with a voluptuous smile" (Chapter XVI). She then tries to seduce Arthur with her diabolical sweetness, but Van Helsing intervenes with his golden crucifix.

Lucy returns to her coffin and later, with a hammer provided by Van Helsing, Arthur drives a stake into Lucy's heart. As Dr. Seward describes it, "The Thing in the coffin writhed; and a hideous, bloodcurdling screech came from the opened red lips. The body shook and quivered and twisted in wild contortions ... whilst the blood from the pierced heart welled and spurted up around it" (Chapter XVI). For a few minutes, the four rest but when they turn back to the coffin, the pretty and sweet Lucy has returned, finally calm.

The killing of Lucy is one of the high points of *Dracula*, providing an internal climax to the tale before the story returns to the elusive figure of Dracula. Bram Stoker's description of the necessary but grisly killing of Lucy is particularly imaginative, haunting and gory, and to a degree, sexual in nature, a return after many pages to the tone of the first chapters of the novel. The story of the life and death of Lucy is so compelling that many vampire films, even ones not based on Stoker's novel, such as *Brides of Dracula* (1960), *House of Dark Shadows* (1970) and *Count Yorga, Vampire* (1970), incorporate the side story of the creation of a second vampire, usually a female.

After Dracula dispatches Lucy, he turns to Mina Harker, the bride of Jonathan Harker, sucking the blood from her body on at least two occasions without the knowledge of the other characters or the reader. On the third occasion, however, the reader receives an explicit description of what happens, from the writings and words of Dr. Seward and Mina. With the paralyzed Jonathan Harker looking on, Dracula once again sucks Mina's blood through the puncture wounds on her neck. After what seems to Mina a very long time, Dracula removes his mouth from Mina's neck and Dracula's lips seem to drip with fresh blood. He then says to Mina,

> And you, their best beloved one, are now to me, flesh of my flesh; blood of my blood; kin of my kin; my bountiful wine-press for a while; and shall be later on my companion and my helper [Chapter XXI].

Dracula then pulls open his shirt, opens a vein in his chest with his long sharp nails and when the blood began to spurt out, presses Mina's mouth to the wound, forcing her to swallow some of the blood. When it is over, Mina feels that she is unclean and polluted.

This is the most overtly sexual scene in the novel. While the sucking of blood from a beautiful female's neck can be sensual in the extreme, the forcing of Mina to drink Dracula's blood directly from his body is much closer to rape than sex. Stoker adds to the effectiveness of the scene by having Dracula rephrase a portion of the Bible, Genesis 2:23–24, where Adam, after the Lord created Woman from Adam's rib, describes Woman by stating, "This is now bone of my bones and flesh of my flesh." The linking of a winepress and blood may also come from the Bible, Isaiah 63:2–3. In a sense, Dracula is not only attacking Mina's virtue, he is attacking the Christian faith of Mina and the others, by distorting some of its premises. Both sensual and horrifying, this scene with Mina and Dracula is one of the enduring images of the novel and as good an example there is of the evil that is Dracula.

The narrative format of *Dracula* is one that is rarely used in literature, as the entire story is conveyed by the documents in the case, such as newspaper articles, diaries and letters, rather than from one or more points of view from the characters or from the omniscient third person of the author. It is an interesting technique, similar to overlapping flashbacks used in films, although in this case, Stoker has arranged the documents in such a way that they generally relate the story of Dracula in a linear manner. Unfortunately, no matter the document or the writer, Stoker tends to write in the exact same style, undercutting some of the value of his method. For example, the purported newspaper article about the *Demeter* could just as easily have been written by Jonathan Harker than a reporter. It is clearly not written in the style of a newspaper article.

Another technique of Stoker's is to relieve the horror of the novel by inserting events of a much more commonplace nature between the terrifying ones, such as inserting between the story of Harker's experiences in Transylvania and Dracula's deadly ship ride to England a vignette of Lucy's three different marriage proposals which are made to her on the same day. Other examples of this technique are the vignette of Mina's marriage to Jonathan, the escape of a wolf from the zoo and even the unusual antics of Renfield, the resident of Dr. Seward's asylum.

As part of Stoker's style, Dracula himself is missing from most of the novel and when he appears, he is often just a fleeting impression of one of the characters, or he appears as a bat or other animal, rather than as a real flesh and blood creature. To some degree, that is the nature of Dracula, as described by Stoker, as vampires generally operate in the shadows rather than out in the open. It also enhances Dracula's horrifying nature when he does appear in the flesh, because the reader never becomes so accustomed to the character throughout the long novel that he becomes blasé about him. As a result, the moment when Jonathan Harker suddenly spots Dracula on a street in London, after the character's long absence from the novel, is quite horrifying even though nothing of a horrific nature happens. This technique, which works well for the novel, would never have worked as effectively in a film and it is a rare Dracula movie that does not have Dracula as the central character.

Dracula, of course, whether present or not, is the overwhelming figure in the novel. He is an unforgettable creation of Bram Stoker and the principal reason why the novel has maintained such enduring fame. In addition to Dracula, Stoker has created several other memorable characters who add to the effectiveness of the work, such as Renfield, the man who eats the spiders and the flies and seems to become a disciple of Dracula upon occasion, and Mina Harker, a strong woman who does battle with Count Dracula. Then there is Dr. Abraham Van Helsing of Amsterdam, an expert in obscure diseases. He is called in by Dr. Seward on Lucy's case and remains on the job long enough to kill Count Dracula.

Van Helsing is portrayed as polite, caring of others, analytical and brilliant. While he often seems slow moving, Van Helsing is always indefatigable in his pursuit of vampires. He is able to overcome the initial skepticism of others so that he acquires a quintet of assistants to help him in his cause. Van Helsing is more than a match for Dracula, first driving him from England by destroying the refuge that his numerous coffins bring him and then relentlessly tracking him back to Transylvania and destroying him there. The character of Van Helsing is such an important personality of the story of Dracula, and an engaging one at that, that a number of notable actors have played the role in films, including Edward Van Sloan, Peter Cushing (who played the part the most times), Laurence Olivier and Anthony Hopkins.

Dracula is also a primer of vampire lore, containing all of the elements that one expects in the undead. There are the two bite marks on the victim's neck and the use of a crucifix and garlic to dissuade the vampire from attacking. Dracula's reflection is not seen in a mirror, he never eats food, he has immense strength and he can turn into various animals such as a bat and a dog. And, of course, the best method for permanently slaying Dracula is a stake through the heart. With some variation, these are the classic elements of a vampire of the cinema, still employed over 100 years after the novel was first published.

There are also some interesting aspects of vampire lore in *Dracula* that do not often show up in films. Dracula is originally described as a tall, old man with a long white mustache (Chapter II). As the story progresses and he receives his nightly nourishment on a regular basis, Dracula seems to grow younger, so by the time Harker first spots Dracula in London, Harker is not even sure that it is Dracula because Dracula seems so young. In order to attack a victim, Dracula has the ability to arrive in a mist that he creates and to enter a room through a small opening in a door frame. When Harker first comes to Castle Dracula, Dracula is unable to take any action with regard to Harker until Harker crosses the threshold of his own free will. Likewise, Dracula is unable to enter Renfield's cell until Renfield voluntarily invites him in. Dracula can only cross running water at low tide. And, in Bram Stoker's version of vampirism, Dracula does have a limited ability to be out and about during the day.

For a novel that has been in existence for over 100 years and still retains much of its fame, it is not surprising that scholars have attempted to discern some themes or hidden meanings in the book. Some have suggested that the novel addresses topics such as feminism, in the person of Mina Harker, sexual predators, fear of foreigners, repression of sexuality in Victorian times, and Dracula as the anti–Christ. And, while there is some support for all of those ideas in the novel, nevertheless, the people who proffer those notions seem overly analytical about a novel which is primarily a first-class vampire story, with a strong plot, memorable dialogue and unforgettable characters. Unlike Mary Shelley's *Frankenstein*, which clearly contains much thematic material, *Dracula* is simply a book to read and enjoy, and to leave the analysis to the academics.

"Dracula's Guest" by Bram Stoker

"Dracula's Guest," first published in 1914, two years after Stoker's death, is widely believed to be the original first or second chapter of *Dracula*, which was cut from the manuscript as a result of the length of the novel. If so, it must have been re-written by Stoker, as the style of the short story does not quite fit into the published version of *Dracula*.

"Dracula's Guest" involves an unnamed narrator who could be Jonathan Harker who goes walking in the woods on Walpurgis Night in Munich, possibly before setting out on his journey to Transylvania. Walpurgis Night, according to the story, is a night when all of the graves open and the dead, along with the devil, come forth and walk. The narrator gets lost in a snowstorm in the woods and seeks refuge in a tomb. There he sees a sleeping woman with rounded cheeks and red lips. The narrator is then hurled out of the tomb by what seems to him the hand of a giant and then when he falls asleep in the woods, he is attacked by a large dog or wolf which lies on top of him and licks his throat. The narrator is rescued by some soldiers who were sent there by the *maitre d'* of the narrator's hotel in response to a letter from Count Dracula, who requested that the narrator, who is Dracula's guest, be protected at all costs.

In the novel *Dracula*, when the three vampire women at the castle in Transylvania attack Jonathan Harker, he seems to recognize the fair one with the golden hair, although he cannot remember exactly where he has seen her (Chapter III). No further explanation is given in the novel. According to Barbara Belford, in her biography of Bram Stoker, a prior draft of *Dracula* contained this line, in describing one of the three vampire women: "As she spoke I was looking at the fair woman and it suddenly dawned on me that she was the woman—or her image—that I had seen in the tomb on Walpurgis Night." On the other hand, the sleeping woman in "Dracula's Guest" is not described as fair; the narrator says only that she was "a beautiful woman with rounded cheeks and red lips, seemingly sleeping on a bier."

The Films

Nosferatu (1922)

As the credits state, *Nosferatu* (sometimes referred to as *Nosferatu: A Symphony of Horror*) is a free adaptation of Bram Stoker's *Dracula*. Since the producers never obtained permission from Stoker's widow to use *Dracula* as a basis for the film, all of the names of the characters are changed and the title of the book is not used. Thus, Dracula becomes Count Orlok, Jonathan Harker becomes Hutter and Mina Harker becomes Ellen. The word "nosferatu" means undead in Romanian, or at least it has acquired that meaning over time, and so *Nosferatu* is an appropriate substitute name for the film. In fact, the word, "nosferatu," is used several times in Stoker's novel and in the 1931 film version of the story.

Nosferatu was directed by F.W. Murnau, one of the most famous directors of silent films and an important figure in the Expressionism movement in the German cinema of the 1920s. Murnau is still well-known today for his German masterpiece, *The Last Laugh* (1924), about an aging doorman at a prominent hotel, and his American masterpiece, *Sunrise* (1927), about an extramarital affair that almost leads to violence. *Nosferatu* consistently receives excellent reviews, even today, but that may result more from the resume of its director than the quality of the film. In fact, *Nosferatu* is vastly overrated.

That is not to say that *Nosferatu* does not have any positives. After a weak opening, the film improves substantially when it turns to the events on Dracula's boat ride from his native land to Germany, a scene clearly inspired by the novel. First, the captain is told that a sailor below deck has become sick and is delirious. A slight image of Orlok is then shown in the hold, seeming more like an impression of the Count rather than the image of a flesh and blood being. Then, the entire crew becomes sick and dies. As the first mate goes below to try to determine the cause of the tragedy, he sees rats in the coffins and then, in the best effect in the film, Orlok's coffin lid swings open on its own and Orlok's prone body rises directly up to a standing position, as if by magic. The tall, long-fingered body with the horrifying face drives the first mate mad. He jumps off the ship to his death, leaving the captain no choice but to tie his arms to the wheel. The scene ends with a striking shot from the hold looking up to Orlok on the deck, as he walks, hands spread, toward the captain, with the horror of the situation being realized on the captain's face.

Murnau also uses an effective plot device of merging two stories of travel into one. After Hutter, the Jonathan Harker character, recovers from his experiences in Transylvania, he tries to return as soon as possible to the town of Wisborg in Germany where his wife, Ellen, lives. Count Orlok is also moving as fast as possible to get to Wisborg, in order to set up his new place of abode, but also to get to Ellen. The juxtaposition of the converging story lines adds some excitement to the film.

Another of the strengths of the film is the makeup worn by Max Schreck as Count Orlok, makeup that has become iconic in the horror film genre, almost in a league with Lon Chaney's makeup in *The Phantom of the Opera* (1925) and Boris Karloff's makeup in *Frankenstein* (1931). Orlok is completely bald, with a triangular face, oversize pointed ears and a long thick nose, giving him the appearance of a rat. His fingers are long and pointed and Schreck makes good use of those fingers to add to the repulsive nature of his character, much like Bela Lugosi would in the 1931 sound version of Bram Stoker's novel. Schreck is good in the part of Count Orlok. Unfortunately, most of the rest of the performances in the film are poor, brought down by the constant overacting.

A unique aspect of *Nosferatu* comes with its opening title card, which states that the film is a chronicle of the great plague of 1838 in Wisborg, Germany. Given the nature of a vampire, it seems likely that if there were ever such a creature, its effect on a community would be just like a plague, with numerous dead in a confined area. Here, vampirism is treated as the Black Death, with townspeople told to stay in their homes, not to bring the afflicted to a hospital for fear of spreading the epidemic, and so many dying that there seems to be a daily procession of coffins through the streets of Wisborg. The film thus brings a unique perspective to vampirism, making the condition a community-wide horror, not just a story of its effect on a few individuals.

The ending of *Nosferatu* is completely original to the film. Since there is no Van Helsing character in the movie, first Hutter and then Ellen learn about vampire lore from a book that Hutter discovers at the inn on his journey to Castle

Orlok. The book states that there is no way to obtain salvation from a vampire unless "a woman without sin should cause the vampire to forget the first cock crow. Of her own free will she should give him his blood." Recognizing the severity of the plague in town, Mina attracts Orlok to her home by opening the window and then she sends Hutter away so that she can be alone with Orlok. As the vampire bends over Ellen, the cock crows, the dawn comes through the window and Orlok disappears. Hutter is just able to return to Ellen to embrace her before she dies. Ellen's heroic actions have rid the town of the plague.

Although the ending of *Nosferatu* is slightly different from conventional vampire lore, it is quite effective. It displays a bit of the feminist attitude of the novel, as the strong-willed Ellen deliberately distracts Orlok to save her community and her husband. It is a rare occurrence in a vampire film for a woman to cause the death of the vampire. This is similar to the novel, where it is the strong-willed Mina Harker who is the prime cause of the death of Dracula, although she does not do the actual slaying. Also, the ending of *Nosferatu* has its surprise, with the heroine of the film dying in the arms of her husband. The ending also relates back to the end of the novel, where Quincey Morris dies after stabbing Dracula in the heart with a knife, much like Ellen dies after killing Orlok.

All of that being said, much of *Nosferatu* is disappointing. While one of the best parts of Stoker's novel is its opening, the beginning sections of *Nosferatu* are its weakest. So much time is spent in Hutter's hometown before Hutter leaves on his journey to Transylvania that the film is quite boring right from the start. Not much happens on the trip to the castle and it takes a full 20 minutes of film before Hutter reaches his destination. At the castle of Orlok, there is some similarity to the events of the novel, even to the episode of Hutter cutting his finger in the presence of Orlok. However, that incident seems like surplusage, just like several other events from the novel which are incorporated into the film, with no payoff to the incidents, almost as if the filmmakers felt they had to include them in the film despite their lack of interest in them.

Nosferatu is supposed to be an example of German Expressionism, and there are many opportunities in the opening scenes for the use of that style of filmmaking. Unfortunately, it is never actually employed. Showing a wolf after someone mentions a werewolf and having plenty of rats at the castle and later on the ship back to Germany is not Expressionism. Obvious stylistic techniques fall flat, such as the film running in fast motion to show the ride of Orlok's stagecoach and the use of stop motion photography to show Orlok piling his caskets in preparation for his journey to Germany. Given the manner in which these scenes are shot, they are more humorous than horrifying. At one point, the stagecoach ride is seen in a negative print, which only calls attention to the direction of the film, without adding anything to the effectiveness of the scene.

Also, why is only one part of the ride shown in negative and the rest of the ride shown in positive? To illustrate Murnau's lack of understanding of the material, he makes a major blunder when he allows Hutter to go outside of the Orlok castle during the day, in the bright sunlight and in a pleasant location, immediately diffusing the oppressive and horrifying atmosphere of the inside of Orlok's abode.

There is much that is outright silly about *Nosferatu*. Orlok has a clock in his castle and when the alarm rings, a miniature skeleton on top of the device strikes the bell. When Orlok sees a picture of Ellen that Hutter is carrying on his person, Orlok actually says, "Your wife has such a beautiful neck." Then there is the section of the film where Professor Bulwer lectures his students on "the horrible habits of carnivorous plants," first showing a fly-trapping plant and later a polyp with tentacles. Bulwer, who substitutes for the Van Helsing character, never becomes a significant character in the feature. What are these scenes doing in the film?

Perhaps the silliest aspect of the film is that the Renfield character of the novel is replaced by Knock, the real estate agent for whom Hutter works. Once Orlok begins his journey from Transylvania, Knock, who is many miles away, starts to become crazy. He is sent to a lunatic asylum where, for no apparent reason, he starts talking about his master and begins spouting sayings such as "Blood is life! Blood is life!" Knock eventually escapes from his confinement by killing a guard who actually turns his back on him just to light a cigarette. None of this makes any sense, particularly because Knock never meets Dracula at any time. It as if the filmmakers wanted to include a Renfield-like character in the film, but could not devise any practical way to include him. Or, they simply needed some incidents to pad the length of the feature.

So, while *Nosferatu* has its attributes, it is still significantly overrated. With little inventive or expressionistic camera work, a flimsy plot and silly, superfluous and inconsistent elements, the reputation of *Nosferatu* is far greater than the actual quality of the film.

Dracula (1931)

For modern film audiences, accustomed to big budget color productions with expensive special effects, *Dracula* (1931) must seem creaky and dated. Even though it received good reviews upon its release, its stature in the horror film genre has unquestionably fallen over time. And yet, even more than 80 years after its original release, the Bela Lugosi version of Bram Stoker's story remains the most famous film version of the novel and in some small ways, it is still the best film version of them all.

Almost everyone agrees that the opening scenes of *Dracula*, most of which come directly from the novel, are the high points of the movie. The film commences with Renfield, in place of Jonathan Harker, arriving in Transylvania by stagecoach and being warned by the villagers about proceeding onward to the Borgo Pass at night. When Renfield insists on continuing his journey, an older woman gives him a crucifix, for whatever protection it might bring him.

At this point, the film becomes almost silent, first in the basement of Castle Dracula, where the Count and the female vampires exit their coffins with rats and bugs looking on and mist and spider webs filling the scene, and later, with a long shot looking down on Renfield as he enters the Castle on his own, walking through one of the most magnificent and high sets in all of horror films. There is then a striking long shot of Dracula, holding a candle, walking slowly down the never-ending steps of his castle, as Renfield approaches him. Renfield starts to interact with Count Dracula, giving Dracula the opportunity to state some of the most famous dialogue from the film—"I am, Dracula.... I bid you welcome," and when the wolves howl, "Listen to them—Children of the night. What music they make." Even though those lines come from the novel (Chapter II), Bela Lugosi, with his unusual speaking style, makes them immortal.

In addition to the magnificent sets at Castle Dracula and the sharp dialogue, the effectiveness of these opening scenes must be attributed to director Tod Browning. He employs unusual camera angles such as high angle shots, includes extra inanimate objects in his shots such as a candelabrum, a wine goblet or a chair, and employs montage as he intercuts shots of bats, vampires and the like into the story line. His camera moves somewhat in these scenes, including one striking shot as the camera slowly moves in on the cloaked-in black Dracula, with only his pale face and bright eyes showing. Other memorable moments from these early parts of *Dracula* are the cut on Renfield's finger that attracts Dracula and the female vampires' attack on Renfield, both of which are incidents from the novel. There is a missed opportunity on the ship ride back to London, with not much happening there, although there is an accidental homage to the style of Stoker's novel, when part of the ship's story is conveyed through a newspaper article. (This also happens later in the film when a part of the story of the Woman in White is read in a newspaper.) The story picks up in an atmospheric and almost silent scene in which Dracula walks through the foggy streets of London and attacks a flower girl, before Dracula meets Mina and Lucy at the opera house.

The opening of *Dracula*, which comprises about one-third of the movie, is not just the best part of the film, it is one of the strongest sections of any vampire movie ever made. It conveys a non-ending mood of horror, without any outright moments of horror, from the meeting with the villagers in Transylvania through the beginning of the story in London. And then it all stops.

Part of the problem is that much of the rest of the film is based more on the stage play by Hamilton Deane and John L. Balderston than on the novel by Bram Stoker. Another significant problem is the direction of Tod Browning which, once the story moves to London, suddenly becomes static and unimaginative as if Browning has lost touch with much of the mood of the story. A comparison of the shot selection in the contemporaneously shot Spanish version by director George Melford with the shot selection by Tod Browning highlights some of the deficiencies in Browning's work in the latter part of the film. A good example occurs in the scene near the end of the movie on the steps of the basement of Carfax Abbey. Browning generally employs only long shots; Melford varies his shots including long shots, close-ups and unusual angles. While Browning chooses to have Dracula push Renfield down the steps and the actual pushing is not shown, Melford chooses to have Dracula throw Renfield over the high side of the steps, a much more dramatic ending.

In addition to the disappointing direction of Tod Browning once the story moves to England, the English portion of the film is a tale of missed opportunities. The whole story arc of Lucy being killed by Dracula and then becoming a vampire goes by so fast that it has little impact. Also, Van Helsing seem to have forgotten that he must dispose of Lucy with a stake through the heart, as no such scene is shown in the film. On one occasion, when Dracula flees the house, Jonathan Harker tells Van Helsing and Seward about seeing a wolf running across the estate. On another occasion, Renfield tells the others about a red mist being spread over the lawn, coming on like a flame of fire, and that when Dracula parted the mists, Renfield saw thousands of rats with their eyes blazing red. Mina begins to tell Jonathan about the time Dracula forced her to swallow his blood but Mina never finishes the story. While some of these ideas come from the novel and work very well in that format, *Dracula* (1931) is a movie and these events should have been shown to the viewer, not merely described. How wonderful would the film have been if the filmmakers had taken the time to reproduce those incidents onscreen? The biggest disappointment, however, is undoubtedly the killing of Dracula, which occurs off-screen, amounting to not much more than a groan from Dracula, making the end of the film anticlimactic and, in fact, frustrating.

For most viewers, their opinion of *Dracula* depends substantially on their evaluation of Bela Lugosi's performance as Count Dracula. Some people love it; some people hate it. There are seldom any opinions in between those extremes. And, on a purely technical level, Lugosi's performance is poor. Lugosi often emphasizes the wrong word in a sentence or the wrong syllable in a word. Sometimes there are strange pauses in his delivery; other times he seems to be trying to remember his lines when he is delivering them. Yet, for all of that,

Realizing that Dr. Van Helsing and Jonathan Harker are in hot pursuit, Dracula (Bela Lugosi) quickly carries Mina Harker (Helen Chandler) across the basement of Carfax Abbey, near the conclusion of *Dracula* (1931).

Lugosi's performance works for this film. Count Dracula is an alien, first to Renfield in the Carpathians and then to the others in England. His evil nature is exaggerated by his strange manner of speech, not all that surprising for a person for whom English is not his native language. The Dracula of the book studied English history, language, manners and speech so that he could blend into London culture. The Lugosi Dracula has done none of that and his stiffness, formality, the use of his cape to enhance his mysterious nature and the fact that he is a foreigner enhances the monster that he is.

For modern horror fans, and particularly those who are familiar with Lugosi's career, it is hard to appreciate the sensual nature of his looks to 1930s audiences, but the danger in Dracula was oddly attractive to the females in the audience, providing a sensual subtext to the film that did not exist in the script. The contrasting aspects of Lugosi's Dracula are conveyed in the discussion between Lucy and Mina after their first encounter with the Count. Mina makes fun of his foreign demeanor, desiring a man who is more normal; Lucy, on the other hand, is attracted to him. Thus, Lugosi is both repulsive and attractive as Dracula, a different characterization of the Count than in Stoker's novel.

Lugosi usually gave good performances in good films, whether he had major roles in them, such as *The Black Cat* (1934) and *Son of Frankenstein* (1939) or minor roles in them, such as *The Wolf Man* (1941) and *The Body Snatcher* (1945). His poor performances tended to be in poor films, such as the Monogram features from the 1940s, or when his health was weak. True to that observation, Lugosi's performance in *Dracula*, strange as it may be, is particularly appropriate for this film version, making the film always fascinating, even when the story becomes stage bound. Lugosi's portrayal of Count Dracula is still a part of popular culture while the performances of undoubtedly better actors are long forgotten.

Edward Van Sloan plays Professor Van Helsing and it is another memorable performance in the film. Professorial, slow moving yet indefatigable, it is similar to the characterization of the Van Helsing of the novel. The film, however, cleverly allows some direct interplay between Van Helsing and the Count, leading to several memorable moments, including the one when Van Helsing tricks Dracula into revealing that he does not have any reflection in a mirror. Lugosi and Van Sloan, who performed these roles in the original Broadway production, play off of each other beautifully and the tension in their encounter is palpable. The scene ends with another memorable line of dialogue from Dracula—"For one who has not lived even a single lifetime, you are a wise man, Van Helsing."

In the novel, Renfield is almost a throwaway character, interesting though he may be. He contributes nothing to the prime story line until late in the book when he warns Van Helsing and the others that Dracula has already attacked Mina Harker. In the movie, it is Renfield, rather than Jonathan Harker, who goes to Transylvania to meet Count Dracula at the beginning of the story, making Renfield's subsequent lunacy and allegiance to Dracula a more logical plot point. Renfield is played by Dwight Frye, who gives one of the most famous performances in all of horror films. With his maniacal laugh, scrunched up body, wide eyes and toothy grin, Frye is always believable in the role of an unbelievable character.

With Renfield elevated to a more important role in *Dracula*, Jonathan Harker becomes the film's superfluous character. Harker is no more than the ineffectual juvenile of the movie, the type of character that was soon to become a horror film cliché. Likewise, Mina Harker has also been reduced to minor status in the film. As played by the bland Helen Chandler, Mina exudes no vibrancy or sensuality and with the filmmakers foregoing the "blood of my blood" scene from the novel, they have robbed the film of most of the novel's sexual impact.

Deficiencies aside (and there are many of them), *Dracula* is still an enticing film, even after all of these years, because of the opening sequences, the performances, the dialogue, the sets and the inherent strength of Bram Stoker's story. The film is well worth a view, even for modern film audiences who are accustomed to big budget color productions with expensive special effects.

Dracula's Daughter (1936)

With the success of *The Bride of Frankenstein* (1935), a sequel to *Dracula* (1931) was inevitable and in 1936, Universal released that sequel, *Dracula's Daughter*. Of course, it is not quite clear what it means for a vampire to have a daughter and it is not quite clear that a vampire's offspring, if there could be any, would be vampires. Those questions did not deter Universal from producing *Dracula's Daughter* and, of course, a few years later, Universal brought another supposed offspring of Dracula to the cinema in *Son of Dracula* (1943).

The credits to *Dracula's Daughter* state, "Based on a work by Bram Stoker." The work is not identified but most film historians believe that the reference is to the short story, "Dracula's Guest," primarily because Universal paid handsomely for the rights to the story. However, the final product on the screen takes nothing from Stoker's short story, except perhaps for the concept of a female vampire, which comes from the brief moment in the story when the unnamed narrator sees a woman in a tomb who could be a vampire.

Dracula's Daughter owes more to the film, *Dracula* (1931), than to any work by Bram Stoker. The film commences in the basement of Carfax Abbey, just after Dracula killed Renfield and Van Helsing killed Dracula in the 1931 film version, scenes that were original to that movie. In the novel, Dracula kills Renfield in his cell at Dr. Seward's asylum and Dracula is killed in Transylvania. *Dracula's Daughter* does correct one flaw from the ending of the prior film; it finally shows Dracula with a stake through the heart.

As *Dracula's Daughter* develops, there are many reminders of the 1931 film. Van Helsing, whose his name is misspelled and mispronounced "Von Helsing" for some reason, reappears from time to time to educate the participants about all the particulars of vampirism.

Countess Zaleska, who self-identifies herself as Dracula's daughter, is usually shown on the prowl dressed entirely in black with only her eyes showing. When offered a drink, Zaleska turns it down, saying, just as her father once did, "I never drink ... wine."

In terms of the direction of the two films, they have much in common. The shots of Zaleska exiting her coffin are shown just as they were of her father in *Dracula*, with first a hand coming out of the coffin, the camera panning away and then the standing vampire revealed. A high shot of an operating room amphitheater seems to have been lifted directly from *Dracula*. At one point, Zaleska is announced at a party, and the sound of her name completes a sentence of another character. There was a similar occurrence in the 1931 film.

One of the many differences between Bram Stoker's novel and *Dracula's Daughter* is the film's homosexual underpinnings, something not present in the book. When the Dracula of the novel desires to dispose of Jonathan Harker at his castle, he leaves the dirty work to the three female vampires who inhabit his abode. In England, Dracula goes after two attractive young women, first Lucy and then Mina.

Dracula's Daughter is substantially different. While it may be improper to analyze an older work of fiction through the lens of modern ideas and themes, there does appear to be a distinct lesbian element to *Dracula's Daughter*. While Countess Zaleska does not go after women solely, she does seem to prefer them, first in the person of Lili, a poor girl found on the streets of London, and then in the person of Janet, Jeffrey Garth's secretary. Indeed, the downfall of the Countess results from her rejection of Sandor, her male assistant, in favor of Garth but, perhaps, also in favor of Janet.

Of course, *Dracula's Daughter* was released in the era of Hollywood censorship as manifested in the Motion Picture Production Code, and Universal was hardly going to rock the boat with one of its horror films. Nevertheless, there are some subtle erotic and sensual moments in the film. When Lili arrives at Zaleska's studio, Zaleska, who is a painter, tells Lili that she is working on an artist's study of young girl's head and shoulders. At that moment, Zaleska is being honest because Zaleska is then trying to curb her vampire tendencies by encountering them head on. However, when Lili removes her blouse and bares her shoulders, Zaleska's expression reveals a distinct attraction to Lili. Zaleska cannot restrain herself; she has to go after the young girl.

Later, when Zaleska kidnaps Janet and takes her to Transylvania, she becomes attracted to Janet's prone, sleeping body. Even though she is using Janet to attract Garth, once again Zaleska cannot help herself, slowly and sensually bending down low to provide the kiss of death to Janet. Thus, while *Dracula's Daughter* does not directly address the subject of lesbianism, it is clear that the film has homosexual underpinnings.

The ending of *Dracula's Daughter* corrects another weakness of the 1931 film. In the novel, Dracula escapes England and heads back to Transylvania, with Van Helsing and the others on the trail. Van Helsing makes it to Castle Dracula first and kills the three female vampires who inhabit the edifice. Dracula is then killed in an ambush on the road; he never makes it to his castle. The chase of Dracula across Europe and the ending in Transylvania are some of the highlights of the novel. Those events were skipped in their entirety in the 1931 film.

In the exciting ending of *Dracula's Daughter*, the story of the Dracula family finally does return to Transylvania, with scenes in the village near Castle Dracula, Borgo Pass and the castle itself, although the novel's slow, painstaking journey of Van Helsing and the others across land while Dracula travels by sea is replaced by both sides' rapid travel by airplane, coach and even automobile. Zaleska is then killed in the family castle, bringing the story of Count Dracula's trek to England full circle, with the death of Dracula's daughter occurring in Dracula's native land.

While the reputation of *Dracula* (1931) has fallen over time, the reputation of *Dracula's Daughter* has only grown in the many years since it was released. *Dracula's Daughter*, while owing little to Bram Stoker's original novel and nothing to "Dracula's Guest," is a worthy sequel to the 1931 film starring Bela Lugosi.

Horror of Dracula/Dracula (1958)

There is nothing subtle about it. The people who made *Horror of Dracula* wanted their audience to know right away that this was a new type of vampire movie. Immediately at the end of the credits, the camera closes in on Dracula's casket. Suddenly, and for no reason, blood drips from the ceiling onto the casket, blood which is bright and red. It is if the filmmakers were warning the audience—this Dracula movie is shot in color and the gore is going to be right up there on the screen.

When Jonathan Harker meets Dracula for the first time, Dracula states, "I am Dracula and I welcome you to my house." There is none of the archaic and European style of speaking from the novel, where Dracula states, "I am Dracula and I bid you welcome" (Chapter II). Here, the filmmakers seem to be saying—even though the film is set in the late 1800s, this is going to be a modern version of Bram Stoker's *Dracula*, and fidelity to the original story line, setting and point of view should not be expected.

Not surprisingly, then, the plot of *Horror of Dracula* is different in many ways from the story line of the original novel. The Jonathan Harker who comes to Castle Dracula at the beginning of the film already knows that Dracula is a vampire. Harker is on a secret mission to kill Dracula. While he succeeds in killing a fetching female acolyte of Dracula's, Harker is in turn caught by Dracula and turned into a vampire. Van Helsing, a friend of Harker's, then goes searching for Harker at Dracula's castle and when he discovers the body of his good friend, fangs showing in an open casket, Van Helsing is forced to put a stake through the heart of his ally to end his existence as one of the undead. Renfield, one of

At Castle Dracula, one of Dracula's brides (Valerie Gaunt) tries to cozy up to Jonathan Harker (John Van Eyssen) in order to attack him, in *Horror of Dracula* (1958).

the most intriguing characters from the book, is missing. Dracula's journey on the *Demeter* from Eastern Europe to England is completely overlooked. Indeed, it is not quite clear where the events of the film occur. Lucy and Mina seem to live within a reasonable distance from Dracula's castle, as the film's participants are able to travel back and forth in a horse drawn carriage or hearse.

Other moments from *Horror of Dracula* are clearly inspired by the novel. The opening story sequences are told by way of Jonathan Harker's diary. In Harker's hometown, Dracula first goes after Lucy and attacks and kills her, before turning his attention to Mina. In order to protect Lucy from Dracula, Van Helsing has the room filled with garlic and the windows shut, but a maid, at the entreaty of Lucy, removes the garlic and opens the windows, allowing Dracula to make another attack. Mina is saved at one point by blood transfusions from Arthur. At the denouement, Dracula is chased back to his castle in his native land and killed there, similar to the ending of the novel.

One of the most effective sections of *Horror of Dracula* is the interlude

Shortly thereafter, when Dracula (Christopher Lee) learns about the attack by one of his brides (Valerie Gaunt) on Jonathan Harker, he becomes angry with her, in *Horror of Dracula* (1958).

with Lucy and her bout of vampirism. Just a few days after her death, Lucy rises from her casket and goes after Tanya, the young daughter of the Holmwood maid, much as the Lucy of the novel attacked young children in the area. After learning about vampires from Van Helsing and hearing Tanya's story of seeing Lucy alive, Arthur Holmwood, Lucy's brother and Mina's husband, goes to

Lucy's coffin in its vault and finds it empty. The next night Arthur returns to the outside of the tomb with Van Helsing. Lucy starts to attack Arthur, but Van Helsing intervenes with a crucifix, causing Lucy to flee to her casket. Van Helsing then drives a stake through her heart. Lucy screams, her face becomes contorted and then she expires for good. A few seconds later, and just as in the novel, when Arthur and Van Helsing look in the casket, Lucy is composed and beautiful, just as she was before her encounters with Dracula.

The moment when Van Helsing brandishes a large crucifix to stop Lucy's attack on Arthur is one of the most striking moments of the film's story arc involving Lucy. As Lucy tries to walk backwards, away from Van Helsing, Van Helsing touches her forehead with the crucifix. It burns into her skin, leaving a large mark on her forehead. The sizzle and the screech are horrifying. This unforgettable moment in *Horror of Dracula* is inspired by a moment in the novel when Van Helsing tries to protect Mina, who is the under the influence of Dracula, by touching her forehead with a Sacred Wafer. As Jonathan describes it in his journal, "There was a fearful scream which almost froze our hearts to hear. As he had placed the Wafer on Mina's forehead, it had seared it—had burned into the flesh as though it had been a piece of white-hot metal" (Chapter XXII). In the film, Lucy's mark disappears when she is killed. In the novel, the mark on Mina's forehead and a later burn on Mina's hand from a crucifix disappear when Dracula meets his death.

Lucy's story of the undead is handled in a manner that is very faithful to the story line of the novel. That is one of the reasons why it is one of the most effective sections of *Horror of Dracula*.

In addition to the killing of the undead Lucy described above, there are three other vampire killings in *Horror of Dracula*. All four are handled in a different manner. The first one is of the female vampire in Dracula's Castle. The prone figure of the girl, played by the beautiful and amply endowed Valerie Gaunt, is shown from her right side with the camera looking up at Harker as he is about to drive a stake through her heart. After some screams, the next shot is directly down into the casket, with the beautiful girl now an old hag, with a stake through the heart and blood gushing from the wound. It is both a gory and surprising scene.

The next killing is that of Jonathan Harker by Van Helsing. This is shown in the more traditional manner, with Van Helsing picking up a stake and hammer and then the scene fading away with nothing else shown. The third one is the killing of Lucy, described above.

The fourth killing, of Dracula himself, is one of the most effective vampire killings ever filmed. During a fight between Van Helsing and Dracula at the castle, Van Helsing suddenly leaps to a window and pulls the drapes off. The sun of the dawn hits Dracula; Van Helsing paralyzes Dracula with a makeshift cross. As a result, Dracula's left hand falls apart and crumbles, his right hand and face crumble to dust even as his hand continues to move down his face, his chest caves in and then the winds blow away the remains, leaving only Dracula's clothes and ring behind. It is a startling special effect, as impressive today as it was back then, and still the most spectacular demise of Dracula ever filmed.

While the Dracula of the book is slayed by the traditional stake through the heart, unlike the film Dracula who is exposed to sunlight, the demise of Dracula in *Horror of Dracula* is actually inspired by the novel. As Mina Harker describes it in her journal, after the bowie knife of Quincey Morris plunged into the heart of Dracula, "before our very eyes, and almost in the drawing of a breath, the whole body crumbled into dust and passed from our sight" (Chapter XXVII). What does not occur in this Hammer film version is the surprise look of relief on Dracula's face when he is killed in the novel. As Mina also writes, "[E]ven in that moment of final dissolution, there was in the face a look of peace, such as I never could have imagined might have rested there."

For a film whose reputation rests on its graphic use of blood, gore and violence, *Horror of Dracula* is surprisingly restrained in some of its potentially gory moments. When Dracula surprises Harker in the vault just after Harker has killed the young vampire woman, Dracula walks in the doorway and seems to fill the opening. The last shot is of Dracula closing the door; the rest is left to the viewer's imagination. Later, when Dracula goes after Lucy, the only action shown is Dracula entering Lucy's room and bending down over her body in bed. The biting of her neck or whatever else occurs is cloaked from view by Dracula's cape. On the night of Dracula's last attack on Lucy, the Count's presence is implied but never shown. The staking of Jonathan Harker, as referenced above, is not shown at all.

Also, and in keeping with the tone of Bram Stoker's novel, the character of Dracula is actually missing from the film for almost its entire length. Indeed, after his initial conversation with Harker at the castle, Dracula never utters another word in the movie. While Dracula is frightening at his castle, with the mad and animalistic expressions on his face when he gets angry, his fangs showing, streams of blood coming from his mouth and displays of his incredible strength, he is never quite as frightening once he travels out of his native land. This is caused partly from his long absences from the film. His persona is also not helped by the fact that he seems unreasonably frightened of Van Helsing, even fleeing back to his castle at the first counterattack by the very mortal Van Helsing, undercutting some of the fear that Dracula is supposed to engender.

In Bram Stoker's novel, as described above, even though Dracula is missing from much of the narrative, the fear of the character never dissipates for the reader, because Stoker provides constant reminders of his character's propensities throughout the story, slowly building up to the "blood of my blood" scene and then to the death of Dracula. This demonstrates, once again, that literature is different than film and in a film version of Stoker's novel, Dracula should always remain the prime focus or the horror of Dracula can slip away.

While not a complete success, primarily because of the use and characterization of Dracula, *Horror of Dracula* is an excellent entry in the long line of cinematic adaptations of Bram Stoker's famous novel. Along with *The Curse of Frankenstein* (1957), *Horror of Dracula* started the third important horror cycle of the sound cinema, just as *Dracula* (1931) and *Frankenstein* (1931) started the first horror film cycle of the early sound era. *Horror of Dracula* is different than Bram Stoker's novel and different from the two prior film adaptations, *Nosferatu* (1922) and *Dracula* (1931), illustrating the fact that Bram Stoker's vision was strong enough to survive and even flourish as different filmmakers produced their own interpretations of Stoker's famous work of horror.

Bram Stoker's Dracula (1992)

For a film that claims to be the definitive version of the novel, the opening sequence of *Bram Stoker's Dracula* is not very promising. Before the title, there is an introductory section set in 1462 showing a very human Dracula going off to war, impaling many of his foes in the manner of Vlad the Impaler, and then returning to his castle to find his fiancée, Elisabeta, dead, having committed suicide in the mistaken belief that Dracula died in battle. This causes Dracula to turn against God and vow to return after death to seek vengeance for Elisabeta's death, making Dracula into, presumably, a voluntary vampire or, perhaps, the first vampire of all time, assuming someone can permanently turn himself into a vampire by simple declaration.

The opening has a tenuous relationship to Chapter III of the novel, in which Dracula explains his family's heritage, but the film version of that heritage is totally made up. It is shot and acted in a pretentious and overly stylistic manner and with inappropriate and excessively dramatic music, ending in a surfeit of blood and Dracula proclaiming, "The blood is the life," for no apparent reason other than the fact that some character in just about every Dracula movie either says that line or something very similar.

The credits to the movie are finally displayed and then after some irrelevant scenes in London, the film turns to the main story line, as Jonathan Harker travels to Transylvania to sell some prime real estate in England to Count Dracula. From this point forward, the plot hews closely to that of Bram Stoker's novel, with some of the action laid out in journals or diaries of the participants. From time to time, phrases from the book are incorporated into the dialogue. However, despite the strength of Stoker's plot, the problems with the opening of the film continue throughout the main body of the film—*Bram Stoker's Dracula* is all style and no substance, resulting in an ineffective movie.

Many of the difficulties with *Bram Stoker's Dracula* arise from its presentation, which has so many problems that it is hard to identify them all. There are the crazy transitions between scenes, such as the time when Mina and Lucy are talking happily in a beautiful garden in England. A storm suddenly rises in the sky and the plot segues to the stormy ride of Dracula on the *Demeter* as it travels from Transylvania to England. But, why was there a sudden storm back in England? The only reason was to create the segue, which is hardly a sufficient reason.

At Castle Dracula, three beautiful vampire women, much like the novel, attack Jonathan Harker but in this case the three creatures of the night seem to mystically rise from the sheets and blankets of one of the largest beds ever made. In the stylized direction, with strange camera angles and confusing point-of-view shots, the attack on Harker is overtly sexual but, paradoxically, without any sensuality at all, perhaps because it is so confusing. One of the female vampires is able to destroy Harker's crucifix with her mind alone, something Dracula was unable to do just a few minutes before. What is going on here?

The trip on the *Demeter* is relayed in a perfunctory manner, with possibly less horror to that portion of the tale than there was in *Dracula* (1931), even though the earlier film also skipped over most of that incident. Indeed, this section of *Bram Stoker's Dracula* is told in such a confusing manner, with jump cuts and fast motion and point-of-view photography, that it appears that Dracula makes his first attack on Lucy in England while Dracula is still on board the ship.

The opening sequences in Transylvania in *Bram Stoker's Dracula*, directed by Francis Ford Coppola, pale in comparison to those same sequences in the 1931 version directed by Tod Browning. The scenes on the *Demeter* in *Bram Stoker's Dracula* are far less effective than those same scenes in *Nosferatu* (1922), directed by F.W. Murnau. The attacks on Lucy by Dracula and the final slaying of Lucy in Coppola's version are dwarfed by the same effective moments in *Horror of Dracula* (1958), directed by Terrence Fisher, and as for the ultimate demise of Dracula, nothing in *Bram Stoker's Dracula* comes close to *Horror of Dracula*.

It is amusing to see Dracula in Transylvania figuratively drooling over Jonathan's picture of Mina, eventually leading him to attack Mina once he travels to England. This incident does not come from the book; it was first used in *Nosferatu*. Dracula says to Harker, to explain why he will not dine with him, that he does not drink—wine. This line comes from *Dracula* (1931), not from

Stoker's novel. There is a section of cross-cutting between the marriage ceremony of Jonathan and Mina in Rumania with Dracula's last vicious attack on Lucy in London, similar to the cross-cutting between a religious ceremony and brutal killings at the end of *The Godfather* (1972), also directed by Coppola. Since Winona Ryder plays both Dracula's fiancé back in 1462 and Mina Harker, and since Mina and Dracula already have a connection before they meet, there is an overriding theme of reincarnation in the film, similar to *The Mummy* (1932). These examples raise the question as to why the film is called *Bram Stoker's Dracula*, when it incorporates incidents from so many other sources.

A significant difference between the novel and this film is the reincarnation issue and the courtship by Dracula of Mina in London while, at the same time, Dracula is attacking Lucy at night. The courtship scenes, some occurring in a primitive movie theater of the late 19th century, as if Dracula and Mina are teenagers on a modern date, are not very convincing. More importantly, they undercut the horror of Dracula, as here he seems quite human, such as in the moment he learns that Mina has left him to marry Jonathan Harker. Dracula actually starts to sob. Would Christopher Lee's Dracula ever cry in a film? At a moment like this, Gary Oldman's Dracula has become Jonathan Frid's Barnabas Collins, the quintessential wimpy vampire.

Bram Stoker's Dracula has first class production values, but those values are dissipated by the bravura direction, immense sets and impressive special effects that proclaim the skill of the director and the technicians but do not contribute to the success of the film. The cast is first-rate but the acting is poor. Anthony Hopkins is forgettable as Dr. Van Helsing, lost among the quick cuts, special effects, strange camera angles, insensitive dialogue and lack of involvement of Hopkins in his character. Gary Oldman, as Dracula, is more difficult to understand in the opening scenes in Transylvania than Bela Lugosi was in the 1931 film, a hard feat to accomplish, although Oldman's performance does improve substantially once the tale moves to England. Nevertheless, for all of the production assistance that enhances Oldman's performance, he is never as frightening as Christopher Lee was in *Horror of Dracula*. Indeed, the image of Max Schreck of *Nosferatu* lingers longer in the viewer's mind than any of the different visages of Gary Oldman in *Bram Stoker's Dracula*, other than the weird hair that adorns his head when he first meets Harker at his castle, perhaps one of the reasons why the villagers are afraid to come close to the edifice.

All is not bad in the film, from small matters to large. Dracula has incredibly long fingers with incredibly sharp fingernails, flowers wilt in Dracula's presence and Dracula's shadow appears to operate independently of the vampire, nice effects all. Dracula grows younger once he transitions from Transylvania to England, a nice touch from the novel. Jonathan Harker, on the other hand,

In the top photograph from *Bram Stoker's Dracula* (1992), Jonathan Harker (Keanu Reeves) says goodbye to his fiancé, Mina Murray (Winona Ryder), just before he leaves on his journey to meet Count Dracula. In the bottom picture, from left to right, Arthur Holmwood (Cary Elwes), Quincey Morris (Bill Campbell), Dr. Seward (Richard E. Grant) and Professor Van Helsing (Anthony Hopkins) hide and watch as the recently deceased Lucy returns to her coffin with a child in her arms.

grows grayer, a nice counterpoint also from the book. When Dracula licks the blood off of Jonathan's razor at Castle Dracula, it is a clever but disgusting touch to the film. Dracula changes into many different forms during the film, one of the best occurring during his final attack on Lucy, when Dracula appears in the shape of a vicious wolf, and another good one occurring at the time Dracula attacks Mina, presaged by a colored mist travelling from Carfax Abbey to Mina's room.

The ending of the movie is quite good, effectively showing the chase across the Continent to Transylvania, where Van Helsing disposes of the three vampire women and Quincey Morris delivers a blow to Dracula's chest with his long knife. These scenes, based on very similar events near the end of the novel, are as exciting as they were in the book. Then, in the type of defect that recurs often in this film, the effectiveness of those scenes immediately dissipates with an added scene, when Mina (as Dracula's reincarnated fiancée) voluntarily goes off with Dracula by herself. Dracula then requests relief from his life of evil and Mina thrusts the knife into his heart again, kisses his dead lips and slices off his head. The film ends with a high shot looking down on the two of them and then a shot of the original Dracula and Elisabeta in a stained-glass ceiling of the castle, all with church-like music playing. Talk about pretentious. This is the killing of a vampire, not a religious event.

Many questions are raised by the ending of *Bram Stoker's Dracula*, none of them complimentary to the movie. Is anyone completely sure as to what happens at the end of this film? Even upon repeated viewings, questions remain, although the main question still is—what does all of this have to do with *Dracula*, by Bram Stoker?

A few good moments aside, *Bram Stoker's Dracula* is poorly written, acted and directed. It follows the plot of Bram Stoker's novel but is nowhere near as successful in creating an epic tale of horror. What purports to be the most definitive film version of Bram Stoker's novel is only the most pretentious one.

Other Adaptations

Much like other classic works of horror such as Mary Shelley's *Frankenstein*, Robert Louis Stevenson's *Dr. Jekyll and Mr. Hyde* and Gaston Leroux's *The Phantom of the Opera*, Bram Stoker's *Dracula* has been filmed so many times in so many different formats that all of the adaptations could not be covered in this book. In addition to *Nosferatu*, there have been other silent film versions of *Dracula*, now unfortunately lost. In addition to George Melford's Spanish *Dracula* of 1931, there have been other foreign language adaptations of the novel, from countries as diverse as Turkey and Korea. And, of course, there have been several television adaptations of the novel, both on commercial and public television. At both Universal and Hammer, there were numerous sequels to their respective screen interpretations of the novel, most of which brought less and less of Bram Stoker to the screen as the series progressed. There have also been film satires of the character, in *Abbott and Costello Meet Frankenstein* (1948) and *Dracula: Dead and Loving It* (1995).

Chapter 6

The Phantom of the Opera by Gaston Leroux

Gaston Leroux was inspired to write *The Phantom of the Opera* after visiting the Paris Opera House and exploring its many subterranean levels. Leroux was able to observe a subterranean lake in the bowels of the building, which was actually a flood control system used to control the extensive ground water beneath the edifice. Leroux was also aware of an accident at the opera house in 1886, when one of the chandeliers' counterweights fell into the audience, killing a woman and injuring a number of people. Leroux incorporated these details and the history of the opera house into *The Phantom of the Opera*, a novel that became so popular that it inspired numerous horror films and an incredibly successful stage musical.

Background

Gaston Leroux was born in 1868 in Paris, France, although he grew up in Normandy where his family had shipbuilding interests. Despite earning his law degree, Leroux began work on newspapers, first covering court trials and later travelling the world, reporting on significant historical events such as the Russian Revolution of 1905. In 1904, his first of many books was serialized and by 1907, he was working full time as a writer of fiction with his early fame in fiction arising from a series of detective stories he created about Joseph Rouletabille, a journalist-detective. *The Phantom of the Opera* was serialized in the newspaper *Le Gaulois* from September 1909 through January 1910. It was published as a novel later in 1910. Leroux passed away in 1927.

The Literature

Given Gaston Leroux's background as a reporter and mystery writer, it is not surprising that *The Phantom of the Opera* is written in the nature of a true crime, non-fiction work, with the unnamed narrator investigating the alleged ghost of the Paris Opera House and several unsolved murders that occurred in the edifice some 30 years before. He discovers that the "ghost" was Erik (whose last name is never disclosed), who was born with a countenance so hideous that his mother gave him a mask so that she did not have to look at his face. After a life on the run, Erik built a secret lair in the basement levels of the Paris Opera House. From those rooms, Erik terrorized the edifice's occupants for many years, including a young opera singer named Christine Daaé, eventually leading to her kidnapping by the Phantom and a strange journey of discovery deep in the bowels of the Opera House before Christine's escape with her lover, Raoul.

That short summary of the plot of *The Phantom of the Opera* does not do justice to the scope of the entire novel, which is complex in many ways. The book also displays quite a bit of humor, particularly in the reactions of the new managers of the opera house to the ghost of the opera. However, the true strength of *The Phantom of the Opera* arises from its setting, both in the opera house and in its underground catacombs, and by some striking moments that linger long in the reader's memory.

One of the most memorable sequences in the novel begins when Erik first brings Christine to his subterranean lair. Erik lures Christine through the passageway behind the mirrors in her dressing room and puts her on the back of a white horse. He then walks her down the circular gallery of the cellars of the opera house, where Christine sees demons with shovels and pitchforks in front of the red fires of the furnace. After a walk down "a spiral stair into the very heart of the earth" (Chapter 12, "Apollo's Lyre"), they reach an immense dark lake with a bluish glow lighting up the bank. Erik places Christine in a boat and then rows them across the noiseless lake to his drawing room and other living quarters. In some ways, the underground of the opera house is the ultimate old dark house.

It is in Erik's quarters that the most unforgettable moment of the novel occurs. Erik is playing the piano and Christine is singing for him. As Christine then describes it, "Suddenly, I felt a need to see beneath the mask. I wanted to know the *face* of the voice, and, with a movement which I was utterly unable to control, swiftly my fingers tore away the mask. Oh, horror, horror, horror!" (Chapter 12, "Apollo's Lyre"). Christine is shocked from the visage she sees. Eric is so furious that he forces Christine to continue looking at his face, even forcing Christine to dig her fingers into his corpse of a face, to prove that the hideous face is not another mask.

The unmasking of the phantom is the highlight of the novel. It is clearly the most cinematic moment of the story and would be used in all of the film interpretations of Leroux's novel. Interestingly, there is no detailed description of the phantom's face at that moment and throughout the novel, there are conflicting descriptions of the face, depending on which character is describing the phantom's countenance. The best description comes early in the novel from Joseph Buquet, the soon-to-be-murdered chief sceneshifter. He says that the ghost is extraordinarily thin, with a skeletal frame, two big black holes for his eyes in what seems like a dead man's skull, nasty yellow skin stretched across his bones, no nose and hair consisting of only three or four dark locks on the forehead and behind his ears (Chapter 1, "Is It the Ghost?").

Other remarkable moments in the novel include Carlotta, the opera's lead performer, singing on the opera stage but her voice sounding like the croaking of a frog and Christine disappearing from the opera stage in the middle of a performance, after the stage turns dark. Then there is the falling of the opera house chandelier during a performance, which is the ghost's revenge for Carlotta appearing on stage despite the ghost's threats. The chandelier plunges from the ceiling and smashes into the seating area, "amid a thousand shouts of terror" (Chapter 7, "*Faust* and What Followed"). Many are injured and one is killed by the ghost's act of horror.

Significantly, most of these highlights occur in the first half of the novel, with the quality of the second half of the novel falling significantly, becoming less of a mystery or horror story and more of a melodrama, and a disappointing and unconvincing one, at that. For example, when Raoul and his associate, the Persian, pursue Erik and Christine into the cellars of the opera house, they become trapped in a torture room of mirrors, mirages, a heat ray, and a hidden exit. In a story of implausibles, this one is the most implausible. How did Erik build such a room at the opera house and why? Even if the reader willing to suspend his disbelief, this section of the novel is still quite boring, with Raoul and the Persian finally making their inevitable escape from the torture chamber after two tedious chapters of effort. Then, for the most minor of reasons, Erik, who until that time has been the epitome of evil, changes personalities. Despite his love for Christine, Erik frees Christine and Raoul and allows them to go off and marry. In a fairly long novel, this transformation of Erik is quite rapid; it is over in just a few pages. Erik's conversion to the side of good is unconvincing, resulting in an unsatisfactory conclusion to the novel, which ends not with a bang but with a whimper.

As part of these concluding sections of the novel, Leroux attempts to humanize the phantom. Erik tells Christine that he is tired of living in his subterranean retreat. He says, "I want to have a nice, quiet flat, with ordinary doors and windows and a wife inside it, like anyone else! A wife whom I could love and take out on Sundays and keep amused on week-days" (Chapter 23, "The Torture Begins"). Obviously, Eric can never achieve that goal because of people's reaction to his shocking countenance. This theme, that society's horrified reaction to a hideous face can result in evil, is similar to a theme of both the novel, *Frankenstein*, and many of its film adaptations, and it is very effective in most of those works. It does not succeed, however, in *The Phantom of the Opera*, primarily because Erik is evil throughout the story, causing many deaths, and his transformation seems like a rushed twist to provide a finish for the tale, rather than a conversion that has arisen naturally from the story that has gone before.

Early in the novel, the narrator comments that the lives of all Parisians "are one masked ball" (Chapter 3, "The Mysterious Room"), and, in fact, *The Phantom of the Opera* is a novel of masks and mirrors. Obviously, the most important mask is the one worn by the Phantom throughout the novel, but it is interesting to learn that his mother gave him one at an early age, so that he has worn a mask almost his entire life. An important scene in the novel occurs at a masked ball, where Raoul is dressed as a black domino, Christine as a white domino and Erik as the Red Death, surely an accurate symbol for him. Raoul and Christine often mask their affection for each other and it is only when Erik voluntarily removes his mask in the presence of Christine that Erik can become human again. Similarly, Erik uses the mirrors in Christine's dressing room to enter and exit at will, Erik has a mirrored torture chamber in his downtown lair but he has no mirrors on the walls of his dwelling. Even Erik cannot bear to look at his own face.

The Phantom of the Opera, by Gaston Leroux, whether it is considered a tale of ghosts or horror, mystery or romance, has its faults as a novel and that may be one of the reasons it is no longer read today. However, its dramatic potential is obvious and film, television and stage adaptations of the novel have been frequently made, starting in the silent era and continuing to the present day.

The Films

The Phantom of the Opera (1925)

Lon Chaney's version of *The Phantom of the Opera* is a surprisingly faithful adaptation of Gaston Leroux's novel, even down to some of the details, such as Erik playing his own work, *Don Juan Triumphant*, on his organ in his basement lair, Raoul and Inspector Ledoux (the replacement character for the Persian) holding their hands high in front of their faces as they search through the opera cellars so that Erik cannot strangle them with a quick lasso, or Erik using a long reed to swim underwater to upset a boat on the cellar lake, in this case, killing Raoul's brother who has gone into the cellars looking for Raoul.

Of course, there are some changes from the novel. The book relates the story of Raoul's and Christine's meetings earlier in their lives, the influence of her father on Christine and the Phantom's blackmailing of the new opera managers for payments of 20,000 francs. These moments are all missing from the film. The horse which first transports Christine into the phantom's cellar lair is black, not white. However, the most significant change is at the end, where the Phantom no longer repents and lets Raoul and Christine go off and marry. Instead, a more exciting ending is substituted, with all of the employees of the opera storming the cellars of the edifice, bearing torches just as the villagers in *Frankenstein* (1931) would soon do, to seek revenge against Erik for the murder of Joseph Buquet, an opera house employee. Erik escapes with Christine, steals a carriage and the chase is on. The carriage overturns, Christine is saved and the mob finally catches up with Eric, pummeling him unmercifully and then throwing his dead body into the Seine River. This film version ends with a bang, not with a whimper.

Indeed, the last part of *The Phantom of the Opera* (1925) seems more like a movie serial than a horror film with, in addition to the final chase, Raoul and Ledoux trapped in the torture chamber of mirrors and then almost drowned in the flood waters of the opera house cellars. Unlike the novel, the second half of the film, while still weaker than the first half, does not disappoint.

The change in ending does undercut a partial theme of the film, which is slightly different from the theme of the novel. In Leroux's version, there is an attempt to postulate that the hideousness of Erik's face has caused his evil nature and that love can reverse the effects. This idea is repeated in Erik's early statement in the film to Christine, where he says, "If I am the Phantom, it is because man's hatred has made me so." However, later in the film, Erik reverses the idea, saying to Christine, "Now, you shall see the evil spirit that makes my evil face!" However, whether it is the face that causes the evil or the evil that causes the face, with the change in the ending of the film from that of the novel, these ideas are left hanging. They are completely forgotten by the end of the movie.

The Phantom of the Opera (1925) has a structural problem, caused by its over-reliance on Leroux's storyline. The climax of the film comes halfway through with the unmasking of the Phantom, a moment made for the cinema. Because of its significance and impact, it probably should have been deferred to the end of the film when Christine reaches the Phantom's hideaway for the second time. Thus, even with the improvements to the story line in the second half of the film, as contrasted with the novel, the second half of the film is still a letdown, since the unmasking is such a remarkable cinematic moment. Indeed, the unmasking scene of *The Phantom of the Opera* (1925) is some of the best five minutes of horror ever put on the screen. It is an iconic moment of the horror film genre.

The scene is set up by the fact that only traces of the phantom are revealed earlier in the film. Early on, the phantom materializes most often as a shadow on the wall or sitting in Box 5 wearing a cloak and a hat, as if he may not be real. He then appears to Christine as a melodious voice from behind the walls of her dressing room. Then, when Christine follows the voice through the sliding mirror of her dressing room, she first sees the masked and hatted Phantom, and even that figure is frightening enough to shock Christine.

In the Phantom's subterranean hideaway, Christine receives a note warning her never to touch the Phantom's mask. That is all the encouragement she needs and she immediately sneaks up on the Phantom while he is playing the organ and, after some suspenseful hesitation, pulls off his head covering and mask. The audience sees the hideous face first, with the effect heightened by the expression of horror on Chaney's face. He turns and faces Christine and the shock on her face is apparent. Then it is back to a half-shot of Chaney, who then points an accusing finger at Christine, with Chaney embellishing the moment with his wide toothy mouth and round eyes. There is then a shot of Chaney from below as he walks toward the camera, as the horrid face fills the screen. He grabs Christine and repeating a line from the novel (Chapter 12, "Apollo's Lyre"), says, "Feast your eyes—glut your soul on my accursed ugliness!"

The scene continues for a few minutes longer, with the face of the Phantom holding the viewers' attention whenever it is shown, as if the viewer needs to re-confirm that such a thing is actually up there on the screen. While Chaney's makeup does not match the description of the Phantom from the novel, it is better than Leroux could ever have imagined. Chaney's acting skills only add to its effectiveness. In addition, Chaney's makeup becomes more horrific as the film progresses, particularly in the darkening of his face around the eyes, so that the audience never becomes blasé about the Phantom's countenance.

Another striking moment in the film is the sudden drop of the chandelier into the opera audience. The huge chandelier in the front of the hall and high above the audience is a prominent fixture in every long shot of the stage. Then, when Carlotta is singing on stage as a challenge to a direct threat by the Phantom, the lights suddenly blink, the shadow of the Phantom is seen and a voice shouts, "Behold! She is singing to bring down the chandelier." The immense fixture shakes and then it rapidly falls into the audience at great speed. Panic ensues.

While the journey by Erik and Christine through the cellars of the opera

The Phantom (Lon Chaney) exults over his capture of Raoul and Ledoux as Christine (Mary Philbin) cowers on the steps, near the conclusion of *The Phantom of the Opera* (1925).

house is also quite good, a better scene in the film is the retreat by Raoul and Christine to the roof of the edifice for a private conversation. Although this incident does come from the novel, it is much more effective in the film because of the visuals. As Raoul and Christine talk, the rooftop statue of Apollo dwarfs them. Suddenly there is a shot of the Phantom, perched high on the statue, his red cape flapping in the breeze, as he eavesdrops on the two lovers. In a film of many unforgettable images, this is one of the best.

The sets for *The Phantom of the Opera* (1925) never cease to amaze, even more than 85 years after the film was released. The auditorium is huge, with multiple tiered seating along the sidewall, a high stage curtain, large chandelier and realistic orchestra pit, allowing impressive long shots of the stage from several different angles from within the theater. According to author George Perry, the backstage part of the set contains all of the necessary equipment, scenery and props for the staging of a real opera. The roof, including the impressive statue of Apollo, is built to scale. The Grand Foyer, the setting for the masked ball, with the double staircase leading to a central staircase, is spectacular. The lower catacombs contain high sets with columns and arches and a black, shiny lake.

While the aboveground sets for *The Phantom of the Opera* (1925) are not exact replicas of the Paris Opera House, they are strikingly similar. The opera house set is so impressive that it stood for 90 years, having been used in a number of other Hollywood productions over the years. In addition, the use of color in the masked ball scene, to highlight the Phantom's masquerade as the Red Death, is particularly effective, and the tinting of numerous scenes also adds to the interest of the film.

The Phantom of the Opera (1925) is far from a perfect film. Mary Philbin, as Christine, overacts outrageously, with exaggerated hand and body movements. When she is in the Phantom's presence, she appears to be in a trance or sleepwalking, which makes no sense within the context of the story line. Because of problems during production, the plot has lapses in logic and the ending comes quite suddenly, with the audience never learning what happens to Raoul, Christine or the opera house. And, as noted above, the second half of the film is somewhat of a letdown. Nevertheless, even though there were many subsequent adaptations of Leroux's most famous novel, the 1925 version starring Lon Chaney remains the best, even after all of the time that has passed since its release.

Phantom of the Opera (1943)

When film fans think of Claude Rains, they seldom remember his strong resume in horror films. Rains is better remembered for his important roles in non-horror films, such as Prince John in *The Adventures of Robin Hood* (1938), Senator Paine in *Mr. Smith Goes to Washington* (1939), Mr. Jordan in *Here Comes Mr. Jordan* (1941), and, of course, his most famous role as Captain Renault in *Casablanca* (1942). Yet, Rains had three of the most important horror film roles in the classic Universal era—the title character in *The Invisible Man* (1933),

Larry Talbot's father in *The Wolf Man* (1941) and the title character in *Phantom of the Opera* (1943). Strangely, in both the first and last films in that trio, Rains's face was not shown throughout much of the films.

Based on the title of Gaston Leroux's novel, a screen adaptation of *The Phantom of the Opera* can emphasize one of two elements—the phantom or the opera. For the 1925 version that was silent, it would have been difficult to emphasize the opera and therefore the film emphasizes the horror aspects of the tale, to the movie's benefit. For the 1943 version, Universal decided to emphasize the singing portion of the story, to the chagrin of horror film fans everywhere. The musical scenes in *Phantom of the Opera* (1943) are lengthy, impressive and pleasant enough to watch, but, frankly, there were better Hollywood musicals to view in the early 1940s, such as *Hollywood Inn* (1942), starring Fred Astaire and Bing Crosby and *Meet Me in St. Louis* (1944), starring Judy Garland. People going to see *Phantom of the Opera* in 1943 were interested in a remake of a classic horror film, not another movie musical.

The masked Phantom (Claude Rains) arrives unannounced at the home of opera singer Biancarolli, ordering her to leave Paris so that Christine can sing in her place at the opera, in *Phantom of the Opera* (1943).

In addition to being a musical, *Phantom of the Opera* (1943) is also a musical comedy, as Anatole Garron, the lead male singer in the opera, and Raoul, the police inspector, simultaneously vie for Christine's affections, often acting quite silly in the process, such as bringing the identical presents for Christine at the same time or trying to enter a room through a door at the same time. Since the film plays more like a musical than a horror story, it actually brings back more memories of *42nd Street* (1933) than *The Phantom of the Opera* (1925) because after the lead singer is drugged by the Phantom, Christine goes out on the opera stage as a youngster but must come back a star.

Gaston Leroux's famous novel was somewhat old-fashioned by 1943 and it made sense to update the narrative for a relatively big budget film that was intended to be bright and colorful, rather than dark and shadowy. As a result, the set-up for the 1943 film is substantially different from the one in the novel. Erique Claudin, a violinist for the opera orchestra, has been secretly funding the singing lessons for Christine Dubois, a singer in the chorus who has now worked her way up to be the stand-in for the opera's prima donna. In the process, Erique has gone broke. When he is fired from the opera, Erique tries to sell the manuscript for his new concerto to a music publisher. When it appears to Erique that the publisher is stealing his work, Erique snaps and kills the publisher. The publisher's girlfriend then throws a vat of acid into Erique's face, sending him into hiding in the opera house, where he starts to steal food, terrorize the occupants and continue to promote Christine's career, this time by less than honest means. The ghost of the opera has been born.

Even though *Phantom of the Opera* (1943) sometimes seems to be only a musical, there are several impressive non-musical moments in the film, such as the shot of Erique in the basement of the Opera House listening from afar to Christine delivering her stunning debut performance, and the film's final shot of Eric's violin, bow and mask lying amid the rubble of the opera house's cellar. The best section of the film, however, is the fall of the chandelier and the events leading up to it. Raoul has decided to draw out the Phantom by going against his wishes and having another ingénue sing the lead in the opera *Le Prince de Caucasie*, a film original based upon the music of Tchaikovsky. Raoul fills the opera house with policemen, some wearing stage masks so that they can be on stage during the performance. The entire scene is played out while the opera is being performed on stage so that there is minimal dialogue as the plot moves forward.

Erique strangles a guard and takes his place in his mask and costume, Raoul finds the dead policeman, Erique sneaks up the ladders toward the chandelier, Raoul and another policeman search along the catwalks for the Phantom, and Erique finally reaches the ceiling and starts to saw through the chain holding the fixture in place, high above the audience. The scene is primarily done in pantomime and is therefore an accidental homage to the Chaney version, although the soundtrack is hardly silent, with the sounds of the opera and strains of Tchaikovsky heard throughout the house as the events are occurring.

The scene ends with a stunning use of sound. The new female singer starts her solo just as Erique is about done with his work. As she hits and holds a very high note on the scale, her singing suddenly turns to a high-pitched scream as the chandelier falls into the crowd. It is a moment worthy of Alfred Hitchcock. This section of the picture alone makes *Phantom of the Opera* (1943) worth a view.

The unmasking of the Phantom is moved to the end of the feature, where it should be, to provide a maximum climax to the story. Unfortunately for this film version, the unmasking does not provide a climax; it provides a letdown. When Christine whips off Erique's mask, the camera moves in for a close-up, showing the disfigured right side of the Phantom's face and not much else. Erique has a full head of hair and a normal nose, left eye and mouth. He is far from good-looking but his face is only partially mutilated. In a comparison with Lon Chaney's version, well, there is no comparison.

The scene is also shot without style. After the short close-up of Claude Rains's face, there is a longer shot of Susanna Foster as she backs away from the Phantom in fright. There are only a few more shots of the Phantom before he is killed in the collapse of the basement roof. This scene becomes more of a throwaway than a climax, as if the filmmakers knew that Rains' make-up was nothing

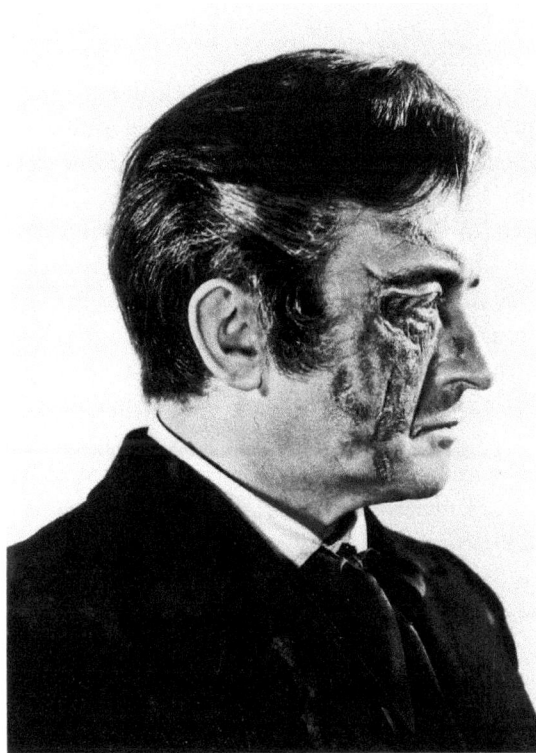

This publicity photograph for *Phantom of the Opera* (1943) shows the unimpressive makeup worn by Claude Rains for a brief moment in the film.

special and that it was important that the film shift away from the requisite unmasking scene as soon as possible.

Phantom of the Opera (1943) is not a horror classic. Indeed, much like the 1925 version, it is not really a horror film. Yet, for all of its faults, the remake is a pleasant diversion, entertaining enough even for the avid horror film fan, but not compelling enough to erase memories of the 1925 silent version.

The Phantom of the Opera (1962)

Horror film fans know what to expect from a Hammer Films production of a classic work of horror. The film will seem big budget, with luscious color photography, impressive sets, beautiful women and period costumes. There is likely to be a bit of violence. Those fans also know that the script will be, at most, a loose adaptation of the source material. Hammer was never afraid to make significant changes to the plots of famous works of horror that it brought to the screen.

The Phantom of the Opera (1962) is no exception, with the film actually providing two different villains in place of the one ghost of the opera house. One of those villains is a dwarf-like creature who roams the catacombs of the opera house, perhaps as an assistant to the Phantom. The other is Lord Ambrose D'Arcy, the opera's chief composer, who chooses the lead female singers for the opera based upon whether or not they will sleep with him. In the case of Christine Charles, D'Arcy has her fired from the opera when she refuses to act positively to his advances. Hubris and lechery are not D'Arcy's only sins, however, as it turns out that he stole the score for his new opera from a Professor Petrie, who was then accidentally disfigured by acid in a fire at a music publishing house. Since there is a masked man at the opera committing pranks, such as slashing opera posters, destroying the sheet music and perhaps committing murder (as a stage hand's body swings onto the stage during an opera performance), most viewers will conclude that the Phantom is Professor Petrie.

Another expected attribute of Hammer horror films is a buxom young actress as the female lead and in this case, Heather Sears, as Christine, fits the bill. However, other than her obvious attributes, Sears is really not that attractive and she is bland in the role. It is hard to understand why so many male characters are interested in her. Michael Gough, who is well-known to horror film fans from *Horror of Dracula* (1958) and a number of other horror films over his long career, is dominating and deliciously villainous as D'Arcy. It is the performance of the film.

The best-known performer in the film is probably Herbert Lom, who plays the Phantom. Although Lom appeared in several genre films in his long career, he is best known today for his role as Dreyfus, Inspector Clouseau's boss, in the *Pink Panther* films. As is often the case in the film adaptations of Gaston Leroux's novel, the character of the Phantom is, by necessity, off screen for much of the film and thus it is difficult for an actor to stand out in the role. Nevertheless, Lom does a nice job in the few scenes in which he appears and he makes effective use of his voice when he is under the mask.

With the exception of the strong production values and generally good performances, *The Phantom of the Opera* (1962) is a misfire in almost every other regard. While the 1925 silent version was about horror and the 1943 version was about music, the 1962 version seems to be more about romance (between Christine and the opera's young production manager, Harry Hunter) and backstage intrigue (when D'Arcy fires Hunter and tries to run the entire opera by himself). While each of these story lines is somewhat interesting, they also seem like filler material, having little to do with the ghost that is terrorizing the opera house.

The back-story of the Phantom's disfigurement from acid does not come from Gaston Leroux's novel. It actually has its origins in the 1943 film version, where the Claude Rains's Phantom was disfigured by acid in a fight at a music publishing house when he thought one of his compositions was being stolen. Since the Phantom in the 1962 film version is a totally sympathetic character, he is given a dwarf-like assistant who lives in the cellar of the opera house and seems to have committed all of the bad deeds shown in the film, including killing a rat-catcher for no reason. No explanation is ever given as to who the Dwarf is. (None can be given; he is only in the film to commit several random acts of villainy, which a sympathetic Phantom cannot do or he would not be a sympathetic character.) Replacing the Phantom of the Opera with two characters, D'Arcy, an unpleasant gentleman, and this Dwarf, whose actions make no sense, is not an even trade. As a result, there is almost no true horror in *The Phantom of the Opera* (1962).

Structurally, the film is a mess. Since the Phantom never even knew who Christine was until the day she auditioned for the lead role in the Opera once the prior female lead fled in fear, it makes no sense for the Phantom to have done (or allowed the Dwarf to commit) any of the acts of violence or pranks that are shown throughout the film. The Phantom's original motivation was to have his opera performed, not cancelled. Then, because the Phantom is a good guy, there is no tension at the end of the film. Unlike the very clever scene in the 1943 film, where elements of the plot unfold throughout the theater while an opera is performed on stage, the end of *The Phantom of the Opera* (1962) is a straightforward performance of an opera based on the life of Joan of Arc. That means that the climax of the film is the excommunication of Joan of Arc, not all that interesting to horror film fans.

Of course, the filmmakers were smart enough to realize that *The Phantom of the Opera* (1962) could not just end with a successful performance of an opera and so, in a sense, an epilogue was added. The Dwarf is discovered along the high catwalks above the stage and chased by a stagehand. (The only reason the Dwarf is there is to provide an ending to the film. No logical reason can be provided for him being high in the theater.) The Dwarf then jumps onto the opera house chandelier, which eventually crashes to the ground. (The only reason the Dwarf jumps onto the chandelier, one of the puniest in all of *The Phantom of the Opera* history, is because this is *The Phantom of the Opera* and there has to be a chandelier somewhere in the story.) As the chandelier is about to crash to the stage, the Phantom removes his mask (why?), jumps onto the stage from a side box, pushes Christine to safety and is himself crushed to death by the falling fixture.

It is hard to evaluate Herbert Lom's makeup as the Phantom because if the viewer blinks, Lom's unmasked face will be missed. It is shown for just a few seconds, once right before Lom jumps and twice when he is lying on the floor of the stage. Given the full mask that Lom wears throughout most of the film, as contrasted with the partial mask worn by Claude Rains in the 1943 version, the viewer is justifiably expecting a spectacular face of the Phantom when his mask is removed. Instead, Lom's "scary" visage consists mainly of a closed eye and scars on his forehead, once again confirming the uniqueness and effectiveness of the Lon Chaney makeup in the silent version. Much like the 1943 version, the quality of the makeup undoubtedly suggests the reason why the filmmakers were hesitant to show the Phantom's face to the viewer for any significant length of time.

Hammer Films did a nice job with their versions of the Frankenstein monster, Dracula, the mummy and the werewolf, but it missed the mark with *The Phantom of the Opera* (1962). Faults and all, it is hard to top the 1925 silent version with Lon Chaney. This version does not come close.

Other Adaptations

It has been estimated that, on a worldwide basis, there have been over 50 feature films and television movies inspired, in whole or in part, by *The Phantom of the Opera* by Gaston Leroux. Despite those many and varied adaptations, Lon Chaney's silent film is still the most famous cinematic version, probably because of the iconic makeup employed. These days, however, the most famous adaptation of Gaston Leroux's novel is Andrew Lloyd Webber's musical, *The Phantom of the Opera*, which opened in London in 1986 and then premiered on Broadway in January 1988. The critically acclaimed production won nine Tony Awards. As of this writing, it is still playing in London and on Broadway. In 2004, a film version of the musical was released.

Chapter 7

The Magician by W. Somerset Maugham

Aleister Crowley, an Engishman who was born in 1875 and died in 1947, was a poet, painter, novelist, theologian and philosopher but today he is only remembered as a professed magician, occultist and Satanist. In a 1950s intoduction to a reissue of *The Magician*, W. Somerset Maugham wrote that the title character of *The Magician*, Oliver Haddo, was based upon Aleister Crowley, down to the description of the character. In fact, Maughm's description of Oliver Haddo in the novel is more grotesque than Aleister Crowkey in real life and the real Aleister Crowley was never proven to have powers of the occult. Thus, while Crowley was the inspiration for Haddo, the story of *The Magician* is all Maugham's.

Background

Although of English descent, William Somerset Maugham was born in Paris, France, on January 25, 1874. After graduating from medical school and passing his exams, Maugham decided to pursue a career in writing instead of medicine. In 1897, Maugham's second book, *Liza of Lambeth*, a tale of working class life in London, became very popular and for the next decade or so, Maugham continued writing novels, including *The Magician* (1908), but none were as popular as *Liza of Lambeth*. At that point, Maugham turned to play-writing, achieving a very popular hit in 1907 with *Lady Frederick* and then with many subsequent works for the stage. W. Somerset Maugham passed away at the age of 91 in December 1965.

The Literature

In the first third of *The Magician*, W. Somerset Maugham introduces the reader to Arthur Burden, his fiancée, the beautiful Margaret Dauncey, and the infamous Oliver Haddo, a self-proclaimed magician or alchemist. In this section of the novel, Maugham also spends some time on the history and lore of magicians, the latter being used by Maugham to lend some credibility to the later exploits of Haddo's. This section of the story is both well-researched and incredibly imaginative but it is also boring in the extreme. The characterization of the evil Haddo is lost in the excessive verbiage and the uninteresting tales of past "real world" incidents of the occult, with *The Magician* sometimes seeming more like a textbook than a novel. It is difficult to get through this section of *The Magician*, particularly because the book, published in 1908, reflects the old-fashioned writing style of the era.

Thereafter, *The Magician* starts to focus on its story line and its supernatural elements, including the bewitching of Margaret by Haddo, the highlight of the novel, Margaret dumping Arthur and marrying Haddo, the death of Margaret and the destruction of Haddo and his creations by Arthur. Unlike the first part of the novel, Maugham no longer goes on detours related to historical figures and events of the occult as he did earlier in the novel. He does a much better job focusing on the plot of his novel.

There is also a decided sexual element to the story at this time which adds to its interest, with Haddo hypnotizing Margaret into real or imagined ribald journeys or Margaret becoming more sensual and attractive while under Haddo's trance than she ever was while interacting with the boring Arthur. The discovery in Haddo's lab of living flesh, semi-formed humans and a child-like body with two monstrously large but distinct heads creates unforgettable images of horror. There is also a good moment where Dr. Porhoët, a friend of Arthur's and Margaret's, uses his own magic incantation to raise an image of Margaret from the dead.

In these latter sections of the book, Maugham's writing style is the same as it was at the beginning of the novel but because events are now unfolding at a much faster rate and the story has an intrinsic interest, Maugham's style is no longer an impediment to the enjoyment of the novel. Indeed, at this point, Maugham's inventiveness, strong vocabulary and striking imagery add to the effectiveness of the tale, cleverly painting the scenes, pictures and people of the narrative.

For example, as Maugham describes the bewitching of Margaret, he writes that Haddo subtlety hypnotizes her and then tells her tales of fantasies of strange worlds, of famous figures from the world of art, literature, mythology and mathematics and of "legendary monsters and foul beasts of a madman's fancy" (Chapter VIII). As another example, human though he may be, Haddo is a true monster, even including his physical appearance, originally described by Maugham as his "vast obesity" (Chapter III). By the end of the novel, as Maugham describes him, Haddo's corpulence had become a positive disease. "His chin was a mass of heavy folds distended with fat, and his cheeks were puffed up so that his eyes were preternaturally small." His eyelids were swollen, his ears were bloated, his lobes were swelled, his hands were repulsive, his balding head was now a great shining scalp and he sweated profusely (Chapter XIV). Surprisingly, Maugham's description of Haddo is more specific and substantially more abhorrent than either Mary Shelley's description of the Frankenstein monster or Robert Louis Stevenson's description of Dr. Jekyll in their respective famous works of horror.

There are some interesting references in the book that would later become associated with classic horror films. At one point Haddo states that the alchemist seeks "power over the whole world, power over all created things, power over the very elements, [and] power over God Himself" (Chapter VII). This manifestation of megalomania may have inspired some of the dialogue from *Frankenstein* (1931) and *The Invisible Man* (1933).

Animals seem to be particularly frightened of Haddo and the motif of animals being frightened of a person long before the human characters realize that there is a monster in their midst shows up in many films such as *Cat People* (1942). Haddo recounts incidents of magicians generating homunculi—little humans in bottles with horrible countenances. This brings thoughts of Dr. Pretorius and his more successful creation of little human beings in beakers in *Bride of Frankenstein* (1935). At the end of the novel, when it is learned that Haddo has created larger versions of some life forms, the analogy to *Frankenstein* (1931) is obvious.

In "A Fragment of Autobiography," W. Somerset Maugham wrote that when his publisher asked his permission to reissue *The Magician*, he felt that before consenting to the reissue, he should read the novel again, since nearly 50 years had passed since he had last read it and he "had completely forgotten it." Maugham may not have realized it but that was an illuminating observation on his part.

While many of Maugham's other works are still well-known today, *The Magician* is almost completely forgotten. In fact, if it were not for the movie version of Maugham's novel, *The Magician* (1926), the book would be, as Maugham wrote, completely forgotten today, long overshadowed by the famous works of horror of Mary Shelley, Bram Stoker, Edgar Allan Poe and many others.

The Film

The Magician (1926)

W. Somerset Maugham's only tale of the supernatural was adapted for the cinema in 1926 in a film directed by Rex Ingram and titled *The Magician*. Ingram was a well-known director of silent films; his output included such famous films as *The Four Horseman of the Apocalypse* (1921) and *Mare Nostrum* (1926). Although *The Magician* was made for a Hollywood studio, it was filmed in France, the location of most of the story in both the novel and the film, adding some authenticity to the film's presentation. At one time, *The Magician* was believed lost but today it is available for viewing in a high quality print.

The film version of *The Magician* is surprisingly faithful to Maugham's novel, at least until the end. Margaret Dauncey, the niece of Dr. Porhoët, is seriously injured when part of a huge sculpture of a faun she is working on falls, severely injuring her spine. Arthur Burdon, a leading surgeon, performs the surgery as many other doctors observe the operation in the hospital's amphitheater. After the operation, Arthur and Margaret fall in love and intend to be married.

One of the people observing Margaret's operation is Oliver Haddo, a student of the occult who, despite his interest in Burdon's work, is more interested in creating life than saving lives. One day, while perusing a musty old book of alchemy in the ancient Library of the Arsenal, Haddo discovers the formula for generating life. The formula requires the heart blood of a maiden who has fair skin, golden hair and eyes that are blue or grey. That description fits Margaret so perfectly that Haddo sets out to bewitch the young girl. The deed is done, Margaret marries Haddo and then Haddo takes her to his tower laboratory in order to use her virginal blood to create life. However, Arthur arrives just in time to kill Haddo and rescue Margaret.

As can be seen from that short plot summary, the movie takes much from the book by W. Somerset Maugham. Although some of the relationships between the parties are different and the last third of the movie focuses on Haddo's desire to create life, which is a part of the novel but not its prime focus, many scenes in the movie, in addition to its general plot, are clearly recognizable from the book. For example, the movie adapts a scene from Maugham's novel in which Haddo demonstrates his powers of the occult in a snake charmer's tent by being bitten by a poisonous snake and surviving. Also, Haddo's accumulation of wealth at the gaming tables of Monte Carlo by use of bets he orders Margaret to make are shown, as is the moment when Margaret cruelly advises Arthur that she has married Haddo by the impersonal use of a telegram delivered to Arthur at a time when Arthur has no reason to doubt that their marriage is going forward.

One of the highlights of the novel is also one of the highlights of the film. When Haddo bewitches Margaret in the film, he directs her to look at the statue of a faun, which magically turns into a living god playing a musical instrument. Next come scenes of people dancing in an orgiastic ritual. Suddenly Oliver Haddo, bearing horns that give him the appearance of the devil, and Margaret, with her hair down and wearing virginal white, are in the scene. There are then flashes of what seem to be men raping women with the men, in particular, being close to naked. One grabs Margaret and takes her into his embrace. In the background, there is a smoky haze, giving the impression that the entire scene is occurring in Hades.

Much like the similar scene in novel, it is unclear whether these incidents actually occurred or whether Haddo simply created them in Margaret's mind. Whichever it is, these were shocking scenes for the 1920s leading, according to film historian Carlos Clarens, to negative reviews upon the film's release for reasons of tastelessness. Almost 90 years later and after many more frank examples of sexuality on the screen, these scenes from *The Magician* still have the ability to surprise and even titillate the viewer. There was never anything quite like it again in the cinema of horror, even after Hammer Studios and then others started to emphasize the sexual element in horror films starting in the late 1950s.

Rex Ingram cleverly ties portions of his film together with the imagery of the faun, i.e., a Roman god of the forest who is half man, half goat. Margaret is injured by a sculpture of a faun; a different statue of a faun starts the scene in which Haddo first bewitches Margaret. A faun even adds interest to the first shot in the film, which is a straightforward establishing shot of Paris, but with a statue of a faun jutting out on the right side of the screen for no apparent reason other than to establish a motif of the film.

It is difficult for someone born long after the end of the silent film era to evaluate the acting in silent films. It is so much different than the performances expected in sound movies and on television. Nevertheless, the film seems well-acted, without any of the over-acting generally associated with silent films. Alice Terry, the wife of director Rex Ingram, is strikingly beautiful as Margaret Dauncey, and Iván Petrovich is believably earnest as Arthur Burdon. The actor who carries the film, however, is Paul Wegener, as Oliver Haddo. Wegener was one of the leading actors of the silent cinema of horror, playing the Golem in two film versions of the tale and starring in *Student of Prague* (1913). Wegener is an imposing person, tall and carrying some excess weight, although never becoming the hideously obese figure of Maugham's novel. With his unusual manner of dress and overly dramatic mannerisms, Margaret correctly observes that Haddo "looks as if he had stepped out of a melodrama." Haddo's bulging eyes, permanent frown and slanted head make him seem like the personification of wickedness, even before he does anything evil. Paul Wegener seems to embody the character of the iniquitous magician rather than acting the part, thereby becoming the perfect screen personification of Maugham's malevolent magician of print.

The similarities of *The Magician* (1926) to *Frankenstein* (1931) and other films of director James Whale cannot be overlooked by any horror film fan. The conclusion of the film occurs during an electrical storm, in a tower laboratory with winding stone steps, apparently the ideal setting for man to create life. Haddo has a dwarf-like assistant to help him, similar to Dr. Frankenstein's hunchback assistant, Fritz. The destruction of the laboratory in the concluding scene of the film begs comparison with the end of *Bride of Frankenstein* (1935). Also, Rex Ingram seems to love adding bits of humor to his story, such as the man in the snake charmer's tent whose hat floats to a ceiling because of a balloon that has gotten inside it, or Haddo's dwarf, after the explosion of the tower at the end of the film, hanging from his clothes on the side of a partially destroyed wall. This is similar to the humor that Whale inserted in his horror films, particularly *The Invisible Man* (1933) and *The Bride of Frankenstein* (1935), but also *Frankenstein* (1931), in that unique moment when Fritz takes a quick break from the action to pull up one of his socks.

The finishing sections of *The Magician* involve a chase across country to rescue Margaret, a last second save of Margaret, a brutal fight between Arthur and Haddo in the sorcerer's tower, the fiery death of Haddo and then the spectacular explosion of the laboratory tower. These concluding scenes do not come from Maugham's novel; they are screen concoctions. They contrast well to the film's always fascinating but somewhat laid back and atmospheric presentation. Unlike the novel, *The Magician* delivers some rousing excitement at its end, making the film an exceptional treat for the horror film fan.

Those who discount silent films and believe that the horror film genre began at Universal in the early 1930s are depriving themselves of many significant horror thrills. Whether viewing *Dr. Jekyll and Mr. Hyde* (1920), *The Phantom of the Opera* (1925), *The Magician* (1926) or several others, there is much to enjoy in the lost art of the silent horror film.

CHAPTER 8

"The Fall of the House of Usher" by Edgar Allan Poe

House of Usher (1960) is a seminal film in the history of horror films. It was the first adaptation of a Poe story by Roger Corman, previously a producer and director of second feature horror films and other low budget genre titles for American-International Pictures. It was the first film made by Corman in color; thereafter most American horror films were made in color. The film signified an important step in Vincent Price's ascent to horror film icon. It was also the first in a series of Poe film adaptations of the early 1960s. However, despite the historical significance of *House of Usher*, the film is ultimately disappointing, not nearly the equal of the 1928 adaptation of Poe's short story by director Jean Epstein.

The Literature

Not unexpectedly, given that Edgar Allan Poe wrote it, "The Fall of the House of Usher" is primarily a story of setting and mood rather than of plot. The first paragraph of the story immediately sets the mood of the tale. As the unnamed narrator approaches the Usher mansion, he describes the area as a "singularly dreary tract of country," with the clouds hanging "oppressively low in the heavens." He sees the house of Usher as melancholy and bleak. With the first glimpse of the building from afar, "a sense of insufferable gloom" pervades the spirit of the narrator. He feels a sinking, sickening and iciness in his heart.

The gloomy mood of the first paragraph of the story continues throughout the narrative, as Roderick Usher is very ill, suffering from acute nervousness and depression caused by the impending death of his sister, Madeline, who is suffering from a severe and long-standing illness. When Madeline finally dies, Roderick decides that before finally burying Madeline, her corpse should be preserved for two weeks inside one of the numerous vaults within the main building of the house of Usher.

One night, as the narrator is reading a story to Roderick, Roderick hears sounds throughout the house and concludes that his sister was buried alive. Suddenly, "the lofty and enshrouded figure of the lady Madeline of Usher" appears, with "blood upon her white robes, and the evidence of some bitter struggle upon every portion of her emaciated frame." She then falls upon her brother and during her final convulsions Roderick also dies, perhaps by a heart attack caused by the terror he feels. The narrator runs out of the house in fear. Then, as he looks back at the house of Usher from a point of safety, he sees the house, whether caused by a whirlwind or lightning or some mysterious force, seem to split into two and fall to the ground, completely destroyed.

Poe structures "The Fall of the House of Usher" in pairs, with even the name of the story having a double meaning. The title clearly refers to the actual destruction of the Usher mansion at the end of the story, as it literally falls to the ground, but it also refers to the end of the ancient race of Ushers, as Roderick and Madeline are the last surviving Ushers of all time. The noises of Madeline as she somehow escapes her tomb are heard only after the narrator reads about those same sounds in the story he is reading to Roderick, each of the sounds thus appearing twice in the story. Madeline and Roderick are not just sister and brother; they are twins. In the end it is one twin who causes the death of the other and they both finally die at about the same time, just as they were born at about the same time.

This twinning of items by Poe has led commentators to search for other parallelisms in the tale, thereby discerning a psychological element in "The Fall of the House of Usher." Some believe that Roderick and his sister reflect two parts of one personality, with Roderick the intellectual and Madeline the physical counterpart. That is why one of the siblings cannot live without the other. At the beginning of the story, the narrator notices a barely perceptible zigzag fissure in the structure of the Usher mansion that will eventually lead to its destruction. It has been argued that this fissure is a reflection of the fracture of Roderick's mind.

Others, such as your author, believe that analyzing "The Fall of the House of Usher" as a story of the psychological and finding twinning items that may not really be there may be stretching matters a little bit too much. In most ways, "The Fall of the House of Usher" is simply a tale of the supernatural and of the unknown. No explanation is proffered as to how Madeline, even if she were buried alive, escaped from her shut coffin and the locked tomb. The actual fall of the structure of the House of Usher seems to arise from mystical, rather than corporeal means. Roderick's strange illness is never explained.

At the end, the narrator narrowly escapes the fall of the house with no more understanding of the Usher family than when he first arrived at the mansion on that "dull, dark, and soundless day in the autumn of the year." Is it madness or the mystical? Poe leaves that question unanswered and the ending of the tale is an enigma, to both the narrator and the reader.

The Films

The Fall of the House of Usher/La chute de la maison Usher (1928)

Jean Epstein, one of France's most respected silent film directors, made the most famous silent film adaptation of Poe's "The Fall of the House of Usher" in his native land in 1928. Epstein is considered one of the leaders of French avant-garde or Impressionist style of filmmaking. That sub-genre of film, which flourished during the 1920s, is hard to define. Most movies that fall within that category demonstrate experimentation in narrative, editing and camerawork, without trying to appeal to the interests of a mass audience. *The Fall of the House of Usher* clearly falls within that broad category of experimental films, whether or not it is truly Impressionistic in style.

While Epstein has taken several important licenses with the plot of Poe's story, *The Fall of the House of Usher* is nevertheless a faithful adaptation of "The Fall of the House of Usher." Roderick Usher, who is suffering from severe depression, partially as a result of the impending death of his wife, Madeline, has written to his childhood friend, Allan, and asked him to come to the Usher mansion for company and support. Shortly after Allan arrives, Madeline, while Roderick is painting her portrait, collapses to the floor, dead. Even though Roderick believes Madeline may still be alive, her body is placed in a nailed coffin and entombed in a vault far from the family home. Roderick, however, still has his doubts and one night, as a storm encloses the Usher house and Allan is reading a story to Roderick, Madeline suddenly appears at the mansion. Her appearance coincides with the ratcheting up of the ferocity of the storm. Just after Roderick, Madeline and Allan escape from the structure, the house of Usher completely collapses.

While clearly based on Poe's "The Fall of the House of Usher," Epstein's *The Fall of the House of Usher* also has similarities to Oscar Wilde's *The Portrait of Dorian Gray*, as Madeline's personality seems to leave her and become a part of the lifelike portrait that Roderick is painting. The film also draws significantly from "The Oval Portrait," a short story of Poe's published in 1850. This may be the shortest short story Poe ever wrote, comprising only six paragraphs. In the story, a painter continually paints his young bride over many weeks, not realizing that he is drawing the life from her. When the painting is finished, the bride is dead. This film seems to have been lifted this plot point directly from "The Oval Portrait" and inserted into the story line of "The Fall of the House of Usher," to create *The Fall of the House of Usher*.

If Poe's "The Fall of the House of Usher" is primarily about mood and setting rather than plot, then Epstein's film is all about style and effect rather than story. Epstein employs tracking shots so that the viewer feels he is in the Usher house, double images to convey the madness of Roderick, superimposed images of candles or the flowing dress of the dead Madeline to remind the viewer of the apparent death of Madeline, and the insertion of other shots to upset the timing of the feature, such as a clock pendulum swinging back and forth, windswept waves on a lake and frogs in a forest. There is a surreal quality to the film, aided by the extreme close-ups, subjective shots, scenes shrouded in vapor and even that peculiar moment when a dog runs away from Allan during Allan's walk outside the Usher mansion. In addition, the lack of sound actually contributes to the dreamlike world and imagery that is so critical to Poe's writings. Epstein has cleverly used the silence of his cinema to add to the gloomy and oppressive mood of the Usher mansion, where everything seems to be slow moving, somber, grayish and depressingly quiet. Epstein effectively recreates Poe's image of the Usher edifice as melancholy and bleak.

The highlight of the film is Madeline's funeral scene, strikingly photographed from the time her body is placed into her coffin at the Usher house and then as her body is slowly transported across land and water to the Usher family vault. Epstein has chosen to move the entombment of Madeline away from the Usher house, where the deed was done in the story, so as to provide the opportunity for this stunning moment of film experimentation. The scene has no title cards to interrupt the flow. The procession walks and floats among shots of dead trees, with the camera sometimes bouncing and sometimes viewing the convoy in tight close-ups or from unusual camera angles. The funeral scene stands as one of the notable moments of horror of the silent cinema, with the overwhelming silence adding to the surreal quality and mood of the tableau.

All of those attributes notwithstanding, *The Fall of the House of Usher* is overrated. Because Epstein has not added any substance to Poe's insubstantial plot, the film drags in places, even though it has a short running time of approximately 65 minutes. When the story line drags, it also becomes confusing. *The Fall of the House of Usher* has cinematic style; it lacks cinematic substance. While the silence of the silent cinema is a positive in conveying the mood of a Poe story, it is a detriment to the end of the film when the surprise reappearance of Madeline occurs. Just as in Poe's story, the sounds of Madeline exiting her tomb and returning to the house follow exactly the sounds in the story being read by Allan, a spooky moment in the story. In a silent film, the entire effect is lost.

Another missed opportunity is the fall of the house of Usher itself, which is shrouded in vapor and clouds as it collapses. The special effects, which are primarily vapors and steam geysers in and around the house, are only fair, and the haze in the scene makes it somewhat unclear as to what is actually happening. The element of sound as the house slowly crashes to the ground could have made a difference in this scene, once again illustrating the problems inherent in adapting to the silent cinema a story that has important sound aspects.

While the changes from the plot of "The Fall of the House of Usher" are minor, they do eliminate many of the parallelisms in the tale. Roderick and Madeline are no longer twins; they are married. They do not die at the same time; both survive. The title does not have a double meaning; it can only refer to the physical collapse of the House of Usher. These changes do not necessarily detract from the effectiveness of the film since, in any event, they are merely subtexts of the story and not essential to the story itself. The elimination of the doubling simply makes the film different from the story.

Someone once wrote that the only great silent films that were also great movies were the comedies. While that is a clear understatement as to the entertainment value of silent films, even in these days of color, wide screen, stereo sound and computer-generated imagery, the comment applies somewhat to *The Fall of the House of Usher*. While the 1928 film by Jean Epstein may be a great silent horror film, with the visuals always memorable, the film is no better than average when compared to all of the horror films of the classic era, both silent and sound. Simply stated, *The Fall of the House of Usher* is a film to admire, not to enjoy.

The Fall of the House of Usher (1949)

This first sound version of Poe's "The Fall of the House of Usher" was produced at the very end of the 1940s, on the eve of the science fiction film wave of the 1950s, when Hollywood was no longer in the horror film business but the British were still turning out some good pictures of the supernatural, such as *Dead of Night* (1945) and *The Queen of Spades* (1949). However, *The Fall of the House of Usher* (1949), made on a minuscule budget at G.I.B., a long-forgotten film studio, is, despite a few tantalizing moments, a severe disappointment.

Both the beginning and ending of the film are based on Poe's short story.

However, in this version of the tale, the illnesses of the Usher siblings and the eventual destruction of the Usher mansion are a result of a curse placed on the Ushers by a man who was killed by Roderick's father. The father discovered the man and Roderick's mother having an affair in a temple on the grounds of the Usher estate. There, Roderick's father, in a rage over the infidelity, cut the man's head off and beat his wife into madness. However, the head of the man still lives and the mother, who is now a mad hag, lives at the temple and protects the head. For no apparent reason, there is also a torture chamber at the temple, although it does not really figure into the plot of the movie.

This detour into the story of the killing at the temple and the curse on the Usher family is pretty strange stuff, indeed. Although it is not based on any writing by Poe, it is nevertheless consistent with the tone and weirdness of a number of Poe stories. Perhaps that is why the reference to the torture chamber was made. Unfortunately, the execution of this portion of the film is particularly ineffective. Sometimes the first half of the movie seems like an amateur production made by a film student, shot on the grounds of a large house that was borrowed for a few days. The direction is commonplace, without any style. The acting is abysmal, which is particularly disappointing for a British film. The musical score, which is inappropriate for the mood of the story, is also jarring at times, particularly when it starts and stops for little reason.

Unlike the Jean Epstein film version of the story, which stretched Poe's short story into a full length film without adding any new story lines, the tale of the curse in the 1949 film version adds some substance to the narrative, justifying the longer length of the feature. But this added story line does not fit well with the core plot of "The Fall of the House of Usher," and, indeed, for most of the second half of the film, which concentrates on Poe's original story line, the mother is completely missing from the story and the living head only reappears in a shot or two. It is as if two separate stories were filmed inside one movie, without any cohesiveness between the two. It simply does not work.

For the second half of the film, which reverts back to Poe's basic plot, it is as if the director of the film, Ivan Barnett, got his second wind and decided to imbue his movie with some cinematic style. There is a good shot from inside the coffin as Madeline is placed in the vault and the lid positioned on her coffin, with the effectiveness of the shot aided by the sound of the nails being hammered into the lid. There is also a neat shot when Madeline returns from her tomb, as the walking, ghostlike Madeline forces Roderick up the curved steps of the mansion, with the hag suddenly appearing in the shot, adding a bit of horror surprise. However, the strength of these latter scenes is enhanced by the clever use of sound, such as a clock ticking, the wind howling, thunder crashing, rain beating and a door knob turning. Sound is often an important attribute of a horror film and its clever use near the end of the 1949 film version illustrates the potential that sound could have had for Jean Epstein in parts of his version of the story, if sound were then available.

Given this effective use of sound in the 1949 film version, it is particularly disappointing that the key scene in Poe's story, the sounds of Madeline escaping her coffin and tomb just as a character is reading about those same sounds in a story he relates to Roderick, are handled very poorly. In the story, as the narrator reads about the sounds and the same sounds are heard in the house of Usher, it is unclear what those sounds signify, adding to the horror of the story. In the film version, however, as the sounds are heard, Madeline is shown escaping from her coffin and the tomb, severely undercutting the effectiveness of the moment. Val Lewton demonstrated the effectiveness of sounds without the visuals in *Cat People* (1942) and *The Leopard Man* (1943), among others of his features. Ivan Barnett could have learned much from Lewton's style. The sounds of Madeline escaping her tomb alone would have been much more horrifying if they had not been combined with the visuals of Madeline's escape.

The bookending of the film by vignettes of four gentlemen in an English gentlemen's club is superfluous and is, in fact, quite embarrassing. The acting in those scenes is actually worse, if at all possible, than in the main part of the film. The purpose of those scenes is to proffer the idea that one of the strengths of Poe's works was that he often had enigmatic endings to his stories. That is a good point to make for this film because, as discussed above, the ending of Poe's "The Fall of the House of Usher" leaves several questions unanswered.

In this film version, however, the four English gentlemen miss the primary enigma that the film cleverly posits, i.e., whether Madeline actually returned from her coffin (after being buried alive) or was she a ghost or just an imagining of Roderick. After Roderick's demise, there is a shot of Madeline's coffin back in the vault. Even though the viewer previously saw the coffin being opened by Madeline and heard the sound of the cracking of the wood of the coffin, the coffin is now undisturbed with the lid secured to its top. That would seem to indicate that Madeline was not buried alive and that her body still remains in the coffin. Also, and unlike Poe's story, the returning Madeline clearly sets out to kill Roderick. This is another implication that Madeline is only a ghost or an imagining by Roderick, perhaps caused by the living head at the temple so that his curse can be fulfilled. None of the gentlemen at the club raise this issue, making it apparent that the screenwriters did not understand the one cleverness of their own script.

Part of the difficulty in evaluating *The Fall of the House of Usher* (1949) is that the available prints are washed out and incomplete. Nevertheless, although the film has a few clever moments, mainly near the end, it is definitely a very disappointing version of Poe's short story. While the 1928 Jean Epstein version of the tale is overrated, it is still substantially better than this effort, illustrating, once again, that sound is not always an improvement over silence.

House of Usher (1960)

House of Usher commences with a clever re-working of the story line of Poe's short story. The person who arrives at the Usher mansion is not an unnamed narrator but instead is Philip Winthrop, who has come from Boston to see his fiancée, Madeline Usher. However, Madeline's brother Roderick does all that he can to keep them apart, claiming that Madeline is seriously ill as a result of a curse on the Usher family caused by the evil of generations of Ushers. When Philip rejects Roderick's claims and attempts to leave with Madeline, Madeline appears to die. Roderick then has his sister entombed in the family vault, not advising Philip that Madeline, who suffers from catalepsy, is still alive.

Philip Winthrop (Mark Damon) discovers that his fiancée, Madeline Usher (Myrna Fahey), is dead, as her brother Roderick Usher (Vincent Price) looks on, in *House of Usher* (1960).

At the end, a mad Madeline returns from her tomb. As Madeline tries to kill her brother, the collapse of the house occurs, with Philip the only one escaping death in the fall of the house of Usher.

While *House of Usher* takes little of the story line of Edgar Allan Poe's tale, it does incorporate some the minor aspects of the story. Roderick's morbid acuteness of the senses comes from Poe, but it is emphasized in the movie, with the movie Roderick so sensitive to sound that people cannot wear their boots in the house and so allergic to the taste of food that he can only eat the blandest of fare. The film Roderick plays the lute; in the story it is a guitar. The "barely perceptible fissure" in the house of Usher that the narrator observes near the beginning of Poe's story has been transformed for the movie into a huge crack in the structure of the house that threatens its very existence. In fact, one of the strengths of the film is its foreshadowing of the fall of the house of Usher, by time and again showing manifestations of the structural weaknesses of the edifice and by Roderick and the family retainer Bristol apparently resigned to the fact that the house will eventually collapse.

House of Usher has many other strengths. The use of color, which was still somewhat innovative at the time, adds to the appeal of the story. Purists may argue that black and white photography is better for horror and, of course, there is much to that position. However, films today are all made in color; it is what the audience expects. In this case, the richness of the color adds to the luster of the Usher mansion, an effective contrast to the dead and gray outside. One objection, though, is that both Roderick and Madeline tend to wear very brightly colored clothing, out of keeping with the supposed mood of the film. This anomaly is undoubtedly caused by the fact that, having decided to go to the cost of producing the movie in color, the filmmakers felt they had to employ the brightest colors they could, to exploit the technological advance they chose. Films can never be truly analyzed without considering budgetary and other matters that are only indirectly related to the art of film.

The performances in *House of Usher* are generally outstanding, with Vincent Price particularly good, somehow making the story line of the film make some sense, at least for a while. The eloquent lines he is given seem to roll of his tongue and there is none of the overacting that sometimes seemed to sneak into his later horror film portrayals. Harry Ellerbe is good as Bristol and Myrna Fahey is particularly attractive as Madeline, so much so that it is hard to believe that she is suffering from an incurable illness. Mark Damon as Philip is handsome and earnest but it is a thankless role, having to play opposite the suave Vincent Price who has all of the good lines.

The best moments in the film are the small ones. As Madeline is lying in her coffin, apparently dead, the viewer suddenly notices that her fingers are moving.

Roderick rushes to close the lid on the coffin so that Philip will not notice. The viewer can then hear breathing within the coffin, solidifying the fact that Madeline has been entombed alive. These moments remain in the mind of the viewer long after the exciting climax of the film is forgotten. It is sometimes surprising to realize that subtle moments of horror can be much more effective than spectacular ones.

Roger Corman has cleverly disguised the low budget of his film in an expanse of color and wide screen but it does show through. There are only four characters in the cast (with a few extras appearing in a dream sequence) and there are limited sets, with almost no outdoor sequences in the movie. Instead of showing past events in flashbacks, Vincent Price as Roderick Usher merely describes them. The outside of the Usher house looks like a painting and not a realistic one at that. The long shots of the burning of the house are clearly miniatures.

Ultimately, *House of Usher* simply does not work. The problem is with the script. The most significant change from Poe's story is not the fact that the visitor to the Usher house is the fiancé of Madeline's. Rather, it is Roderick deliberately entombing his sister alive. Why does he do that? The only explanation is that the film is about Roderick's madness, pure and simple. Roderick seems to have had such an obsession with the evil deeds of his ancestors that he has gone crazy, believing that evil occupants can somehow make a house itself become evil. There is no evidence that Madeline is really sick and, as noted above, she seems very healthy as played by the attractive Myrna Fahey. In fact, if Roderick had made a little effort to bring workmen to the site to patch up the Usher mansion, perhaps put on a new roof, brace the structure where the fissure was located and remodel some of the inside, it is unlikely the structure would ever had collapsed. If there is any lesson to be learned from the film, it is that deferring maintenance in order to save money is seldom a good idea.

By making *House of Usher* a tale of madness only, all of the subtlety and enigma of the Poe tale is gone. Madeline's madness and homicidal tirade at the end of the film are clearly caused by being chained in her coffin when she was still alive. While there is a hint of a sexual element in the relationship between Roderick and Madeline, as Madeline is so dominated by her brother that she can never seem to pull herself away and leave with Philip, it is a mere trace element of the film, never developed in any way. It does relate, however, to a trace element of Poe's story, as there is the barest hint of incest within the long line of the Usher family, culminating in the end of the family line with the death of Roderick and Madeline.

Corman attempts to make the house of Usher into the primary monster of the film, but that idea simply does not work. While some sparks from the fire jump onto Philip, a chandelier almost crushes him and a casket almost rolls on him, these incidents seem to be related to problems with the structural integrity of the house and not to any evil in the house. The only significant attempt to personify the house as evil comes from the dialogue spoken by Roderick. For example, he says, "For hundreds of years, foul thoughts and foul deeds have been committed within its walls. The house itself is evil now." Roderick's unusual views about his house convince the viewer that Roderick is mad, not that the house is evil. For a more successful personification of a house as evil, see *The Haunting* (1963).

The story is padded at times, by an irrelevant dream sequence from Philip's mind and by an interminable search by Philip through the house, first looking for, and then trying to follow, Madeline's body. Since the only character in the film that is truly fleshed out is Roderick, the viewer has little emotional attachment to the young lovers, Philip and Madeline. While it is a positive that the film returns to the plot of the Poe story for the ending, with the return of Madeline, her attack on Roderick and the fall of the house, there is little of Poe in this film. The last shot of the movie includes some language from the last lines of the Poe story superimposed on the picture, but even then, the quote is not completely accurate.

House of Usher commences in a strong manner but the silliness of its plot finally does it in. While the film is still watchable, it is ultimately unsatisfying. *House of Usher* has its historical significance but not as an interpretation of a story by Edgar Allan Poe.

CHAPTER 9

"Spurs"
by Tod Robbins

There is an old joke that goes something like this. Two young boys go to the movies and see *Frankenstein*. They are especially frightened by the face of the monster. As the two leave the theater, one says to the other, "That monster was scary. But where did they find an actor who looked like that?"

In the innocence of youth, those two youngsters do not realize, as most people do, that the faces and shapes of movie monsters are almost always created by makeup and special effects. While exceptions to this rule are rare, they do occur. One example, of course, is Rondo Hatton, who suffered from the real life disease of acromegaly, which severely distorted his head and face. Hatton is best known today for the minor horror films in which he appeared at Universal in the 1940s, although most of those films are easily forgettable.

Another exception is *Freaks*, a 1932 film produced at MGM and directed by Tod Browning, the director of *Dracula*. What sets this film apart from just about every other film ever made is that the title characters are portrayed by real-life freaks, with their deformities and handicaps right up there on the screen for all to see. No one viewing *Freaks* has an escape valve to release the tension, by thinking that the film is all make-believe and that the freaks are only actors in makeup. No one viewing *Freaks* would ever characterize the film as forgettable.

Background

Few details are known about the life of Clarence Aaron "Tod" Robbins. He was born in Brooklyn, New York, in 1888. He attended Washington and

Lee University in Lexington, Virginia. His first novel, *Mysterious Martin*, about a serial killer, was published in 1912. Thereafter, Robbins wrote short stories, often for pulp magazines, and other novels (usually of fantasy or crime) and even some poetry. "Spurs" was first published in the February 1923 issue of *Munsey's Magazine*, a popular monthly periodical that also published works by Edgar Rice Burroughs and P. G. Wodehouse. Robbins died in France in 1949.

The Literature

"Spurs" is set in a traveling show of freaks and feats known as Copo's Circus, which has taken up temporary residence in the town of Roubaix in northern France. One of the acts in the show is performed by a midget, Jacques Courbé, who rides into the arena on his large dog, St. Eustache, as if it were a pony and he an intrepid knight of old. Courbé has an interest in Mademoiselle Jeanne Marie, the beautiful bareback rider in Copo's show. Marie, however, has an interest in her partner in the act, a handsome, Herculean young man named Simon Lafleur.

When Marie learns that Courbé has received a large inheritance from his recently deceased uncle, she decides to accept Courbé's proposal of marriage. They are married but when Courbé realizes that Marie does not really love him and only married him for his money, Courbé's love for Marie is gone in an instant. Thereafter, Courbé, with the use of his vicious dog, St. Eustache, terrorizes Marie by requiring Marie to carry him long distances across France on her shoulders. Courbé even manages to kill Lafleur when the circus returns to Roubaix. The story ends on a note of irony as the circus owner, Papa Copo, sees Marie carrying Courbé on her shoulders and worries that she is still humiliating him. Copo thinks, "Ah, but she should not poke fun at Monsieur Jacques Courbé! He is so sensitive; but, alas, they are the kind that are always henpecked!" (Chapter 3).

Fans familiar with the 1932 movie adaptation of "Spurs," re-titled *Freaks*, will expect a number of unusual characters in the story and Robbins does not disappoint. In addition to Courbé, Copo's Circus has Griffo, the giraffe boy, who has a long neck and is covered with spots; Monsieur Hercule Hippo, the giant; Mademoiselle Lupa, the wolf lady with the long, sharp white teeth who growls when she tries to talk; and Madame Samson, who always has her trained baby boa constrictors coiled about her neck and ears. Unlike the film, however, the freaks at the circus are not the focal point of Robbins' short story and Robbins does not describe them to any great degree. Thus, while *Freaks* may be gruesome, "Spurs" is not.

"Spurs" is technically not a horror story, although it has elements of horror, because all of the events of the story could have taken place in real life, although concurrence in that view requires just a little bit of imagination and a lot of willing suspension of disbelief on the part of the reader. Instead, "Spurs" is the tale of a monster, albeit one of the tiniest and meanest of them all. Early on, Jacques Courbé is an object of pity, both because of his size and because of the way he is treated by Marie and the circus audiences. By the end of the story, Courbé is revealed to be a true fiend. By making a midget into the villain and the beautiful Marie and the handsome Lafleur into the victims, Robbins has turned the natural sympathies of the reader on their head, thereby creating a unique story of the unusual.

"Spurs" is a simple and straightforward story, yet Robbins makes a significant point—monsters, heroes and victims come in all shapes and appearances and, in particular, all sizes. Thus, for its unique villain and worthwhile thesis, Robbins' tale of intrigue among circus performers has its special interest.

The Film

Freaks (1932)

The opening credits to *Freaks* state merely that the film is suggested by Tod Robbins' story "Spurs," which implies to the audience that the film is only a loose adaptation of Robbins' chronicle of unrequited love, revenge and murder in a circus setting rather than a strict reworking of the original story. That surmise turns out to be correct, both in terms of plot and point of view.

Unlike the short story, the film places emphasis on its freaks, not its story line. *Freaks* is a true menagerie of the unusual and the unique of mankind. Browning provides to the viewers such "monstrosities," as the carnival's outside talker calls them, as midgets, pinheads, a man with half a body, a man with no arms or legs, a person who is half woman-half man, a bird lady, a bearded lady, female Siamese twins joined near the waist and a human skeleton. The camera shows the audience some unusual events, such as one of the Siamese twins feeling the touches made by a man on her sister, the man with no lower body walking up steps on his hands, an armless and legless man striking a match and lighting a cigarette, and an armless woman eating with her feet.

In showing the human oddities living out their lives communally in the backstage of the circus, Browning emphasizes the very commonplace activities of their real lives, such as the wearing of a new dress, the playing of games such as ring-around-rosie, romantic entanglements and the birth of a child. Within the isolated world of the freaks, everything is normal. In that regard, Browning makes a significant point which is slightly different than that of Robbins'—real people come in all shapes and appearances and, in particular, all sizes.

What plot there is in *Freaks* has its genesis in the short story by Tod Robbins. Hans, a circus midget, is engaged to be married to another circus dwarf, Frieda, but instead, Hans has become infatuated with Cleopatra, a beautiful aerialist who is full-sized. When Frieda accidentally tells Cleopatra of Hans' large fortune, Cleopatra decides to marry the little man and then murder him for his wealth. At the wedding feast, Hans starts to doubt Cleopatra's bona fides when she gives an affectionate kiss to the circus strongman, Hercules, insults his fellow performers and carries Hans around on her shoulders against his will, humiliating him in front of his friends.

This photograph shows some of the guests at the wedding feast in *Freaks* (1932). Clockwise around the table starting at the left, there is a pinhead (Schlitze, a man), Madame Tetrallini (Rose Dione), female midget Frieda (Daisy Earles), the man without the lower half of his body (Johnny Eck), the human skeleton (Pete Robinson), male midget Little Angelo (Angelo Rosito), the Siamese twins (Violet and Daisy Hilton), and Roscoe, the stutterer (Rosco Ates).

Hans falls ill at the dinner from the poison Cleopatra has secreted into his celebration wine. She continues to poison Hans over the next week, but the freaks have caught on. During a trip by the circus caravan in a violent rain, the freaks wreak their revenge on Cleopatra and Hercules. In an epilogue, Hans and Frieda are happily reconciled.

Some of the similarities between "Spurs" and *Freaks* are evident in that short synopsis of the plot of the film. They center on the marriage between the midget and the beautiful circus performer, and the wedding feast, where Hans first learns of the true nature of his new spouse. Both the film and the story turn out to be tales of revenge. In addition, the Hans of the film has the hubris of the Courbé of the story—Hans is always better dressed than anyone else and he believes he is superior to the rest of his friends.

However, the similarities end there. While Hans can sometimes be unfeeling toward Frieda, he is still the prime victim of the film. Cleopatra and Hercules are clearly the villains and, even at the end, when they are viciously punished for their murderous acts and their disdain for the freaks, the audience never has any sympathy for the two. Thus, unlike the short story, the film never goes against type. The villains are the good-looking but cruel characters and the victim is someone for whom the audience has a natural sympathy, i.e., a person who is small and different in appearance than most others.

There are two unforgettable scenes in this movie. The first is at the wedding feast, where the freaks decide to honor Cleopatra by accepting her as one of their own. At the same time as one of the little people dances down the top of the banquet table, allowing each of the freaks to sip some wine from a loving cup as part of a strange ritual, the freaks clap and chant, "We accept her, one of us. Gooba-gobble, Gooba-gobble." The joy of the freaks is contrasted with the alarm on the face of Cleopatra. When she receives the loving cup as a gesture of participation in the ceremony, she shouts, "You dirty, slimy freaks! Get out of here." Then she tosses the wine into the face of the dwarf, picks up Hans and carries him around on her shoulders, shouting, "Giddy up, horsey!"

The scene at the wedding feast is so striking because it is so unexpected. Until this point, *Freaks* has been about an unusual love and some mercenary motives. The film suddenly changes directions, now emphasizing the secret rituals and the strange society of the freaks, with their bizarre chant and weird induction ceremony. For the first time in the film, the freaks seem out of the norm. The scene ends with a moment from the short story and the ultimate humiliation of Hans—Cleopatra involuntarily carrying him on his shoulders, as if he were a little baby.

The incidents at the wedding feast are topped near the climax of the film, when the freaks seek their revenge on Cleopatra and Hercules. In scenes shot through rain, under wagon wheels and often in the dark or with indirect lighting, and with the freaks, many in thug hats, attacking with knives and a gun, as they walk, crawl and slide through the mud in an almost silent montage of strange but determined faces, it becomes quite clear, quite fast, that the code of the freaks, hurt one, hurt all, is real. Because of the number of them, their variety and their single-minded resolve, the attack of the freaks is more shockingly vicious and spine-tingling than the assaults of more traditional movie monsters, such as mummies, vampires or werewolves. It has never been duplicated on the screen.

The actual ending of the film, however, is disappointingly abrupt. Before the film audience can see what the freaks actually do to Cleopatra as they surround her in the woods, the story jumps back to a carnival barker who has been narrating the film, eliminating the climax that was about to occur. The sideshow talker then shows Cleopatra sitting in her cage. She has been changed into a hen lady, with her head sitting on a hen's body and without the ability to speak, only to make quacking noises. It is the striking image of the film, resulting in the most famous still from the movie. Also, the "Gooba-gobble" chant at the wedding feast now has added significance.

Even so, the transformation of Cleopatra raises many questions, the primary one being: how did the freaks accomplish that alteration in Cleopatra's body? Even though the freaks once chanted that they accepted her and she was one of them, that does not explain how Cleopatra became even more bizarre than most of them. Lingering questions such as that, along with the abrupt ending to the main part of the movie, contribute to the disappointing conclusion of the film.

Despite the problems with the finish, *Freaks* is still one of the most incredible movies ever made. The real life sideshow performers who appear in the film can never be forgotten. Some of the scenes in the film remain astonishing even 80 years after the film was released. Building on the plot and themes from a good short story, the filmmakers have created an amazing movie, the most unusual one from the classic era of the cinema of horror.

Chapter 10

The Island of Dr. Moreau by H.G. Wells

Since he wrote about time travel, invaders from Mars, a trip to the moon and an invisible man, H.G. Wells was obviously a man of great imagination. Yet for all of Wells's other famous works of science fiction, *The Island of Dr. Moreau* may be his most imaginative story ever. Wells envisioned a scientist who operates on a variety of animals and attempts to transform them into human beings, moving the evolutionary process along with great rapidity. Other science fiction writers wrote about time travel, experiments on the human body and man's interactions with other worlds but few, if any, turned to the horrific idea of changing beast into man.

Background

Herbert George Wells was born on September 21, 1866, in Bromley, Kent County, England. Although Wells published over 80 books during his lifetime, both fiction and non-fiction, he is remembered today primarily for his writings in the field of science fiction, probably in part because of the number of movies that have been based on his works in that genre. Two of those novels are discussed in this book, the very successful *The Island of Dr. Moreau* (1896) and *The Invisible Man* (1897), discussed in the next chapter. Wells died in London on August 13, 1946.

The Literature

The strange tale of Dr. Moreau is told from the perspective of Edward Pendrick, who is lost at sea and then rescued by a ship called the *Ipecacuanha*.

When the *Ipecacuanha* reaches its island destination, the captain, who has taken a dislike to Pendrick, throws Pendrick overboard with Montgomery, the passenger who nursed Pendrick back to health, and his companion, Dr. Moreau. They end up on the unnamed island run by Moreau. There, Pendrick finds that Moreau is operating on animals in an attempt to turn them into human beings. Why Moreau is doing this and what he hopes to achieve from his experiments is never satisfactorily explained, but such is often the case in mad scientist literature and movies.

While Moreau is somewhat successful in his experiments, with his creatures reciting Moreau's laws and trying to abide by them, once Moreau is killed by a puma in the operating room and Montgomery dies shortly thereafter, Pendrick is unable to control the man-beasts of the island. The man-beasts slowly revert to their former selves, losing the ability to speak or to stand upright. By the end of the novel, the society created by Moreau has completely disappeared. Pendrick is barely able to escape from the island with his life.

On its face, *The Island of Dr. Moreau* appears to be a novel of science fiction. In Chapter 14 of the novel, titled "Dr. Moreau Explains," Wells takes the time to provide a scientific explanation for all the strange happenings in his tale, through the words of Dr. Moreau, but the explanation is short and completely unconvincing. It is as if Wells believed that he had to provide some scientific underpinning to his tale even though he had no particular interest in doing so. Also, Wells does not use his story of the beasts of the island as a springboard for a discussion of important questions or themes, as many writers of science fiction do. Thus, *The Island of Dr. Moreau* is primarily a tale of horror, not one of science fiction.

However, to the extent *The Island of Dr. Moreau* is about science and science fiction, it is about the theory of evolution. The scientific experiments of Dr. Moreau are related to the evolution of animal into man, although Moreau is not content to wait for evolution to work. Evolution takes too long for Moreau; he wants his results immediately. Yet, life on Moreau's island is always at a tipping point, with Moreau constantly worried that his creations will reacquire their old characteristics, something they are prone to do over time. As Moreau explains to Pendrick, "[J]ust after I make them, they seem to be indisputably human beings. It's afterwards, as I observe them, that the persuasion fades. First one animal trait, then another, creeps to the surface and stares out at me" (Chapter 14, "Dr. Moreau Explains"). So, with Moreau's experiments partially successful but then finally going awry, has Moreau helped to prove the theory of evolution or has he actually disproved it? There is no conclusive answer in the book.

As brilliant as Moreau may be, he does not understand an important aspect of evolution, i.e., that animals have evolved as a response to the environment in which they live. By overlooking the environmental aspects of evolution, Moreau has severely harmed the island creatures because after Moreau's operations on them, they can no longer adequately deal with their native environment on their own. They now need Moreau to assist them. As Pendrick writes, "Before they had been beasts, their instincts fitly adapted to their surroundings, and happy as living things may be. Now they stumbled in the shackles of humanity, lived in a fear that never died, [and] fretted by a law they could not understand." While Moreau is oblivious to the problem, Pendrick understands the effect of Moreau's experiments on the survival of his subjects, calling this "the viler aspect of Moreau's cruelty" (Chapter 16, "How the Beast Folk Taste Blood").

Some of the strengths of *The Island of Dr. Moreau* are the monstrosities that Wells imagines and describes. There are men who appear to be running on all four legs like animals; three grotesque human figures with fat, heavy, chinless faces with retreating foreheads, giving off the "irresistible suggestion of a hog" (Chapter 9, "The Thing in the Forest"); a childlike thing with a low forehead and slow gestures as if it were a sloth; Beast People with their misshapen heads half-hidden by their shoulder blades; men with the features of a hyena-swine, a dog and a monkey; and other half-animal, half-human creatures. Well's short novel has more horrific monsters in it than any other work of horror.

In addition to his imaginative descriptions of the man-beasts on the island, Wells effectively uses the technique of parallel characters to enhance the impact of his story. Davis, the drunken captain of the *Ipecacuanha*, and Dr. Moreau each believe they are gods in their own world and act accordingly. The black-faced man Pendrick sees on board the *Ipecacuanha* turns out to be one of Moreau's most successful experiments, as the creature can walk on two feet, talk and exist somewhat in human society. Unfortunately, mankind treats him with disgust and the other animals on the ship are completely terrified by him. Moreau, by changing this animal's life against his will, has left him no place of comfort except with the other man-beasts, essentially becoming an almost-leper in a leper colony. Similarly, when Pendrick is finally able to escape the island and return to the civilized world, he feels as out of place with the real people there as he was with the man-beasts on the island. Much like Moreau's creations, Pendrick cannot find a home in either the world of the beasts or the world of men.

With little thematic material, *The Island of Dr. Moreau* is just a tale of monsters and madmen, but as good a tale thereof that has ever been written. The story never becomes boring since the reader knows that there is always another surprise or, at least, another gruesome detail, soon to be read on an upcoming page. Wells's story is different than most other works of horror or science fiction. It was a popular novel in its day and it is still a good read in the present day.

The Films

Island of Lost Souls (1932)

The novel, *The Island of Dr. Moreau*, has no female characters. All of the humans and all of the significant beasts on the island are male. Wells does mention some female creatures in passing, although he never fully describes them. Thus, since the book is quite entertaining without female characters, there was obviously no reason to insert female characters into any film adaptation of the novel.

Nevertheless, is there anyone who is surprised to find that the 1932 film version contains female characters? When a Hollywood movie is about something other than war, a female character is always a necessity. That is one of the significant differences between literature and film or, at least, literature and a Hollywood film.

The primary female character in *Island of Lost Souls* is actually a female creature—Lota, the Panther Woman. She is the most successful "human being" that Moreau has created. Unlike the male beasts of the island, which are hairy and misshapen, Lota is quite attractive, wearing the native garb of a Polynesian, revealing for its time. Lota is attracted to Edward Parker, the Pendrick character from the novel, who accidentally arrives on Moreau's island after the wreck of a ship on which he was traveling. Moreau encourages a relationship between the two because he is interested in determining if his operation on the Panther Woman has been a success. She looks like a real woman, but can she develop real female emotions?

The other female character is Parker's girlfriend, Ruth Thomas. She eventually comes to Moreau's island to rescue Parker. While she is a minor character in *Island of Lost Souls*, she brings a touch of eroticism to the feature, on one occasion gratuitously removing her stockings on camera to show off her legs, but, more importantly, unwittingly used by Moreau in furthering his experiments, as she is a sexual draw for the man-beasts of the island, a blond attraction to the dark natives much like Ann Darrow was to King Kong. There is no question that *Island of Lost Souls* is a pre–Code film, in the interactions between the different sexes and the different species.

Along with *Murders in the Rue Morgue*, released earlier in the year by Universal Studios, *Island of Lost Souls* is the second film of 1932 to address the issue

In addition to *Island of Lost Souls*, the other 1932 Hollywood horror film that dealt with evolution was *Murders in the Rue Morgue*, based on a short story by Edgar Allan Poe, and starring Bela Lugosi as Dr. Mirakle, an evolutionist.

of evolution, a subject that would completely disappear from the screen shortly after the release of this film. The novel, *The Island of Dr. Moreau*, is about evolution, but the word is never mentioned in the text. By contrast, the Dr. Moreau of the film is happy to lecture on the subject of evolution. He tells Parker, "Man is the present climax of a long process of organic evolution.... With these [creatures] I have wiped out hundreds of thousands of years of evolution." Unfortunately, just like the Moreau of the novel, his creatures, including the Panther Woman, often backslide somewhat into their original forms and customs. As Moreau whines to Montgomery, "The stubborn beast-flesh creeping back ... day by day it creeps back."

    Dr. Moreau suffers from an illusion that seems to be common to all mad scientists—he believes that he is God. After he explains his experiments to Parker, Moreau tells him, "Do you know what it means to feel like God?" That line is very similar to the dialogue from *Frankenstein* (1931), when Dr. Frankenstein discovers that his creature is now alive. Frankenstein says to Victor Moritz,

"In the name of God, now I know what it feels like to be God." Since the Moreau of the 1932 movie is killed by his own creatures, just like the Dr. Frankenstein of Mary Shelley's novel was killed by his own creature, Dr. Moreau and Dr. Frankenstein have much in common. Indeed, Moreau has not created human beings. He has inadvertently created the monsters that will destroy him, or, in other words, his own Frankenstein monsters.

The Island of Lost Souls does an excellent job of re-creating Wells's vision of a desolate island filled with the beasts created by Dr. Moreau. The man-beasts seem to be everywhere—in trees, acting as house servants, running a power wheel and unloading a ship. The effect is enhanced by the outstanding makeup on the actors playing the man-beasts, makeup that displays hideous faces, hairy heads and hairy bodies and, upon occasion, oddly shaped ears and malformed feet. On the negative side, the beasts of the island all seem to be of similar backgrounds, usually dogs or apes, and much of the makeup on the individual creatures is similar. The film does not display the variety of creations envisioned by H.G. Wells in his novel.

Despite its title, H.G. Wells's novel does not focus on Dr. Moreau, instead emphasizing Pendrick and the man-beasts of the island. Moreau seldom appears in the written work, has little to say about his experiments and his death is almost anti-climatic. The movie, however, takes a different approach. Once the story reaches Moreau's island, Dr. Moreau is the main focus of the film. He dominates every scene in which he appears, with the camera first focusing on him and then lingering on his visage whenever possible. Moreau's dialogue is eloquent; he defends his experiments with alacrity. As played by the incomparable Charles Laughton, with his short mustache, strangely-shaped beard and all-white outfit except for a black tie, Moreau is alternately gregarious and cold, childlike and ruthless, caring and cruel. In the entire history of horror films, there has never been a madder scientist than Dr. Moreau, as portrayed by Charles Laughton.

After Laughton, the other performer of interest is Bela Lugosi, playing the creature who is the Sayer of the Laws. The Laws that are recited by the beasts in the film are sometimes different than those from the book, although they are similar in attitude. Lugosi does an okay job in the role, but the part is very small until the end, when he does receive a fair share of the dialogue. Lugosi should have had better film roles at this stage of his career, although *The Island of Lost Souls* is one of the best horror films in which he ever appeared. The leggy Kathleen Burke plays the Panther Woman and while not exactly beautiful, Burke is surely exotic in the role. Her dialogue is delivered in a stilted manner, but that is consistent with the way the part is written and the fact that she is playing a woman recently created from an animal. Burke is more than adequate for the role.

The Island of Lost Souls is directed by Erle C. Kenton, well-known to horror film fans for his direction of three movies at Universal Studios during the 1940s in which the Frankenstein monster was a character. Kenton makes the most of the jungle setting of the film, moving his camera among the foliage as he tracks the players, and shooting the story from behind trees, between tree branches, around pillars and through a backlit cave entrance. He also employs a tilted camera upon occasion, has the camera slide in for extreme close-ups of the characters and in one section, shoots the characters by their reflections in a pool of water, all adding to the mysteriousness of the story line. Kenton also makes effective use of sound, in the cracking of Moreau's whip, the clanging of the iron gates of the compound, the snarling of the animals and the cries from the House of Pain. This may well be Kenton's finest directorial effort.

While *Island of Lost Souls* is faithful in many ways to Wells's novel, such as in the meeting of Parker and Montgomery on board ship, Parker being tossed out of the boat by the drunken captain, Moreau's experiments on both domestic and shipped-in animals, the man-beasts of the island, the seeming torture of

This publicity photograph for *Island of Lost Souls* (1932) shows the relationships among the principal characters. Edward Parker (Richard Arlen) loves Lota, the Panther Woman (Kathleen Burke), but Dr. Moreau (Charles Laughton) disapproves.

the animals on the island and the chanting of the Laws, the film's emphasis on the relationship between Parker and Lota makes the film substantially different than the novel. In addition, the ending of the film differs significantly from that of the novel's. In Wells's story, after the deaths of Moreau and Montgomery, which are not caused by a vast uprising on the island but rather, by small, isolated incidents, the "civilization" on the island gradually reverts to what it was pre-Moreau—an island of beasts and not of men. It is an interesting scenario to read but not very cinematic.

The film, on the other hand, ends in true cinematic style, with a revolt of the creatures when Moreau violates the first Law of the island, spilling the blood of Man. As a result, Moreau can no longer control his kingdom. In a scene reminiscent of the end of *Frankenstein* (1931), or, perhaps, more like the end of *Freaks* (1932), the man-beasts, some with torches in hand, chase after Moreau in order to destroy him. There is revenge showing on their distorted faces. Moreau, ineffectively cracking his whip at the creatures, must retreat backwards upon the onslaught of his creations. In a fitting bit of retribution, the man-beasts drag Moreau into the House of Pain; his screams can be heard from far outside the building.

The film ends on a happy note, as Parker and Thomas escape the island, but not before Lota saves them from attack by reverting, in part, to her panther origins and killing a beast of the island. In sacrificing her life to save Parker's, Lota finally displays the human emotions that Moreau desired, proving the potential of Moreau's experiments. Unfortunately, it is too late for Moreau to understand his achievement, as he is then dying in the House of Pain.

The Island of Dr. Moreau (1977)

By all objective standards, *The Island of Dr. Moreau* (1977) should have been superior in quality and enjoyment to *Island of Lost Souls* (1932). The newer film has a large budget, is shot in color and on location and has background music, qualities that are lacking in the first movie version of H.G. Wells's novel. In addition, the 1977 film stars Burt Lancaster, one of the most admired film actors of his generation. The beautiful Barbara Carrera plays the female lead. Yet, for all of these attributes, the newer film is a disaster, far inferior to the 1932 original.

In this version of the story, Andrew Braddock, the Pendrick character from the novel, floats to the shore of a deserted island in a dinghy from the *Lady Vain*, a ship that was lost at sea. There Braddock meets Dr. Moreau, who is doing genetic experimentation with animals in an attempt to turn them into men; Montgomery, an associate of Moreau's; and Maria, a beautiful young woman

Moreau brought to the island at a young age after rescuing her from the streets of Panama City, or, at least, that is the story Moreau tells Braddock. Braddock is appalled by Moreau's experiments on the animals. Dr. Moreau is unhappy with Braddock's inquisitive nature and the fact that Maria has taken an interest in Braddock.

Partly as an attempt to try to understand why his creatures backslide toward their original state and partly in pique for Maria's attention to Braddock, Moreau captures Braddock and starts a regimen of injections that begin to turn Braddock into an animal. That results in a disagreement between Montgomery and Moreau, leading to the shooting death of Montgomery by Moreau. When the creatures of the island realize that Moreau has broken one of the Laws, the prohibition against spilling blood, they attack Moreau and kill him. Braddock and Maria manage to escape the island in the repaired dinghy and at the end of the film, a large ship is about to rescue them.

While that brief synopsis would seem to indicate that the 1977 film is a fairly close adaptation of Wells's novel, the opposite is true. Dr. Moreau, in this incarnation, is interested in genetic engineering, not the evolution of animal into beast. Evolution is neither mentioned in the film nor is it an unspoken theme of the movie, as it was in the book. As another example, Braddock does not meet Montgomery on board ship before reaching the island and, as a result, the Montgomery character is not fleshed out in the film. No information is given to the viewer about him; he is a true cipher. While Montgomery was a significant character in the novel, his only reason for being in the film is to provide Moreau with someone to kill, triggering the finale of the feature.

Maria is a completely new character, created just for this film. She is not the same as the Panther Woman of the 1932 film, who was essential to the plot of that film. Here, there is a slight implication that Maria was created by Moreau, because of the lack of information about her past and the comfortable manner in which she lives on the island, but she speaks completely correct English and has no animal characteristics in her face or body. As played by Barbara Carrera, Maria is incredibly beautiful and striking, hardly the handiwork of Dr. Moreau. The insertion of Maria into the story is solely to create a female interest, some love scenes and not much else. She does, however provide a minor justification for Moreau going after Braddock and attempting to turn him into an animal.

The whole story arc of Moreau trying to turn Braddock into an animal is original to this film, and it is not very convincing. Moreau's reasons for experimenting on Braddock are not the least bit credible. Why Moreau would have a serum available to accomplish the dubious task of turning Braddock into an animal when, for the last many years Moreau has been working in the opposite direction, is unexplained. Once again, it seems to be just a brazen plot device to create a climax for the film, leading to a justification for the man-beasts deciding to overthrow Moreau and then accidentally destroying all that he has created.

The ending of the 1977 film, of course, does not come from H.G. Wells's novel; it comes from the 1932 film. (In fact, the Law against spilling blood comes from the 1932 film; there is no specific Law on that subject in the novel.) Since the insertion of a love interest for Braddock also comes from the 1932 film, *The Island of Dr. Moreau* (1977) sometimes seems to take more from the earlier film than it does from the novel. However, the conclusion of the 1932 film has some logic and symmetry to it, with the creatures taking Moreau to the House of Pain to punish him for breaking the Laws. The ending of the 1977 film is similar, except that Moreau does not even make it to the House of Pain. He is mauled before he gets there. The man-beasts then destroy Moreau's laboratory, starting a fire in the process, and then, for no apparent reason other than to create an exciting conclusion to the film, let all of Moreau's real jungle animals out of their cages. The real animals immediately attack the man-beasts, with the result that every beast and man-beast is destroyed in the conflagration that has already started.

This ending of *The Island of Dr. Moreau* (1977) is not the spectacular finish that the filmmakers apparently desired. Instead, it is confusing and illogical. The climax to *Island of Lost Souls* (1932) is infinitely more satisfying.

Even after the destruction of the island, there is one more disappointing climax to the film. The makers of *The Island of Dr. Moreau* (1977), along with many other filmmakers, have stolen the surprise moment from *Wait Until Dark* (1967), when the apparently dead killer in that film jumps up to make another attempt on the life of the blind heroine, Suzy Hendricks, scaring both Hendricks and the movie audience. Similarly, in *The Island of Dr. Moreau* (1977), a man-beast attacks Braddock and Marie as they try to escape in the dinghy. Braddock and Maria appear to have killed the creature, which then slips into the water, apparently dead. The man-beast then jumps up three more times for additional unexpected attacks, before it is finally killed. Yet, are there any movie fans who do not anticipate each "surprise" move of the man-beast and think to themselves, "Been there; seen that before"?

It is not just the conclusion of the 1977 film that is problematic. Throughout the film, there is little or no significant tension between the characters and the plot elements are essentially non-existent. That is one of the reasons why the ending of the film seems so contrived, as if certain characters were placed in the tale just to create a climax and for little other purpose. Indeed, the film seems more like a travelogue than a horror film, with Braddock vacationing on a beautiful island with the opportunity to view some exotic animals and the lucky chance to find a beautiful woman with whom to spend some quality time.

The one significant improvement over *Island of Lost Souls* is that there are a variety of man-beasts on the island, much like H.G. Wells' novel. While the earlier film limited its man-creatures to those who were formerly dogs and apes, the later film has man-creatures in the shapes of dogs, apes, bears, lions and several other animals. The makeup is excellent and often quite convincing. This is the lone attribute of the 1977 film that brings it more in line with Wells' novel than the 1932 film.

Burt Lancaster plays Dr. Moreau. The part is written differently than the Charles Laughton version, in which Moreau seemed intelligent, crazy, flakey and bipolar. For Lancaster, the role of Dr. Moreau is more similar to that of the traditional mad scientist, smart but severely unrealistic, impractical and strong-headed. Lancaster, though miscast in the role, is good in the film but his performance is instantly forgettable. It is difficult to comprehend the reasons why he would want the role, except as a chance to play a great villain from popular culture. It would be hard for anyone to top Charles Laughton as Dr. Moreau and Burt Lancaster falls short.

Color, music, better makeup, better special effects, location shooting and updated science do not always a better movie make. After all of these many years, *Island of Lost Souls* (1932) is still the best film version of the H.G. Wells novel about Dr. Moreau and the man-beasts of his island.

Other Adaptations

The third major film version of Wells's novel about Dr. Moreau was *The Island of Dr. Moreau* (1996). The film starred Marlon Brando as Dr. Moreau and was directed by John Frankenheimer.

Chapter 11

The Invisible Man by H.G. Wells

The Invisible Man, originally published in 1897, was Wells's fourth science fiction novel. In his preface to *The Complete Science Fiction Treasury of H.G. Wells* (1934), Wells noted that while the seven novels in that compendium were placed by the publisher in the order in which they were written, Wells recommended reading the third or fourth books, *The Invisible Man* or *The War of the Worlds*, before the first two, *The Time Machine* and *The Island of Dr. Moreau*. Wells wrote that a reader who is unfamiliar with his writings will probably find the latter two novels more agreeable than the first two works in the book.

The Literature

The Invisible Man commences with striking language. Wells writes, "The stranger came early in February, one wintry day, through a biting wind and a driving snow … over the down … carrying a little black portmanteau in his thickly gloved hand" (Chapter I).

And, the stranger who arrives in the village of Iping that winter day is an unusual individual, indeed. By use of bandages, gloves, blue spectacles with sidelights, the brim of a hat and a piece over his nose, every inch of his body is covered. Over the next several weeks, the stranger will remain in his room above the Coach and Horses pub, conducting experiments with his laboratory equipment and talking to himself. Who the stranger is and why his body is completely concealed at all times is a mystery that will tantalize the residents of the village of Iping for quite some time.

The first seven chapters or so of *The Invisible Man* are more mystery than horror story as the villagers search for the dark secret of the stranger. Of course, for the reader, there is really no mystery because the title of the book gives the secret away. In any event, on the day of a holiday celebration in Iping, matters come to a head. Griffin unleashes the total power of his invisibility, taking off all of his clothes and becoming completely invisible, beating some of the villagers and making his escape.

Griffin flees Iping and after he tells his story to Doctor Kemp, a scientist he once knew slightly in his early days at the university, Kemp betrays Griffin. Griffin, in his madness, decides to wreak his revenge on Kemp and after a terrifying round of cat and mouse and some violence, Griffin is captured and then killed. In death, his body slowly becomes visible again, to the shock of the onlookers.

The Invisible Man is structured as a mystery but there is also a farcical element to the story. The descriptions of the visible effects of Griffin's invisibility are humorous in and of themselves, such as bed-clothes gathering together and leaping into the air and a fistful of money traveling through the countryside on its own. Then there are the villagers tumbling down the steps to get away from the invisible man, and Griffin's sneezing at the most inappropriate times. Wells often mocks his characters, such as the villagers who think Griffin is the bogey-man, a criminal who has escaped from justice, a piebald (his flesh spotted with different colors) or a creature of the supernatural. Mrs. Hall waters down her patrons' beer with sarsaparilla, Mr. Marvel wears socks with holes in them and Colonel Adye, the chief of the Burdock police who knows he is chasing an invisible man, thinks it would be unsporting to spread powdered glass on the street to catch him. The novel concludes with a joke, as the tramp Marvel ends up with Griffin's notebooks, hoping that he will eventually be able to understand them and then turn himself into an invisible man some day. It may be the humorous components of *The Invisible Man* that convinced director James Whale, who was always interested in the humor in horror, to become involved in the film adaptation of the novel.

The Invisible Man is also science fiction, in the section of the novel where Griffin tells his story to Kemp. In the first part of his tale, Griffin provides the scientific explanation for his discovery of the secret of invisibility, by way of a detailed, boring and unconvincing account. The next part of Griffin's story is particularly fascinating, as he finally uses the drug on himself. After a "night of racking anguish, sickness and fainting" (Chapter XX), Griffin's body gradually becomes invisible. But, where is he to go and how is he to survive? Griffin realizes that so long as he remains in London, he can have no safe shelter, no clothing (which if he had it, would forgo all the advantages of invisibility) and that he can seldom eat (because when he eats, he becomes grotesquely visible again for a time). It is at that point that Griffin decides to don his disguise and move out of the big city to continue his experiments in a small village. Griffin later concludes that "invisibility, in fact, is only good in two cases: It's useful in getting away, it's useful in approaching. It's particularly useful, therefore, in killing" (Chapter XXIV).

The Invisible Man is a tale of power and madness. Almost as soon as Griffin becomes invisible he becomes power mad, with his head "teeming with plans of all the wild and wonderful things I had now impunity to do" (Chapter XX). Griffin displays his madness on his flight out of Iping, breaking many of the windows in the village and cutting the telegraph wires. More alarming, Griffin tells Kemp of his plans to go on a reign of terror, with judicious slayings of those who disobey him so that he can terrify and dominate the countryside (Chapter XXIV). Wells does not make it clear whether Griffin's madness arises as a side effect of the invisibility drugs or as a result of the invisibility itself, but since there is little discussion of the drugs Griffin imbibed, it appears that it is the invisibility itself that causes the madness. Wells seems to be saying that absolute power not only corrupts absolutely but may also cause madness.

That thesis is undercut significantly by the fact that Griffin, even before his experimentation with invisibility, was not a person of high character. He once stole money from his father to obtain the funds necessary to keep his research going, resulting in his father's suicide. Griffin is forced by societal convention to attend his father's funeral but he shows no remorse. Also, most "mad scientists" believe their experiments are intended for the good of mankind, or at least delude themselves into thinking so, despite the unlikelihood of that result when viewed from a disinterested perspective. By contrast, Griffin moves forward with his research either because he just wants to see what he can accomplish or to obtain that absolute power that he mentions. Griffin was probably slightly touched before he became invisible, undermining any theme of the novel tying power to madness.

The Invisible Man is truly about isolation and degradation. Griffin must move out of London and into the tiny community of Iping because there is too much danger for him in London. Yet, Griffin must still live in isolation within that isolated village, hiding in his room above the pub and limiting his conversations with the villagers. Until he accidentally meets up with Kemp, Griffin says that there was "no human being in the world in whom I could confide" (Chapter XXII). Griffin must be suspicious of everyone and, of course, in the end, Kemp betrays him also.

The isolation that Griffin experiences relates to, and is a part of, the degradation that he suffers. Griffin has a strong academic background. Although he was just an instructor at a small provincial cottage, he is obviously a superior scientist. Even before his experiments are successful, he has the hubris of a noted scientist. Returning to his hometown for his father's funeral, he sees a girl he had known ten years before. He does not talk to her because, as he puts it, she was just a very ordinary person. Whether justified or not, Griffin has the pride of the wealthy and the educated. Yet, after becoming invisible, Griffin must hide himself in Iping, where, when he runs out of money, he turns to stealing cash from the vicarage, just like a common thief. In fact, the clothes he wears and most of the food he eats are all stolen. As superior as Griffin believes himself to be, his plans are continually thwarted by those he believes to be inferior. As he tells Kemp, "Every conceivable sort of silly creature that has ever been created has been sent to cross me" (Chapter XXIII).

Thus, the life of an invisible man is both degrading and isolated, not what Griffin ever expected. Before Griffin started his research, he believed that once he became invisible, he would have unlimited power. He believed that he would be able to obtain everything that a man desires. Griffin found, to his dismay that

> invisibility made it possible to get them, but it made it impossible to enjoy them when they were got. Ambition—what is the good of pride of place when you cannot appear there? What is the good of the love of a woman when her name must needs be Delilah? [Chapter XXIII].

The end of *The Invisible Man*, while intriguing, exciting and somewhat gruesome, is actually a tragedy, as the lonely and degraded Griffin finally meets his end, ultimately realizing that the discovery of invisibility could never provide him with the power that he sought. *The Invisible Man* is also a tale of horror, science fiction, mystery, comedy and adventure, an unusual combination for any novel, and more than enough to make *The Invisible Man* a work that is still read today.

The Film

The Invisible Man (1933)

The film version of *The Invisible Man* commences with the same striking image as the book, with a dark figure in the distance carrying a suitcase down a small hill in a driving snow and a brisk wind. As the stranger wipes the snow from the road sign to the village of Iping, the audience sees a figure with his face covered by bandages and glasses and not one part of his body left exposed.

Griffin takes a room at *The Lions Head* inn in the village of Iping, where he attempts to conduct his research and experiments in order to find the secret of returning to the life of the visible. His hopes of being able to work in peace, however, are shattered by the inquisitiveness of the villagers and the beginning of his madness. One day, in a fit of pique, Griffin unravels his bandages and reveals his true condition to the villagers. He avoids arrest and flees the village, then going to the home of his former associate, Dr. Kemp. Prior to Griffin becoming wrapped up in his invisibility experiments, he and Kemp had been working for Dr. Cranley, the father of Griffin's fiancée, Flora. Kemp reveals Griffin's location to the police and after Griffin kills Kemp, is himself killed by a policeman's bullets as Griffin walks out of a barn in which he was sleeping onto the snow-covered ground.

While the opening sequences of *The Invisible Man* in the village of Iping hew closely to the events related in the novel, there was simply no time to treat the film story of the invisible man as a mystery. Instead, the film moves quickly from the invisible man's introduction to the revelation of his true nature, making the film version of Wells's novel into a horror story only, without any mystery

Jenny, the landlady (Una O'Connor), almost discovers Griffin's secret in *The Invisible Man* (1933). The Invisible Man is played by Claude Rains.

elements. Once Griffin flees the village of Iping, the story generally goes off on its own, unrelated to events in the book, except for Griffin's meeting up with Kemp, his desire for Kemp to be his confederate, his betrayal by Kemp and, in this version, the killing of Kemp by Griffin. There are no flashback sequences in which Griffin explains the science behind his experiments or his early days coping with his invisibility. Apparently, every film from the 1930s needed a love interest, so Griffin is given Flora Cranley, a Hollywood concoction. Flora is played by Gloria Stuart, usually a fine actress, but the part of Flora in this film is a throwaway, unrelated to the main story, and Stuart has little to do.

Another important change from the novel is that in the film, there is no question as to the cause of Griffin's madness. It is Griffin's use of a plant extract known as monocane in his invisibility drug that causes the change in Griffin's personality. Thus, the film does not raise the question of the possible deleterious effects on the psyche of a person who believes he wields close to absolute power. The film makes it clear that Griffin began his experiments with invisibility only so that he could accomplish what no man had ever done before. It is only after he first takes the invisibility drugs that he is consumed by the power he now believes he can wield over all of mankind.

Similarly, the film version of *The Invisible Man* is not about degradation and isolation. The film viewer never experiences Griffin stealing money to live or food to eat. The fact that Griffin is living close to poverty is glossed over in the film. Griffin is arrogant at the beginning of *The Invisible Man* and that carries through to the very end. Also, the story moves too quickly to create a sense of isolation for Griffin and since he has two people interested in his well-being, Flora and her father, the invisible man never seems totally isolated from society. Thus, the two factors from the novel that created some sympathy for Griffin are missing from the movie. As a result, and unlike the novel, the story of the invisible man is not a tale of personal tragedy. There is no sadness in his killing. Griffin's death by gunshot is merely the traditional killing of a movie monster at the end of a horror film, an event cheered by the audience.

As one might expect, director James Whale emphasizes the humor that is inherent in the Wells story and also adds a few bits of his own. On several occasions, the invisible man mocks the villagers, by dancing around partially dressed and singing songs such as "Here we go gathering nuts in May." Then there are the people calling into the police to make some fairly ridiculous suggestions on how to catch the invisible man, and Griffin's explanation of the rules of being an invisible man—never go out until an hour after eating; be careful about the rain because water can be seen on your head and shoulders; and avoid smoky cities because the soot sticks on you until a dark outline of your body can be seen. (Some of the latter ideas come from the novel, Chapter XXIII.)

In terms of the production, *The Invisible Man* is a first-class effort by Universal. The first uncovering of the invisible man is still stunning for modern audiences, with effects that have never been improved upon, even with all of the recent technological advances in film making. Who does not believe that there is really an invisible man under those bandages, as first the nose comes off, then the glasses, next the head bandages and then the wig? The viewer can actually see through the spot where the head is supposed to be. The villagers run away but when they come back, all they see is a shirt dancing in the air and all they hear is a voice that is mocking them. It is at moments such as these that the cinema surpasses literature. Imagination is important but seeing (or, perhaps, not seeing) these special effects on the screen is a moment of cinema magic. Later, there are convincing manifestations of the invisible man riding a bicycle, lifting the cash drawer from a bank, working the brakes and gears of a car and lighting and smoking a cigarette. The special effects created by John P. Fulton for this film never cease to amaze, even upon repeated viewings.

The direction of the film by James Whale is outstanding with, for example, angled shots from the floor up to the invisible man to increase his stature and the alarm he generates, and Whale's camera lingering on the villagers and other bystanders for reaction shots, adding both humor and horror to the film. These minor characters are usually played either by common looking actors or strange looking actors, making them seem to be genuine people of the countryside and not really paid performers. With the exception of Una O'Connor as Mrs. Hall, Griffin's landlady, whose performances in horror films are always a matter of personal taste (but see her fabulous performance as Janet in *Witness for the Prosecution* [1957] as she is cross-examined by Charles Laughton on the witness stand), the performances, even down to the very small parts of the villagers and the police, are outstanding.

However, the film would never have worked without a commanding performance in the title role. Claude Rains is marvelous as Griffin, using his cultured voice, rolling tongue and modulations of the volume and tempo of his speech to convey the different aspects of Griffin's character, from serious to humorous and sane to mad. Note the scene in which he reunites with Flora, first talking to her quietly in a rational manner and gradually becoming more excited and loud, revealing the insanity within him to the woman who loves him. Rains manages to convey all of the variety of emotions of Griffin without the use of any facial expressions and with very few hand gestures. Along with Boris Karloff, Rains was the second performer in a James Whale monster film who became a star even though his face was not shown throughout all or most of the film.

The dialogue of *The Invisible Man* is often cited in reviews and it is truly memorable. Primarily written by playwright and now screenwriter R.C. Sherriff, it bristles with the madness of Griffin. Examples are "Suddenly I realized the power I held; the power to rule, to make the world grovel at my feet." Later, "We'll begin with a reign of terror, a few murders here and there; murders of great men, murders of little men, just to show we make no distinction. We might even wreck a train or two." Still later, "Even the moon is frightened of me, frightened to death, the whole world frightened to death." Rains is marvelous as Griffin but without the stunning dialogue, his performance could never have been so striking. The one minor defect in the dialogue, though, is Griffin twice using the old horror film chestnut—that he should never have meddled in things better left alone. Luckily, that idea is not emphasized in the movie.

The ending of the film is better than the novel, as a story that opened in the snow comes full circle, with Griffin betraying himself to those who are chasing him by the footsteps he creates in the snow. Griffin is shot at close range by a policeman; he falls to the ground. As he dies, his body becomes visible again, in a good special effect for its time. *The Invisible Man* ends, as the film versions of *Dr. Jekyll and Mr. Hyde* previously had and the film version of *The Picture of Dorian Gray* would in the future, with the mad monster reverting to his true self upon his death.

While the film version of *The Invisible Man* does not display the depth of characterization or the subtle thematic material of the novel, it has a crackling good story that is better than the one in the book. The 1933 film is a fine adaptation of H.G. Wells's famous novel.

Chapter 12

"The Black Cat," "Morella" and "The Facts in the Case of M. Valdemar" by Edgar Allan Poe

Edgar Allan Poe generally wrote poems and short stories; the only novel he ever penned was *The Narrative of Arthur Gordon Pym* (1838). Poe's writings are therefore difficult to adapt to a full length movie because there is never enough of a plot in his short works to fill the running time of a feature film. Nevertheless, Poe's name is such a significant draw for horror film fans that filmmakers cannot resist associating Poe's name with their horror films, even if the film has little to do with Poe. As film historian William K. Everson wrote, in *Classics of the Horror Film*,

> The number of horror films claiming to be based on stories by Edgar Allan Poe is prodigious; but those that can claim real kinship to his original stories are few, while those that may be considered to have done them justice are rarer still.... For the most part ... Poe's name was cavalierly attached to films which borrowed the *titles* of his work, and perhaps a single incident to justify the pillaging of that title.

The Black Cat (1934), one of the great horror films of the classic era, provides support for Everson's thesis. There is little of Edgar Allan Poe in the movie, despite a reference to Edgar Allan Poe in its credits. Indeed, it was not until the 1960s, when multi-part adaptations of works of horror became commonplace, that cinematic justice could potentially be done for some of Poe's short works, including "The Black Cat." Unfortunately, most of those short film adaptations have little of Edgar Allan Poe in them, either.

The Literature

"The Black Cat"

"The Black Cat" is the tale of an unnamed narrator who, one night when he becomes intoxicated, becomes so angry at his black cat, Pluto, that he cuts an eye out of one of the animal's sockets and one morning, "in cold blood," the narrator slips a noose around Pluto's neck and hangs the cat from a limb of a tree. Many months later, matters repeat themselves with another black cat that has mysteriously appeared. When the narrator attempts to kill the animal and his wife attempts to defend the animal, he buries an axe into his wife's brain, instantly killing her. The narrator hides his wife's body in a wall of the cellar and then re-lays and re-mortars all of the bricks, so that no one will suspect that anything lies behind the partition. However, when the police arrive and they are talking to the narrator, a cry is heard from behind the wall. The police tear down the wall and discover the corpse of the wife, with the black cat, very much alive, sitting on her head. The narrator has accidentally walled up the monster cat with the dead body of the wife.

"The Black Cat" has a familiar structure for a Poe story. The narrator is unnamed. He has few redeeming features. He seems to be writing solely to justify some horrific acts he has undertaken for no apparent reason. The reader is never sure if the tale involves real events or is just the distraught imaginings of a crazed individual.

The plot itself is also familiar, being somewhat similar to "The Tell-Tale Heart," first published in the same year as "The Black Cat." Both stories involve a murder for which the killer has no explanation. In both, a dead body is hidden in a house, either behind a wall or under a floor. Both narrators are discovered by the police as a result of real or imagined noises in his house. There is a question in both stories as to whether the tale is one of the supernatural or simply one of overwhelming guilt.

However, "The Black Cat" is more horrific than "The Tell-Tale Heart," with "The Black Cat" featuring the deliberate gouging out of an eye of a cat, the hanging murder of the cat, the deliberate axe murder of the narrator's wife and the constant ranting and ravings of the narrator as he relates his story. There is also a true monster in the tale—the mysterious unnamed second black cat, which no one has ever seen before the night he first mysteriously appears at a bar.

The cat then follows the narrator home, as if stalking him. The cat is one-eyed, as if he is the reincarnation of Pluto. Over time, the white splotch on the cat's body gradually changes into the shape of a gallows, as if the cat were a specter of revenge. It is not too difficult to suspect that the narrator did not, in fact, accidentally wall the cat in the tomb. The creature seems to have deliberately gone there on its own, in order to consummate its revenge for the killing of Pluto.

Poe's story is fuelled by its strange images, such as the phantasm of Pluto on the only remaining wall of the narrator's house that has burned down and the apparition of a gallows on the chest of the new cat. There is the hatred of the narrator toward the new cat, describing the cat by using words such as "odious" and "pestilence" and describing his attitude to the cat with words such as "bitterness" and "unutterable loathing." There is also a graphic description at the end of the story when the dead wife's body is discovered behind the wall. Poe describes the body as "greatly decayed and clotted with gore." There is no humor in the story to relieve any of the tension.

"Morella"

If "The Black Cat" is one of the best known tales of Edgar Allan Poe's, "Morella" is one of least. Here, another unnamed narrator tells of his marriage to Morella, a brilliant and learned woman who teaches her husband about mysticism and ancient philosophies. When Morella becomes seriously ill, she tells the narrator, on her deathbed, "I am dying, yet I shall live." She is referring to the child she is carrying, which was previously undisclosed to the reader.

Once Morella dies, her daughter is born. She is an image of her mother and she grows more so over the years. Initially, the narrator makes the child a recluse from society; he never even gives the child a name. Many years later, the narrator changes his mind and decides to have the child baptized. However, at the ceremony, when asked the name of the child by the priest, the narrator cannot think of any name other than "Morella." Upon hearing that name, the child's features convulse, a hue of death spreads over her face and as she falls, the child responds, "I am here!" She then dies and when the narrator brings her to the ancestral tomb and lays her to rest, he finds no traces of the first Morella, even though she had been buried there some years before.

"Morella" has themes that will be familiar to those who have read the stories of Poe's that were the inspiration for several 1960s horror films. The transmigration of the soul of one character into another is the basis for "Metzengerstein," a dying wife is the cornerstone of "Ligeia" and the doubling of characters can be seen in many stories including "The Fall of the House of Usher" and "William Wilson." Unlike most of Poe's other tales, however, "Morella" has little genuine horror in it, except for its surprise ending. Instead, amidst discussions of ancient philosophies and philosophers, the tale is most concerned with the inconsistent and unreal emotional relationships of its characters, not horror. "Morella" is a minor work of Poe's and, justifiably so, is not well known by the reading public.

"The Facts in the Case of M. Valdemar"

Edgar Allan Poe wrote many strange tales but "The Facts in the Case of M. Valdemar" has to be one of the strangest. The narrator, a mesmerist, believes that he can delay a person's death by hypnotizing that person close to his expected demise. M. Valdemar is the perfect subject for the experiment; he has a fatal disease and his physicians have the ability to closely estimate his date and time of death. Valdemar is receptive to the idea of being mesmerized and when Valdemar's end is near, the doctors call in the narrator, who proceeds to hypnotize Valdemar. Valdemar continues in a state of hypnotic sleep for seven months, with true death somehow being delayed by the hypnotic trance. At that point, the narrator and the attending doctors decide to awaken Valdemar. The deed is done and then, "amid ejaculations of 'dead! dead!' absolutely *bursting* from the tongue" of the body, Valdemar's whole frame shrinks, crumbles and rots away, leaving on the bed a nearly liquid mass of loathsome, detestable putrescence.

Unlike many of Poe's horror stories, the unnamed narrator in this tale is not giving an explanation for one of his crimes. Rather, he is describing a scientific experiment gone wrong. He is trying, according to him, to give the true facts of an event that has been inaccurately talked about and misrepresented in society and which has resulted in "a great deal of disbelief."

Despite his intent, the chronicler does not succeed in convincing anyone that the story of M. Valdemar has any basis in reality. The thought that a person with an incurable disease can be kept alive by mesmerism is hard to accept. Yet, oddly enough, "Valdemar," more than 150 years after its publication, has more bases in reality today than it did when it was first written, with modern medical techniques able to keep a body alive long after the mind cannot effectively function. In his own way, within the context of a horror story, Poe has raised questions concerning the scientific and moral basis of keeping a person alive while in a coma (as Valdemar was for seven months) or whether it is better to pull the plug and let nature take its course.

Then again, perhaps one should not read too much into a Poe story, particularly from the perspective of an era long after Poe's death. It may be best to simply observe that "Valdemar" is one of Poe's most gruesome tales, in the vivid description of Valdemar when he first crosses the line from life into semi-death and then in the crumbling of his body at the end of the story.

The Films

The Black Cat (1934)

Edgar Allan Poe did not invent black cats, although it sometimes seems like he did. Black cats have been around for a long time, long enough to have many superstitions attached to them. In America, many people believe that if a black cat crosses your path, it is bad luck. In other countries, a black cat is deemed to be a portent of good luck. Therefore, it may be that the title of *The Black Cat* (1934) refers to the superstitions rather than to Poe's story, particularly since there is next-to-nothing of Poe's short story in the film. That would make substantial sense except for one fact—the credits of the movie specifically state that the feature was suggested by the immortal Edgar Allan Poe classic, which is a reference, presumably, to his short story titled "The Black Cat." So, is the use of Poe's name and the title of his short story just a marketing ploy or is the 1934 film actually inspired in any way by either Edgar Allan Poe or his famous tale?

One thing is clear—the plot of the 1934 film owes nothing to Poe's short story of the same name. In fact, the film has almost no plot at all, being more a tale of atmosphere, setting and personalities than of coherence, with a bit of necrophilia, Satanism, torture, acts of revenge and perhaps some incest thrown into the mix. There is no black cat accidentally walled up with a murder victim, resulting in the discovery of the murderer. Clearly, the plot of Poe's short story has been jettisoned for this film.

Some have suggested that *The Black Cat* (1934) captures the mood of Poe's short stories, even if it does not employ the plot of any of them. In *Classics of the Horror Film*, William K. Everson wrote that "in its mood and in its oppressive, claustrophobic and generally unhealthy atmosphere ... [*The Black Cat* (1934)] does evoke a very definite feeling of Poe." However, while Everson is correct in that observation, it really misses the point. Many horror films have that same atmosphere and mood; it is a quality of horror films, not just those purportedly based on works of Poe's.

By contrast, in terms of point of view, the film does not capture the style of Poe's tales. Poe generally employs an unnamed narrator who relates his tale from a biased and sometimes hysterical point of view. There is none of that in *The Black Cat* (1934) so at least in that regard, the film does not capture the spirit of Poe.

Perhaps the link between short story and film is the black cat that their titles share. In the movie, Dr. Vitus Werdegast, a Hungarian psychiatrist, is deathly frightened of cats. When Werdegast first sees a cat, which happens to

In the conclusion of *The Black Cat* (1934), Bela Lugosi, playing Dr. Werdegast, has a rare career victory over Boris Karloff, playing Hjalmar Poelzig, as Werdegast intends to skin Poelzig alive.

be black, at the mansion of his rival, Hjalmar Poelzig, an Austrian architect, he kills it with a thrown knife. Later, when Werdegast is about to shoot Poelzig, the sight of a second black cat causes him to drop his revolver. Werdegast's irrational fear of cats is similar to the narrator's fear of the second cat in Poe's short story, so there may be a trace element of Poe in the film. However, after these two instances of Werdegast's interactions with some cats, the black cats, for the most part, disappear from the film. Despite the title of the film, black cats are not important to any aspect of the film, further indicating that the title is a marketing ploy, used to trade on the name of Edgar Allan Poe.

Indeed, it is stretching to find any link between Edgar Allan Poe and this film, even though the film bears the title of one of his short stories and has his name in the credits. Better comparisons for *The Black Cat* (1934) can be found in a trio of horror films from 1932, *Dr. Jekyll and Mr. Hyde*, *Island of Lost Souls* and *Murders in the Rue Morgue*, all of which display the characteristics of pre–Code films in terms of either subject matter or sexuality. There is a decided eroticism to *The Black Cat* (1934), in moments such as Werdegast, with a hungry expression on his face, touching the hair of the sleeping young newlywed, Joan Alison, on a train; Poelzig embalming beautiful women and hanging their bodies in glass cases in the basement of his mansion; Poelzig marrying the daughter of his wife; the healthy banter of the young newlyweds; a gratuitous shot of a nude bronze statuette; and the legs that Joan Alison displays in her short dress as she flees the Poelzig mansion near the end of the film. This is not Edgar Allan Poe; it is Hollywood of the early 1930s.

The Black Cat (1934), whether or not it is Edgar Allan Poe, is one of the best-remembered Universal horror films of the early 1930s. The film may be all style and no substance but it is effective, as long as the story line is not considered too closely. *The Black Cat* (1934) was also Universal's highest grossing movie of the year. Part of the reason for that box office success was undoubtedly the star power of Karloff and Lugosi in the early 1930s, but part must also be attributed to the marketability of the name of Edgar Allan Poe to fans of horror films.

Tales of Terror (1962)

Tales of Terror was Roger Corman's fourth in a series of eight film adaptations of works by Edgar Allan Poe. What sets *Tales of Terror* apart from the previous Corman films is that *Tales of Terror* is a compendium of three short films, with the only links between the three being Edgar Allan Poe and the introduction by Vincent Price. In an interesting homage to Poe, the names of the three female characters in the short films, all of whom are original to the films, are inspired by works of Poe's. The "Lenora" of "Morella" comes from either the "Lenore" of the poem "The Raven," or the short story "Eleonora," about the love of a woman who dies. The "Annabel" of "The Black Cat" comes from the poem "Annabel Lee," about a young lover who dies. The "Helene" of "The Facts in the Case of M. Valdemar" comes from the three-stanza poem "To Helen," about a beautiful woman.

Corman, by turning to this three film format, provided himself with a unique opportunity to produce faithful adaptations of three of Poe's tales. He could choose any story he desired from the many stories Poe wrote, and he did not have to stretch out the plots of those stories to fill the length of a feature film. Unfortunately, in many ways, Corman squandered that opportunity.

"Morella"

For the first part of *Tales of Terror*, Roger Corman and screenwriter Richard Matheson apparently decided to forgo the chance to produce a faithful version of a Poe short story and, for some reason, decided to bring an original work to the screen. The short film involves a man named Locke who, after the death of his wife Morella 26 years before, banished his daughter Lenora from the house because Morella, in her dying breath, blamed her demise on Lenora. As the film opens, Lenora returns to the house and learns that Locke has kept Morella's mummified body in its bed, not in a tomb. That night, Morella's spirit rises from its body and enters Lenora's body. Lenora turns into a very alive Morella, and Morella's body becomes a very dead Lenora. Morella then attacks her husband, seeking revenge for something unstated. Locke and Morella then die in a fire accidentally started by a dropped candle.

The entire story makes little sense. What was Morella trying to avenge by her return from the dead and her attack on Locke? How did Morella obtain the power to enter and then take over Lenora's body? If Locke was so much in love with Morella, why was Morella so angry with Locke? None of these questions are answered in the film, making the film version as confusing as the short story. There is also sloppy plotting near the end of the feature, with a dropped candle providing an easy climax to the film, probably in attempt to paper over the fact that the writers could not provide convincing responses to any of the reasonable questions raised by the story line.

The most important question raised by the film version, however, does not concern its convoluted plot. Rather, it is why the filmmakers would choose a story for *Tales of Terror* that they apparently believed could not be faithfully adapted for the cinema, even in a short film version. Poe's "Morella" and the film share the subject of transmigration of the soul after death, with the spirit of the cinema version of Morella once again transferring into her daughter's body, although with decidedly different timing and results than in Poe's version. Other than that, the two tales have nothing in common except for the name of the title character.

Tales of Terror has the same standard of production values that most of Roger Corman's Poe adaptations have. The film appears to have a big budget, with its use of color and its large indoor sets. However, they are mere façade. The shot of the Locke mansion by the sea, used several times in the film, is an obvious drawing. When Locke tells the story of the death of Morella many years before, there is no flashback (which would require a large cast) but instead, it is all talk, limiting the size of the required number of actors (and paychecks) for the movie. Some of the footage of the burning mansion comes from *House of Usher* (1960). Who, other than Roger Corman, was still using stock footage by the 1960s?

"Morella," by Edgar Allan Poe, is nothing special and therefore few readers would expect that any film version of the story would be anything special. In that regard, at least, the film adaptation does not surprise or disappoint.

"The Black Cat"

Unlike "Morella," Poe's "The Black Cat" is something special and therefore, because the middle portion of *Tales of Terror* has little to do with Poe's short story, it is a major disappointment. The short film involves a slovenly alcoholic named Montresor who has no job and is happy to live on the money he takes from his pretty wife, Annabel, who works as a seamstress. When Montresor learns that Annabel is having an affair with his friend, Fortunato, Montresor kills Annabel and then entombs the dead Annabel and the live Fortunato behind a brick wall that Montresor builds in the basement of his house. However, when the police come to investigate the disappearance of Annabel, they hear Annabel's black cat wailing behind the wall, betraying Montresor's crimes.

Except for the ending, this second part of the trilogy takes nothing from "The Black Cat." In fact, this middle section of *Tales of Terror* is based more on another Poe story, "The Cask of Amontillado," first published in 1846, than

A publicity still for "The Black Cat" section of *Tales of Terror* (1962). A drunken Montresor (Peter Lorre) is dreaming about Fortunato (Vincent Price) and Annabel (Joyce Jameson) pulling Montresor's head off his body.

on "The Black Cat." In "Amontillado," a man named Montresor murders a wine-taster named Fortunato by walling him up alive in the catacombs of an Italian city. The reasons for Montresor's killing of Fortunato are the "thousand injuries of Fortunato" that Montresor has borne over a long period of time. There is no black cat in the story; Montresor gets away with his crime. The story has a light tone, similar to that of the film.

"The Black Cat" section of *Tales of Terror* attempts to tell a story with humor, not horror, with the light tone being just the opposite of that of Poe's "The Black Cat." The first story in this trilogy, "Morella," while not successful, at least tried to capture the mood of Poe's stories of horror. "The Black Cat" section of the film goes in the opposite direction, undercutting the effectiveness of its surprise ending. For example, there is nothing of a supernatural nature in the short feature, such as the image of a gallows appearing on the chest of the cat, as in the Poe story. The black cat of the film is not an avenging monster; he is more of an afterthought.

In fact, the short feature is not even a horror film. It is merely the story of a perfect crime gone wrong, with Montresor making one fatal mistake—not realizing he entombed the black cat behind the wall. One almost expects Columbo or some other television detective to appear and conduct the investigation into the disappearance of Montresor's wife.

"The Black Cat" section of *Tales of Terror* has a few good moments of humor, particularly in the wine-tasting scene. It is enjoyable to see Peter Lorre with a good film role late in his career. Other than that, there is little to like in this short film allegedly based upon "The Black Cat," by Edgar Allan Poe but in essence, an original work.

"The Facts in the Case of M. Valdemar"

This last section of *Tales of Terror* is the best of the three and not surprisingly, it is the one that is closest to the plot and spirit of the Poe story on which it is based. In this film version of "The Facts in the Case of M. Valdemar," a mesmerist named Carmichael has been regularly mesmerizing Mr. Valdemar to relieve Valdemar of the pain he is experiencing as a result of an incurable disease. Carmichael then proposes that he hypnotize Valdemar *in articulo mortis*, i.e., in the clutches of death (a phrase from the short story), in order to determine how long the moment of death can be postponed by mesmerism. The deed is done and Valdemar seems to linger on after death in a comatose state.

Carmichael is interested in Valdemar's wife, Helene. She is interested in her husband's physician, Dr. James, although Helene remains faithful to her husband, even though he is not entirely alive. Finally, Carmichael threatens Helene, saying that if she does not marry him, he will leave Valdemar in limbo forever, not dead and not alive. Valdemar then rises from his bed and in order to protect

Helene, attacks Carmichael, When Dr. James finally breaks into the room, Carmichael is dead and the body of Valdemar has turned into a liquid slime.

Obviously, liberties have been taken with the original Poe story but they are generally for the better, or, at least, they are more cinematic. The hypnotist, Carmichael, is a figure of evil. By contrast, in the original Poe story, since he was the narrator, the mesmerist portrayed himself as a rational scientist. Valdemar's wife, Helene, is a new character. As performed by Debra Paget, she adds some pulchritude to the story. More importantly, she provides the key motivation of the story, both in the evil nature of Carmichael and in the return of Valdemar from the dead.

The ending of the short film is generally well-handled. When Valdemar first rises from his bed, it is a truly eerie moment. Valdemar's appearance starts to degenerate but the creepiness of the scene is undercut by some cheesy special effects, as the screen blurs and wavers, instead of employing modern trick photography. The climax is then cleverly delayed, as the film cuts to Dr. James in the downstairs foyer of the house. He hears a cry, rushes upstairs and breaks down the door. He then gathers Helene and then the two look at the floor, with obvious disgust on their faces. It is only then that the viewer is shown the remains of Mr. Valdemar, in a surprise ending taken from Poe's short story.

The "Valdemar" section of *Tales of Terrors* displays the potential of a multi-part adaptation of some of the works of Edgar Allan Poe's. The script shows no evidence of padding, as all of the additions to Poe's story are important to the revised plot of the film. The mood of the film is similar to that of Poe's tale, although slightly less dark in tone. The script gives a chance for the performers, and particularly Basil Rathbone as Carmichael, to shine. While there have been several modifications to the plot of Poe's tale, the basic premise and the climax are the same.

This short film is clearly inspired by Poe's tale of M. Valdemar. It is a shame that the first two stories were not inspired by their source material. They would have been far better films.

Other Adaptations

In 1941, Universal released another film titled *The Black Cat*, also with a credit to the short story by Edgar Allan Poe. However, once again, the newer film has almost nothing to do with Edgar Allan Poe, except for some cats that appear from time to time in the feature and a small incident in the movie where the crying of a cat, which is trapped in a crematorium where the villain is attempting to dispose of the heroine, alerts the hero to the situation and allows for a rescue.

Chapter 13

Black Moon
by Clements Ripley

The most famous zombie and voodoo movie of all time is *White Zombie* (1932), an independent production starring Bela Lugosi. The film was also a surprising financial success. *White Zombie* led to several more independent films about voodoo but for the major studios, Columbia Pictures was the only one to release a film about voodoo in the early 1930s, namely *Black Moon* (1934). Perhaps because the voodoo craze had already waned by 1934 or perhaps because the film did not contain any actual zombies, *Black Moon* never came close to either the financial or critical success of *White Zombie*.

Background

Clements Ripley was born in Tacoma, Washington, in 1892. After college, a stint in the Army and a few years as a farmer, Clements decided to pursue a writing career on a full time basis. Clements Ripley wrote seven novels, three of which were made into movies: *A Devil with Women* (1930), based on Ripley's novel *Dust and Sun*, published in 1929, *Gold Is Where You Find It* (1938), based on Ripley's novel of the same name published in 1936, and, of course, *Black Moon* (1934), based on Ripley's novel of the same name which was published in book form in 1933. Clements Ripley passed away in 1954.

The Literature

The villain of *Black Moon* is Amalia Perez, the leader of a voodoo cult on the Caribbean island of San Cristobal. The secondary villain of the novel is

Amalia's uncle, Dr. Perez, who attempts to blackmail Stephen Lane, a friend of Amalia's from New York City, into marrying Amalia and taking her away from San Cristobal. Matters do not go well once Stephen travels to the island. When Stephen breaks up a voodoo ceremony by shooting a papalois who is about to sacrifice a young girl in a pagan ritual, Stephen is forced to go on the run with Gale, the secretary to Dr. Perez. There are then numerous twists and turns to the story, with Amalia finally being killed by an unexpected person after Stephen has escaped at least two death traps. Stephen and Gale are then able to safely flee to the States, where presumably they will be married and live happily ever after.

Black Moon is only a light tale of horror, relying more on atmosphere than outright incidents of terror. The mood is created primarily by the incessant beating of the voodoo drums, in various levels of intensity, and by the separation of the black culture and the white culture on the island, creating an overbearing feeling of tension and foreboding. That feeling is augmented by the natives' apparent involvement with voodoo.

The atmosphere is also enhanced by small incidents that occur once Stephen comes to the island, such as the strange nocturnal walks of Amalia and the discovery in the night of a dark blotch of blood on a pathway, which spot disappears by the next morning. (This actually relates to the murder of Father Anselmo, the priest who was supposed to marry Amalia and Stephen.) There is also the appearance on a walkway of a coconut shell, bottom up, with five little pegs anchoring it into the ground. Upon closer examination, however, the pegs are fingers and based on a scar on one of the fingers, it is clear that the fingers are those of the deceased Father Anselmo. Gale explains that the object is a bad luck charm known as an ouanga, used against an enemy by having the papalois cook up an ouanga and put it on a trail where the adversary will pass. The victim promptly shrivels up and dies. Fortunately, that does not happen to Stephen, even though he appears to be the target of the ouanga.

Some of the atmosphere of the island is undercut, at least for a modern audience, by Ripley's disconcerting treatment of the black masses on San Cristobal. An unfortunate underlying premise of the novel is Ripley's apparent belief that blacks, by their nature, are substantially different and inferior to the whites on the island and that their lives are not as important as those of the whites. In describing the black population of the island, Ripley uses language that is unacceptable today, such as darkies and, of course, the n-word. Ripley has a true colonial attitude toward the native population. On the other hand, one of the most interesting characters in *Black Moon* is Lunch, a black man whom Stephen meets on the boat ride to San Cristobal. Although Lunch speaks in dialect and sometimes seems subservient to the whites, he is actually smart and courageous, rescuing Stephen and the others on several occasions. While the white characters are unable to defeat Amalia, a native woman, Maman Célest, is able to kill her. The characters of Lunch and Célest ameliorate at least some of the racist attitude in the remainder of Ripley's novel.

Indeed, some of the strengths of Ripley's story are the interesting characters that he creates. In addition to Lunch, there is Dr. Perez, alternately kind, vicious, protective of others, out to kill others, telling stories of danger in the island and then attempting to lessen the effects of his tales. At the end, after escaping from Amalia's clutches with the others, Perez turns on his companions and attempts to kidnap Gale from the island. Perez is always the most intriguing, yet puzzling character on San Cristobal.

Despite his success in the characterizations of Lunch and Perez, Ripley misses an opportunity in his portrayal of Amelia. The reader learns that she is beautiful and later that she is evil, but other than that, there is not much else to her portrayal. Amalia seldom appears in the first half of the book, so the reader never learns why Stephen fell in love with her, and she seldom reappears in the latter half of the book, even when her evil nature is exposed. Since the reader learns very little about Amalia and her character, Amalia's impact on the tale is reduced. Since Amalia is the principal villain of the narrative, Ripley erred in his storytelling by keeping Amalia hidden in the background of the tale.

Black Moon can never be accurately described as scary, gripping, exciting or enthralling. Its main interest lies in Stephen's actions to avoid being killed on San Cristobal and then to escape the island with his new love, Gale. The novel is more like the short story, "Most Dangerous Game," by Richard Connell, where a sadistic Russian general pursues unsuspecting people on a Caribbean Island as if they are wild game he is hunting, than one of the many famous horror stories covered in this book. While *Black Moon* is mildly entertaining, it promises more in the area of voodoo than it delivers. Ripley's novel was apparently never reissued in paperback and received little distribution in its time. Its sole claim to fame today is that it is the basis for a horror film, itself long forgotten, produced at the height of the horror film craze of the early 1930s.

The Film

Black Moon (1934)

There is an interesting relationship between the plot of the film, *Black Moon*, and the plot of the novel, *Black Moon*. In the novel, Dr. Perez is extremely worried about his niece's interest in voodoo and therefore devises a scheme whereby Stephen Lane and Amalia will marry and immediately move to the States for good. Perez believes Amalia will become westernized and be able to shed the superstitions of her island. The reader never learns if Perez' plan will work, since Amalia secretly opposes the idea and, in any event, Amalia is killed on the island.

As the movie version of the novel opens, Stephen and the Amalia character, re-named Juanita, are married and living in New York City. The couple has a little girl named Nancy. Stephen is a successful businessman. Juanita, however, is still drawn to the mysteries of the islands, often playing her voodoo drums in the household to the chagrin of the staff, since the drums reverberate quite loudly throughout the very large house. Even though her uncle opposes the idea, Juanita is set to return to San Christopher (note the change in name) for a visit but, in reality, for the underlying purpose of returning to her voodoo roots.

Thus, the movie version of the novel illustrates that the Perez scheme of the novel would never have worked. Juanita has been unhappy in New York for years. Even in the big city of New York, Juanita is unable to divorce herself from the religious cults and the voodoo that were so much a part of her younger days on San Christopher. When she finally returns to her homeland, she says that it is the first time she has been at peace in years.

Once the story moves to San Christopher and Stephen eventually comes to the island, the novel and the film have much in common, including the fact that Juanita is, in fact, the high priestess of the native voodoo cult. Just as in the novel, Stephen causes problems when he interrupts the ritual sacrifice of a young native woman by shooting the priest who is about to do the killing but in a striking change from the novel, Juanita completes the killing once Stephen departs. Later, the whites on the island protect themselves from attack by Juanita and the natives by securing themselves in the high tower on the island built for just such purpose. Juanita, however, smokes them out, capturing Stephen, Gail Hamilton (Stephen's secretary) and the child. These scenes from the film are clearly inspired by similar events in the novel. The end of *Black Moon* then diverges from that of the book, as the natives determine that Nancy must be sacrificed to avenge the shooting of their priest. Reluctantly, Juanita participates in the ceremony and as she brings her machete high to kill her own daughter, she is shot in the back by Stephen. As Dr. Perez buries Juanita in her homeland, Lunch, Stephen, Gail and Nancy escape the island.

Given its relative unknown status in the world of classic horror films, *Black Moon* is a surprisingly effective film. There is actually a little more brutality in the film than in the novel, although both handle the killings and attempted killings off-screen. The plot of the film version constantly moves forward, with no time spent on the irrelevancy of comic relief. The introductory section in New York City, completely original to the film, with voodoo drums beating and the sudden killing of Macklin, a man sent to New York by Dr. Perez to convince Juanita not to return to San Christopher, effectively sets the stage for the horror that is about to come. Just as in the novel, the atmosphere on San Christopher is established by the constant beating of the voodoo drums, but the sounds of the island are more effective in the film than the novel, because the beating of the drums can actually be heard, not just imagined. Voodoo movies, by their nature, tend to be demeaning to the black characters, and, of course, in the novel, that was a serious deficiency. In the movie, however, the difficulty is handled better, with the natives characterized as being very dangerous, not as a result of their race, but as a result of their interest in voodoo. Also, the offensive language from the novel is missing. It is a fine line to walk, but here the filmmakers succeeded in making an effective voodoo movie, without making it seem racist in nature.

Much like the novel, any racist attitude in the movie is ameliorated somewhat by the character of Lunch, who is treated as an equal by Stephen. Lunch is portrayed as completely different from the natives on the island, perhaps because Lunch is American-born. It must have been hard for the filmmakers to refrain from using Lunch as comic relief, although that is more a phenomenon of the 1940s than the 1930s. (If *Black Moon* had been made in the 1940s, chances are good that Mantan Moreland would have played the part of Lunch and his not-very-funny fear of voodoo would have taken up much of the running time of the film.) Much like the novel, Lunch is one of the most interesting people in the film, particularly since he is well-played by Clarence Muse, who gives the best performance in the movie.

As to the other performers, Jack Holt is good as Stephen Lane but he seems somewhat old for the part. He does manage to deliver the line, "the natives are restless," without breaking into a smile. Dorothy Burgess seems bland in the role of Juanita, until she morphs into the High Priestess of the cult, at which time she becomes more alive and more beautiful than before, somewhat similar to Ripley's characterization of Amalia in the novel. The 1930s horror film queen, Fay Wray, plays Gail, the unassertive good girl of the movie. Since Gail is a less interesting role than that of Juanita, the part is not very challenging for Wray. With her dark hair and unpleasing hairstyle, the usually very attractive Wray is somewhat of a disappointment in the film.

There are no zombies in *Black Moon*. Indeed, there is little mention of voodoo in the film, except for the use of some native voodoo terms and the discovery of a doll with pins in it. For all of the mysticism associated with the island cult, its implements of murder are common ones—knives, machetes and hangings. Some have compared *Black Moon* to the 1940s horror films of Val Lewton, with their reliance on atmosphere rather than on their slight plots to create a feeling of horror in the audience. That is a good association for any horror film and it is justified in this case. Setting and atmosphere carry the film. Not well-known today, *Black Moon* is an effective piece of horror, surely deserving of the status of a minor classic of the horror film.

Chapter 14

"The Raven" by Edgar Allan Poe

Adaptations of works from other media have always been an important component of motion picture production but there have only been a few films that have used poems as their source material. Some examples are *Clancy of the Mounted* (a 1933 serial based on a poem by Robert W. Service), *Gunga Din* (a 1939 adventure film based upon a poem by Rudyard Kipling), *The Set-Up* (a 1949 boxing film based upon a poem by Joseph Moncure March) and, of course, for horror film fans, at least two films purportedly inspired by "The Raven," a poem by Edgar Allan Poe.

The Literature

"The Raven" is an 18-stanza poem about unnamed poet who yearns for his deceased love, Lenore. Hearing a tapping and a rapping at his chamber door and then at his window, the poet opens a shutter and in steps a stately Raven, who speaks only one word, "Nevermore." Whether over the poet's grief for his loss of Lenore or because he has become slightly daft since that loss, the poet perceives the Raven as a prophet of bad news—that he and Lenore will never be reunited, even after the poet's death. For the rest of his life, the poet remains deeply depressed while the Raven watches over him from his stately perch.

"The Raven" is so famous that those who have never read the poem will recognize its opening lines, "Once upon a midnight dreary, while I pondered, weak and weary, Over many a quaint and curious volume of forgotten lore," and its refrain, "Quoth the Raven, 'Nevermore.'" Other phrases from the work are also well-known, such as "[S]uddenly there came a tapping, As of someone gently rapping, rapping at my chamber door."

"The Raven" is a wonderful poem, even for those who are not connoisseurs of poetry in general. Much of its impact stems from Poe's skillful use of several effective literary techniques of poetry. He employs alliteration, as in "weak and weary" and "grim, ungainly, ghastly, gaunt." There is internal rhyming, such as "napping," "tapping" and "rapping," and "Eagerly I wished the morrow;—vainly I had sought to borrow / From my books surcease of sorrow." There are almost identical lines repeated one after the other, such as "It shall clasp a sainted maiden whom the angels name Lenore—Clasp a rare and radiant maiden whom the angels name Lenore." There is the refrain of each paragraph, usually "Nevermore," but sometimes something similar such as "nothing more" or "evermore."

However, it is the image of the Raven, more than anything else, which makes the poem so memorable. The ebony bird is first announced by his sound— the gentle rapping, rapping at the poet's chamber door. When the shutter is opened, the stately Raven steps into the room in a saintly manner and with the demeanor of an aristocrat. He then perches above the poet's chamber door on a bust of Pallus Athena, the Greek goddess of intellectual wisdom. The poet then decides to put a chair in front of the bird and try to divine the meaning and purpose of the Raven. While the poet grows more hysterical over time, the Raven never reacts, sitting still and never flitting, displaying the seeming eyes of a demon. The Raven's response is only one word, "Nevermore."

There is the hint of the supernatural in the tale as the Raven can talk, even though he has only one word in his vocabulary, and he stays perched on the bust of Pallus forever. The Raven could be deemed to be a messenger of the devil, although the very existence of the bird could be the simple imaginings of the poet, depressed after the loss of his lover, Lenore. As was often the case in Poe's works, either interpretation concerning the genuineness of the Raven is a possibility, so it is up to each reader to decide on his own.

The Raven is a symbol of evil and death in the poem, and it has remained so in the mind of many readers ever since the poem's publication, but whether a full length feature film could be inspired by the words and imagery of the poem, as effective as they are, was unclear in 1935. Yet Universal Studios attempted to do just that, in a film starring Bela Lugosi and Boris Karloff.

The Film

The Raven (1935)

Although *The Black Cat* (1934) had nothing to do with Edgar Allan Poe, at least there were some black cats in the film. *The Raven* (1935), on the other hand, has no real ravens in it. Yet, paradoxically, there is more of Edgar Allan Poe in *The Raven* than in *The Black Cat*.

Of course, the plot of *The Raven* does not come from Edgar Allan Poe's poem. The poem is a story of atmosphere, imagery and writing style; it has no true story line. The filmmakers therefore chose to jettison all that could be found in the poem and create an entirely new tale for the cinema.

As the film opens, pretty Jean Thatcher is severely injured in an auto accident. Her father, Judge Thatcher, convinces Richard Vollin, a retired doctor, to perform the requisite surgery to save Jean's life. The operation is successful. During the recovery period, Vollin falls in love with the much younger Jean, but she does not return his interest. She is already engaged to Dr. Jerry Halden. When Judge Thatcher opposes Vollin's interest in Jean, Vollin blackmails an escaped criminal, Edward Bateman, into assisting him with his scheme of revenge. Vollin accomplishes his blackmail by using a form of plastic surgery on Bateman's face, turning him ugly, but promising to rectify the situation once his night of revenge is complete. However, on the night of Vollin's revenge against Jean and her

Dr. Vollin (Bela Lugosi), right, orders Bateman (Boris Karloff), left, to put Judge Thatcher (Samuel S. Hinds) onto the table with the swinging pendulum death trap high above, in *The Raven* (1935).

friends, Bateman turns on Vollin and it is Vollin who is killed in one of his own deathtraps.

While there are no ravens in the film's storyline, ravens do dominate the feature. The credits state that the film was suggested by Edgar Allan Poe's immortal classic, which is the same wording of the credit for Edgar Allan Poe in both *Murders in the Rue Morgue* (1932) and *The Black Cat* (1934). Presumably, the reference here is to the poem "The Raven." Under the opening credits, there is a statuette of the black bird.

When the movie first turns to Dr. Vollin, played by Bela Lugosi, the initial image is a shadow of the raven statuette, with Vollin reciting some lines of "The Raven" to a representative from a museum who is visiting his house to discuss Vollin's Poe collection. Vollin then tells his guest that the raven is his "talisman" which, given Lugosi's purported difficulty with the English language, must have seemed like a strange word to him, as it would be to most viewers, including your author, who have to look the word up in the dictionary to discern its meaning. Vollin appears to be saying that the raven is his lucky charm, which is surprising to the representative of the museum since he understands the raven to be a symbol of death.

The raven references continue thereafter. When Jean Thatcher dances a special dance onstage for Vollin, which is titled "The Spirit of Poe," the dance is performed while some lines of "The Raven" are read to the audience. The reading is primarily from the second stanza of the poem and it ends with the language, "For the rare and radiant maiden whom the angels name Lenore." While it is not quite clear, Jean is probably dancing the part of Lenore in the stage production. This interpretation is supported a bit by the fact that when Vollin comes backstage to congratulate Jean, he kisses her on the hand, looks her in the eyes and says, "Whom the angels call Lenore," once again implying, at least to Vollin, that Jean is the radiant and lost Lenore. Interestingly enough, Vollin's statement is a slight misquote of Poe's poem, calling into question Vollin's bona fides as a Poe expert.

On the night of Vollin's revenge, with all of the house guests gathered at his house, Jean asks Vollin for his interpretation of the poem "The Raven." Vollin explains that Poe had something great in him but he then fell in love with Lenore. Thereafter someone took Lenore away from him, and when a man of genius is denied his great love, he goes mad, causing him torture, and so he decides to torture those who torture him.

Now, one of the strengths of Poe's works is that they are often subject to multiple interpretations, many of which can be valid. No one, however, in the 90 years since "The Raven" had been published by 1935, ever reached the interpretation that Vollin apparently had, once again calling into question Vollin's bona fides as a Poe aficionado. Of course, Vollin may have misinterpreted Jean's request about "The Raven" and thought she was asking for an explanation of the plot of the film in which they were then appearing, also titled *The Raven*. That is the only explanation that makes sense.

From this point forward, the motif of the raven disappears from the film and the viewer is left with the specious opinion by Vollin that Poe's writings describe many torture devices. Obviously, when Judge Thatcher is locked on a bench with a swinging pendulum slowly dropping down on him, that device is taken from "The Pit and the Pendulum," an 1842 story of Poe's about a prisoner who is subjected to several torture devices, including a swinging pendulum sword. The closing walls used in *The Raven* also come from "The Pit and the Pendulum," although the walls in the story are red hot. The other tortures in Vollin's basement, shown for an instant and never mentioned again, are a stretching rack, a small wooden cage and some chains with weighted balls. None of these appear to come from Poe's short stories. Apparently Vollin forgot to recreate other tortures from Poe's works, such as a person being buried alive (from several stories, including "Premature Burial," published in 1844) and walling a man who is still alive in a place where no one can find him ("The Cask of Amontillado," first published in 1846). However, Vollin's impression that Poe's works rely heavily on torture devices is seriously misplaced.

If *The Raven* falls short on its use of Edgar Allan Poe, it makes up for it by its entertaining screenplay and first class production. The film plays more like a serial than a horror film, as swinging pendulums and closing walls have provided many exciting cliffhangers for many serials over many years. The makeup for Bateman is excellent and somewhat inventive. The night of revenge set on a dark and stormy night sets just the right mood for what has become, by the last half hour of the film, an old dark house mystery.

Director Louis Friedlander has been criticized for his work in this film, but that is usually a result of comparisons with Edgar Ulmer's work in *The Black Cat* (1934), a contest few directors could win. Friedlander is more than competent in *The Raven*, as demonstrated by the scene in which Bateman first sees his disfigured face in a series of mirrors, arranged on a curve, with Bateman shooting out the glass of each in turn, as if to destroy the image that he sees in them. It is an unforgettable moment. There are also varied and effective shots of the pendulum as it drops (although the blade seems kind of puny) and a good use of close-ups, particularly of Lugosi and Karloff. Friedlander does a nice job in this film.

The real joy of *The Raven* is the performance of Bela Lugosi, in his last major film role in the initial horror film cycle of the 1930s. In the prior film *The Black Cat*, Lugosi was still strikingly handsome, even though he was over 50 years of age. In *The Raven*, however, Lugosi is more creepy than handsome, not

Also in *The Raven* (1935), Dr. Vollin (Bela Lugosi) forces Jean Thatcher (Irene Ware) and Jerry Halden (Lester Matthews) into a room with closing walls, one of Vollin's many torture devices.

just in his maniacal fascination with Poe but also in his advances to the much younger Jean Thatcher. Lugosi's screen persona adds to the disturbing nature of these scenes. Lugosi, of course, had a tendency to overact in his horror films, but here that propensity works splendidly, as Vollin gets crazier and crazier over the length of the film. Could any other actor have delivered the line, "Poe, you are avenged," and have it make at least a little bit of sense?

The Raven is not art; it is not even Edgar Allan Poe. It is, however, one of the most fun horror films of the early 1930s, so long as the viewer is not expecting any relationship between the film and Poe's most famous poem.

Other Adaptations

In 1963, as part of his Edgar Allan Poe cycle, Roger Corman produced and directed another film entitled *The Raven*. When the movie commences, it appears that it will be a fairly close adaptation of Poe's poem, with Erasmus Craven pining for his deceased wife, Lenore, and a raven tapping and rapping at the door and a window. Craven lets the raven in but at that point, the similarity between the film and the poem ends. In response to a question from Craven about Lenore, the raven responds in a voice that sounds suspiciously similar to Peter Lorre's and with a vocabulary substantially greater than "Nevermore." The film is more of a comedy than a horror film, and it has aged greatly since it was first released.

CHAPTER 15

The Hands of Orlac
by Maurice Renard

Although the 1930s and 1940s were the glory days of the Universal horror film, surprisingly few of the studio's horror films were adaptations of written works. After *Dracula* (1931), *Frankenstein* (1932) and *The Invisible Man* (1933), ten years went by before Universal adapted another work of horror literature to the screen, namely, *Phantom of the Opera* (1943). (Universal's alleged adaptations of Poe short stories in the early 1930s are best overlooked for purposes of this discussion.)

MGM is not well-known for its horror films during the first two decades of the sound era, but, in fact, it produced several, all of which were based on works of literature. (A possible exception is *Mark of the Vampire* [1935], but by the end of the film, it becomes quite clear that *Mark of the Vampire* is not really a horror film.) *Freaks* (1932), *Dr. Jekyll and Mr. Hyde* (1932 and 1941), *The Devil-Doll* (1936) and *The Picture of Dorian Gray* (1945), produced at MGM during the classic era, are all horror films based on works of literature. Another is *Mad Love* (1935), considered to be the best of the many adaptations of *The Hands of Orlac* by Maurice Renard.

Background

Maurice Renard was born in Châlons-en-Champagne, France, in 1875. In his teens, after reading works by Edgar Allan Poe, Renard became interested in literature and particularly works about the supernatural. He eventually wrote more than 18 novels and over 100 short stories in a variety of genres, but to the extent he is remembered today, it is for his science fiction writings. Indeed, according to the *St James Guide to Science Fiction Writers*, Renard is considered a pioneer of French science fiction and one of the most important science fiction writers of the period from 1910 through 1930. Renard died in 1939.

As an aside, Dr. Cerral, the famous surgeon who performs the hand transplant surgery on Stephen Orlac in the novel, was inspired by Dr. Alexis Carrel, a real French surgeon who experimented with biological transplants and grafting procedures. Carrel won the Nobel Prize in 1912 in the category of Physiology or Medicine.

The Literature

Most horror film fans will be familiar with the general plot of *The Hands of Orlac* from its many film adaptations. Stephen Orlac, a famous French pianist, is severely injured in a train collision just outside Paris. Orlac has serious wounds to his head, legs, arms and hands. He is operated on by the noted surgeon, Professor Cerral, and while the operation is a success, the question remains—will Orlac ever be able to play the piano again?

The mystery and horror in the novel come from the fact that during the operation, Cerral grafted the hands of Vasseur, a murderer who was guillotined for his crimes, onto Orlac's arm. Over the course of the novel, there are two murders that are investigated, the second one being that of Stephen's father, and because of the operation, Orlac is worried that he may be the killer in both crimes. In several surprise twists at the end of the tale, the actual murderer of Orlac's father is discovered and then it turns out that Vasseur was inno-

Peter Lorre, in one of his most recognizable roles, plays the obsessive Dr. Gogol, in *Mad Love* (1935).

cent of his crimes, so that Orlac does not actually have the hands of a murderer attached to his body.

That short synopsis of *The Hands of Orlac* would seem to indicate that the novel is quite exciting, but, in fact, it is boring in the extreme. Instead of focusing on the new hands of Stephen Orlac and whether they are affecting his mind and character, the main plot of the novel takes a back seat to the random acts of horror and the supernatural, such as the unsubstantiated premonition of danger at the train station by Stephen's wife, Rosine, and a bloody knife with an × on it mysteriously appearing on the doors of two apartments. As a result, not much happens in the first part of the novel, even though it is over 150 pages long.

Another problem with *The Hands of Orlac* is that while it is not written in the first person, it is primarily written from the perspective of Rosine's, with the reader experiencing the inner thoughts of Rosine's over and over again. She is concerned about her husband's health, his mental state, their finances, phantoms and unsubstantiated problems her husband may have been experiencing before the train accident. Maurice Renard describes Rosine as beautiful and while that may be true, she is also incredibly boring, resulting in the novel being filled with pages and pages of nothing happening.

Then there is an abrupt switch of point of view later in the novel, with the story no longer being narrated from the perspective of Rosine's, but instead, being written in the first person by M. Gaston Breteuil, a court reporter who happens on the scene of the first murder. This is a sloppy style of writing, as if Renard regretted writing the story from Rosine's perspective and decided to create a new character to pick up the tale. (A similar switch in narrator also occurs near the end of *The Phantom of the Opera*, by Gaston Leroux, and it is not wholly successful there, either.)

Later, when Stephen's father, Edourd Orlac, is found murdered with a knife with an × on it protruding from the body, Inspector Cointre of the Paris police takes over the two murder investigations. At that point, *The Hands of Orlac* becomes a classic detective story, with Cointre the Sherlock Holmes character and Breteuil the Dr. Watson figure. That is fitting because, in a sudden transformation, the story becomes a mystery, not a tale of horror or science fiction, with the murders finally solved and Orlac allowed to have a happy ending from his predicament.

The Hands of Orlac really picks up in the last 30 pages, with twists and turns similar to those of the best detective stories. Unfortunately, it is a long time coming and one suspects that many readers of *The Hands of Orlac* will never quite make it to the end. And, while it is an interesting mystery, it still contains the ultimate cheat resolution for horror fans—that everything that went before has a rational explanation.

The Hands of Orlac is a difficult book to locate, as it had a limited publication in the United States and was never re-printed in paperback. Frankly, given its boring nature, lack of a significant plot and cheat ending, the book is not worth the effort to find. In addition, the novel is a challenge for those who desire to adapt it to the screen. Should they turn the movie into a straight horror film of a man turned into a killer when he receives a transplant of a murderer's hands, or should the story be treated as one of the rational, as in the Maurice Renard original? For avid horror film fans, the choice is obvious. Unfortunately, all of the filmmakers, with one minor exception, have chosen the opposite approach.

The Film

Mad Love (1935)

Maurice Renard's novel was first adapted to the cinema in an Austrian silent film, *The Hands of Orlac/Orlacs Hände* (1924), which starred Conrad Veidt as Stephen Orlac and was directed by Robert Wiene. While the 1924 film shows some aspects of German Expressionism, the film is really a mystery, not a horror film.

Mad Love, the first sound adaptation of *The Hands of Orlac,* was released in 1935. It is a clever reworking of the plot of *The Hands of Orlac,* with the emphasis now placed on the doctor who does the hand transplant surgery, rather than on the famous pianist, Stephen Orlac, or his wife, Yvonne (using the first name from the 1924 film). The surgeon is Dr. Gogol, a physician with incredible skills but one who is the ultimate mad doctor. Gogol is sexually frustrated, a condition that deteriorates once he learns that Yvonne Orlac, the beautiful young theater star with whom he is obsessed, is married. When Yvonne's husband is severely injured in a train accident, Gogol performs transplant surgery and gives Orlac the hands of a recently executed murderer. Despite his success as a surgeon, Gogol is mad and after the operation on Orlac, Gogol's downward spiral of madness accelerates. In a crazed attempt to win Yvonne's affections, Gogol decides to eliminate Orlac by killing his father and then by trying to convince both the police and Orlac that Orlac is the killer. When that scheme fails, Gogol attempts to strangle Yvonne, who is saved at the last instance by a knife thrown by Stephen Orlac into the back of Gogol.

Mad Love is the best film version of Maurice Renard's novel. There are many reasons for this but one of the most important is that there is a bit of the unreal or supernatural to the tale. The hands that Orlac receives are those of the murderer, Rollo, who was an expert in knife throwing. After the operation by Dr. Gogol, while Orlac can no longer play the piano with any expertise, he suddenly becomes a natural knife thrower, in the style of Rollo, for no realistic medical reason. No attempt is made to provide a rational explanation for this unexpected phenomenon, making *Mad Love* into a true tale of the fantastic, unlike Renard's novel or its other film adaptations.

When Dr. Gogol observes Orlac's newfound knife throwing ability and the effect it is having on Orlac's psyche, Gogol decides to use that information to drive Orlac completely mad. While in the Renard novel, it is the con man, Eusebio Nera, who tries to convince Orlac that Orlac has the hands of the murderer, in *Mad Love*, it is a disguised Dr. Gogol who undertakes that part, making the film version at least a little more realistic, if that is at all possible in this crazy tale. On the other hand, Orlac's own descent into madness after the operation and his piano playing difficulties arise quite suddenly in *Mad Love*; it is given much more attention in both the novel and the silent film version. However, given that Orlac's mental deterioration is such an unconvincing storyline in both the book and its many film versions, *Mad Love* deals with it in the best way possible, by emphasizing Gogol's insanity and not that of Orlac's.

Dr. Gogol is the maddest of mad doctors. He enjoys watching guillotinings, attends Yvonne's stage performances in a horror show for 47 consecutive nights, and takes a life-size wax figurine of Yvonne from the show to his home, where he plays the organ for it and confides his secrets to it on several occasions. Gogol seems to confuse the waxwork with Galatea of Greek mythology, a carved statue that came to life. Adding some spice to a mid–1930s film, there is a rare sexual component to the tale, as Dr. Gogol has a perverse attraction to Yvonne, demonstrated at the theater when Gogol grabs Yvonne and violently kisses her in front of others, and later by his attraction to her wax statue and his desire at the end of the film to kill her since she is the one he loves. *Mad Love* was made at a time in Hollywood when these sexual issues could not be fully developed, but they provide an important and effective subtext to the main story line of the movie.

Mad Love was directed by Karl Freund, who directed only a few other films during his long career in the cinema. One of those films was *The Mummy* (1932), his only other horror film and along with *Mad Love*, another classic of the genre. Freund began work in silent films in Germany as a cameraman, including working on many Expressionist films such as *The Golem* (1920). Freund's experience in silent films is demonstrated in sequences in *Mad Love* without dialogue, such as the Orlac's dreams after Stephen's operation and a montage illustrating the treatments for Stephen's hands and the large expenses that accrue as a result thereof. Freund's background in cinematography and lighting is displayed in several scenes in the movie, such as, for example, the moment when half of Lorre's face is shown in shadow as he watches Yvonne perform on stage, presaging

Gogol's split personality, or when Gogol's face is shown in extreme close-up when he first expresses his love to Yvonne, with the audience experiencing the same discomfort that Yvonne feels. German Expressionism is evident in the high arched ceilings in Gogol's operating facilities, the non-rectangular door and curved banister in the shop of Orlac's father, and Gogol appearing in several differently shaped mirrors wearing different clothes and talking to himself, as he finally loses it all after Yvonne calls him a liar and a hypocrite.

Even with all of the skilled craftsmen working behind the camera, including Freund and the great cinematographer, Gregg Toland, soon to be known for his work on *Citizen Kane* (1941), *Mad Love* would never have worked without an excellent performance in the role of Dr. Gogol, and Peter Lorre, in his first American film role, more than rises to the occasion. With his shaved head and nasal, lisping voice, Gogol, in Lorre's hands, is the epitome of the sinister, a mad doctor who becomes madder and madder as the film goes on, until he is a raving maniac at the end.

Lorre is particularly effective in the scene in which he meets with Orlac and pretends to be the murderer, Rollo. The scene is shot primarily from behind Gogol as he whispers his story to Orlac. Suddenly, Gogol pulls open his coat and there is a shot of the front of Gogol, who is wearing the contraption that presumably keeps his guillotined head onto his body. The scene finishes with the maniacal laugh of Gogol's. While *Mad Love* is filled with many creepy moments, including the costumes of the cashier and the ushers at *Le Théatre des Horreurs* at the beginning of the film, the stage play of torture performed by Yvonne in that theater and the guillo-

Gogol (Peter Lorre) masquerades as Rollo, the knife thrower, whose hands were transplanted onto Stephen Orlac's body and whose neck was severed from his body when he was guillotined, in *Mad Love* (1935).

tining of Rollo, nothing tops this scene which is particularly effective, partly because of the staging and lighting, but primarily because of Peter Lorre's performance, which is mostly voice and not much else.

This scene could have been the climax of the film, with the rest of the movie becoming a letdown but, instead, the excitement continues, with Orlac arrested, Yvonne trapped in Gogol's apartment and forced to pretend that she is the wax figurine that Gogol worships, and then Gogol attempting to strangle Yvonne as an expression of his love. The name of the film, *Mad Love*, is actually appropriate, as it describes Gogol's perverted attitude to Yvonne. Nevertheless, it is fitting that Gogol is actually killed by the hands of Orlac, which relates back to the title of Renard's novel. *Mad Love* realizes the potential that Maurice Renard's novel had, turning a third-rate novel into a first class horror film, considered by many to be a classic of the cinema of horror.

Other Adaptations

There have been at least two more other official, or, perhaps, unofficial screen adaptations of the novel. *The Hands of Orlac* (1960) is a French-English production which stars Mel Ferrer as Stephen Orlac and features Christopher Lee in an important supporting role. The film exhausts most of Maurice Renard's plot in its first 10 minutes and then goes off on a story line that has little to do with the transplanted hands of a murderer. *The Hands of Orlac* was justifiably panned wherever it played.

Another remake is *Hands of a Stranger*, an American movie made in 1962. Maurice Renard does not receive any mention in the credits and all of the characters' names have been changed, perhaps to avoid claims of copyright infringement. The film is a talkathon, with not much happening throughout.

Chapter 16

Burn Witch Burn! by Abraham Merritt

Sometimes horror comes from monsters or ghosts or science fiction experiments gone awry. Other times it comes from everyday creatures, such as birds or cats or flies. Upon occasion the horror arises in babies or young children. And once in a while, it comes from everyday objects, such as pieces of paper, paintings or playing cards. In *Burn Witch Burn!*, the horror comes from some unexpected, yet terrifying everyday objects—children's dolls. And, because dolls are such commonplace yet beloved items, the horror they generate can be especially disturbing.

Background

Abraham Merritt, who was born in Beverly, New Jersey, in 1884, wrote science fiction and fantasy stories as a sideline to his main career as a journalist. Some of his novels concerned aliens, lost races, beautiful princesses, underground caverns, ancient ray machines and fantasy worlds.

Burn Witch Burn! was a little different than Merritt's other works, since it was written partially as a mystery and partially as a tale of witchcraft. The novel was published in 1933, with the author designated only as "A. Merritt." Merritt wrote a sequel of sorts, *Creep, Shadow!*, published in 1934, but thereafter Merritt completed only one more novel prior to his death in 1943 at the age of 59.

The Literature

In its early stages, *Burn Witch Burn!* is a straightforward medical mystery, as Dr. Lowell (his first name is never given) tries to discover why Thomas Peters, the right hand man to Julian Ricori, a notorious gangster chieftain, dies abruptly in a hospital, with rigor mortis immediately settling into his body and then disappearing almost as quickly as it appears, an unusual medical phenomenon. Lowell writes letters to other physicians in the area to see if they had ever encountered similar cases. He receives a number of responses, including those involving the similar deaths of a spinster, an acrobat, a banker and a trapeze artist. Yet, Lowell cannot discern any obvious ties between all of the victims, until Ricori notices that all of the victims had interactions with children. That leads to the dolls that each of those children was given as presents and then to the strange doll store of Madame Mandilip.

It seems that Madame Mandilip has created dolls that can walk and kill, the latter accomplished with a quick dagger thrust into the head of the victim. After a killing, Mandalip creates new killer dolls with the face and spirit of the last victim, continuing the killing spree. In the end, Lowell, Ricori and another decide to directly attack the doll maker at her shop. At the point that Mandilip is concentrating on her human foes, a doll in the image of Nurse Walters, the only one that seems to be able to thwart Mandilip's will, gathers the strength to repeatedly thrust a dagger through the doll maker's throat, twisting it savagely into Mandilip's body. As the dolls disintegrate and catch on fire, Mandilip's body is trapped in the flames. Ricori shouts, exultantly, "Burn witch burn!" (Chapter 17, "Burn Witch Burn!").

While some have criticized Abraham Merritt's writing style in his other works of fantasy, his writing in *Burn Witch Burn!* is quite effective. His descriptions of the dolls as alive, with the malicious expressions on their faces, their human-like mannerisms and the way in which they attack are all stunning and disturbing. Merritt uses the oppressive and strange silence before some of the attacks to add to the horror of his tale. The use of the witch's ladder (a knotted cord of woman's hair) hidden on a victim as a marker for the dolls to attack and the flute-like musical sounds to signal the dolls to return to their master are unnerving.

In one of the most striking scenes in the novel, Lowell decides to enter Madame Mandilip's shop on his own, on the ruse of buying a beautiful doll for a grandchild. There he loses the battle of wills with Mandilip, coming under her deep hypnotic influence. The doll shop then seems to turn into an immense chamber, filled with mellow light, ancient tapestries, carved screens and a halfglobe of a mirror of the purest water reflecting the images of the carvings around its frame. Lowell also sees the doll made in the image of Nurse Walters, which seems so alive that it is "like seeing the girl herself through a diminishing glass" (Chapter 13, "Madame Mandilip"). Since the Walters doll has been disobedient, Mandilip has nailed the doll into a cabinet in a strange crucifixion tableau.

Thereafter, in a striking scene, four dolls come to attack Ricori. Lowell actually observes a doll creeping over a window sill, sliding head first into the room and performing a double somersault. It is the doll of the circus acrobat that Lowell learned of early in the tale. The next to arrive are the banker, the spinster and the other acrobat, each holding the dagger pins of death. The incident ends with the death of Dr. Braile, an associate of Lowell's, from a dagger thrust and a falling chandelier.

The novel is weakest when Lowell takes too long to accept the fact that the supernatural is involved, resulting in several talky passages in which Lowell tries to rationalize the facts or hold debates with others. In the real world, it might take forever to convince a doctor that the supernatural is genuine. In the literature and cinema of horror, skeptics must be convinced quickly or the tale can become boring. Here, Dr. Lowell is a character in a book titled *Burn Witch Burn!* which was written by a noted author of fantasy fiction. The good physician should have accepted the validity of the supernatural much earlier in the novel, just as most characters do, for example, in vampire movies.

No explanation is ever given as to why Mandilip does what she does or kills innocent people who have done her no harm. It may simply be that she is a witch and that is what witches do. There is also no explanation as to why Nurse Walters is the only one who can stand up to Mandilip's will, at least after she is turned into a doll. Perhaps the explanation is that since the doll has Walters' soul, it also has her exceptionally strong will. After the death of Mandilip, there is a superfluous last chapter of the book, which tries to give a scientific and historical explanation of all that has gone before. Since that chapter comes after the rousing climax to the tale and the surprise death of Mandilip, most readers probably just skim over the words of that extra chapter, having already received their fill of horror with the burning death of the witch.

Those criticisms are nitpicks, at most. Abraham Merritt has woven a remarkable tale of witchcraft and horror by employing commonplace items as Mandilip's instruments of evil. What a disturbing concept—dolls that come to life and kill. Can any reader of *Burn Witch Burn!* ever look at a doll again, as cute and lovable as it may be, and not have at least a little suspicion and at least a slight feeling of dread?

The Films

The Devil-Doll (1936)

Abraham Merritt's novel of an evil doll maker seemed a natural for adaptation to the cinema and just three years after its publication, *The Devil-Doll* was released by MGM. The credits specifically state the film was based on the novel *Burn Witch Burn!* by Abraham Merritt but the cast list does not disclose any characters in common with the book. When the film opens with two prisoners escaping from Devil's Island, it is clear that the storyline of the film will have little in common with that of the novel.

The two escapees are Paul Lavond, an innocent man wrongfully imprisoned for 17 years for embezzling from his own bank and killing a night watchman, and Marcel, an old and perhaps mad scientist, whose reason for imprisonment is not disclosed. The two arrive at the home of Malita, Marcel's wife, and Malita and Marcel immediately pick up their old hobby of reducing animals to doll-like size, on the specious theory that if all humans were reduced to a similar size, the food supply of the Earth would never run out. Apparently the two are early environmentalists. However, Marcel's experiments have not been totally successful because with their reduction in size, the animals lose all independent thought and can be controlled by the will of the scientists. When the same result occurs with a young servant girl, Lavond decides, after Marcel's sudden death, to use the dolls to wreak his revenge on the three bankers who had framed him for the crimes that had wrongfully sent him to prison.

Lavond's plans meet with success. He transforms one of the bankers, Radin, into a tiny doll who can then be used for killing; he uses a different doll to permanently paralyze the second banker. As the Radin doll is just about to attack Charles Matin, the third banker, Matin confesses, clearing Lavond of all wrongdoing. However, because of all that he has done, Lavond must still flee Paris, never telling his daughter who he really is.

There is little of *Burn Witch Burn!* in *The Devil-Doll*. When Lavond goes undercover in Paris, he pretends to be an old woman who operates a doll shop under the name of Madame Mandilip. At least two of the dolls in the doll shop come to life and attack and try to kill with small daggers. When banker Emil Coulvet is paralyzed by one of the dolls, the newspaper reports a "look of constant terror in Monsieur Coulvet's expression," which is similar to the expression on Peters' face as described at the beginning of the novel. Those are just about the only elements from the novel that make their way into the film. However, that expression on Coulvet's face is never really shown to the viewer, because no matter how actor Robert Greig could have contorted his face, it could never have equaled the description of a face of terror contained in the novel or in the newspaper account read in the film.

Part of the problem with *The Devil-Doll* is that it was produced at MGM instead of, say, Universal. As a result, the filmmakers treat the film almost purely as a mystery, rather than a horror story. While evading the police, Lavond is intent on clearing his name and obtaining revenge for his false imprisonment.

Lionel Barrymore in a publicity photograph for *The Devil-Doll* (1936), playing Devil's Island escapee Paul Lavond, who is here disguised as Madame Mandilip, the owner of a doll shop that produces killer dolls, such as the ones shown.

The police almost catch him by accident on a few occasions, such as when a policeman is in Mandilip's shop where some stolen jewels are out in the open. This is standard fare for mystery movies and because much of the film focuses on those elements, the story of the dolls sometimes seems superfluous.

Most of the rest of the tale involves Lavond's interactions with his elderly mother, who always thought he was innocent, and with his young daughter, who has been ashamed of him and humiliated by him throughout her life. At the end, Lavond, without revealing his true identity, provides his daughter with enough closure concerning her feelings about her father that she can renew her life and marry the young French businessman with whom she is in love. When *The Devil-Doll* is not a mystery, it is a heartwarming story of family relationships.

That is not to say that there are no horror elements to the story. In fact, the few scenes of horror in the film work quite effectively. Mandilip sells the doll of a female dancer with a beret to Madame Coulvet, who gives it to her daughter. That night, Lavond uses his mental powers to awaken the doll from a distance. Then, in an almost silent sequence (with the exception of Franz Waxman's effective score), the doll squirms out of the grip of the young child, climbs on to Madame Coulvet's desk, steals two strings of Madame's jewelry and drops them off a balcony into a basket carried by Lavond, climbs onto the banker's bed, stabs him with the paralyzing dagger and makes her escape. Later, while the police are surrounding the home of the third banker, Charles Matin, the killer doll of the first banker, Victor Radin, stealthily enters the Matin residence and makes his way upstairs. As the living doll is about to stab Matin, Matin confesses.

Both of these sequences are fascinating; they are the highlights of the film. Their effectiveness is diminished somewhat, though, by the special effects employed. It is painfully obvious that the dolls are played by real human actors, with their images reduced and then superimposed on the screen with the full sized actors. It can be difficult for the viewer to suspend disbelief when the effects are so artificial. (The effects work substantially better when the doll actors walk among sets of enlarged props, such as chairs and toy blocks.) In the novel, each walking doll was really a doll, made in the likeness of a human and magically imbued with the soul of that human. A walking doll is much more disturbing than a walking person, particularly a person substantially reduced in size.

The motivations of Marcel's wife, Malita, are somewhat confusing. The experiments of Marcel and Malita were intended for the betterment of mankind, however misdirected their theories might have been. Why then does Malita throw in with Lavond's scheme of killing or paralyzing people? Why does she suddenly turn on him at the end? The answer to that last question is, of course, to provide a method of destroying Malita and all of the dolls, ridding Paris of a mad scientist and some deadly creatures, a necessary ending for horror films of the era. Monsters and their makers must be destroyed. The ending does hearken back to the ending of the novel though, as in the novel, Madame Mandilip and all of her deadly dolls are also destroyed in a deadly inferno.

Reading *Burn Witch Burn!* before viewing *The Devil-Doll* illustrates one of the perils inherent in that approach to classic horror film viewing. *Burn Witch Burn!* is a stunning novel of horror, one that appears to be an excellent candidate for adaptation to the cinema of horror. *The Devil-Doll* is not truly an adaptation of Merritt's novel, making the film disappointing to a reader of the novel.

Viewed independently, however, *The Devil-Doll* is a very likable little horror film. There is nothing inherently wrong with combining mystery elements and a tale of interpersonal relationships with a horror film and it is a nice contrast to the approach usually taken by the Universal horror films of the era. The mystery and personal elements go well with the story of the dolls. Even for someone who has a preconceived notion as to how *Burn Witch Burn!* should have been adapted into a film, *The Devil-Doll* is an entertaining viewing experience.

Curse of the Doll People/Muñecos infernales (1961)

Twenty-five years later, *Burn Witch Burn!* was adapted into a horror film made in Mexico, titled *Muñecos infernales*, which literally translates to "Hellish Dolls," an appropriate title, indeed. The film was regularly seen in a dubbed version on American television in the 1960s and 1970s, usually under the title, *Curse of the Doll People*, although it was also shown under the title *Devil Doll Men*. Abraham Merritt and his novel did not receive any mention in the credits to the Mexican film even though the film is clearly inspired by, if not an actual adaptation of, *Burn Witch Burn!*

This film version corrects one of the problems with the Merritt novel. In the novel, there is no explanation given as to why Madame Mandilip is killing people and then turning them into dolls. In *Curse of the Doll People*, the explanation is given up front, at a dinner party in which Karina, a doctor with an interest in voodoo and cults, is told a story about the adventures of four archaeologists in Haiti who were cursed by the high priest of the voodoo cult after they stole a sacred idol from his temple. As soon as Karina hears the story, she explains to the four that, in addition to the high priest setting out to retrieve the stolen idol, it is likely that he will attempt to kill all of the adventurers and their families, as revenge for the desecration of the sacred temple.

Karina knows of what she speaks. The means of the voodoo priest's revenge are the hellish dolls. When they are in boxes or are carried around, they seem just like ordinary dolls, although perhaps a little bit larger than usual. However, when they walk around on their own, climb on furniture and, most importantly, use a long needle to murder their victims with a quick thrust through the neck or the heart, it is clear that these are no ordinary child's playthings. Once a murder is accomplished, the voodoo priest is able to track the soul of the dead person and plant it into a previously prepared new doll that has the face of the victim. Thus, each victim in turn becomes a new murderer, through his or her spirit in the new doll, as controlled by the witch doctor.

While the back-story of *Curse of the Doll People* involving the theft of the idol from the voodoo temple is original to the film, the movie takes substantial material, large and small, from Abraham Merritt's novel. One of the intended victims, Molinar, appears to be a crime boss. He has a number of assistants who can both protect him and search for the doll maker. Molinar is based on the character of Julian Ricori from the novel. In fact, the opening scene from the novel, where Ricori brings one of his men to the hospital because of both a sudden illness at dinner and the strange, frightened expression on his face, is repeated in the film almost exactly as it occurs in the novel.

Much like *Burn Witch Burn!*, a braided coil of human hair, the witch's ladder (called the sorcerer's ladder in the film), is used to mark the intended victims for the dolls. It also foreshadows the death of an upcoming victim. The sound

Luis (Jorge Mondragón) shows an idol that he has stolen from a sacred temple in Haiti to Karina (Elvira Quintana) and Dr. Amando Valdés (Ramón Gay) in *Curse of the Doll People* (1961). Karina warns about the curse attached to the idol.

of a flute brings the dolls back after the completion of their murderous tasks. After death, some of the victim's hands and faces strain and clench, similar to the quick onset and dissipation of rigor mortis in the victims in Merritt's novel. Also, much like Dr. Lowell in the novel, Karina visits the doll shop of the high priest on her own, challenging the priest at great risk to herself and thereby coming under the hypnotic influence of the priest.

Karina's trip to the house of the voodoo priest in the film, while similar to Dr. Lowell's visit to the doll shop of Madame Mandilip's in the novel, both of which seem brave but incredibly foolish, does highlight an important difference between the film and the book. Karina is more than the Dr. Van Helsing of the story; she is the heroine of the film— beautiful, educated, courageous and wise. The other male characters generally follow her lead. Even by 1961, it was rare for a woman to be the person that brings about the destruction of a movie monster. In this case, Karina accomplishes the task almost single-handedly. (Another rare example of a female character taking down an unearthly creature occurs in *Nosferatu* [1922].) The change in the protagonist in the metamorphosis of Merritt's novel from literature into film makes *Curse of the Doll People* somewhat unique in the cinema of horror, even more than 50 years after its original release.

Curse of the Doll People is a low budget film, as all of the Mexican horror films from that era seem to be. This is particularly apparent near the opening of the film, when the story of the stealing of the idol and the curse of the voodoo priest is related by Luis, one of the thieves. As eloquently as Luis tells the story, the incident would have been far more effective if shown on screen. It could have been the highlight of the film. In most other ways, however, the low budget of the film is an asset, not a detriment, as was often the case with horror films or B-crime movies. For example, by 1961, most horror films were produced in color. *Curse of the Doll People* is in black and white, which adds to the haunting nature of the subject material and also allows contrasting shadows and light to contribute to the mood of the film.

Without a large budget, the special effects and miniatures of *The Devil-Doll* (1936) and other films such as *Dr. Cyclops* (1940) could not be employed. Instead, the murderous dolls appear to be played by little people or children, wearing the fright masks of a prior victim, eerily similar to the faces of the actors who played the victims. This technique is surprisingly effective, with the immobile faces of the dolls contrasting with the dolls' easy mobility when they walk and attack. It is much easier for the viewer to buy into the concept of murderous dolls when they are not an obvious creation of special effects, as they were in *The Devil-Doll*. In this instant, the not-so-special effects of this Mexican film are far more effective than the sometimes very special effects of *The Devil-Doll*.

When one of the walking dolls is run over by a car, it is taken to the hospital, leading to a kind of autopsy. The simple effect here is to substitute an actual doll for the actor under the mask, with the doll having the same visage as the actor's mask. In a shiver-inducing moment, Karina and Armando decide to cut open the doll's body. First Karina slices off the doll's head, "because it was necessary." Then, as cuts are made by the doctor in the body of the doll, the witch's ladder somehow magically rolls into the doll's head and the eyes of the head light up, ensnaring Karina in a hypnotic trance. She then throws the head on the ground, tramples it with her high heel and sets it on fire. The rest of the body then self-destructs in fire, leaving behind a pattern of dust in the shape of a little body. This is probably the most memorable scene in the film, with some simple special effects being far more ghastly than anything that could be done in a big budget film.

Other good scenes involve an attack by two dolls on Karina at a time when she cannot scream because of a prior hypnotic command of the voodoo priest, and the voodoo priest creating one of his murderous dolls, this time using a doll with the face of a recently killed hospital nurse and capturing the soul of that nurse in the doll. Then there is the interesting shot of the tall zombie collecting one of the dolls after a murder and the two walking down the street hand-in-hand. Much of *Curse of the Doll People* is original and clever.

The ending of the film, however, is disappointing. Karina, Armando, Molinar and a henchman decide to attack the high priest at his shop. He entrances all of them; their cause seems to be lost. Karina then pulls out a crucifix, somewhat immobilizing the priest and then the disobedient doll, previously pinned in the cabinet, stabs the priest. The temple of horror goes up in flames, killing the priest, his zombie and all of his dolls.

While the conclusion of *Curse of the Doll People* is surprisingly similar to the ending of Merritt's novel, the ending of the film seems rushed, particularly after the previously measured pace of the narrative. Also, the insertion of a crucifix into the story to thwart the high priest's use of voodoo, a plot point not contained in Merritt's novel, is jarring and unconvincing. This is not, after all, a tale of vampires but is one of voodoo and witchcraft. It would have been better to stick with Merritt's surprise ending, with the villain dispatched solely by one of his doll creations, rather than being dispatched by a *deus ex machina*.

Disappointing ending aside, *Curse of the Doll People* is still one of the best of the Mexican horror films. One of the reasons for the film's enduring success may be that while most of the Mexican horror films employed original scripts, Curse *of the Doll People* was based on a minor classic of horror literature, *Burn Witch Burn!*, by Abraham Merritt.

CHAPTER 17

"The Devil and Daniel Webster" by Stephen Vincent Benét

The storyline of a person selling his soul to the devil, or making a pact with Satan, is a familiar theme of literature, perhaps most famously employed in the story of Faust, a scholar who makes a bargain with the devil to obtain, in various versions of the tale, worldly pleasures, knowledge or power. The legend of Faust is so famous that a deal with the devil is sometimes referred to as a Faustian bargain.

While movies about the devil have become quite common in recent decades, they were virtually nonexistent in the 1930s and 1940s. With the possible exception of *The Picture of Dorian Gray* (1945), in which there is a hint of a Faustian bargain, the only Hollywood film of those decades that deals with the selling of a soul to the devil in a serious manner is *All That Money Can Buy* (1941), sometimes known as *The Devil and Daniel Webster*.

Background

Stephen Vincent Benét was born in Bethlehem, Pennsylvania, in 1898. A graduate of Yale University. Benét's literary output during his relatively short career included novels, short stories, screenplays, and radio broadcasts. "The Devil and Daniel Webster" was first published in the *Saturday Evening Post* in 1936. It was later adapted into a play, a film and an opera. (Benét contributed the libretto for the opera, which was composed by Douglas Moore.) Benét suffered a heart attack and died on March 13, 1943, at the age of 44.

Of course, Daniel Webster was a real person, born in Salisbury, New Hampshire, in 1782. He was admitted to the New Hampshire bar in 1805 and eventually became known as a constitutional scholar, arguing over 200 cases before the United States Supreme Court. He became a member of the House of Representatives, a senator from Massachusetts and a Secretary of State under three presidents. Webster passed away in 1852.

The Story

"The Devil and Daniel Webster" tells the tale of Jabez Stone, a down-on-his-luck New Hampshire farmer who one day, when his situation is at its lowest ebb, sells his soul to the devil in exchange for seven years of prosperity. Immediately thereafter, matters turn around for Jabez and he becomes a wealthy man. Unfortunately, though, there is that problem of the stranger turning up each year on the anniversary of their bargain to check on Jabez' situation. When Jabez' time is just about up, he seeks out the services of the famous attorney, Daniel Webster, who agrees to take his case. After some back and forth between Daniel Webster and the devil, it is decided that the case will be argued in court before an American jury of the quick or the dead. At first, the trial does not go well, as Webster loses every objection that he makes. But, when Webster stands up to give his closing argument, his silver-tongued oratory carries the day and the jury finds in favor of Jabez.

Although the story has a few horror elements, "The Devil and Daniel Webster" is not primarily a horror story, in part because of its light tone. The first few paragraphs of the narrative establish the plot as more of a tall tale or made-up yarn than a narrative that will curdle the reader's blood. The writing has a whimsical quality, particularly in the descriptions of Daniel Webster. Webster's oratory skills are purportedly so great that "when he stood up to speak, stars and stripes came right out of the sky, and once he spoke against a river and made it sink into the ground." Jabez sets out to meet Webster early one morning and Jabez finds that Webster is "up already, talking Latin to the farm hands and wrestling with the ram, Goliath, and trying out a new trotter and working up speeches to make against John C. Calhoun." It is hard to terrify a reader when the story has such a light tone.

Benét's story turns more serious when the devil finally meets Daniel Webster in the kitchen of Jabez' house. There the devil, known as Scratch for the evening, is characterized as clever but not necessarily evil, although he does trick Webster in allowing himself to choose the jury. Because of Scratch's jury selection of the dead, villains all, Webster has a difficult case. Seven of the jurors are identified by name and most are real historical figures. For example, Walter Butler was an English Loyalist during the American Revolution who led a raiding party on colonists in 1778 that became known as the Cherry Valley Massacre. Many women and children were killed during the attack. Simon Girty was another Loyalist, who in 1779, along with a large force of Indians, ambushed a number of American troops and according to Benét, whooped with the Indians as white men burned at the stake. The judge is Justice Hathorne, who in real life presided at many of the Salem witch trials and never repented of his acts as others did. When Scratch asks Webster if he is satisfied with the jury, Webster facetiously answers that though he is satisfied, he misses Benedict Arnold. Scratch advises Webster that Benedict Arnold is engaged in other business. (In the film version of the story, Benedict Arnold is one of the jurors.)

The setting of the trial and the grim tableau of the jurors and the judge constitute the primary horror element of the story. However, while the jury and the judge add an element of the grotesque to the story, Benét, because he is writing a homespun story, not a tale of the grotesque, emphasizes Webster's speech at the trial, not the jurors or the trial's setting. This goes to show that even though a plot about the devil incarnate, losing one's soul to Satan and a jury of the villainous dead would seem to be the stuff of a good horror story, emphasis, characterization and writing style are often the most important elements of good literature. Thus, even though "The Devil and Daniel Webster" is not a tale of horror, with a different emphasis, characterization and directorial style, it had the potential to be adapted into a good horror film.

The Film

All That Money Can Buy/The Devil and Daniel Webster (1941)

In the first and last parts of the film, *All That Money Can Buy* is faithful to Benét's "The Devil and Daniel Webster," as Jabez Stone, a hardworking but unlucky farmer living in the state of New Hampshire, sells his soul to the devil in exchange for seven years of prosperity (all that money can buy) and is saved at the end of the film by the famous trial lawyer, Daniel Webster. However, there is a long story arc in the middle that is original to the movie.

In Benét's story, Jabez is always a good person, even after he becomes a wealthy man. The reader's sympathies are always with him. In the movie, however, there is a significant change in the story line in the middle of the film, as prosperity changes Jabez' personality and values. He becomes a loan shark himself, brings a mistress into his house, builds a large mansion to show off his wealth to the neighbors, starts to gamble and no longer goes to church. He also treats his wife Mary with contempt. While the change in demeanor and outlook of Jabez is clearly caused by the devil, it still makes Jabez a much less sympathetic figure than he was in the story with, perhaps, some viewers hoping he will receive his final comeuppance at the end, rather than Daniel Webster winning his case for him.

Stephen Vincent Benét was one of the screenwriters on *All That Money Can Buy*, so it is not surprising that some of the dialogue in the movie comes from the short story. When the Scratch of the cinema comments on the demise of Miser Stevens, another of his clients, he says, "In the midst of life, one really hates to close these long-standing accounts, but business is business." When Daniel Webster accuses the devil of not being an American, Scratch responds that he is, pointing out, "Am I not still spoken of in every church in New England? It's true the North claims me for a Southerner, and the South for a Northerner, but I am neither." In agreeing to challenge the devil in court, Webster says, "If two New Hampshire men aren't a match for the devil, we'd better give the country back to the Indians." These lines and others come almost verbatim from the story.

All That Money Can Buy is sparked by several outstanding performances. While the nominal leads are good, i.e., James Craig as Jabez and Anne Shirley as his wife Mary, the film is stolen by the feature players. Walter Huston is outstanding as Scratch, with his devil-may-care attitude as he plays the devil, impish in nature, bemused most of the time but always ready to turn serious when there is a soul that can be taken. Huston makes great use of his funny hat, his cigar, his wide mouth seemingly full of more teeth than can fit inside, his short laugh and his scrunched up face. Edward Arnold plays Daniel Webster. The fine character actor, whether being serious or humorous, fits the part perfectly, convincing the audience that Daniel Webster is, indeed, a figure larger than life. Jane Darwell plays the mother of Jabez,' always matronly and loving, but often disapproving of her son's conduct, even trying to convince Mary to become more aggressive in defending her marriage. Has Jane Darwell ever given a bad performance in a movie?

For horror film fans, there is one interesting bit of casting. Simone Simon, best known for playing the lead in *Cat People* (1942) and reprising the role in its sequel, *The Curse of the Cat People* (1944), plays the part of Belle, the devil's temptress and the woman who becomes Jabez' mistress. Simon is pretty and flirtatious, but it is her French accent and her foreignness in the farmlands of New Hampshire that gives a touch of menace to her character, making her very believable as the devious agent of the devil.

When lists are made of the Hollywood horror films of the 1940s, *All That Money Can Buy* is often overlooked, probably because its story is more folktale than horror story. The opening slide of the film, which is similar to the introduction in the short story, sets the initial tone of the film. It states, "It's a story

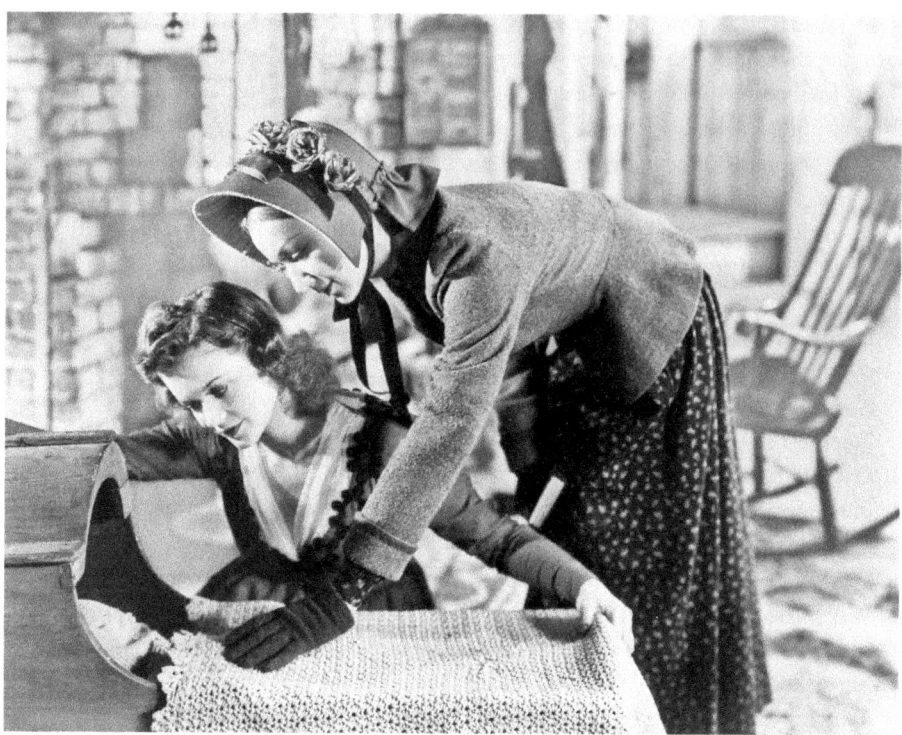

In this scene from *All That Money Can Buy* (1941), Mary Stone (Anne Shirley) looks at her baby in the carriage while the baby's nurse, Belle (Simone Simon), who is really the devil's temptress, gets between mother and baby.

they tell in the border country, where Massachusetts joins Vermont and New Hampshire. It happened, so they say, a long time ago." Also, the film addresses issues of wealth and poverty, patriotism and even collective action by the working class, in this case in the form of a grange for the farmers to protect themselves from loan sharks. These are hardly the usual themes of horror films. All of these elements disguise the fact that, unlike the short story, the film is, in essence, a tale of horror.

Some of the horror of the film comes from incidents in the feature that were not in the short story. There is the tree into which Scratch burns the date of April 7, 1847, the date seven years in the future when Jabez must relinquish his soul. Jabez is unable to nick the tree with either a knife or an axe, because a bargain with the devil is for all time. There are the friends of Belle from "over the mountain," ghostly figures that Jabez first sees with their faces pressed against his window, and who then come to his party to eat and dance. There is a ghostly dance with Belle and Miser Stevens, with Belle flinging Stevens around the dance floor like a whirling dervish, just before Stevens meets his death. There is the dance in the barn, with Scratch playing the fiddle at a violent speed, yelling, "Faster. Faster," as Jabez pursues Belle around the dance floor, never quite catching up with her. The end of *All That Money Can Buy* fits comfortably into the horror genre as, after the conclusion of the trial, a fire of spontaneous combustion burns down the new mansion of Jabez, forcing him to return to live in his small cottage. In horror films, fire is a destructive but often cleansing element, ridding the countryside of movie monsters and, in this case, the devil himself.

The horror of the story really comes to the fore in the trial sequence. The setting is the barn of Jabez', with hay on the floor and not much light. The jury consists of the dead—ghostlike figures as they march into the barn. Judge Hathorne is dressed all in black, with a shaved head and a monotone voice, seemingly more executioner than jurist. The score by Bernard Herrmann is spooky. Until Daniel Webster gives his stirring closing argument, there is little lighting in the scene and, at all times, the ethereal nature of the jury contrasts forebodingly with the real world setting of Jabez Stone's farm. Indeed, director William Dieterle infuses just about every scene in the film with a feeling of gloom, with either the entire scene shot in the almost dark or a shadow appearing on a wall or on a face or in the background, once again providing the film with an atmosphere of horror.

Stephen Vincent Benét's "The Devil and Daniel Webster" is not a horror story; its light style contains no atmosphere of horror and there are no images of horror, except in the persons of the jury and the judge. By contrast, folktale though it may be, *All That Money Can Buy* is, in its added plot elements, style and atmosphere, one of the most entertaining horror films of the 1940s.

Chapter 18

The Edge of Running Water
by William Sloane

With the arrival of the second horror film cycle in 1939, Columbia Pictures decided to capitalize on the renewed popularity of Boris Karloff by signing the horror movie icon to star in a quartet of modestly budgeted "mad scientist" films. The first three films of the series, *The Man They Could Not Hang* (1939), *Before I Hang* (1940) and *The Man with Nine Lives* (1940), were directed by Nick Grindé and sometimes seemed to be copies of each other, with Karloff working on experiments he believed would help mankind, the authorities being somewhat skeptical of Karloff's processes and actions, the authorities prosecuting Karloff (unfairly so in the mind of Karloff), and then Karloff's revenge on those he believed had persecuted him or those, in his madness, he desired to kill.

The last film in the series, *The Devil Commands* (1941), was different in many ways from the first three films, including the basic plot and the director of the film. And, perhaps most importantly, *The Devil Commands* did not have an original screenplay. It was based on *The Edge of Running Water*, a minor horror classic written by William Sloane.

Background

To most horror film fans, including this author, William Sloane is a little known contributor to the science fiction genre. Born on August 15, 1906, in Plymouth, Massachusetts, William Milligan Sloane, III, was better known during his lifetime as a publisher rather than as an author. Sloane wrote only sporadically during his career, with the majority of his works penned during the 1930s. Most of his writings were plays, but he also wrote one short story and two novels that fall in the broad categories of science fiction and horror, including his second novel, *The Edge of Running Water* (1939). Sloane passed away in 1974.

The Literature

The Edge of Running Water tells the story of Dr. Julian Blair, a former university professor who several years before the story commences moved from New York to an isolated house at Setauket Point in Maine, along the Kennebec River (one of the justifications for the title of the book). There, Blair secreted himself with the mysterious Mrs. Walters in order to conduct some experiment, the nature of which he is reluctant to disclose. Late in the novel, however, Blair finally reveals his secret when he allows Richard Sayles, a former student of Blair's, into his secret laboratory. There, Sayles is confronted by seven mechanical men created by electrical wire, seemingly holding hands and sitting around a table, as if a séance were being conducted. Sayles is justifiably shocked by the image and so is the reader, as Blair, in his crazed attempts to contact the dead, has created a scientific séance, more powerful than a common séance, because of the introduction of the electrical force.

When Sayles tries to prevent Blair from continuing with his experiments, Blair knocks Sayles unconscious, runs to his laboratory and turns his invention on at full speed. From the force of the noise and the vacuum, the Blair mansion collapses. Upon investigation, Blair's body has completely disappeared. Presumably, he has been sucked into another physical world through a hole that was created by his strange apparatus.

William Sloane employs a number of writing techniques to make *The Edge of Running Water* into an effective novel of horror. The book is narrated in the first person by Richard Sayles, allowing the author to delay the entrance of Julian Blair into the story for as long as possible, creating a sense of anticipation in the reader. Thus, through the eyes of Sayles, the reader first becomes acquainted with the town of Barsham Harbor and then the dark, dowdy and ill-cared-for house at Setauket Point. These contrasting settings will become important focal points for later developments in Sayles' chronicle.

At the house at Setauket Point, Sayles meets Anne, the younger sister of Blair's deceased wife, Helen. Sayles had known Anne when her sister and Blair were married. It was Helen's sudden death from pneumonia several years before that caused Blair to leave the university and set out on the path that led him to the isolated site in Maine. Anne is in the story primarily as a romantic interest for Sayles, a common cinematic device, but she and Sayles are also employed as a contrast between the lunacy of Blair and Walters. Anne and Sayles are naturally attracted to each other, are likable when together and provide a real world counterpart to the other world experiments of Blair's. Sayles, of course, also functions as the representative of rational science, a counterpoint to Blair's very unusual views on the uses of science.

As Sloane delays the appearance of Dr. Blair, he spices the tale with Sayles' expressions of foreboding, much like the "Had-I-But-Known" school of mystery writing. In the opening pages of the novel, Sayles writes that the knowledge that Blair acquired "rips the fabric of human existence from throat to hem and leaves us naked to a wind as cold as the space between the stars" (Chapter 1). That is pretty strong stuff for the beginning of a novel, horror story though it may be. Throughout the remainder of the tale Sayles continues in this style, writing that his story is about "a thing both violent and terrible" (Chapter 2), or that he and Julian were "between us and without knowing what we did, creating a horror" (Chapter 7). While these types of foreshadowing and foreboding are initially effective in turning the mood of the novel to the mysterious, they do start to become repetitive at times as they continue throughout the book, even after it is very clear what Blair is up to in his laboratory.

The first climax of the novel occurs when Sayles and Anne are returning from a swim. They hear a loud, unusual noise, described by Sayles as a "sort of roaring, pulsing, crashing sound" (Chapter 13). When the two enter the house, they find the limp body of Mrs. Marcy, the housekeeper, at the foot of the stairs, with Dr. Blair and Mrs. Walters looking down at her. At this point in the story, *The Edge of Running Water* becomes a traditional mystery, as the exact cause of Mrs. Marcy's death and the complete circumstances thereof are unknown. The matter is investigated by the local sheriff and then similar to the order of events in more traditional mystery stories, there is a coroner's inquest at which all four inhabitants of the Blair house are called to testify. While it originally appeared that Mrs. Marcy had accidentally fallen into the river, the difficulty for the coroner's jury is that the autopsy shows that Mrs. Marcy did not drown. She died from a terrible blow across the chest which resulted in a fractured sternum, ruptured spleen and two broken arms. No one is quite sure how she could ever have received those injuries, from either a fall at the house or a fall into the river where her body was discovered (another justification for the title of the book).

The Edge of Running Water is particularly strong in this section, being more like a howdunit than a whodunit. Of course, the reader, recognizing the book is a horror story and not a detective story, can easily guess that something happened when Mrs. Marcy was cleaning Blair's lab, which caused the loud blast and the death of Mrs. Marcy. The reader's special knowledge, however, does not take away from the quality of the puzzle, because there is still the question of what exactly caused Mrs. Marcy's death and how her footprints in the mud showed that she had left the Blair house under her own power. Also, there is an inherent interest in the tension between the very real and very logical criminal process being applied to the fantastic and somewhat illogical quest of Dr. Blair to contact the dead. (In this regard, there is similarity between *The Edge of Running Water* and the first three films in the Columbia horror series with Boris Karloff.)

The horror of the tale returns when Sayles and Anne are awakened that night by another strange sound, which starts as a cold humming whisper and then grows continuously louder. It is accompanied by the hiss of moving air being sucked into Blair's laboratory. Here, and indeed throughout the novel, there is a somewhat rare case of horror in literature being created only by sound, somewhat similar to the loud banging, presumably by ghosts, in *The Haunting of Hill House* by Shirley Jackson.

However, in its climax, *The Edge of Running Water* is primarily a novel of sight, not sound. The tableau of the seven mechanical men, not actually sitting in chairs but attached directly to the table and each other, is the haunting image of the novel. Blair has actually given names to the mechanical men. Sayles is justifiably shocked by the image and so is the reader, as Blair, in his crazed attempts to contact the dead, has created the most horrific scientific séance of all time.

This climax to *The Edge of Running Water*, as Blair goes off the deep end just as the true power and dangerous quality of his invention are realized, is quite intense. The effectiveness of the ending is aided by the fact that the climax is interwoven with the townspeople and the sheriff coming back to the mansion with more suspicions about the death of Mrs. Marcy, adding a double intrigue to the conclusion of the story. Nevertheless, the ending is subtlety disappointing. Blair was supposed to be making an attempt to contact the dead, surely a compelling idea for the culmination of the tale. There are many exciting permutations for what could have happened if Blair had actually contacted the dead through his device, none of which occur in *The Edge of Running Water* because Blair never comes close to his goal.

Instead, Blair's experiments are misdirected, as he has essentially created the greatest tornado of all time, instead of being the first to contact the spirit world. Thus, the story's slow build to a climax of horror fizzles out somewhat. Blair's work does not rip the fabric of human existence from throat to hem, as promised by Richard Sayles in the first chapter of the book. Blair turns out to be just another mad scientist engaged in a project that is not so much science fiction as lunacy, a severe disappointment for the reader.

While *The Edge of Running Water* is enjoyable enough and is well worth reading, as the horror moments, though few and far between, build crescendo-like to the ending, the work as a whole disappoints to some extent, because the payoff for the reader's investment is simply not there. Yet, the novel's cinematic elements, such as the troubling loud noise that emanates from Blair's lab and the séance of mechanical men, made the book a natural for a transfer to the cinema. And, indeed, just two years after its publication, it was made into a horror film starring the most recognizable horror star of the day, Boris Karloff.

The Film

The Devil Commands (1941)

The Devil Commands is a clever reworking of *The Edge of Running Water*. The film opens as Dr. Julian Blair is demonstrating to his colleagues his latest discovery—that each human brain emits individualistic brain waves that can be charted on paper, much like the electroencephalogram (EEG) from today. Blair demonstrates his machine on his wife, Helen, with her brain waves being charted on a screen. Thereafter, Helen is killed in a car accident and when Blair returns to his lab after the funeral, the brain wave machine continues to chart Helen's brain waves, convincing Blair that Helen is trying to communicate with him.

Blair is then off on his long quest to develop a device which can contact the dead. Blair flees to an old house on the coast near Barsham Harbor, so that he can conduct his research in peace. Along the way he picks up a fake medium, Mrs. Walters, who Blair believes will be useful to his experiments. Once at Barsham Harbor, Blair robs graves to find bodies to assist in his pursuit of the spirit world which, among other strange occurrences at the mansion, arouses the suspicions of the natives. At the conclusion of the film, in a mechanical séance similar to that of the novel, Helen's voice is finally heard. Just at the moment of his success, however, Blair pushes his machine to its highest power, causing the collapse of the house and the disappearance of Blair.

Although one of the strengths of the novel was its device of telling a story of horror as if it were a mystery, the filmmakers cleverly eschewed that approach in favor of relating a relatively straightforward horror tale. With a short running time of approximately 65 minutes, there would not have been enough time to develop the mystery properly and the slow pace of the novel would have seemed deadly on film. Thus, from the beginning, Blair's mission and the reason for it are shown to the reader. Similarly, Mrs. Walter's involvement in the plot is made very explicit once she enters the narrative. The core mystery of the novel, the death of Mrs. Marcy, is shown to the viewer as it happens. The trick of creating false footprints with a pair of her shoes, a surprise plot point of the novel, is overtly indicated to the audience. Thus, *The Devil Commands* is clearly a horror film, not a mystery.

In the novel, the least developed character is Julian Blair. His entrance into the chronicle is delayed until significantly into the story and his next significant appearance occurs at the climax. With Boris Karloff in the lead, that approach could not have worked for the movie, either financially or aesthetically, and therefore Blair is the main character in the film from the very beginning. That is an asset to the story as Karloff gives his usual good performance. It also allows the picture to focus on its horror elements. As a result, the pace of the film is quite brisk.

With the emphasis on Julian Blair, Richard Sayles and Anne (now Blair's daughter rather than his sister-in-law) become minor characters. Many films of this era often have a side romance amid the horror. There is none of that in *The Devil Commands*, even though there was a romance between Anne and Sayles in the Sloane novel. For some reason, Anne replaces Sayles as the narrator in the film, which is surprising because she adds almost nothing to the feature in that capacity. Oddly, with Anne's voiceover at the beginning of the movie and the camera moving in slowly toward an old dark house, the opening of the film seems like the opening to *Rebecca* (1940). The similarity is enhanced later in the film, when Mrs. Walters becomes a kind of Mrs. Danvers character, as she dominates the dark mansion and all of its inhabitants.

For a minor genre film, *The Devil Commands* is surprisingly effective. The death of Mrs. Marcy, as she is trapped in the laboratory when Blair's mechanism starts to run, is one of the best scenes in the film. In a tense moment, her pounding on the door is not heard until it is too late. In the novel, Mrs. Marcy's death was not described. In addition to Karloff's performance as Blair, Anne Revere gives a dark and ominous performance as Mrs. Walters, the malevolent medium, willing to do anything for a buck, even covering up a killing. Usually dressed in black, Walters is pure evil, without any redeeming qualities. In many ways, Anne Revere steals the film from Boris Karloff. Another important attribute of the film is the understated performance by Kenneth MacDonald as Sheriff Ed Willis. With Richard Sayles no longer important to the narrative, it is Willis who provides the counterpoint to Blair's and Walters' irrational ideas.

The direction of Edward Dmytryk cannot be overlooked. His steady hand on the story contributes to the success of the film, particularly once the plot moves to the candle-lit house on the coast. The use of candles at the house comes from the novel, but Dmytryk uses that attribute to create shadows on the walls of the house and across the faces of the performers, which he combines with low key lighting, making *The Devil Commands* into a true horror story. A

Dr. Julian Blair (Boris Karloff) conducts another experiment in contacting the dead through electricity, with the help of Karl, the lab janitor (Ralph Penney), and Mrs. Walters, a fake medium (Anne Revere), in *The Devil Commands* (1941). Since Karl is not played by a star of the film, there is a chance that this experiment could go awry for him.

low budget film can often seem like a higher budget production by effective use of shadows, lighting and camera angles.

It is a rare film from this early in horror film history that still has the power to scare an audience but the climax of *The Devil Commands* has that effect even today. The Julian Blair of the film has not created a hole in the physical universe; he actually contacts the dead. The voice of Helen Blair is clearly heard by the audience during Blair's final operation of his contraption, leaving no doubt that Julian Blair has contacted the spirit world. Modifying the image from the novel, the film uses a séance of mechanical men, made not of electrical wires but of dead bodies encased in what seems like old-fashioned metal diving helmets. As the power of Blair's device is increased, the mechanical men lean forward and seem to come to life. With the special effects vortex created in the middle of the screen, at least a slight chill must come down the backs of a modern viewer. It is a striking climax to the film, unlike the climax to any other film of its era and continuing up to this day. As in the novel, the ending is intercut with the townspeople making their attack on the mansion, adding to the effectiveness of the film's conclusion.

The Devil Commands provides an excellent blueprint for adapting a good horror story to the cinema, paring down the plot to its best horror elements and then telling the tale in a straightforward narrative, with no side trips for humor or romance. Good performances and an attention to detail in the direction are also essential attributes. Though it may have a low budget, *The Devil Commands* is still well worth a view today, something that cannot be said of many of the other low budget horror films of the 1940s.

Chapter 19

The Undying Monster
by Jessie Douglas Kerruish

For those who are most familiar with werewolves from the Universal horror films of the 1930s and 1940s, the novel, *The Undying Monster*, will seem very strange. The werewolf of the title does not receive his affliction from the bite of another werewolf, cannot be killed by a silver bullet fired by someone who loves him, kills only in very limited circumstances and is not affected by the full moon. This undying monster does, however, have its own legends and rules, contributing to the mystery inherent in the story and also to the moments of violence and terror that erupt from time to time.

Background

Jessie Douglas Kerruish was born near Hartlepool, County Durham, England, in 1884. She started writing for periodicals as early as 1907 and by 1915, was regularly contributing 20,000 word novellas to the *Weekly Tale-Teller*, an English periodical. She then turned to writing novels, the most famous of which is *The Undying Monster*, originally published in England in 1922. It was not published in the United States until 1936. The short novel has also been published under the title *The Undying Monster: A Tale of the Fifth Dimension*. The subtitle is a reference to the discussion in the book about a dimension one removed from the dimension of the supernatural. Jessie Douglas Kerruish died in 1949.

The Literature

The Undying Monster starts out very quickly. Swanhild Hammond is at the Hammond home, worried about her brother, Oliver, who is out very late on a starlit winter night. It is just the kind of night described by the ancient family rhyme: "Where grow pines and fir amain, Under Stars, sans heat or rain, Chief of Hammond, 'ware thy Bane!" (Chapter I, "The Thunderbarrow Shaw"). The subject of the verse is the Undying Monster of Dannow, which sporadically over centuries has suddenly appeared and murdered people by horribly mutilating their bodies. The incidents always occur at night in a wooded area when the weather is chilly. True to the family curse, when Swanhild drives down to the woods, she discovers Oliver's dog dead, Oliver knocked unconscious and Oliver's companion, Kate Springer, barely alive. The curse of the Hammonds has returned.

At this point, *The Undying Monster* turns from a tale of horror into an historical mystery, with Luna Bartendale, an expert at hunting down ghosts and other manifestations of the supernatural, trying to trace the curse of the monster back through the Hammond family tree to its origins several centuries before. The novel becomes a difficult read in this section, partially because it is quite boring, but also because it is hard for the reader to keep all of the strange names and ancient events in mind over the course of many pages. This is a common problem with historical mysteries, even those that have received a measure of fame, such as *The Daughter of Time*, a 1951 novel by Josephine Tey.

The novel returns to the quality of its strong opening near the end, when the mystery of the monster is solved. The undying monster is Oliver who, like his male ancestors, turns into a werewolf under the conditions set forth in the family verse and just like those ancestors over many centuries, Oliver attacked and killed Kate Springer, his companion of the moment, in the Shaw. After turning into a werewolf and attempting one final attack, Oliver is cured by Luna and the curse of the Hammonds is broken.

While the novel *The Undying Monster* is the source material for only one horror film, its influence on the genre seems to go far beyond that. The rhymes and other sayings that embody the curse of the Hammond monster may be the inspiration for the verse that sparks the Wolf Man legend of the 1941 film. In *The Undying Monster*, the pentacle, a five pointed star, drawn on the ground, provides some protection from the undying monster. That concept will be seen once again in *Devil's Bride* (1968). The references to the Fifth Dimension bring back memories of some of the introductions to *The Twilight Zone* episodes— "There is a fifth dimension beyond that which is known to man." The idea that a man's curse to his god started the line of werewolves in the Hammond family may have been the inspiration for the explanation of the origin of Count Dracula's vampirism as posited in *Bram Stoker's Dracula* (1992). However, the concept that lycanthropy is a mental disease, although with very physical manifestations, contradicts the cure provided to Larry Talbot in *House of Dracula* (1945).

Luna Bartendale is the Dr. Van Helsing character of the novel, although she is much younger and prettier than the vampire hunter from Amsterdam. Nevertheless, Luna is just as intelligent, even managing to trace the beginning of the Hammond monster to events that occurred in 700 B.C. and devising her own cure for the Hammond curse. It is refreshing to have a female character in this pivotal role, making *The Undying Monster* sometimes seem more modern in attitude than one would expect from a novel first published in 1922.

The opening of *The Undying Monster* is stunning, as Swanhild discovers Oliver's dog lying on the ground, its body "twisted and squeezed to an almost shapeless mass before being flung against the tree." Next she finds Oliver near a tree, "sprawled over the roots with his head in a puddle of blood," and then Kate Springer, with a "pair of pale blue eyes opened in that mutilated thing that had been the prettiest face in the village" (Chapter I). As a result of Kerruish's effective language, the opening sequence of *The Undying Monster* is striking, horrific and brutal.

Oliver's transformation into a werewolf at the end of the novel and his attack on Goddard Covert, the fiancé of Swanhild, is as stunning as the opening of the novel. The undying monster, which appears when only one other person is present, suddenly materializes in the body of Oliver, with a "droning snarl" from Oliver which then swells "into a crackling, roaring, screaming, demonic howl." Goddard then sees Oliver "drop to all fours and crouch back in momentary defensiveness while his eyes lit up and glowed red." The monster attacks Goddard, with "red-hot slavering jaws that strove to get at his throat." Goddard is only saved by the beast biting into his artificial arm, a relic of the past war. When Luna then arrives and paralyzes the monster, Goddard finally gets a good look at it. The monster has the face of Oliver Hammond, but with ears laid back, a mouth that is distended and sucked in at all sides, a protruding jaw with big teeth and an upper face that slopes back into insignificance (Chapter VIII, "In the Fifth Dimension"). With other people present, Oliver quickly flicks back to his normal appearance.

This climax to the novel is aided immensely by Jessie Douglas Kerruish's ability to describe the grotesque in a vivid manner, as can be seen from some of Kerruish's language quoted above. Kerruish adds sound and setting to the gruesome events, adding to the terror of the situation. She cleverly delays the appearance of the monster until the end of the novel, piquing the reader's interest throughout the story. The story is more gruesome and violent than one would expect from a story written in the 1920s, although the violence is not as explicit as it probably would have been if the story were written today.

If the reader can get past the central section of the novel, which is primarily an historical mystery, the book is very entertaining. For those who have only learned about lycanthropy from the cinema, *The Undying Monster* provides an interesting and unexpected variation on the legend of the werewolf.

The Film

The Undying Monster (1942)

Much like the novel from which it is adapted, the strongest part of *The Undying Monster* is its opening sequence, in part because the beginning of the film is based on the initial chapter of the novel. As the film opens, Helga Hammond is worried about her brother Oliver, who is working late at the laboratory of Dr. Geoffrey Covert. The night is starlit and frosty, just like the night when a monster attacked Helga's grandfather 20 years before on the path by the edge of the cliff. That monster is the subject of a family legend, as set forth in the poem recited by the butler, "When stars are bright on a frosty night / Beware thy bane on the rocky lane." That verse has obvious similarities to the one quoted in the novel.

Suddenly the cry of the wolf is heard. Helga quickly rides down to the rocky lane by the cliff near the shore. There she discovers the dead body of Oliver's spaniel, a dazed and bloody Oliver and then the almost dead body of Covert's nurse, Kate O'Malley. Oliver survives but he cannot remember all of what happened because of a blow to his head.

After the excellent opening, the film, much like the novel, switches from a horror story to a mystery. Unlike the book, however, the film is not an historical mystery but rather, is a contemporaneous detective story, with the lead detective being Bob Curtis, the head of the police laboratory. At this point, the film has all of the accouterments of a standard mystery, with an inquest, clues that appear to be significant but are in fact related to a different crime and inexplicable acts on the part of the suspects. Although this section of the film does not involve ancient events and difficult names, it is every bit as boring as the similar segment of the novel.

While it may seem disappointing that the female Van Helsing of the novel, Luna Bartendale, has been replaced by the more traditional and male Bob Curtis of the film, that is not really the case. Curtis is simply a police detective with an expertise in science. There is no Van Helsing character in the film. In fact, there is no one in the film who has any special knowledge of werewolves or the supernatural. (Curtis's flighty assistant, Christy Christopher, hardly suffices.) That is one of the problems with the ending of the film—there is never any context provided for the unearthly events that are discovered.

The problems with the plot of *The Undying Monster* are masked somewhat by the excellent direction by John Brahm, aided by the film's magnificent sets. Both attributes can be seen in the opening shots of the film, first with the dramatic establishing shot from a distance of the Hammond House sitting on a rocky cliff above a turbulent sea, and then as the camera silently roams the Hammond mansion without a single cut, showing magnificent stained glass windows, a large staircase, sculptures and the large seal of the Hammond family, all bathed in contrasting shadows and light. These scenes set the somber, eerie tone of the story to come, even though nothing happens in these opening sections of the film.

Brahm never lets the direction of *The Undying Monster* become boring, mixing standard shots with high shots of the interior of the mansion, high and low angle shots on the cliffs, subjective shots from the view of the monster and even a shot through a fireplace of two characters conversing. In the latter scene, instead of shooting the characters through the fireplace fire as is commonly

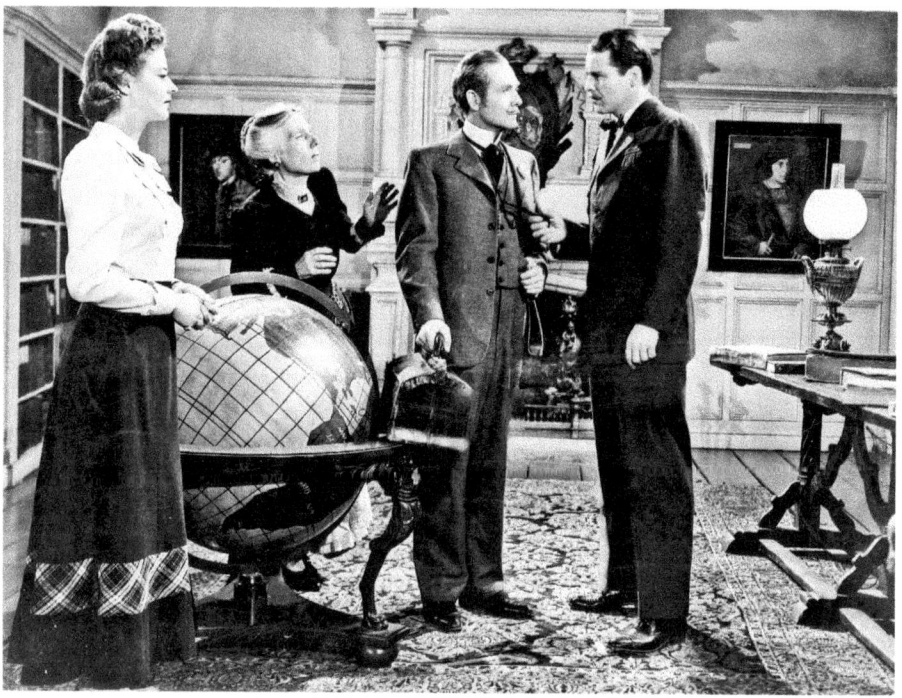

In this publicity photograph for *The Undying Monster* (1942), Bob Curtis of Scotland Yard (James Ellison), on the far right, questions Dr. Covert (Bramwell Fletcher) about his alibi on the night of the attack on Kate O'Malley, while Helga Hammond (Heather Angel), on the far left, and Mrs. Walton (Eily Malyon) look on.

done, Brahm shows the characters veiled in billowing smoke, giving the moment a ghost-like quality even though, once again, not much is happening in the scene. Adding to the ghostliness of the film is a Hammond House filled with shadows even during the daytime and its outside always masked in fog.

Despite the quality of the production, there are some amazingly amateurish moments in the film. A fistfight between Curtis and Stredwick, a poacher, becomes a dance of missed punches, fake overreactions and a lot of rolling around on the ground. In the scenes with the werewolf carrying Helga on his back, the monster often walks and runs too quickly to be believably carrying such a heavy burden on his back.

Those moments can be forgiven because of some clever touches in the film, such as the good use of Helga's dog sensing evil before it actually arrives. This is a slight horror movie cliché but it is used effectively in *The Undying Monster*. Even better is the scene in Curtis' laboratory, where he subjects some hair found at the scene of Kate's attack to a spectrum analysis, projecting a chemical analysis of the hair into different lines appearing on a screen. Curtis proves that the hair found at the scene is wolf's hair by comparing the subject hair to the hair of a real wolf. Suddenly, the lines of the spectrum on the hair found at the scene disappear from the screen. The lights are turned on and Curtis discovers that all of the hair he collected at the scene of the attack has disappeared. The discerning horror film fan knows that the hair has disappeared because it is werewolf hair, which tends to disappear at times. The scientist in Curtis, however, cannot understand what has happened.

The boring nature of the long middle section of the film is redeemed somewhat by its exciting conclusion, but it is a conclusion that is unsatisfying, unlike the memorable ending of the novel. As the climax of the film begins, the monster, seen only in shadows, sneaks into Helga's room and kidnaps her. This is inconsistent with all of the historical sightings of the undying monster, which has always horribly mutilated its victims on the rocky lane, not merely kidnapped them from their home. (What werewolf has been known to abduct its victims and kill them at a different place?) It is also inconsistent with the story line of the film for the monster to go after a Hammond family member. Here, the screenwriters are simply manipulating the script in an illogical manner, just to provide an exciting conclusion to the film. Unfortunately, they are not successful. Instead, they have merely re-used the horror film cliché of a pretty heroine attacked by the vicious monster but then saved at the last instance. There is also no payoff to the ending, as the supposedly horrible monster is killed easily by regular bullets and Oliver's transformation from werewolf back to man is done in a cursory and unconvincing manner. Also, once the deed is done, no one appears to be the least bit surprised that there was a werewolf in their midst.

Jessie Douglas Kerruish's novel laid a framework for Oliver to be disclosed as the undying monster at the end, based on the exhaustive investigation by Luna Bartendale. The surprise in the book makes sense. In the film, the same surprise makes little sense, as a curse through the male side of the Hammond family is not even mentioned until after Oliver is killed. Nevertheless, even though there is no good reason for the viewer to guess that Oliver is the monster, the fact that Oliver totally disappears from the movie near its end will be clue enough for most movie fans.

John Brahm's direction is still excellent during these concluding scenes of the film but excellent direction can only go so far in a film. A compelling plot is also required and in this category, *The Undying Monster* comes up short. That is one of the reasons why horror film fans, when they think of werewolf films from the classic era, do not include *The Undying Monster* in the mix. Despite the fact that the film is based on a novel that, in its day, was well-known and despite the excellent production values, the film itself is quite disappointing and nowhere near as interesting as the Universal Wolf Man films of the same era.

CHAPTER 20

Uneasy Freehold by Dorothy Macardle

During the 1930s and 1940s, the classic era of the Hollywood horror movie, there were surprisingly few horror films about ghosts and those few Hollywood films that involved ghosts were generally light in tone, such as *Topper* (1937), about a deceased couple that returns to the real world to do a good deed, and *Beyond Tomorrow* (1940), a Christmas story about a ghost who helps two young lovers. Thus, *The Uninvited* (1944), a serious story of ghosts and horror, must have been a major surprise to moviegoers in the mid–1940s.

Background

Dorothy Macardle was born in 1899 in Dundalk, Ireland, a town located about halfway between Dublin and Belfast. In 1937, Macardle published *The Irish Republic*, a well-regarded history of Ireland. Macardle started penning novels in the 1940s, writing a total of four between 1941 and 1953. One of those books is about a wartime romance but the other three had supernatural themes. *Uneasy Freehold* (1941) is about ghosts and a haunted house, *The Unforeseen* (1946) is about person with psychic powers and *Dark Enchantment* (1953) concerns witchcraft. In addition to her novels and works of nonfiction, Macardle also wrote plays and short stories. Macardle died in 1958 at the age of 69.

The Literature

Uneasy Freehold is the story of the ghosts that haunt Cliff End, a large house that is located on the edge of the North Devon Cliffs by the sea in the southwest corner of England. The protagonists of the novel, Roderick Fitzgerald, a writer, and his sister, Pamela, purchase the mansion from Commander Brooke, a local resident whose family had lived in Cliff End for five generations. Once the Fitzgeralds move into Cliff End, they are constantly terrorized by what appears to be a ghost, or perhaps two ghosts, haunting the house. The two investigate the backstory of Cliff End, discover who is really haunting the house and by the end of the novel, rid Cliff End forever of its ghostly apparitions.

There is an inherent interest in the alternating stories of *Uneasy Freehold*, as the Fitzgeralds, in the present, try to lead their own lives in a haunted house while also trying to discover the true story of what happened at Cliff End many years before, with the hope that the backstory of Cliff End somehow relates to the current ghosts of the manor. Nevertheless, the novel is slow moving for most of its length, with the main storyline of the present-day ghosts interrupted by story arcs of Roderick working on his new play, Roderick and Pamela entertaining their friends from London and Roderick's somewhat unconvincing love interest in the 18-year-old Stella, the Commander's granddaughter. Also contributing to the slow pace of the story is the fact that the ghost story is sometimes presented in a clinical fashion, as Roderick and Pamela keep discussing and analyzing, and then re-discussing and re-analyzing, the various possible explanations of the strange occurrences in Cliff End. In the introduction to the novel, Roderick, writing in retrospect, regrets his "slow-witted refusals to face the truth." Most readers will agree, wishing the climax of the story had occurred about 50 pages earlier.

As with many novels of horror, *Uneasy Freehold* is sometimes more like a detective story than a ghost story, as Roderick and Pamela interview many people to determine the truth behind the backstory of the ghosts of the manor. These witnesses include Commander Brooke, Stella, Miss Holloway, Stella's nurse and governess, and Father Anson, the local priest. The backstory involves the Commander's daughter, Mary, universally described as kind, gentle and religious, her husband Llewellyn Meredith, a painter, their daughter Stella and a dancer named Carmel whom Meredith used as his model for his paintings. One night, Carmel ran out of the house at Cliff End in a seeming panic. Mary Meredith chased after her, apparently trying to save Carmel from committing suicide or from something else unknown. The wind took Carmel and flung her into a gnarled tree on the edge of the cliff. The fast-running Mary could not grasp the tree and she fell over the high cliff to her death. Carmel died a few weeks later and when Llewellyn moved to Europe (where he drowned few years later), the Commander raised Stella on his own. It seems apparent that Carmel, universally reputed to be the evil person who broke up Mary's and Llewellyn's marriage, is the ghost haunting Cliff End.

The investigation sequences are engaging, as the Fitzgeralds are, in essence, conducting a cold case investigation of events that occurred many years before. At the end of the novel, the ghost story merges with the detective story. The Fitzgeralds conduct two séances, with the assistance of Garrett Ingram, an attorney with some knowledge of the spirit world, in an attempt to talk to Mary Meredith or whichever other spirit is haunting the house. The scenes are the highlights of the novel, with the cold case investigators discovering new witnesses in the world of the spirits.

During the first séance, which is held in the artist's studio, the room becomes incredibly cold and the participants' strength weakens. After the participants leave the studio, the sound of sighing is heard and a "phosphorescent figure, like a mummy," draws out of the studio door and gradually crystalizes into the figure of a woman, with a head of hair hanging down. As Roderick describes it, "I saw the classic brow; the lips, fine and stern; smooth eyelids veiling the eyes.... She opened her eyes—great, ice-blue eyes, alight with so fierce a flash of power and purpose that I closed my own" (Chapter XVIII, "Mary"). And then the figure disappears. A second séance is then held in the nursery, with more information provided by the spirits' use of a spelling glass. This story arc includes the spirit of Carmel possessing Pamela; the plot twist that Stella is Carmel's daughter, not Mary's, and that Mary was the evil person many years ago; Stella and the ghost of her mother conversing in Spanish, allowing the ghost to finally leave the house in peace; and Roderick, armed with the knowledge of the true backstory of Mary and Carmel, permanently driving the spirit of Mary away from Cliff End although, in a last act of revenge, Mary starts a small fire in the house. In contrast with the slow pace of the novel in the earlier sections, the conclusion of *Uneasy Freehold* is both thrilling and chilling.

Horror film fans will desire to compare *Uneasy Freehold* with *The Haunting of Hill House*, by Shirley Jackson, just as they will want to compare the screen versions of the two, that is, *The Uninvited* (1944) and *The Haunting* (1963). Each film is well-respected by genre fans although it is unlikely that *Uneasy Freehold* has been read by many of them. *Uneasy Freehold* has been long out-of-print and it is difficult to locate a copy of the book. *The Haunting of Hill House* is much more recent, having been published in 1959. It seems to never have gone out-of-print. *The Haunting* is the more famous of the two movies, another probable factor in the continued popularity of Shirley Jackson's novel, as contrasted with *Uneasy Freehold*.

A comparison of the two novels is probably unfair. Although they both involve ghosts that haunt an old dark house, they are written in different styles and probably with different intents. *The Haunting of Hill House* is the darker of the two, with Shirley Jackson inexorably building her story from small supernatural incidents to a frightening conclusion. The story takes place almost entirely within the confines of the eerie Hill House. It is always a horror story, never a mystery.

Uneasy Freehold is lighter in tone, with much of the action occurring outside the much less frightening Cliff House, usually in a bright setting by the sea or in a small village. There is no inexorable sequence of events in *Uneasy Freehold* that leads to a horrific climax. Rather, there are perplexing manifestations from the spirit world that must be investigated and then dealt with. Both novels are well worth reading but for most horror fans, such as your author, the frightening Jackson novel is a better read than the interesting, but slow moving Macardle book.

The Film

The Uninvited (1944)

The Uninvited is a faithful adaptation of Dorothy Macardle's novel of ghosts and hauntings. Early in the film, siblings Pamela Fitzgerald and Roderick (Rick) Fitzgerald purchase a mansion known as Windward, located high on the cliffs above the sea, from a Commander Beech. The Fitzgeralds intend to make Windward their new home. The Commander has a granddaughter named Stella whose mother, Mary Meredith, died by a fall over the cliffs of Windward when Stella was only three. The spirits of a person or persons unknown are now haunting Windward house but by the end of the film, the Fitzgeralds discover the truth about the hauntings, finally ridding Windward of its ghosts for all time.

Readers of *Uneasy Freehold* will be familiar with most of the manifestations of the ghosts in the film, such as the smell of the scent of mimosa in Windward from time to time; a dog and cat who are frightened of something in the house; the atmosphere of the artist's studio which causes a severe depression in those who occupy it; the sounds of a sobbing woman which sometimes seem to dominate the edifice; and the incredible cold in some of the rooms of Windward, a cold that Roderick describes in the introduction to the film as "no mere matter of degrees Fahrenheit, but a draining of warmth from the vital centers of the living." *The Uninvited* also employs some original devices, such as wilting flowers in the artist's studio, candles dimming and going out on their own and a ghost turning the pages in a notebook to direct the Fitzgeralds' attention to some important information.

Film is obviously different than prose and even though *The Uninvited* is a faithful adaptation of the Macardle novel, several changes were made. Some are

Pictured are the three main characters in *The Uninvited* (1944), from left to right, Rick Fitzgerald (Ray Milland), Pamela Fitzgerald (Ruth Hussey) and Stella Meredith (Gail Russell), in the countryside near the haunted house known as Windward.

inexplicable, such as the modifications of the names of characters and places and Roderick's transformation from a writer into a composer. Others are understandable, such as eliminating many of the extraneous characters from the novel, thereby, for example, requiring Dr. Scott to participate in the séance near the end of the film, as contrasted with a new character to the novel, Ingram, conducting the séances in the book. As a result of the elimination of extraneous matters, the storyline from the novel has been tightened and so, unlike the novel, *The Uninvited* does not have a slow pace. Even with the cuts, there is still a lot of story to pack into the film's 98-minute running time. Nevertheless, the film displays some lighter moments which are original to the film, such as Rick getting sick on a sailboat and a scene with a batty resident of Miss Holloway's sanitarium. There are also some personal moments between Rick and Stella, such as a date on the sailboat, that make the romance between the two much more convincing than it was in the novel.

As was usually the case when a horror novel was written in the form of a mystery, the screen version of *Uneasy Freehold* generally eschews the mystery elements of the story, concentrating instead on its horror components. The Fitzgeralds' investigation into the history of Mary and Carmel does not occur until late in the movie and is cursory, at best. In fact, there is so little attention paid to the backstory of Windward throughout the film that when the story's big surprise, that Carmel was the good soul and Mary the evil one, is finally revealed, it is hardly a high moment for the viewer. By contrast, that same revelation is one of the highlights of the novel, because of the mystery nature of the novel and the fact that so much time was spent in the book in the investigation of the backstory of the mansion.

The Uninvited adds Miss Holloway, Carmel's nurse from many years before, as an additional evil spirit who haunts Windward, but in her own corporeal manner. Miss Holloway was a minor character in the novel but in the film, she is a major character and a true villain. It is clear in *The Uninvited* that Holloway murdered Carmel those many years before, by allowing her to die of pneumonia when she was Carmel's nurse. (There are implications of that in the novel but no definitive answer is given.) Late in the film, Holloway sends Stella back to Windward when she knows that no one else will be there, with the expectation that the ghost of Mary will drive Stella to jump of the high cliff, a death matching the fall of Mary to her own death many years before. Mary had once tried to kill Stella because she was Carmel's daughter and Miss Holloway has now made an effort to assist the ghost of Mary in finally accomplishing that malevolent deed. (This is an original story arc for the film.)

The Uninvited has a strong conclusion. As part of Miss Holloway's plot against Stella, the young woman is driven by the mists of a ghost that appears onscreen for only the second time in the movie to the high cliffs of Windward. Stella is just rescued by Rick before she would have fallen to her certain death. Then, while Rick, Pamela, Stella and Dr. Scott are calmly discussing the incident in a downstairs room at Windward, the doors of the room suddenly burst open, accompanied by a surge of background music, shocking the viewer. It is the arrival of the spirit of Carmel, evidenced by the smell of mimosa in the room, the breeze in the room and the turning of the pages in a doctor's old notebook. Carmel is never seen but she is surely there. Stella then learns that Carmel was her mother, not Mary. Since Stella is happy with the news, the spirit of Carmel is satisfied. It is able to leave Windward forever. The film has come to a happy ending.

But suddenly, accompanied by another sharp spike of the soundtrack music, the audience is surprised once again when Rick suddenly sees the ghost of Mary outside the door. The cold has unexpectedly returned. Rick then leaves the room and with a candelabrum in hand, walks up the steps of Windward, challenging the spirit of Mary. The swirling mist re-appears but quickly resolves itself into the face and body of a human, with a flowing dress, similar to the figure of Mary in her several portraits painted by her husband (and also similar to the description of the ghost of Mary in the novel). Rick defies the spirit of Mary, telling her that now that everyone knows the truth about her, they are not afraid of her. In fact, they now laugh at her. Rick tells the mist, "From now on, this house is for the living." He throws the candelabrum at the figure; the mist disappears, apparently forever. Windward is now a happy dwelling, finally free of its ghosts. As a manifestation of that change, the house cat is finally willing to go up the steps of the mansion.

The Uninvited is often compared favorably with the Val Lewton horror films of the 1940s, which were known for creating an atmosphere of horror by the use of sound, shadow and atmosphere. Viewers who make that comparison, however, decry the fact that the ghost of Mary is shown in *The Uninvited*, rather than just implied. However, while the Val Lewton approach is one method of creating a good ghost movie (see *The Haunting* [1963], shot in the Lewton style), it is not the only technique. The actual appearances of the specter of Mary in *The Uninvited* are some of the highlights of the film, providing the proverbial chill up the spine of the viewer. (In any event, the ghost of Carmel, as contrasted with the ghost of Mary, is handled in the Val Lewton manner in *The Uninvited* and in the only ghost movie produced by Val Lewton, *The Curse of the Cat People* (1944), the ghost is shown onscreen.)

By today's standards, *The Uninvited* can hardly be considered a frightening film, but it still has those two great shock moments and the eerie special effects of the ghosts of the mist. It is made with high production values such as its famous score and Academy Award nominated cinematography. The cast includes two Academy Award winning actors, Ray Milland (*The Lost Weekend* [1945]), playing Rick Fitzgerald, and Donald Crisp (*How Green Was My Valley* [1941]), playing Commander Beech. Yet despite these attributes, the film seems to have been overlooked by most horror film fans, perhaps because it was produced at Paramount Pictures, a studio not known for its horror output. Whatever the reason for it often being overlooked by genre fans, *The Uninvited* is a forgotten gem of a horror film, one of the best of the 1940s.

CHAPTER 21

"The Body Snatcher" by Robert Louis Stevenson

In November 1884, the *Pall Mall Gazette* commissioned Robert Louis Stevenson to write a Christmas story, but he was unable to complete the assignment in a timely manner. Instead, Stevenson gave the *Gazette* "The Body Snatcher," a previously unpublished story that he wrote back in 1881. The *Pall Mall Gazette* published the story in its 1884 Christmas "Extra" in place of a holiday story. Stevenson thought so little of his short story that he refused to accept the entire 40 pounds that had been offered to him by the *Gazette*, believing that his piece was unworthy of the full fee. Today, that short story is well-known to horror film fans as the inspiration for one of the best of the 1940s horror films.

Background

"The Body Snatcher" derives some of its inspiration from the true life crimes of William Burke and William Hare, which they committed over an approximate 12 month period in Edinburgh, Scotland, in the late 1820s. Burke and Hare were grave robbers who supplied bodies to Dr. Robert Knox, an Edinburgh teacher and researcher in human and comparative anatomy. Although the first cadaver Burke and Hare supplied to Knox died from natural causes, the next 16 were murdered by Burke and Hare, usually by suffocating or "burking" them, as the type of killing eventually became known. The police finally arrested the two for the murders and William Burke was eventually executed for the crimes. Dr. Knox was not prosecuted because there was no proof that he had knowledge of the origins of the cadavers, even though Knox clearly must have known that they were illegally obtained.

The Literature

"The Body Snatcher" is narrated by a man who is intrigued by a chance meeting he observes between an old drunken Scotsmen named Fettes and a London doctor named MacFarlane. The narrator conducts an investigation and determines that MacFarlane and Fettes, when both were medical students in Edinburgh, became involved with grave robbers, who were not above killing people and delivering the bodies to the dissecting room. One of those grave robbers was an acquaintance of MacFarlane's named Gray, who often referred to MacFarlane as "Toddy MacFarlane." MacFarlane eventually killed Gray and when the body was delivered to the dissecting rooms, Fettes, even though he recognized the body as that of Gray's and knew that Gray had been murdered, nevertheless handled the body just like any other unknown body he received, providing it to the medical students for dissection.

A few days thereafter, Fettes and MacFarlane, now short one grave robber with the death of Gray, set out on their own to rob the grave of a recently deceased farmer's wife. They did their deed in the dark because their lantern was broken. Fettes and MacFarlane dropped the woman's body into a sack and placed it on the carriage seat between them. During the ride back in the rain across rutted roads, the body bounced off of each of them. It also seemed larger than remembered. The two were so frightened that they stopped the carriage to check their baggage. They opened the sack and to their horror, the body turned out to be that "of the dead and long-dissected Gray."

Robert Louis Stevenson's style of writing is very effective throughout. At the beginning of the story, Stevenson's descriptions of the contrast between MacFarlane ("he became his years, breathing, as he did, of wealth and consideration") with Fettes ("bald, dirty, pimpled and robed in his old camlet cloak") are striking. Stevenson is particularly eloquent in describing the degradations of grave robbing, stating, "The wife of a farmer ... was to be rooted from her grave at midnight and carried, dead and naked, to that far-away city that she had always honoured with her Sunday best ... to be exposed to that last curiosity of the anatomist." Also, Stevenson cleverly uses the story of Burke and Hare as the background to the tale. Their story was notorious in its day and Robert Louis Stevenson, who was born in Edinburgh in 1850, must have become very familiar with the tale as he was growing up. There is a reference to the execution of Burke in the story and the doctor who runs the facility at which Fettes and MacFarlane are medical students is referred to as Mr. K—, a possible reference to Dr. Robert Knox, the medical researcher for whom Burke and Hare worked.

The end of "The Body Snatcher" is powerful. Its setting is classic for a horror story: a grave yard at night in an incessant rain, lit only by the light of one of the gig lanterns, amid dripping trees and huge and moving shadows. MacFarlane hurts his hand on a stone and tosses the stone aside, hitting the gig lamp and knocking it down a hill. As a result, the remainder of their grave robbing is done in complete darkness. Once the sack with the body is placed on the gig seat between Fettes and MacFarlane and they start to ride, farm dogs accompany their passage with howling and wailing. With each bounce of the gig, "the thing that stood propped between them fell now upon one and now upon the other. At every repetition of the horrid contact each instinctively repelled it with greater haste." As Fettes looks at the bundle, it seems larger than it first appeared. Once the sack is opened and the body of Gray is disclosed, the horse bounds off on its own toward Edinburgh, bearing only the dead body.

"The Body Snatcher" is somewhat frightening at the end, not only because of its surprise ending but also because of the setting and mood created by Stevenson. While not much happens at the end of the tale, Stevenson is still able to mold all of the story's elements into a frightening conclusion. It is a true horror story because Fettes and MacFarlane cannot both be simply imagining the presence of Gray's body. Two people are unlikely to imagine the same incident at the same time. So was it the ghost of Gray coming back to haunt the two or is it some other supernatural occurrence? Stevenson leaves the answer to the imagination of the reader.

With its graveyard scene, dead bodies and surprise ending, "The Body Snatcher" would seem to be a natural for adaptation to the cinema. Nevertheless, it took until 1945, at the very end of the second horror film cycle in America, for a film adaptation to be produced.

The Film

The Body Snatcher (1945)

The Body Snatcher is set in Edinburgh, Scotland, in 1831, just a few years after the misdeeds of Burke and Hare were committed. It may seem strange to relate a tale of a body snatcher operating in Edinburgh so soon after the scandal of Burke and Hare was discovered, but surprisingly, the film is factually correct. As historian Lisa Rosner writes, in *The Anatomy Murders* (Chapter 2, "The Anatomy Wars"), anatomy lecturers in Surgeon's Square in the medical district of Edinburgh returned to their prior practice of obtaining cadavers by illegal means just a few weeks after the conclusion of the trial of William Burke.

The Body Snatcher concerns an Edinburgh grave robber named John Gray, who provides bodies to the noted surgeon and medical school teacher, Dr. Mac-

Farlane, with the assistance of MacFarlane's new protégé, a student named Donald Fettes. At first, Fettes is shocked to learn that Gray provides his bodies illegally but with the guidance of MacFarlane, he eventually becomes used to the situation, just as MacFarlane has. However, when Gray turns to the murder of a street singer as a source for a body and later murders MacFarlane's servant Joseph to prevent Joseph's blackmailing, MacFarlane has had enough. He murders Gray and has his body dissected by his medical students. However, when MacFarlane and Fettes turn to grave robbing on their own, Gray seems to reappear, leading to the death of MacFarlane.

The Body Snatcher is not a fictional version of the real life story of Burke and Hare but it is a clever re-working of some of its elements, primarily the grave robber turning to murder for the purpose of supplying a body for medical school dissection. The memory of Burke and Hare is always in the background of *The Body Snatcher*. A medical student brings their names up in jest, causing outrage in Dr. MacFarlane. Gray tells the story of Burke and Hare to Joseph and even sings a rhyme to him about the two grave robbers, just before killing Joseph. MacFarlane is later exposed as a former student of Knox, who was also involved with grave robbers, but who was shielded at the trial by Gray. That is the event that has enabled Gray to blackmail MacFarlane by threatening to tell Gray's secret to the world. When Gray makes another threat against MacFarlane, MacFarlane points out to Gray that if Gray tells his story, Gray is more at risk than MacFarlane because, while they hanged Burke and mobbed Hare, Dr. Knox is now living like a gentleman in London. (This statement is historically accurate, although Dr. Knox did not move to London until after the time period of the film.)

There are a number of well-staged and directed scenes in the movie, such as Gray robbing the grave of a young boy and killing his dog in the process, shown mainly in shadows and emphasizing the sounds of a spade digging in the earth and the dog growling, and the killing of Gray by MacFarlane, as Gray's cat looks on. However, there are three scenes of particular interest in the film.

One involves the blind street singer, a character who is beautifully handled in the movie. As the camera pans down the city street in the opening sequence of the film, the street singer is shown, singing wonderfully, dressed all in black and holding a tin plate for the coins of the passers-by. She seems an insignificant character, inserted into the scene just to provide some color to the setting. The singer next turns up as MacFarlane and Fettes pass her by on the street, once again seeming to be there solely to provide some added interest to the street scene. A few days later, Fettes starts to walk past her, asks if she knows where Gray is and then puts a coin on her plate. She is next seen when Gray spots her, at a time when he needs a fresh body for the doctors. Gray saddles up his horse and starts in pursuit of the woman. As the camera holds in a stationary position, the singer is then seen from behind, all in black, as she walks down the dark street away from the camera, with the white horse and dark carriage of Gray following her. First the singer disappears in the blackness, then the carriage does, and then in mid-high note the singer's voice is cut-off.

This section of *The Body Snatcher* is striking in its use of shadows and sounds, epitomizing the best of what the Val Lewton horror films are all about. The scene lingers in the viewer's mind, long after the rest of the film may be forgotten, not only for the way in which it is shot, but also because the viewer has gradually come to know the street singer and become used to her presence on the streets, before her brazen killing.

Another interesting incident in the film is the killing by Gray of MacFarlane's servant, Joseph. Once again Robert Wise beautifully directs the scene, which is shot mainly in shadows with, this time, the figures lit by a single candle burning in Gray's living quarters. Boris Karloff plays Gray and Bela Lugosi plays

Grave robber John Gray (Boris Karloff), on the left, has come to discuss business with Dr. MacFarlane (Henry Daniell), on the far right, while MacFarlane's servant, Joseph (Bela Lugosi) looks on, in *The Body Snatcher* (1945).

Joseph, in their final screen appearance together. Lugosi has second billing in the film, above Henry Daniell as MacFarlane, but the role of Joseph is small, hardly befitting Lugosi's former status in horror films. As sad as it is to see Lugosi in such a minor role, he is very good in the scene with Karloff, supporting the observation that Lugosi always performed well in good films, no matter how small his part was.

The ending of the film has been justly praised. MacFarlane and Gray proceed to a wind-swept church graveyard lit only by moonlight, where they rob a grave of a recently deceased woman. They put the body in a sack and place it on the seat between them as they ride back to town in a horse-drawn carriage. A terrific storm of rain and thunder accompanies them on their ride. As the body in the sack continually falls on MacFarlane, he seems to hear the voice of Gray calling him "Toddy" and telling him that he will never be rid of Gray. MacFarlane stops the carriage and Fettes gets off. MacFarlane remains on the carriage. MacFarlane then opens the sack to see who is inside. The camera moves quickly in on the face of Gray. MacFarlane is so shocked by what he has seen that he scares the horse, which runs off in a panic. As the horse drags the carriage on its own with only Macfarlane and the body on board, the body of Gray almost seems to grab MacFarlane. The carriage eventually crashes over a hill, killing MacFarlane. After Fettes determines that MacFarlane is dead, he checks the body that was in the sack and finds that it is that of a middle-aged woman, not of Gray.

As effective as the conclusion of *The Body Snatcher* is, the ending of the short story is better. The short story's ending is one of horror; the film's ending is one of madness. In the film, MacFarlane, because of the cumulative effect of years of guilt over his deceptions, grave robbing and involvement in murders, imagines he has dug up Gray's body, even though it was previously dissected. Thus, unlike the short story, where the body in the sack was definitely that of Gray's, the conclusion of the film is somewhat of a letdown. Also, Stevenson's descriptions are so effective in the story, particularly the body bouncing back and forth on MacFarlane and Fettes, a truly creepy moment, that the film cannot match it, even in the hands of an excellent director such as Robert Wise.

The Body Snatcher has several first-rate performances, including Henry Daniell in the film's lead role of Dr. MacFarlane, even though he is listed low in the credits. It is a rare starring role for the fine character actor and he is excellent in the part. Acting honors, however, go to Boris Karloff, as Gray. It may be the best non-creature performance Karloff ever gave, surely better than his mad doctor performances of the 1940s. Karloff's performance is aided by the quality of the dialogue that he is given but Karloff adds shading and nuance to the script, as he moves effortlessly through the characterizations of Gray as evil, sly, and vengeful, yet affectionate to a sick child. It is a shame that Karloff did not have better roles in non-horror films. His reputation among horror film fans might then have spread to other film connoisseurs.

There are other positives to the feature. There is the touching side-story of the little girl who is cured by MacFarlane and begins to walk. There are some interesting issues of medical ethics raised in the story. Is it acceptable for MacFarlane to refuse to operate on little Georgina, and perhaps save her life, so that he can continue to teach medical students who might save thousands of lives? Is a little grave robbing okay, if it leads to the improvement of medical science so that others may not have to go to the grave so early in life?

The filmmakers have done a wonderful job in opening up Stevenson's short story for purposes of a feature length film, without any obvious padding. All of the added story lines and characters add to the impact of the main story. *The Body Snatcher* is an excellent film and yet, because of its subtlety disappointing ending, it is not quite the classic it is purported to be. Fans of the movie should read the Stevenson short story in order to obtain another, perhaps better, take on the same basic plot.

CHAPTER 22

The Picture of Dorian Gray by Oscar Wilde

When readers think about the significant horror novels of the 19th century, *Frankenstein* (1818) and *Dracula* (1897) immediately come to mind. *The Picture of Dorian Gray* (1891) is rarely considered. When film fans speak about the important horror films of the 1940s, *The Wolf Man* (1941) and *The Cat People* (1942) are usually mentioned. *The Picture of Dorian Gray* (1945) is seldom cited. The reasons for these omissions may be that Oscar Wilde is not usually thought of as a writer of horror fiction and MGM is not usually thought of as a producer of horror films, particularly in the 1940s. Thus, even though horror fans may have some basic idea of the story of Dorian Gray, they may never have actually read the novel or viewed the film. If so, that is a shame because they are missing out on one of the strangest tales of the macabre ever told.

Background

Oscar Wilde was born on October 16, 1854, in Dublin, Ireland. Wilde attended college at Oxford, where Wilde became a participant in the Aesthetic movement which, in an over-simplification, promotes art for art's sake, one of the underlying ideas addressed in *The Picture of Dorian Gray*. Interestingly, the 1945 film version of *Dorian Gray* was produced at MGM, whose logo above the roaring lion states, "Ars gratia artis," which translates to "Art for art's sake."

Wilde's first significant work was *The Picture of Dorian Gray*, the only novel he ever wrote. The story was serialized in *Lippincott's Monthly Magazine* in Philadelphia, Pennsylvania in 1890 before it was published in book form with a revised text in England in 1891. Thereafter, Wilde had great success writing stage plays for the London theater. Wilde died of cerebral meningitis in Paris on November 30, 1900.

The Literature

Given the title of the novel, it is appropriate that Dorian Gray is introduced to the reader through his portrait. As the painting sits in the studio of painter Basil Hallwood at the beginning of the story, Dorian is described as "a young man of extraordinary personal beauty," having a "gracious and comely form" (Chapter I). When Dorian arrives in person at the studio, Lord Henry Wotton, an old Oxford friend of Hallwood's, observes that Dorian is "certainly wonderfully handsome, with his finely curved scarlet lips, his frank blue eyes [and] his crisp gold hair" (Chapter II).

Hallwood completes the painting of his young subject and when Dorian looks at his portrait for the first time (and after some goading from Wotton), Dorian makes the statement that will color the rest of the book:

> How sad it is! I shall grow old, and horrible, and dreadful. But this picture will remain always young. It will never be older than this particular day in June.... If it were only the other way! If it were I who was to be always young, and the picture that was to grow old! For that—for that—I would give everything! Yes, there is nothing in the whole world I would not give! I would give my soul for that! [Chapter II].

And, with that statement by Dorian Gray, a novel of manners and upper class attitudes turns into a novel of horror, as Dorian has apparently made a pact with the devil to preserve his good looks throughout his lifetime.

From that point forward in the story, while Dorian never seems to grow older, the painting not only grows older but also reflects the debaucheries of Dorian's hedonistic lifestyle and evil ways on its painted face. Dorian's personality also changes. He mistreats the actress and his lover, Sibyl Vane, so badly that she eventually commits suicide. Later, for no apparent reason, Dorian viciously murders Hallwood by repeatedly stabbing him with a knife. When Dorian soon realizes that the only clue left to his true self is the portrait, he grabs the knife he used to kill Hallwood, and attempting to kill the painter's work as he had killed the painter, stabs the portrait. From outside the room, a cry and a crash are heard. When the servants enter, they discover the splendid portrait of Dorian as they had last seen it, with Dorian pictured as young and beautiful, just as on that day in June when Hallwood completed his work. On the floor is a dead man in evening dress, with a knife in his heart. "He was withered, wrinkled and loathsome of visage" (Chapter XX). Until they examine the rings on the body, they are unable to determine who the dead man is.

It is doubtful that Oscar Wilde, in his own mind, was writing a novel of horror when he penned *The Picture of Dorian Gray*. Wilde was most interested in society and its attitudes toward people, art, material possessions and the like. As such, the novel is studied in universities and is also the subject of numerous articles and other commentaries on the style, wit and themes of the work. Among proffered theses of the novel are the corruption of morals, the vacuity of the sophisticated classes, the proper place of art in society and the ideal of aestheticism.

As a result of the non-horror themes and writing style, *The Picture of Dorian Gray* can be a bit of a hard read for the avid horror fan. Nevertheless, perhaps unbeknownst to Wilde, an engrossing tale of horror gradually unfolds within the society of sophisticates that Wilde describes and observes. Treating the novel as a work of horror rather than as a novel of manners also highlights several of the horror themes that are inherent in the book.

One is the issue of what is real and what is façade. Because of the painting, Dorian Gray maintains his youthful looks well into his late thirties, still turning heads with his divine-like features. Yet, because of his decadent and wicked lifestyle and despite his good looks, he is shunned by much of society. It seems that the portrait of Dorian Gray, though it prevents the physical aging of Dorian, is a curse on the life of Dorian, compelling what was once a good person into doing evil things, similar to the traditional vampire or werewolf story. Nevertheless, while the portrait both reflects and causes the evil in Dorian, it is the acts of the real Dorian that truly reveal his wickedness. In a sense then, both the picture and his face are part real and part façade.

Another subject of the novel is the Jekyll-Hyde theme of good and evil co-existing in the same person. Similar to what happens in Robert Louis Stevenson's novella *The Strange Case of Dr. Jekyll and Mr. Hyde*, the evil in Dorian Gray has, at least on a superficial basis, been put on the canvas while the good in Dorian remains on his face, dividing the good from the evil in one person. As Dorian says to Hallwood after showing him the painting, "Each of us has Heaven and Hell in him" (Chapter XIII). This is also a theme of the traditional werewolf story, as well as many other horror films that deal with split personalities. Indeed, when Dorian's body returns to its true self upon his death at the end of the film, the happening is reminiscent of the ending of werewolf movies, not to mention vampire movies, invisible man movies and other film variations on Dr. Jekyll and Mr. Hyde.

The Picture of Dorian Gray is not a traditional horror story in the style of, say, a *Dracula* or *The Haunting of Hill House*. One obvious horror element that is missing from Wilde's tale is an explanation for the strange changes in the portrait over the course of Dorian's life. If Dorian has, in fact, sold his soul to the devil in exchange for not growing older, why doesn't the devil or a messenger of Satan make an appearance in the book? In a more traditional horror story, the devil himself would likely be an important character and there would be some explanation for the metamorphosis of the painting. Also, unlike most novels that fall broadly into the category of horror fiction, *The Picture of Dorian Gray* is filled with witticisms, one of the several charms of the book. Many of the adages are spoken or thought by Lord Henry Wotton, who is both clever and cynical. Examples of his observations are "The only way to get rid of a temptation is to yield to it" (Chapter II); "I can sympathize with everything, except suffering" (Chapter III); "Nowadays people know the price of everything, and the value of nothing" (Chapter IV); and "The one charm of the past is that it is the past" (Chapter VIII).

Even though the story is not told in the style of a horror novel and the horror elements are not emphasized, make no mistake. Whatever else *The Picture of Dorian Gray* is, and it is many other things, it is definitely a novel of great horror. And, in 1945, a major studio, MGM, decided to bring the work to the silver screen in a large budget production.

The Film

The Picture of Dorian Gray (1945)

The Picture of Dorian Gray is a faithful adaptation of the Oscar Wilde novel on which it is based. All of the major characters are present and almost every major scene from the novel is incorporated into the film. However, as was often the case when transferring a novel to the cinema, the events and scenes in the written work had to be streamlined for the film version, which in the case of *Dorian Gray* is a positive, as the filmmakers could concentrate on Wilde's plot and ignore his many diversions from the story line.

As faithful as the 1945 film adaptation is, some changes were made to the Wilde's original plot or concept. The very first alteration in the film is the strangest. The preface to the film is not a quote from Oscar Wilde but rather is a saying from *The Rubaiyat of Omar Khayyam*. It says:

> I sent my soul through the invisible,
> Some letter of that after-life to spell;
> And by and by my soul returned to me.
> And answered, "I myself am 'Heaven and Hell.'"

Interestingly, in both the novel and the film, when Dorian shows the changed painting to Basil Hallwood, Dorian says, "Each of us has Heaven and Hell in him." Dorian may himself have been quoting Omar Khayyam when he makes that statement but the verse adds little to the understanding or mood of the film. Surprisingly, the verse returns in the last shot in the film, in an open book in Dorian's house.

In the novel, Dorian rejects Sibyl Vane because of her poor performance on stage, which is related to her preference for the reality of life over the artificiality of life as performed on the stage. This was important to the novel as it relates to one of its themes, the idea of aestheticism or art for art's sake. By contrast, in the film, Dorian rejects Sibyl because after a test cruelly devised by Lord Henry that Sibyl fails, Sibyl no longer appears to be as virtuous as Dorian believes she is. The film version is the more realistic and more cinematic, and although it does result in removing a theme of the novel from the film, i.e., the issue of aestheticism, that is not a detriment to the film as, in fact, few of the themes of the novel are carried into the film.

A new character is added to the film, in the person of Basil Hallwood's niece, Gladys, who has loved Dorian since she was a little girl, when she watched her uncle paint the picture of Dorian Gray. Gladys is all grown up now and is quite pretty and since Dorian has not aged at all, a marriage seems in the offing. The addition of Gladys to the story adds little to the film; she is probably in the story just to add another pretty face and a second romantic interest to the feature.

As a result of other changes to the story, the film version of *Dorian Gray* has more horror elements in some aspects and less in others. In an eerie moment early in the film, emphasized by the atmospheric score, Basil explains to Wotton that there is something mystic about the painting. He says, "Whenever Dorian poses for me, it seems as if a power outside myself is guiding my hand, as if the painting had a life of its own, independent of me." No further explanation is given in the film, but this statement sets the mood for what is to come.

When Dorian makes his statement about selling his soul in exchange for his youth, he makes it in front of a statue of a cat, which Wotton warns is one of the 73 great gods of Egypt and is quite capable of granting his wish. Basil then gives the statue to Dorian, along with the portrait, and the cat statue reappears throughout the film, seemingly watching over Dorian and his painting, perhaps causing the curse of Dorian rather than the picture. It is a tantalizing horror motif for the movie, inserted into the frame when Sibyl has to make her choice about staying the night with Dorian, when Dorian first sees the changed canvas and when Dorian blackmails Alan Carpenter, a chemist, into helping dispose of Basil's body. With the exception of the painting itself, the cat statue is the enduring image of the film, even lingering into the last shot of the feature.

On the other hand, when Dorian kills Basil Hallwood in the film, it is to protect his romantic interest in Basil's niece, Gladys. Dorian knows that if Basil ever tells Gladys about the portrait, she would reject him in an instance. Thus, the killing of Basil in the film version is a pragmatic decision by Dorian. In the novel, Dorian feels compelled to do so because of the influence of the painting. In this instance, at least, the book is more true to its horror elements than the movie.

As fine a film as *The Picture of Dorian Gray* is, it has its shortcomings. Although the film does move at a quicker pace than the novel, it does seem slow moving at times. Possibly because of the censorship concerns of the time, the viewer never really learns much about Dorian's hedonistic and wicked activities that have caused London society to turn against him, except for his trips to the opium dens. Also, the use of a narrator throughout the film, unusual in any film but particularly in a horror film, illustrates the limitations of the script and the production, as the filmmakers are essentially conceding that they could not adequately convey their story just through the visuals and the dialogue. As an example, after the killing of Basil, the portrait is shown with one of the hands dripping blood, surely a nice effect on its own. Not satisfied with the visuals conveying the image, the narrator describes the painting by quoting language from the novel, that the painting had sweated a dew of blood. Really, the viewer does not need that assistance.

The presentation of the portrait is also somewhat confusing. While it may have seemed clever at the time to occasionally show the painting in Technicolor, from today's perspective, it makes little sense. Why not shoot the entire film in color? Also, the second of the three portraits of Dorian's changed face is so stylized as to be unconvincing. The portrait is supposed to show the age and sin on Dorian's face; the painting is not intended to be an imaginary rendering of an horrific face.

Hurd Hatfield gives a wooden and unemotional performance as Dorian Gray. While that is clearly what the director desired, it seems an unusual way to portray a narcissist onscreen. Angela Lansberry was nominated for an Oscar for Best Supporting Actress for her portrayal of Sibyl Vane and while she is fine in the role, her part is so small and unchallenging that the honor is surprising. The rest of the cast, from large roles to small, is excellent with George Sanders receiving acting honors playing Sir Henry Wotton. Sanders always seemed to be a bit of a cad in any role that he played, so he is particularly good as the cynical and unfeeling Lord Henry.

The direction by Albert Lewin and the cinematography by Harry Stradling are exceptionable. Two scenes in the film illustrate their effectiveness. The first is when Dorian enters *The Two Turtles* pub and begins to interact with Sibyl

Vane in the presence of her brother. While the prior scenes in the bar have been shot in bright light, now many of the faces are in shadow or shot from the rear, as if in silhouette, providing a foreboding mood for what should have been a happy moment, presaging the sad ending to the relationship of Dorian and Sibyl.

Later in the film, when Dorian stabs Basil in the back, he accidentally hits the lamp that hangs from the ceiling, causing it to swing back and forth. The effect is stunning, with the action now taking placing within and without the dark, with some of the figures again appearing in silhouette. The swinging lamp returns at the end of the film, when Dorian's true face is finally revealed, tying the end of Dorian's life into the finish of Basil's life. Alfred Hitchcock used this same effect, although with a naked light bulb, in *Psycho* (1960).

From the time of the killing of Basil Hallwood through the end of the film, *The Picture of Dorian Gray* moves quite quickly, a combination of mystery and horror story, with the thematic material, what little there is, entirely gone. During these moments, the film is always engrossing, capped by the stunning ending from the novel, where Dorian stabs the painting in order to release his soul. As the picture of Dorian Gray changes back to its original form, the last shot of the real Dorian on the ground is of his hollowed out, ravaged face, as shocking in person as the picture on the canvas once was. The makeup on Dorian's face is superb, creating a sickening effect in the viewer.

While *The Picture of Dorian Gray* is seldom included in discussions of horror films, much less classic ones, it is hard to classify the movie as anything other than a horror film. The painting is a supernatural and unexplained phenomenon, there is the curse that follows Dorian throughout his life and there are several killings related to the portrait. For the horror film fan steeped in the tradition of the Universal horrors, *Dorian Gray* is a special viewing experience, demonstrating an alternative approach to bringing a horror classic to the silver screen.

CHAPTER 23
"Casting the Runes" by M.R. James

Many of M.R. James's ghost stories were written for purposes of reading on Christmas Eve. While that practice must seem like an anomaly to most Americans, the telling of ghost stories on Christmas Eve was once a tradition in England, one that is memorialized in the opening of *The Turn of the Screw*, by Henry James. In fact, long after James's death in 1936, his ghost stories were still being read on the radio in England on or near Christmas.

Background

Montague Rhodes James, who published under the name M.R. James, was born in 1862 in Kent, England. His father was a pastor and James lived most of his early years at his father's rectory. In academic circles, James's expertise in classical languages and his work as a medieval scholar of early Christian manuscripts is still well-known today. For the general reading public, James's fame arises from the 40 or so ghost stories that he wrote.

The Literature

Mr. Karswell (no first name given) is the villain of "Casting the Runes" and the implement of his villainy is a parchment with Runic symbols on it. Whenever Karswell desires revenge, he hands the deadly paper to the target and thereafter the problems for the victim begin. In "Casting the Runes," Karswell's intended victim is Edward Dunning, an expert for the British Museum, which recently rejected a paper of Karswell's on the subject of alchemy. Dunning does not even know Karswell but his personal troubles, including his household staff becoming seriously ill, sounds heard in his house at night, objects felt under pillows and an inability to sleep, commence after Dunning receives the parchment from Karswell. Dunning also learns of a prior victim of Karswell's, one John Harrington, who died in unusual circumstances, three months after receiving a similar parchment from Karswell. Dunning's death could therefore be imminent.

Dunning and Henry Harrington, who wants revenge against Karswell for the death of his brother John, devise a scheme to slip the parchment in Dunning's possession back into the hands of Karswell. When Karswell's ticket case with the tickets in it accidentally drops to the floor on a train, Dunning returns the case to Karswell, with the Runic paper hidden inside. A few days later, Henry and Dunning learn that an English traveller by the name of Karswell was visiting an English church under repair, when a stone falling from a scaffold struck him on the head, killing him instantly.

The Runes in the title refer to the letters in a series of alphabets that were used to write German from around the third to the 13th century, before the adoption of the Latin alphabet. To those unfamiliar with the symbols, Runes look very strange. Perhaps as a result of their appearance, the Runes have, over time, acquired a reputation of being associated with magic and the occult. Surprisingly, none of the Runes are shown to the reader in James's story. Instead, James writes that when Dunning and Henry looked at the symbols on the piece of paper in Dunning's possession, "the characters on it were more like Runes than anything else, but not decipherable by either man." Thus, the reader never learns the meaning of the Runes or why they have the power that they have.

In fact, James reveals few of the details of his story directly to the reader, often leaving them to the reader's imagination. The only times the reader gets into the mind of a character is with Dunning. One of the occasions occurs early in the story on a train ride home from work, when Dunning sees an advertisement within one of the panes of glass on the train, which reads, "In memory of John Harrington, F.S.A., of The Laurels, Ashbrooke. Died Sept. 18th, 1889. Three months were allowed." The other time occurs in Dunning's home, after he has received the Runic paper, and even then, most of Dunning's experiences only concern noises he may have heard, images he may have seen and his own bad feelings.

There is little direct action in the story. The death of John Harrington and the condition of his body when discovered are told in retrospect. Similarly, the death of Karswell at the end of the story seems to come from a newspaper article, with few details provided. In Karswell's few appearances in the story, there is nothing evil about him. No demon is ever seen by the reader.

And yet, for all of that, there is a mystery and a foreboding about the narrative that always makes the story compelling. The fact that the story is about the unknown, not the known, and that much is left to the reader's imagination only adds to its effectiveness. Also, it is never quite disclosed what causes John's and Karswell's deaths. Was it a demon or something subtler? Most importantly, if horrific events can really occur to a person just from voluntarily taking possession of a piece of paper, then "Casting the Runes" may have the most terrifying premise of any tale of the supernatural ever written.

The Film

Curse of the Demon/Night of the Demon (1957)

As noted above, "Casting the Runes" is a tale of mood and atmosphere, a narrative of implied horrors, with no demons or killings explicitly described. In other words, M. R. James's style of writing is similar to the style of the filmmaking in the Val Lewton horror films. The director of *Night of the Demon*, Jacques Tourneur, directed several of the Val Lewton films. And so, for those who are familiar with the short story and Tourneur's prior film work, it comes as a complete surprise when *Night of the Demon* commences with a bang.

The film opens with Professor Henry Harrington driving fast in a car, in the dark, on a quiet country road, on the way to the mansion of Dr. Julian Karswell. The scene is shot mainly in shadows, but with very bright lighting on faces and the Karswell abode. There are several point of view shots out of the car. Once Harrington reaches the Karswell estate, he begs Karswell to lift the curse that Karswell has placed on him. Karswell, looking much like a warlock, with his pointed beard and hair in slight disarray, agrees, but when Harrington leaves the Karswell grounds, the figure of a monster emerges from the sky and attacks Harrington. Harrington backs his car into some downed telephone wires and is electrocuted by the fallen wires.

The actual appearances of monsters in horror films often disappoint; the figure of the demon that attacks Harrington does not. The creature emerges from a sudden cloud in the sky, and then gradually takes shape, transforming into a winged creature, with four horns on its head, an angry face with a wide mouth filled with sharp teeth, paws seemingly as big as a car and smoke seemingly coming off its body. It is very impressive.

Thereafter, the main part of the story commences as John Holden, an American authority on paranormal psychology and a skeptic about witches and the supernatural, arrives in London by plane to address a conference of academ-

A poster for *Curse of the Demon* (1957), the American film version of the British film *Night of the Demon* (1957), with a good representation of the title monster.

ics on the subject of the paranormal. Holden is surprised when he learns of the death of Harrington but vows to continue Harrington's research into a cult led by Karswell, even after Karswell asks Holden to discontinue the project. Thereafter, Karswell manages to sneak the dreaded parchment into Holden's belongings and later advises Holden that Holden will die on the 28th of the month. Holden pooh-poohs the idea but Harrington's niece, Joanna, and a hypnotic session with a convict from Karswell's cult, finally cause Holden to change his mind. He slips the parchment back into Karswell's possession on a train and it is Karswell who is killed by the demon on the 28th.

As good as the short story is, it must have been difficult to adapt "Casting the Runes" to the cinema because the story is very brief and there is not much action in it. To a great degree, an original script had to devised for *Night of the Demon*, in order to fill the running time of a feature length film. Nonetheless, it is surprising how many elements of James's short story are included in the film.

Of course, at the heart of both works is the parchment with the Runic symbols on it which must be passed by the potential victim back to the person who gave it to him to avoid a deadly encounter with the demon. Just as in the short story, the parchment passes into Holden's/Dunning's possession in a library and the return to Karswell occurs on a train. Drawings of the demon by the convict Hobart are important clues in the film; the woodcut of a man being chased by a demon enriches the atmosphere of the story. In the film, a card handed by Karswell to Holden has extra writing on it, which says, "In Memoriam Henry Harrington allowed two weeks." The writing then disappears. This is similar to the advertisement about Harrington that Dunning sees within the pane of glass on the train in the short story. The one contrasting element is a children's party thrown by Karswell. In the film, it is a pleasant affair, with Karswell performing magic tricks for the kids. In the story, Karswell scares the children by telling terrifying tales and showing frightening slides on a magic lantern device.

After the introductory sequence of the film, *Night of the Demon* reverts to the storytelling style of James's, becoming a story of atmosphere and implied horrors. For example, Holden experiences chills that others do not feel and his vision becomes blurred on several occasions. There are the pages torn out of Holden's diary for dates after the 28th (something that also occurred to Harrington and an idea that comes from the short story); the prediction of a specific date of death for Holden; a cyclone apparently created by Karswell to scare Holden but which quickly gets out of control; sounds in a dark hallway that cause Holden to feel that he is being followed although nothing can be seen; and a walk through the woods at night and into the dark Karswell mansion highlighted by strange sounds, shadows everywhere and a seemingly disembodied hand following Holden in the house. There is a good effect with Holden, as he runs through the woods, seeing the cloud of the demon materialize in the sky as if out of nothing and then running as the cloud chases after him, before the cloud disappears as suddenly as it appeared. There are also some nice touches in the film, such as the demon's large, smoky footsteps appearing in the dirt outside the Karswell mansion; a small house cat turning into a vicious tiger; Holden trying to slip the paper into Karswell's possession on the train and Karswell parrying each attempt; and Karswell chasing the fluttering parchment down the railroad tracks in an attempt to save his life, when the paper spontaneously combusts and disintegrates.

While the heart of the movie, much like the short story, is atmosphere, mood and foreboding, an important difference between the two is that the reader is never given a description of the demon in the story, assuming there really is a demon in the written work. In the film, the viewer sees the demon in the opening sequence of the film, before the main plot of the film commences. Thus, even in the scenes of implied horror and mystery throughout the movie, the demon is always in the back of the viewer's mind. Since the creature at the beginning of the film is hard to forget, *Night of the Demon* creates a mood of fear and foreboding, not of the unknown, but of a monstrous demon. Then, at the end of the movie, *Night of the Demon* does not disappoint. The monster appears once again, materializing much as it had done before, brutally attacking, mutilating and killing Karswell.

One of the controversies about *Night of the Demon* is whether the demon should have been shown to the audience or whether it should have been left to the audience's imagination. Some have no problem with the monster being shown because, unlike *Cat People* (1942), where a quick shot of a panther undercuts the film's ambiguity as to whether or not there really are cat people, no one watching *Night of the Demon* believes that the demon is a figure of someone's imagination. There are many substantiations of the existence of the creature in the film, even without it being shown on the screen. Most critics, however, are on the side of not showing the monster. An example is the noted horror film historian, Carlos Clarens, who, in *An Illustrated History of the Horror Film*, called showing the demon onscreen, "a monumental blunder." (It is therefore surprising that a picture of the demon is shown on the cover of his book.) Most critics who question the use of the demon in the film hold the Val Lewton horror films in the highest regard.

As a group, the Val Lewton horror films are excellent; they deserve the reputation that they have. However, they do not provide the only way to shoot a horror film or even the best way to shoot a horror film. That always depends on the subject matter, the writing and the style of the film. There is no rule of thumb for filmmaking that recommends against showing the monster onscreen and, of course, most horror films do, to great effect. In *Night of the Demon*, the use of the monster in the opening makes the middle of the film much more effective. The contrasting treatments of the demon in the introductory and middle sections of the film add to the wallop that the last scene has when the demon reappears.

M.R. James did not describe the demon in his short story. If Val Lewton had produced *Night of the Demon*, the demon may not have been shown onscreen. Nevertheless, *Night of the Demon* is surely made more memorable because of the appearances of the demon, one of the iconic monsters of all of horror films.

CHAPTER 24

Carmilla by Sheridan Le Fanu

With the exception of *Dracula's Daughter* (1936), a film purportedly based on a short story by Bram Stoker, it sometimes seems as if every horror film featuring a female vampire cites Sheridan Le Fanu's *Carmilla* as its source. However, even in those instances where the films employ some of the names of the characters from Le Fanu's novella and have beautiful actresses playing the female vampire, it is often difficult to find a strong connection between *Carmilla* and any of those films.

Background

The author of *Carmilla* was Sheridan Le Fanu, sometimes referred to as J. Sheridan Le Fanu. He was born in Dublin, Ireland, in 1814, the son of a clergyman. *Carmilla* was first published in *The Dark Blue*, a magazine associated with Oxford University, in four successive monthly issues starting in December 1871. *Carmilla* was then included in a collection of short stories and longer tales of Le Fanu's titled *In a Glass Darkly*, published later that same year. All of the included stories are purportedly selections from the posthumous papers of Dr. Martin Hesselius, an occult detective. Le Fanu died on February 7, 1873.

The Literature

The narrator of *Carmilla* is 19-year-old Laura, who lives with her father and two governesses in a schloss (or manor house) in Styria, which is located in what is now southern Austria. Laura is lonely for friends her own age and she is excited when, by a strange set of circumstances, a beautiful young woman named Carmilla comes to stay at the schloss for a few months. No one knows Carmilla or anything about her before she moves in and after she moves in, strange things start to occur in the schloss and its neighborhood.

Matters come to a head when General Spielsdorf arrives and tells Laura and her father about the circumstances behind the death of Bertha, the General's niece. Although the villain of the General's story is named Millarca, the circumstances are nearly identical to the sudden appearance of Carmilla and her activities in Laura's house. As Bertha became ill and approached death, the General became suspicious of Millarca, believing that she could be a vampire. The General's suspicions were confirmed when he hid in Bertha's bedroom and watched Millarca take the last bit of blood from Bertha's neck. The General chased Millarca off but Bertha died the next morning.

The General has come to the ruined castle of Karnstein in order to locate the grave of Countess Karnstein, who he believes is a vampire, and to destroy the fiend. With the help of Baron Vordenburg, a student of vampirism, the grave of the Countess is located. Inside rests Carmilla/Mircalla, a 150-year-old vampire. A stake is driven through her heart, her head is cut off, and thereafter, the territory is never plagued by any further manifestations of the undead.

The mythology of the vampires, as described in *Carmilla*, contains some of the characteristics of the undead that horror film fans who have read Bram Stoker's novel, *Dracula*, or viewed the Universal and Hammer vampire movies, have come to expect. According to Baron Vordenburg, the Dr. Van Helsing character of the novella, vampires lust for blood, attempt to return to their coffin for at least a few hours each day to revive their life force, and they seem to be able to escape from closed rooms as if by magic. Despite the fact that vampires like Carmilla may have been dead for many years, they appear quite healthy while out in society. Vampires are best dispatched with a stake through the heart and the cutting off of the head from the body.

Carmilla also displays or recites interesting variations on the conventional lore of the vampires. While in their coffins, vampires sleep in several inches of blood. One sign of the vampire is the power of its hand, with a grasp that seems to be made of steel. For their every day victims, vampires go directly to the attack, usually killing their prey in a single strike. On other occasions, vampires are prone to be fascinated by a particular person, who they then pursue with a passion that is in the nature of love. In such cases, vampires employ a clever strategy and display an inexhaustible patience until they reach their quest, which is the domination and ultimate killing of the victim. Vampires are sometimes restricted to using an anagram of their real names in public so that in this case, the vampire, whose real name is Mircalla, uses the aliases "Millarca" and "Carmilla."

Of course, the most important and somewhat unique characteristic of the vampire in Le Fanu's novella, at least at the time, is her lesbian tendencies. All of Carmilla's victims are females, not just Laura and Bertha, but also the village women who are mentioned in passing throughout the story. However, lesbianism alone is not enough to carry the reputation of *Carmilla* and if that were all there were to the novella, the story would have been forgotten long ago or, at least, it may never have been the inspiration for so many horror films. It is the sensual and sexual nature of the tale that lingers longest in the mind of the reader.

All vampire tales are tales of seduction, to a degree, but *Carmilla* emphasizes that aspect of vampire lore. Carmilla is the sophisticated predator; Laura is the innocent prey. As Laura describes it, "Sometimes after an hour of apathy, my strange and beautiful companion would take my hand and hold it with a fond pressure, renewed again and again; blushing softly, gazing in my face with languid and burning eyes and breathing so fast that her dress rose and fell with the tumultuous respiration. It was like the ardor of a lover" (Chapter IV, "Her Habits—A Saunter"). On another occasion when they are walking together, Carmilla draws her arm close around Laura's waist, lets her head sink upon Laura's shoulder and then kisses Laura, saying, "I live in you and you would die for me, I love you so" (Chapter V, "A Wonderful Likeness"). This seduction of Laura by Carmilla, by touch, kiss and language, continues throughout the narrative.

Both the languor of Carmilla's personality and the beauty of her outer being heighten the sensuality of the tale. Carmilla is described as having a rich and brilliant complexion, small and beautifully formed features, large and lustrous eyes and magnificently thick and long hair that she often wears down about her shoulders (Chapter IV, "Her Habits—A Saunter"). Le Fanu's descriptive language also adds to the sensuality of the story, as in the scene where Laura describes a dream she seems to have each night:

> Sometimes there came a sensation as if a hand was drawn softly along my cheek and neck. Sometimes it was as if warm lips kissed me, and longer and more lovingly as they reached my throat, but there the caress fixed itself. My heart beat faster, my breathing rose and fell rapidly and full drawn; a sobbing, that rose into a sense of strangulation, supervened, and turned into a dreadful convulsion, in which my senses left me, and I became unconscious [Chapter VII, "Descending"].

Here, Le Fanu equates the attack of Carmilla on Laura as a seduction, resulting in an orgasmic response by Laura.

For all of the sensuality for which the story is remembered, *Carmilla* always remains a tale of vampires and horror. There is the dream that Laura had when she was six years old, of a young lady who appeared in her bedroom, caressed Laura and then suddenly disappeared after Laura felt the sensation of two needles run very deep into her breasts. When Laura meets Carmilla years later, she realizes that Carmilla was the lady of the dream. In another of Laura's "dreams," she finds a sooty-black animal that resembles a monstrous cat first pacing back and forth in front of her bed and then springing onto her bed. Laura feels two sharp needle prongs in her breasts and when she awakens, she sees a female figure at the front of her bed, which somehow disappears out of the locked room without a trace.

At the end of the story, when Carmilla sees the General for the first time in many months, a brutalized change instantaneously and horribly comes over her, as her true nature is revealed. Then Carmilla is destroyed in her coffin by a stake driven through her heart, causing the body to utter a piercing scream. Carmilla's head is then cut off and as described by Laura, "a torrent of blood flowed from the severed neck" (Chapter XV, "Ordeal And Execution"). The body and head are then burned to ashes, and the ashes are thrown into the river.

Carmilla is known for its lesbian vampire and its atmosphere of sensuality, but it is principally a horror story, and a good one at that. Hollywood took a pass on the story during the classic horror film era of the 1930s and 1940s, probably because of the Puritanism of the Production Code of 1934, but even until recent times, all of the film versions of Le Fanu's novella have been made outside the United States.

The Films

Blood and Roses/Et mourir de plaisir (1960)

Blood and Roses is an Italian-French production that opened in Paris in 1960, under the title *Et Mourir de plaisir*, which means "And Die of Pleasure." The film credits a story by Sheridan Le Fanu as its source material and with a lead character named Carmilla, the title of Le Fanu's story is obvious. The setting of *Carmilla* has been moved from 19th century Austria to modern-day Italy, where wealthy Leopoldo De Karnstein is set to marry the beautiful Georgia Monteverdi. Also present in the house is Carmilla, a cousin of Leopoldo's from the Austrian side of the Karnstein family. The Karnsteins have a history of vampirism in the family tree, but since peasants supposedly attacked the last of the line of vampires in 1765 and killed them all, the modern day family believes it has nothing to worry about.

Georgia Monteverdi (Elsa Martinelli), left, and her fiancé Leopoldo De Karnstein (Mel Ferrer) assist Carmilla (Annette Vadim) who has just discovered the lost crypt where her ancestor Millarca was buried, in *Blood and Roses* (1960). The characters are still in their costumes from the masked ball.

Unbeknownst to the current members of the Karnstein family, one vampire did survive the attack of the peasants those many years before. Her name is Millarca and on the night of a masked ball, when some explosions uncover her final resting place in the graveyard near Leopoldo's villa, Millarca entices Carmilla out to her grave by supernatural means. The spirit of Millarca then takes over the body of Carmilla, turning Carmilla into a vampire. Later, in a quest for blood, Carmilla kills a servant girl and then starts after Georgia. However, instead of killing Georgia, Millarca takes over her body and marries Leopoldo, who she believes is the reincarnation of her lost love from centuries before. As the film ends, Leopoldo has commenced his honeymoon with Georgia, not realizing he has married Millarca, not Georgia.

As can be seem from that plot synopsis, *Blood and Roses* is only a loose adaptation of Le Fanu's famous novella. While there are some lesbian overtones to the story, the lesbian element is muted in the dubbed English language version that was viewed, amounting to not much more than Carmilla kissing Georgia on the lips when she sees a spot of blood on those lips. Apparently, the version shown in Europe placed more emphasis on the lesbian aspects of the tale. In any event, since Millarca is most interested in Leopoldo and not the other females in the story, her purported lesbianism may have been exaggerated for this film, although without seeing the European version, that cannot be confirmed.

When a story about a beautiful woman is transferred to the screen, readers are often disappointed when the actress playing the part of the beautiful woman first appears in the film. It is difficult for any actress to match the reader's imagination of what the character actually looks like. That is one of the reasons why Alfred Hitchcock decided against showing the beautiful and vivacious title character in *Rebecca* in a flashback.

Blood and Roses is a solid exception to that rule. Annette Vadim, who plays Carmilla, is strikingly beautiful in the role and her beauty has not dimmed upon viewing the movie over 50 years after the film was released. In fact, there must be something special about the role of Carmilla, as the part has been played by many beautiful women over many films, including Ingrid Pitt, Yutte Stensgaard and Alexandra Bastedo, and none of them disappoint even after all these many years since their films were first released.

There are some interesting variations on vampire lore in this film. Carmilla/Mircalla can see her reflection in a mirror, but the reflected image shows the blood of a victim on her dress. Vampires must return to their grave for at least a few hours each night to revive their energy (a concept that is similar to the lore recited in Le Fanu's novella). Animals are afraid of them; flowers die in their hands. Of course, the significant plot device of *Blood and Roses*, the ability of a vampire to inhabit the body of another, is original to the film.

Blood and Roses is filled with striking moments, particularly the visions of Carmilla, blond hair down and in a white dress, usually shot from a long distance, walking across the gardens of the Karnstein villa toward the graveyard or the countryside. The most memorable of these shots occurs when Carmilla is walking along a lake as fireworks go off above her. These are remarkable images, aided by the color cinematography of Claude Renoir, the nephew of the famous French director, Jean Renoir. Late in the film there is a dream sequence, shot in black and white, which is surrealistic in nature, another triumph of Claude Renoir. However, the dream sequence, while striking, does not make a lot of sense and it clashes with the mood of the vampire storyline.

There is a lot to admire in *Blood and Roses*, including its direction and cinematography, the use of the great location of the centuries old Hadrian's Villa in Tivoli, Italy, the background music provided by an Irish harp and the beauty of its actresses. However, there is only one death by vampire in the film and not much other action. As a result, *Blood and Roses* is mildly disappointing. It is worth one view by a horror film fan but few will desire to see it again and again.

The Vampire Lovers (1970)

The Vampire Lovers is a close adaptation of Sheridan Le Fanu's *Carmilla*, although with changes in some of the characters' names and with a little padding, particularly in the scene before the credits in which a female vampire is killed by Baron Hartog (the Baron Vordenburg character from the novella), a vignette that does not come from the novella. After the credits to *The Vampire Lovers*, the main story commences. In terms of the narrative order of the film, a significant change from *Carmilla* is that the novella's story arc of Laura (the general's daughter and the Bertha character from the novella) is depicted before the novella's primary story of Emma (the Laura character from the novella). In the novella, Laura's story is told first and Bertha's story is told at the end of the novella, in retrospect, by her uncle, the general. When the general tells the story in the novella, it commands the attention of the reader, since he is accidentally solving the mystery of Laura's situation. By putting them in chronological order in *The Vampire Lovers*, the film, now with two very similar story arcs, seems repetitive.

The lesbianism inherent in *Carmilla* is on display in *The Vampire Lovers*, particularly when Carmilla seduces Emma, by suggestively touching and kissing her all over her body, including her exposed breasts, and expressing her love. Oddly, though, despite the lesbian content, there is very little sensuality in the movie. It is true that the actresses in the film are beautiful and voluptuous, particularly Ingrid Pitt as Marcilla/Carmilla, and they wear low cut dresses to show off their statuesque figures. Upon occasion, the film seems more like soft porn than a horror film, particularly in a gratuitous scene where a naked Carmilla is bathing herself in a freestanding tub while Emma (and the audience) looks on. These types of scenes and others with partial frontal nudity must have seemed shocking in the 1970s. Even today they are jarring for a horror film fan who is expecting to see a straightforward vampire movie. While one can hardly deny an interest in viewing these partially naked and beautiful actresses, the shots add little to the cogency of the plot or the intended sexuality of the movie.

As one would expect from a Hammer film, particularly one from the 1970s, *The Vampire Lovers* is very bloody. Even before the opening credits, the head of a female vampire who is still alive is sliced off by means of a sharp sword across her neck. When Laura's body is shown after an attack by the vampire, the blood of Laura seems to be dripping down her neck, The same occurs with other victims of the female vampire, of which there are so many that the film may have set an all-time record for deaths in a vampire movie. *The Vampire Lovers* emphasizes

Carmilla (Ingrid Pitt), using the alias Marcilla, seduces Laura, the general's daughter, in *The Vampire Lovers* (1970).

the viciousness of the attacks by Carmilla, usually preceded by tight shots of her very sharp fangs. That tight shot is far more effective in creating horror than the sequence before the credits in which the female vampire's head is sliced off, particularly since it is obvious that a dummy was used in the decapitation sequence.

The special effects, to extent there are any, are very disappointing. For full effect, Emma's dreams about the monstrous cat that attacks her each night should have been shown onscreen. Instead, there are some indistinct point-of-view images of a cat whose eyes sometimes alternate with the eyes of Carmilla, some fur shown on her bed and not much else. There is a lot of style in the shots but they are more confusing than frightening. Later in the film, Emma tells Carmilla that at the end of her dreams, the cat turns into Carmilla, a metamorphosis never shown to the viewers. It would have been nice to see that special effect onscreen, instead of just being told about it. A few more dollars in the special effects budget would have gone a long way toward improving this film.

Another problem with *The Vampire Lovers*, which may well be its most significant one, is that the audience never really gets to know and like the female victims, either before or during the time period of Carmilla's attacks. In the first part of the film, Laura is dispatched so quickly that it is hard to remember much about her. More time is taken with the seduction of Emma, but the viewer still never learns much about her. Frankly, she seems like a spoiled rich girl who is far too old to have a full-time governess. The viewer has scant reason to care about Emma and without a reason to care whether Emma survives or not, the film becomes boring. That is also one of the reasons why viewers often root for Carmilla against her victims instead of the other way around.

The acting in the film is only fair, with the notable exception of Peter Cushing, who plays the general. Cushing seems very comfortable in the role, particularly at the end of the film when he returns to Emma's house as a vampire slayer, much like his most famous horror film role as Dr. Van Helsing, a character he played on many occasions in vampire movies for Hammer studios.

There are some elements of the film that do not come from Sheridan Le Fanu, including Carmilla attacking, controlling and then killing Emma's governess and the Morton butler. In addition to some village girls, Carmilla also kills the Morton family doctor (and another male character earlier in the film), so this Carmilla does not limit her victims to the female of the species. There are also some interesting variations on vampire lore. It now seems that a vampire can disappear into thin air right in front of everyone's eyes and that a vampire cannot rest in her coffin unless she is wearing the shroud in which she was interred so that it can cloak her festering body. It is amazing how many different film variations there are on the legends and lore of the vampires.

The ending of the film is strong, with cross cutting between Carmilla's final attack on Emma, interrupted by the necessary killings of the governess and the butler, and the scenes at the graveyard as the General and the Baron search for the coffin of Carmilla. There is a nice touch when the young hero, Carl, after doing battle with Carmilla and stymieing her with a cross at the top of a knife, throws the knife at Carmilla, who fades into nothingness. The knife travels through the faint image of Carmilla and breaks a flower vase on the table behind her. Carmilla escapes. There is also a very nice touch at the end of the film after Carmilla is killed, when the portrait of Carmilla changes into a skeleton with two very sharp fangs.

Even with its strong ending, beautiful women, great locations, and believable period costumes and sets, *The Vampire Lovers* is, overall, a disappointing film, particularly in terms of writing, the shortcuts caused by its low budget and the film's emphasis on nudity. On the other hand, as one of the most faithful adaptations of *Carmilla* ever made, *The Vampire Lovers* is a film that the true horror film aficionado will not want to miss.

Other Adaptations

A number of other films and television productions were purportedly inspired by Sheridan Le Fanu's novella, *Carmilla*. They include the 1964 Italian/Spanish production titled *Crypt of the Vampire/La Crepta e L'incubo*, which included Christopher Lee in the cast, and *The Blood Splattered Bride/La Novia Ensangrentada* (1972), a Spanish production.

Chapter 25

The Werewolf of Paris by Guy Endore

The Werewolf of Paris met with great success when it was first published in 1933. Its author, Guy Endore, then moved to Hollywood where he wrote screenplays for several films, including *Mark of the Vampire* (1935) and *The Devil-Doll* (1936). Yet, when Universal decided to turn to werewolf movies as a part of its horror output in the 1930s and 1940s, the studio opted to forego an adaptation of *The Werewolf of Paris* and instead, devised original screenplays for those films. Thus, it was not until 1961, at a time when Hammer Films was adapting horror novels for the movies on a regular basis, that *The Werewolf of Paris* was finally brought to the cinema.

Background

Guy Endore was born on July 4, 1900, in New York City, where he received his undergraduate degree and his master's degree from Columbia University in the 1920s. In the 1930s, Endore turned to writing novels and short stories, the most famous of which is his only horror novel, *The Werewolf of Paris*, published in 1933. In Hollywood, Endore contributed to the scripts for many films including *The Story of G.I. Joe* (1945), for which he received an Academy Award nomination. Guy Endore died in 1970.

The Literature

After a short preface, the story of *The Werewolf of Paris* begins with two introductory sections. The first involves a feud between the Pitaval and Pitamont families, which results in Jehan Pitamont being thrown down an old well, where he remains for over 50 years, living on pieces of meat given to him three times each week. The next introductory section involves a village girl named Josephine, who is raped by a Paris priest named Father Pitamont. Josephine becomes pregnant by Father Pitamont and when the baby is born on Christmas Eve, Mme Didier, Josephine's employer, is concerned because she believes that a child born on Christmas Eve, particularly one who is the child of a priest, is cursed as it is "a mockery of the birth of Christ" (Chapter Four).

The main part of the novel commences with the appearance of a wolf-like creature in the village of Mont d'Arcy. Over time, it becomes clear that Josephine's son Bertrand is a werewolf, starting from the time he kills animals in the woods, attacks a prostitute in Paris and back home, kills one of his childhood friends. Returning to Paris, Bertrand becomes a member of the National Guard, where he meets a rich and beautiful young lady, Sophie, who is donating her time to assist at the soldiers' canteen. Sophie and Bertrand then start a torrid love affair and, as a result, Bertrand's afflictions seem to have been cured. However, Bertrand's disease is only in remission, a result of Bertrand cutting Sophie's body at night with a knife and then drinking the blood from the wounds. Thereafter, as a result of the vagaries of war, Sophie and Bertrand become separated. Bertrand is locked up in a French sanitarium, where he commits suicide, jumping to his death with another person he believes, in his delusions, to be Sophie.

One of the special interests in *The Werewolf of Paris* is that the reader is sometimes made privy to the innermost thoughts of Bertrand as, for example, when he stalks his friend Jacques along the road to Paris, and once that killing is done, tries to understand the disease with which he has been stricken. In Paris, the reader is with Bertrand as he becomes interested in Sophie while at the same time he worries about what he may unconsciously do to her when his lycanthropy swells inside. *The Werewolf of Paris* is far more successful in creating an understanding of the mental travails of the werewolf than all the complaining that Larry Talbot was wont to do in his feature films at Universal. Understanding the disease from the perspective of the werewolf is something that literature can do best.

While a tale of lycanthropy, *The Werewolf of Paris* is also an historical novel, as the story of Bertrand is woven through events of the Franco-Prussian War (1870–1871), the rise of the National Guard in defending Paris during the war and the temporary ascension of the Paris Commune to power, an attempt by the working class to rule the city. Unfortunately, therein lies one of the problems with the novel. These real life events are not just background material for the story. They are sometimes long and uninteresting diversions to the main plot. These events then lead to a disappointing climax to the novel, as the werewolf is never killed in a spectacular finish, something a horror fan is conditioned to expect. Instead, Bertrand commits one more act of violence, the killing of a guard, and then leaps to his death as a result of a fit of madness, not to end his curse.

In addition to being a story of an affliction that degrades a human being into becoming an animal, thereby necessarily involving bestiality and cannibalism, *The Werewolf of Paris* is a story of other base aspects of the human condition. In its scenes of Father Pitamont raping Josephine, Bertrand's visit to a prostitute in Paris for his first sexual encounter and Bertand and his mother copulating, *The Werewolf of Paris* is a story of the sexual depravity of the clergy, prostitution and incest, some of the more sordid aspects of human sexuality. Cleverly, death comes not only from the werewolf in *The Werewolf of Paris*; it also comes from war and revolution. Aymar Galliez, the nephew of Mme Didier, recognizes the contradiction in chasing after a werewolf amidst the turmoil of class warfare and mass killings in Paris, thinking to himself, "What was a werewolf who had killed a couple of prostitutes, who had dug up a few corpses, compared with these bands of tigers slashing at each other with daily increasing ferocity!" (Chapter Seventeen). Aymar comes to believe that while he once thought werewolves were a rare phenomenon, in a time of revolution, the world is full of them. If *The Werewolf of Paris* has a theme, this is it.

Unexpectedly, since the combination of sex and horror is usually associated with vampires, not werewolves, *The Werewolf of Paris* is, in many ways, a story about sexuality, giving the novel a different feel than most other works about werewolves. The underlying curse of the werewolf comes from sex, albeit rape, and the resulting birth of a young boy on Christmas Eve. Bertrand's first serious attack on a human comes when Bertrand has his first experience with sexuality with the prostitute in Paris, and it comes in a moment of slight kinkiness, when Bertrand tries to take off her last piece of clothing with his teeth, catches a bit of skin between his teeth, feels a drop of blood in his mouth and then goes mad with his affliction. Bertram and Sophie's sexual union involves, in part, Bertrand cutting Sophie and sipping some of her blood at night, adding an element of violence and deviance to their carnal relationship.

As effective as *The Werewolf of Paris* is, the novel is hurt by its side trips into historical events and its detours into the personal stories of some of its unimportant characters, making the book boring at times. Nevertheless, when the novel focuses on its tale of lycanthropy, *The Werewolf of Paris* is original and haunting. Yet, it is also a story that is so rooted in the depravity of all of mankind, not just the werewolf, that it would seem to be a difficult novel to bring to the cinema. Perhaps that is the reason why Universal Studios overlooked Guy Endore's novel in the 1930s and 1940s and that it took until the 1960s to bring the novel to the silver screen.

The Film

The Curse of the Werewolf (1961)

The Curse of the Werewolf follows the general storyline of *The Werewolf of Paris*, as it involves Leon, an unwanted child who is born on Christmas Eve, who grows up and becomes a werewolf. Leon's mother is a mute servant girl who was raped by a beggar who was imprisoned many years ago in a dungeon jail, causing the beggar to become somewhat of a beast himself, similar to the novel's introductory story arc of the imprisonment of Jehan Pitamont. In the novel, the narrator wrote that the story of Jehan Pitamont had little to do with the main plot of his story so it is somewhat surprising that the filmmakers were impressed enough with the incident to incorporate it into the film.

The Curse of the Werewolf is set in 18th century Spain, which means that all of the French historical references and diversions from the novel are not incorporated into the film. That is a decided plus for the movie. However, many other incidents from the novel appear in the film, such as Don Alfredo, Leon's guardian, barring the windows of his room so that Leon cannot escape at night, the mutilation of animals in the village, the local policeman shooting at the wolf and the bullet being found in Leon's leg and Leon pursuing a beautiful and wealthy young woman who is expected to be married to another.

The last third of the film, however, diverges almost completely from the novel, which is understandable since the novel has a weak ending. At the end of the film, Leon is arrested for murder and placed in prison. Then, at the height of the full moon, he changes into a werewolf, attacks his fellow prisoner and breaks out of jail. He is then chased along the rooftops of the town until Don Alfredo shoots him with a silver bullet made by the village watchman from a crucifix many years before. The silver bullet comes from the novel but the exciting conclusion is completely original.

The Curse of the Werewolf employs some nice touches early in the film to foreshadow the horror that the young Leon will become. On the night of Leon's birth, Don Alfredo, sitting downstairs, seems to hear a howl from the room upstairs, before he hears the first cries of the newborn child. At the time of Leon's baptism, when the priest first holds Leon, the skies outside turn black and the inside of the church becomes somewhat dark. As the priest starts to dip Leon's fingers into the water in the font, the water starts to bubble, there is a clap of lightning and the impression of a gargoyle is seen in the water, almost as if the Church does not want to become involved with such a despicable beast. Just as in the novel, when Leon becomes older, hair begins to grow on the palms of his hands.

Oliver Reed in a publicity photograph for *The Curse of the Werewolf* (1961).

Much like the style of *The Werewolf of Paris*, Leon's attacks on animals and humans are not directly shown in *The Curse of the Werewolf*. Sometimes only the results of his actions are shown in the film. On other occasions, his attacks are seen in shadow only or the camera focuses on the victims' faces, with Leon's actions unseen. While the growls and snarls of the beast are clearly heard on the soundtrack, Leon is never shown as a hairy, bestial figure until the end of the movie. By delaying the werewolf's actual appearance until the end of the film, the horror of the figure is greatly enhanced.

The Curse of the Werewolf eschews much of the book's emphasis on the base aspects of all mankind, limiting those ideas to the beginning of the film with the segments involving the sadism of the wealthy marquis and the rape of the mute servant girl. While there is a sexual element to Leon's affliction, in that it is in remission until he begins to engage in sexual activity as an adult, that is only a minor point of the film. In fact, the movie glosses over the relationship between Leon and Cristina, who substitutes for the Sophie character in the novel. The book, on the other hand, seems to emphasize the sexual underpinnings of its tale.

The Curse of the Werewolf addresses lycanthropy in a much different way than *The Werewolf of Paris*. In the book, no one believes Aymar when he tries to explain Bertrand's affliction. In the film, the people of the village are very open to the concept of a werewolf in their midst. In fact, it is the village priest who explains the legend of the werewolf to Don Alfredo. The priest tells Alfredo that the spirit of a wolf sometimes enters a person's body at the moment of birth (often when a person's soul is weak, perhaps from an accident of birth, such as an inherited defect), resulting in a war between the person's soul and the spirit of the beast. Whatever weakens the soul, such as vice, greed, hatred or solitude, strengthens the spirit of the beast and whatever weakens the spirit of the beast, warmth, fellowship or love, strengthens the soul. There is therefore no cure for Leon's affliction except for the love of his family or the love of a woman.

The priest's explanation of the causes and cure of lycanthropy highlights a problem with the novel, *The Werewolf of Paris*. The book never provides the rules of the werewolf, i.e., what strengthens the wolf, weakens the wolf and what will cure or destroy the wolf. The novel has no structure in that regard, making Bertrand's sudden changes from man into beast in the book seem random and arbitrary. On the other hand, most viewers of horror films expect rules for the conduct of their monsters, whether vampires, werewolves or mummies. The priest of the film provides those rules to the viewer, providing an explanation of Leon's conduct in the film and giving the film a measure of cohesiveness. Oddly, the conduct of Bertrand in the novel also conforms to the rules laid out by the priest in the film, paradoxically resulting in the novel making more sense after the film is viewed.

The Curse of the Werewolf uses two horror film motifs to enhance the effectiveness of its story. The priest establishes a Jekyll-Hyde confrontation between good and evil for the soul of the werewolf, thereby incorporating a theme of many horror films, not just those that are adaptations of Robert Louis Stevenson's famous novella. The priest also notes that the spirit of the wolf is strongest during the cycle of the full moon, when the forces of evil have their greatest potency. This is a familiar concept for fans of the Wolf Man films of the 1940s.

In fact, the ending of *The Curse of the Werewolf* owes more to the Wolf Man movies of the 1940s than it does to *The Werewolf of Paris*. Leon makes only one transformation into a wolf during the film and that metamorphosis is primarily shown by the growth of hair on Leon's hands and the change in shape of his hands. In *The Wolf Man* (1941), the first transformation of Larry Talbot is shown by the growth of hair on Talbot's feet and the change in shape of those feet. Leon is killed by a silver bullet shot by the person he believes is his father, surely a person who loves him enough to understand. Larry Talbot is killed by a silver cane wielded by his father, a man who, although he may not have understood his son all that well, loves him very much.

By combining the most cinematic elements of Guy Endore's novel with some good ideas from prior werewolf films, Hammer Studios has created one of the best werewolf movies ever made. *The Curse of the Werewolf* can easily stand alongside *The Curse of Frankenstein* (1957) and *Horror of Dracula* (1958) as excellent adaptations of famous novels of horror by Hammer Studios.

CHAPTER 26

The Turn of the Screw by Henry James

Herman Melville, Virginia Woolf, James Joyce and Henry James—these are frightening names for any high school or college student, and not because of any horror stories they wrote. These authors are frightening because it is just so hard getting through any of their books, particularly ones that have to be read for a school assignment. For horror film fans, however, Henry James is slightly different from the other three. James wrote one ghost novella, *The Turn of the Screw*, which was considered good enough to be adapted for the screen and television on many occasions, including *The Innocents* (1961), a movie that is considered a classic of the horror film.

Background

Henry James was born in in New York City in 1843. During his early writing career, James contributed pieces to magazines and wrote short stories and book reviews, including some short ghost stories. In all, James wrote over 20 novels and novellas, some of the most famous being *Daisy Miller* (1979) and *The Portrait of a Lady* (1881), both about American women in Europe and, of course, *The Turn of the Screw* (1897). Henry James died in 1916. In the preface to the 1908 book edition of *The Turn of the Screw*, James wrote that the story came from a half-remembered anecdote told to him by Edward White Benson, the archbishop of Canterbury, about small children haunted by the ghosts of a pair of servants who wished to do the children harm.

The Literature

After an introductory segment about the telling of ghost stories on Christmas Eve and the promise by a man named Douglas to tell a story "quite too horrible" and beyond "dreadfulness," *The Turn of the Screw* is related through the album of a woman who worked as a governess for two young children, Flora and Miles, in an isolated country home known as Bly. On several occasions while at Bly, the governess sees, or believes she sees, Peter Quint, the valet of the children's uncle, who is now deceased and Miss Jessel, the deceased predecessor of the governess. When Flora becomes sick after one of the governess' sightings of the apparent ghosts, Mrs. Grose, the housekeeper, takes Flora away from Bly for her protection. The governess remains in the large house with Miles but when the ghost of Quint appears again, Miles is so shocked that his heart stops and he dies.

One of the strengths of *The Turn of the Screw* is that over a century after the work was first published, readers are still arguing over whether or not the ghosts are tangible or just imagined. Some readers believe that the governess imagines the visions of Quint and Miss Jessel, making the novella into a psychological tale, rather than a ghost story. No one other than the governess ever sees the two ghosts, even when she sees them in the presence of others. Flora may be lying when she denies their existence, but Mrs. Grose, an honest character in the novel, denies seeing them also. The governess does seem to have an imaginative disposition, so it would not be out of character for her to see things that do not exist.

Other readers believe that the ghosts are real. At a time when the governess had no idea what Quint looked like in life, the governess describes his phantom so clearly to Mrs. Grose that Mrs. Grose identifies the ghost as Quint. Also, if the apparitions are only imagined, why does Miles die at the end of the story?

Still other readers see the novella as one of sexual repression, with the governess imagining the ghosts because of repressed memories and unfulfilled desires in her life. Support for this position comes from the language of the narrative, written by the hand of the governess, which employs unusual words for such a story, such as "intercourse," "throbs," and "climax," the governess' excessive touching of the children and some unusual imagery such as the governess describing Flora creating a boat by finding a small flat piece of wood with a hole in it and sticking another fragment through it to serve as its mast. The problem with this analysis is that there is little in the story about the governess' background and Douglas, the man who introduces the story, has nothing but good to say about the woman. Yet, once again, the novel is ambiguous on this issue, as Douglas implies that the governess was in love with the children's uncle, even though they met on only one occasion, once again providing support for the unrequited sexual longings of the young lady.

In his Introduction to *The Portable Henry James,* Professor John Auchard quotes the writer Joseph Conrad, who liked the work of Henry James, as saying that he could only "imagine with pain the man in the street trying to read it." Others have complained about the "Byzantine syntax" of James and still others believe that his work is "unfathomably slow and dull." Of course, Professor Auchard and many other writers and teachers dispute those claims but, in fact, there is quite a lot of truth in them, at least as to *The Turn of the Screw.*

As to "Byzantine syntax," it is a rare sentence of James's that does not ramble on for line after line, with clauses and subordinate clauses divided by commas, semi-colons and dashes. Thoughts of the narrator are interrupted, mid-thought, with other irrelevant thoughts, thereby causing the story to become very confusing. As to "slow and dull," not much really happens in *The Turn of the Screw.* The governess sees the apparitions of Quint and Miss Jessel on several occasions, the two children seem to be hiding something from her, and the school that Miles attends will not permit him to return for the next session. That is about it. Most of the rest of the novella concerns the ramblings of the governess as she overreacts to everything and imagines that she is in a contest of wills with the two children. This is obviously not the stuff of great horror. If *The Turn of the Screw* had been a short story rather than a novella, it would have worked much better, at least for readers of ghost stories who are not English professors. The one highlight of the plot is the sudden and surprise ending, with the death of Miles occurring in the last seven words of the novel.

The title, *The Turn of the Screw,* is a metaphor used by Henry James to imply that as each plot point in his novel is revealed, the story gets more intense, revealing deeper and deeper layers, just as the turning of a screw by a screwdriver tightens a screw and pushes it deeper into the wood. While the meaning of the title is interesting, it is still generic, having little relevance to the plot of the novel. Perhaps for that reason, the name of the 1961 film adaptation was changed to *The Innocents,* a more appropriate title.

The Film

The Innocents (1961)

The Innocents is a faithful adaptation of *The Turn of the Screw* by Henry James, which is surprising because there is not much padding in the film and, as noted above, there is not much action in the novella. Who would have thought that *The Turn of the Screw* could have ever inspired a critically acclaimed horror film?

Those familiar with *The Turn of the Screw* will recognize the opening of the film, where the uncle hires the governess (who now has a name, Miss Giddens), with the orders never to contact the uncle about the children. Most of the subsequent sequences in the film also come from the story, such as Miles having been expelled from his school; the governess spotting the ghosts of Quint and Miss Jessel on several occasions but having no interaction with them; no one else seeing the ghosts; Miles sneaking out of his room at night with the assistance of Flora; Flora having fits near the end of the movie when the governess tries to convince her to admit that she sees the ghost of Jessel; and Miles dying at the very end of the film when Quint appears for one last time.

The Innocents is a little more explicit than the novella on the backstory of Quint and Miss Jessel. In the written work, Mrs. Grose advises the governess that Quint and Jessel were "infamous" in life, perhaps becoming two familiar with the children. In the film, Quint and Jessel were in a torrid love affair, with Quint often mistreating Jessel, who nevertheless committed suicide after the death of Quint. The film also lays out the plot more overtly, such as at the end of the film, when the governess sends away all of the other occupants of Bly so that she can deal directly with Miles. The governess clearly has a plan to thwart Quint's attempts to possess Miles' soul and to rid the house of Quint. She is successful in the latter goal, but at the expense of Miles' life. Miles' death in the film appears to come as a result of the dispossession of Miles by Quint; in the novella, the cause of death is unclear.

Once again, there is some question in *The Innocents* as to whether the apparitions of Quint and Jessel actually appear at Bly or whether the governess is imagining them. The arguments from the novella as to the reality of the ghosts, pro and con, also apply to the film, particularly because it appears that the governess is the only character in the movie who sees the ghosts. In addition, Deborah Kerr gives a particularly hysterical portrayal of the governess, supporting the belief that the ghosts are imagined. On the other hand, as a result of the way the film is shot, the audience sees the ghosts on the screen and not always from the perspective of the governess. The two children sometimes use very adult language when talking, as if the spirits of Quint and Jessel have already possessed their bodies. Much like the novella, if the ghosts are only imagined, why does Miles die at the end of the film? It is substantially easier to make the argument that the ghosts are real in *The Innocents* than it is in *The Turn of the Screw*.

Whether or not *The Turn of the Screw* is about sexual repression, *The Innocents* is not. The only hint of sexual matters in the film comes from the two occasions when Miles and the governess kiss each other on the lips, once brought about by Miles (and used more to show his deviousness or his possession by Quint, and not for any thematic purposes) and the other occurring after Miles dies. Other than the fact that the governess is a parson's daughter, the audience learns nothing about her background in the film. She does not fall in love with the children's uncle in their short meeting together. The imagery and language of the novel do not carry over to the film. Therefore, it is quite a leap to find issues of sexual repression in *The Innocents*.

As to "unfathomably slow and dull," since the plot of the film is so similar to that of *The Turn of the Screw*, with neither having any memorable shocking moments, that phrase, on its face, could be used to describe *The Innocents*. (Luckily, filmgoers do not have to worry about "Byzantine syntax.") Here, though, the difference between literature and film is most apparent. Even though the film employs many of the same horror incidents as the novella, consisting almost always of the appearances of the apparitions of Quint and Jessel, the film is much more successful in making those appearances into chilling moments. A

The children, Flora (Pamela Franklin) and Miles (Martin Stephens), suggest a game of hide and seek to their governess, Miss Giddons (Deborah Kerr), in *The Innocents* (1961), which may not be such a good idea in the old dark house of Bly.

good example is the first appearance of Quint. The governess is outside in the garden, cutting flowers, with Flora singing and birds chirping in the background. Suddenly, all of the background sounds stops and the governess, slightly blinded by the sunlight, sees a man on the tower of the mansion. After being dismayed by the appearance of the man, the governess drops her cut flowers in a decorative pond. The sound of the flowers hitting the water brings back all of the other background sounds in the scene and the image of the man is gone. What was a perplexing moment in the novella is a haunting moment for the film.

Another example is the second appearance of Quint. The governess is hiding behind some curtains in a large room, playing a game of hide and seek with the children, when the image of Quint suddenly appears in the windowpanes behind her, quickly grows larger until his face fills the screen, lingers for a while and stares at the governess and then mysteriously fades away into blackness. This is an effective restaging of the scene in the novella where the governess spots Quint staring at her from outside the dining room window, once again changing a perplexing moment from the novella into a chilling one for the cinema.

In addition, the tools of the cinema, setting, sound and background music, add to the success of the story. The house at Bly is vast, isolated, lonely and, upon occasion, dark and shadowy. It is a natural setting for a ghost story and contributes significantly to the film's atmosphere of horror. As to the effective use of sound, there are the haunting sounds of Miss Jessel crying in the schoolroom and the melody from the music box that reappears in the film from time to time. Then, in striking contrast, there are a few moments when the film goes almost completely silent, such as in Quint's first appearance, described above. *The Innocents* demonstrates that it is nearly impossible for the written word to employ sound as effectively as the cinema, and that does not even take into account the film's excellent score by George Auric, which adds to the tension of the film, particularly when the phantoms are on the screen.

The film has its flaws. While the performance of Deborah Kerr in the film has been critically acclaimed, the governess often becomes hysterical with little justification, making the character somewhat irritating. Pamela Franklin, as Flora, and Martin Stephens, as Miles, do a fine job, but they make their characters into two of the least appealing children in the entire cinema of horror. Without likable protagonists in the film, it is difficult for the viewer to become invested in the travails and suffering of the characters, undercutting many of the positives of the feature.

The Innocents still receives great critical acclaim today, as does *The Turn of the Screw*. If neither is quite as good as its reputation, the difference is that *The Turn of the Screw* is mainly relegated to the classroom while horror film fans still watch and enjoy *The Innocents*.

Chapter 27

Conjure Wife
by Fritz Leiber

Conjure Wife is about witches, evil spells and manifestations of the supernatural, nothing that one would expect to find in everyday life. Yet, at the core of *Conjure Wife* is the proposition that many women practice witchcraft on a daily basis, to guard their own interests, of course, but also to protect their husbands and push them to success in their careers. It is for that reason that an advertising slogan for the book, which appears on covers of some of the paperback versions, reads, "Behind every good man there's an *evil* woman."

Background

Fritz Leiber, Jr. was born in Chicago, Illinois, in 1910, the son of two Shakespearian actors, Fritz Leiber, Sr., and Virginia Bronson Leiber. The senior Leiber had a long career as a character actor in the movies, appearing in such famous films as *The Hunchback of Notre Dame* (1939) and *The Sea Hawk* (1940). The junior Leiber also acted in a handful of films. *Conjure Wife* was the first novel Leiber wrote. It was first published in the April 1943 edition of *Unknown Worlds*, a pulp fiction magazine, in book form in an anthology in 1952 and then as a stand-alone novel in 1953. Leiber wrote extensively in the science fiction and horror genres, eventually receiving a Grand Master Award from the Science Fiction Writers of America. Leiber died in 1992.

The Literature

The good man of *Conjure Wife* is Norman Saylor, a professor of sociology at Hempnell College, a small college that appears to be located in the mid–Atlantic region of the United States. The not-so-evil woman behind Norman is his wife, Tansy, properly described as a white witch, i.e., a witch that uses her powers for good rather than evil, protecting the innocent rather than harming others. Unbeknownst to Norman, ever since the two first came to Hempnell College several years ago, Tansy has been using her powers of magic to ward of the attempts of three evil witches, Evelyn Sawtell, Hulda Gunnison and Flora Carr, faculty wives all, to cause damage to Norman and his advancing career. However, when Norman discovers that Tansy believes in witchcraft, he orders her to dispose of all of the paraphernalia of her hobby. Immediately thereafter, matters start to go horribly wrong in Norman's life, so much so that Norman, despite his professorial and rational outlook on life, finally concedes to the reality of witchcraft. At the conclusion of the novel, Norman barely prevents the witchcraft-induced suicide of Tansy and then frees Tansy's soul from the mind and body of one of the three witches.

One of the interests of *Conjure Wife* is the analytical way that witchcraft is treated in the novel. The witches do not dress in black, make incantations in front of a cauldron or live in a cave outside society. Instead, the tale occurs in the very real world of a small college, with the witchcraft done on the sly, with few aware of what is happening. Evil in a real, modern setting can sometimes be much more horrifying than evil occurring in the trappings of the traditional horror novel, such as an old dark house with a full moon in the sky and evil creatures roaming the countryside. Indeed, the commonplace nature of the witchcraft in *Conjure Wife* is what makes the novel so effective.

There are, however, some true moments of horror in the novel. There is the striking image of the missing Tansy, once Norman finally discovers her location, as a sort of walking dead character who frightens all who see her. There is a moment where a telephone and its cord seem to come alive, fastening itself tight to Tansy's skin, trying to kill her. There is the time the body of Tansy suddenly attacks Norman in his home, throwing heavy objects at him, trying to hit him with a poker and attempting to slash him with a knife. Most of these and similar horrific incidents are left to the last third of the novel, allowing Leiber to create an atmosphere of commonplace horror before smacking the reader with terrifying manifestations of the supernatural. The slow build in the first part of the novel makes the end of the novel quite dramatic.

Conjure Wife is told solely from the perspective of Norman Saylor; the reader never gets into the heads of the other characters. Telling the story only from Norman's perspective is a decided plus for the effectiveness of the tale. Norman stands in for the reader, first in his obliviousness to what is going on at Hempnell College but primarily as to his skepticism that multiple people at the school are practicing witchcraft simultaneously.

While Norman raises many logical objections to Tansy's theories, once Tansy disappears, Norman is quick to find all of the requisite items that will work to regain Tansy's soul, including going to a graveyard to collect dirt and playing a record with Scriabin's "Ninth Sonata" on it with a new phonograph needle to create the exact item that Tansy needs. Because Norman does not hesitate to begin his epic struggle with the witches, *Conjure Wife* never becomes boring as other horror novels with skeptic protagonists sometimes do. Nevertheless, the story ends with a light line as Tansy, once the battle has ended, questions whether Norman now believes in witchcraft or was he only pretending to believe in witchcraft to cure four women of their delusion of being a witch. Norman responds, softly and seriously, "I don't really know" (Chapter XXI).

Conjure Wife is dated somewhat, not in its horror elements but in its renderings of society. All of the professors at Hempnell College are male. That concept that most women are witches seems sexist by modern standards. The book, however, was first published in 1943 and it is usually unfair to judge an older book by the different standards of a more modern and enlightened society. *Conjure Wife* is a cracking good story about modern witchcraft. Indeed, it is one of the best books on the subject matter, leading the way to stories about other modern day witches and Satanists, such as John Updike's *The Witches of Eastwick* and Ira Levin's *Rosemary's Baby*.

The Film

Burn, Witch, Burn/Night of the Eagle (1962)

Burn, Witch, Burn is the American release version of the British horror film titled *Night of the Eagle*, a film clearly inspired by *Conjure Wife*, but not a strict adaptation of it. One important difference occurs right at the beginning of the movie. While *Conjure Wife* opens with Norman's discovery of Tansy's practice of witchcraft, *Burn, Witch, Burn* defers that scene until later, preferring to set the background for two of the themes of the movie.

The first scene in the film is set in Norman Saylor's classroom at Hempnell Medical College, a small college located in England, where Norman is lecturing on beliefs in superstition and the psychic, debunking the supernatural with a phrase written on the blackboard, "I do *not* believe." This theme reappears throughout the film as Norman, much like many other people, finds it difficult to accept witchcraft as real, but for Norman it is a particularly high leap, since he lectures negatively on the subject at his school. This theme is cleverly tied into the end of the film, when a flying stone eagle chases Norman into his classroom. Norman stumbles into the blackboard, his shoulder accidentally rubs one word out of the sentence, and the blackboard now reads, "I do believe."

The next scene in the film establishes the film's theme of the tensions between college faculty and their wives. The sequence involves an automobile ride with Harvey Sawtelle, a professor at the school who is competing with Norman for the appointment as head of the department, his wife Evelyn, and Flora Carr, the wife of another professor at the college. The women do not hold back their disdain for the Saylors, considering them newcomers and although they play bridge with them and work together, they do not accept them.

These two themes of *Burn, Witch, Burn* derive, of course, from the novel but in the remainder of the movie, the tensions between the faculty and their wives are de-emphasized while Norman's struggles to come to terms with the supernatural become more significant. Near the end of the film, when the witch, Flora, builds a house of taro cards which represents Norman's house and sets it on fire, claiming that Tansy will die in the fire, Norman has difficulty reconciling his beliefs as to the lack of validity of witchcraft with his fear that there is an evil force at work at Hempnell. His worries about Tansy finally resolve the question. He rushes out of the building and tries to get home in an attempt to rescue Tansy.

After the opening scenes, *Burn, Witch, Burn* picks up with the beginning of *Conjure Wife*, as Norman accidentally discovers Tansy's horde of charms and talismans and convinces her to destroy them in the fireplace. Almost immediately, Norman's troubles, similar to the ones suffered in the novel, begin. Tansy eventually disappears from her house and Norman chases after her.

Thereafter, the film moves away from the plot of the novel, almost entirely. There are no story arcs about the stealing of Tansy's soul and no surprise ending about souls switching from body to body. There is one witch practicing at Hempnell, not three, and no spurious contention that most women are practicing witches. Indeed, in the film, Tansy acquired her knowledge of witchcraft from a native witchdoctor during a recent trip to Jamaica. It is not something that was handed down to her by her mother.

Several motifs of the film are original to *Burn, Witch, Burn*. Whenever the camera has a chance, it lingers on the image of the stone eagle, located at a building of the college, presaging its later relevance in the film. The stone eagle replaces the stone gargoyle of the novel, seemingly moving from place-to-place, finally ending on Norman's lawn (at least for an instant), just as it did in the book. The eagle statue comes alive near the end of the film and attacks Norman, something that is original to the film. It also provides the justification for the English title of the film, *Night of the Eagle*. The scene at the end of the film in which Flora Carr, the witch, attempts by magic to burn down Tansy's house while she is locked inside is original to the film and supplies the basis for the American title, *Burn, Witch, Burn*. Nevertheless, the most apt title for the film would have been *Conjure Wife*.

The screenplay for the film comes from Richard Matheson and Charles Beaumont, known for their contributions of scripts to *The Twilight Zone*, as well as several horror films. Their work is usually excellent and for that reason, it is surprising how poorly plotted the film is in its second half, once the film discards the storyline of the novel. The tape of Norman's speech, with the loud noise in the background, seems to cause supernatural events, but why? Flora Carr attempts to kill Tansy from a long distance, by arranging her taro cars into a replica of Tansy's house and setting the cards on fire. The cards burn into ashes, yet Tansy's house never burns to the ground and Tansy survives. Once Norman and Tansy are safe, the witch must be disposed of, so in a *deus ex machina* moment, the stone eagle, for reasons unexplained, falls from a roof and kills the witch, providing an ending for the film but one that makes little sense.

The lead performances in the film are passable, at best. Peter Wyngarde is unappealing as Norman Saylor and Janet Blair is only adequate as Tansy Saylor. The special effects, particularly those of the flying stone eagle, are disappointing.

All of that being said, *Burn, Witch, Burn* is a quality horror film. The story of the film is more modern than the novel, without any sexist attitude. It was a clever idea to reduce the number of evil witches to one, giving the film more focus. The movie appears to have been filmed on location at a small, older college in England. That setting is used to great effect, the equivalent of a very large old dark house, even in scenes shot in the daylight. Produced in an era when most horror films were shot in color, the crisp black and white photography, almost a throwback to a prior era in filmmaking, is very effective. Margaret Johnston, as the witch, Flora Carr, gives an excellent performance in the film. She is sometimes acerbic, sometimes eccentric, but in the end, as quietly malevolent as one can be.

Although the British horror classic of the same era, *Night of the Demon* (1957), was based on a short story by Montague R. James and *Burn, Witch, Burn* was based on a novel by Fritz Leiber, the latter film takes much from the former. Both involve a professor skeptical of the supernatural who finally does believe. Both professors are troubled by evil spells and a demon makes an attack on each of them at the end of their respective films. For most of both films, the horrors remain off-screen. Indeed, it seems that the English title of the latter film, *Night of the Eagle*, is intended to capitalize on the reputation of *Night of the Demon*.

Much like the Val Lewton films of the 1940s, *Burn, Witch, Burn* emphasizes

Under the influence of the college witch, Tansy (Janet Blair) attacks her husband, Norman Saylor (Peter Wyngarde), in *Burn, Witch, Burn* (1962).

contrasting lights and darks, such as the stark lighting in the scenes on the cliffs above the bay where Tansy may decide to commit suicide, and cleverly employs sounds such as the loud noise on the tape of Norman's lecture which is tied into the supernatural, the lapping of the waves on the bay near the Saylors' cottage and the chiming of a church bell to reflect midnight, the hour of death. There are memorable shots such as the footprints in the sand which lead into the bay where Tansy has disappeared and the moment when Tansy attacks Norman with a knife, displaying the physical disabilities of the witch, with a quick cut to Flora Carr practicing voodoo on a doll of Tansy. The film is tied together with recurring motifs, such as fire, a black cat and the stone eagle.

These attributes of classic horror exposition propel *Burn, Witch, Burn* past its obvious script problems and other liabilities, making it a worthwhile film, even today. However, by straying so far from the plot of Fritz Leiber's *Conjure Wife*, the film misses much of what is good about the novel. *Conjure Wife*, with its excellent, straightforward plot and surprise ending, would seem to be a natural for a faithful adaptation to the cinema. Unfortunately, that has yet to occur.

Chapter 28

"The Birds" by Daphne du Maurier

According to Daphne du Maurier's biographer, Martyn Shallcross, the inspiration for "The Birds" arose from an incident that occurred to du Maurier in the town of Pridmouth Beach in Cornwall, England. One day du Maurier was walking down the beach with her dog when two large seagulls flew down and tried to bite the dog. Du Maurier, who was used to large numbers of gulls in the area, was not overly concerned about the incident until suddenly and without warning, the gulls tried to bite her. She had to run into the woods for protection. Du Maurier tied this incident to the time she saw seagulls attacking a farmer who was riding on his tractor. Those two occurrences gave du Maurier the idea of writing a story about birds attacking humans, resulting in a famous short story and a more famous movie directed by Alfred Hitchcock.

Background

Daphne du Maurier was born in London, England, on May 13, 1907. Her first novel, *The Loving Spirit*, was published in 1931. Thereafter, she wrote many novels, short stories, plays and works of non-fiction, including several mysteries. Some of her short stories can be classified as horror stories, such as "The Birds," first published in 1952, and "Don't Look Now," first published in 1971. The latter story and its 1973 film adaptation are discussed in Chapter 36 of this book. Du Maurier passed away on April 19, 1989.

The Literature

Daphne du Maurier's most famous novel, *Rebecca*, opens with one of the most famous lines in mystery fiction: "Last night I dreamt I went to Manderley again." Her most famous short story, "The Birds," also commences with memorable language but in this case it is foreboding in tone: "On December the third the wind changed overnight and it was winter." As simple as that sentence is, it sets the mood for what is to come in the short story. The change in the wind brings more than cold; it brings attacks from birds of every species to a small town off the coast of England, far away from the city of London. The time period seems to be the early 1950s, with memories of the last war still lingering in the minds of the British.

The story focuses on one man, Nat Hocken, who lives with his wife and two children in a small cottage near the sea. During the day, when the tide goes out, Nat secures the windows, rooms and roof of his abode in preparation for the next onslaught of the birds that is sure to come. At night he fights off the attacks of the birds. As the story ends, Nat and his family wait in their house, confident that they can survive the bird attack that is just beginning, but not sure of what the future will bring.

One of the strengths of "The Birds" is the claustrophobic atmosphere of the tale. While Nat is not always trapped in his cottage and there are bird attacks against him on the outside, most of the attacks take place while Nat and his family huddle inside his house, only hearing the attacks of the birds, such as their thuds on the roof, their tapping at windows and the fluttering of their wings and only seeing the results of the birds, such as breaking of glass and splintering of wood. Even some plane crashes are heard from afar but not seen. When some of the birds do get into the cottage, they fly and attack in confined spaces, adding to the helplessness of Nat. The reader experiences the feeling of being enclosed in a small space, because du Maurier puts the reader in that setting with Nat, telling the story only from the perspective and thoughts of Nat.

The overriding tone of the story, though, is not of claustrophobia but of isolation. The story is set on the edge of a coast, in a sparsely populated area. In the beginning of the story, there are some characters other than Nat and his family, such as a few of Nat's neighbors and some school friends of one of Nat's children. There is also some contact with the rest of the country through the wireless broadcasts. By the middle of the story, however, the wireless broadcasts have abruptly ended and as a result of the bird attacks, Nat and his family are cut off from their neighbors, becoming prisoners in their own home. Nat's trips into his neighborhood in between the attacks results in his discovery that all of his neighbors are dead, resulting in a "last man on earth" feeling. In terms of mood and atmosphere, du Maurier cleverly creates a context of both claustrophobia and isolation, adding immensely to the effectiveness of the unexplained bird attacks.

Du Maurier's language is often vivid and dramatic when describing the birds as they ready themselves for attack. On one occasion, du Maurier describes Nat as he looks out to sea:

> What he had thought at first to be the whitecaps of the waves were gulls. Hundreds, thousands, tens of thousands.... They rose and fell in the trough of the seas, heads to the wind, like a mighty fleet at anchor, waiting on the tide.

On another occasion, Nat observes that

> the gulls had risen. They were circling, hundreds of them, thousands of them, lifting their wings against the wind. It was the gulls that made the darkening of the sky. And they were silent. They made not a sound. They just went on soaring and circling, rising, falling, trying their strength against the wind.

"The Birds" was published in 1952, at the start of the science fiction film phenomenon in America, with creatures from outer space, demons from the depth of the oceans and giant insects attacking mankind. "The Birds," however, is not part of that group of stories. No persuasive explanation is provided in the story for what is causing the birds to attack. One farmer says that the Russians have poisoned the birds. The Home Office posits that an Arctic air system has caused the birds to migrate south and that their intense hunger may be causing the birds to attack. Nat believes that the hard weather and the east wind have caused them to go mad. Each of these explanations defies logic, making the attack of the birds into an almost supernatural phenomenon.

Nat Hocken, former soldier and now day laborer, while not understanding the cause of the attacks, perhaps gets it best when he describes the attacks as some instinct of a supposedly lower form of animal. He wonders "how many million years of memory were stored in those little brains, behind the stabbing beaks, the piercing eyes, now giving them this instinct to destroy mankind with all the deft precision of machines."

"The Birds" has no ending; it cannot have one. With no explanation for the cause of the attacks, there is no possibility of finding a solution to the attacks. Nat and his family can only huddle together in their cottage, isolated from the rest of mankind, brace themselves for more attacks and hope for the best.

The Film

The Birds (1963)

The setting of the 1963 film version of Daphne du Maurier's story has been moved from winter to summer and from England to California, with most of the story taking place in Bodega Bay, a small town about a two hour drive up the coast highway from San Francisco. While the location is still by the sea, the time period is the early 1960s, a substantially different era than the early 1950s when memories of war still lingered in the minds of many.

In her short story, Daphne du Maurier provided little personal information about Nat Hocken and his family, and, therefore, the reader never acquired a strong personal connection to the characters. Alfred Hitchcock goes in the opposite direction in his film, spending a substantial amount of screen time introducing the prime characters and describing their inter-relationships before any serious bird attacks occur. This is a technique of several classic horror films, such as *King Kong* (1933) (which spends considerable time on Carl Denham meeting Ann Darrow, Ann working on a movie and Ann falling in love with the first mate, Jack Driscoll, before the story first reaches Skull Island and Kong) and *The Wolf Man* (1941) (with much introductory material concerning Larry Talbot's relationship with his father and Larry's first steps in romancing Gwen Conliffe, before he is bitten by a werewolf). This technique enables the viewer to obtain an emotional attachment to the characters, making their subsequent peril all the more engrossing.

In the film, wealthy newspaper heiress, Melanie Daniels, who has a reputation for being spoiled and out of control, becomes attracted to attorney Mitch Brenner in a San Francisco pet store. Melanie's practical joke on Mitch fails at the store but Melanie is determined to follow it through, bringing a pair of lovebirds to Mitch's young sister Cathy at his family home in the coastal town of Bodega Bay. There, Melanie meets Annie Hathaway, the schoolteacher who still has a crush on Mitch, and Mitch's mother, who is afraid of being abandoned by Mitch, particularly after the death of her husband a few years before. Over the course of the film, Melanie turns out to be a person of surprisingly good character and she and Mitch seem to fall in love.

This backstory has its mild interest but it is not the reason why people went to the theater in 1963 to see *The Birds*, particularly with all of the advertising that was disseminated about the film's true subject. ("*The Birds* is coming!") People went to the film then, and view the film today, to see the birds attack and kill, and so, in order not to lose the audience's interest while the important foundation of the film is being established, birds are almost always present during the early scenes of the film. There are birds fluttering and flying under the credits and birds flying in the sky before Melanie enters the pet store, the second floor of the pet store is filled with caged birds and Melanie's practical joke on Mitch involves lovebirds. While the backstory is developing, a gull hits Melanie in the forehead as she is boating across the bay, drawing some blood. Later, Mitch notices numerous birds ominously perched on some telephone wires.

Once the backstory is fully established and the viewer has become comfortable with the principal characters, the spectacular bird attacks finally commence. (At that point, not coincidentally, most of the backstory disappears from the screen.) The birds attack the children at Cathy's birthday party, causing some damage and personal injury; a neighbor is discovered with his eyes pecked out; schoolchildren are attacked as they run down the road from school; the birds attack at a gas station, resulting in a huge explosion; and there are two

Alfred Hitchcock talks to his cast about one of the final scenes in *The Birds* (1963). From left to right, the actors are Veronica Cartwright as Cathy Brenner, Rod Taylor as Mitch Brenner, Tippi Hedren as Melanie Daniels and Jessica Tandy as Lydia Brenner. Note the bandage on Tippi Hedren's head; it is the result of the final bird attack in the film.

final bird attacks at Mitch's house. To add to their effectiveness, each assault serially increases in severity so that the viewer never becomes blasé about the incidents.

Hitchcock does not try to re-create the mood of du Maurier's story. There is never a feeling of isolation in the film, as Bodega Bay is well-populated, particularly with the people at the diner, an especially talkative lot, and the numerous children of school age in the film. There is generally no feeling of claustrophobia, as Bodega Bay is a wide-open, beautiful area. In fact, Hitchcock creates the opposite mood from the story, by contrasting the beauty and color of Bodega Bay with the terror that is situate there.

The one scene from the story that reappears in the film is the bird attack on Mitch's house late in the film. Mitch, much like Nat Hocken, has boarded up all of the doors and shuttered the windows. He is well-prepared for an attack. When the inevitable assault occurs, the camera always remains inside the house; there are no shots of the outside of the cottage or of the birds attacking. In fact, there are almost no shots of actual birds, just in the one moment when a window shutter opens and Mitch has to reach among pecking birds to close the shutter. The viewer is in the room with Mitch and the others, who never speak. Instead of seeing the attacking birds, the viewer hears the shrieking, cawing, rumbling, fluttering and chirping of the birds. The viewer sees the pecking and splintering of the wood on the door, the holes being poked in the door and the broken glass of a window. While not nearly as claustrophobic as the short story, since Mitch's cottage is so large, Hitchcock handles the scene exactly as du Maurier handles it in the novel, with the viewer always inside the cottage, experiencing the same horror that the characters do, even though the horror is implied and not seen in both versions of the story.

The Birds is filled with famous Hitchcock touches. When Melanie goes to pick up Cathy from school, Melanie waits for Cathy on a bench. Melanie is quietly smoking a cigarette. There is a little park behind Melanie that contains a set of climbing bars. In a scene without dialogue, but with the singing of the schoolchildren in the background, the birds, unbeknownst to Melanie, ominously gather a few at a time on the bars behind her, perhaps preparing for an attack. Melanie then spots a bird high in the sky and visually follows its flight path down to the park apparatus, finally seeing its bars filled with birds. An offensive is clearly imminent. This is the most suspenseful scene in the movie.

Also noteworthy is the high, long distance shot of the fire at the gas station. Suddenly some birds appear in the foreground of the scene, an avian spiking of the ball, as it were. Then there is the memorable last shot of the film, with the four principal characters escaping Bodega Bay in Melanie's car as thousands of birds look on.

The Birds is a marvelous film, one of the best horror films of all time. Yet, paradoxically, it is difficult to recommend *The Birds* to anyone, except for the most devout of horror film fans. The problem lies with the film's ending, a major disappointment in 1963. 50 years later, nothing has changed. The ending is still a severe letdown, perhaps the greatest letdown in the entire cinema of horror.

Part of the problem with the end of the film is what comes just before that ending. After successfully surviving the bird attack on Mitch's home, Melanie and the others fall asleep. Melanie wakes up first, walks up the steps of the cottage to the second floor, opens a door and frightens the birds with her flashlight. They viciously attack her in an unending display of ferocity, causing severe injury to her face, arms and legs. Employing the best special effects of the film, this is a stunning scene. But, there was no reason for Melanie to walk up those steps in the first place. Strong-willed and sharp Melanie has suddenly become the traditional heroine of books and films—doing dumb things so that the hero can rescue her.

Of course, there are reasons for Melanie to walk up those steps; those reasons are just not plot-oriented. Having mastered the use of real birds and bird imagery for the film, Hitchcock wanted one last scene to exploit those techniques, where the bird attacks are not just implied but actually shown. It also gave him a chance to create another gory and bloody sequence for one of his films, similar to the shower scene in his prior film, *Psycho* (1960), for which Hitchcock was justifiably commended. Also, since the writers had no ending for the film, the injuries to Melanie in this last bird attack give Mitch and the others the justification to finally leave Bodega Bay, to locate a hospital for Melanie. As the film ends, everyone is in the car heading out of Bodega Bay but there has been no resolution to the story of the birds.

This is similar to the ending of the short story. Both end with a lull in the action, with the outcome still up in the air. The conclusion of the short story does not disappoint, however, because literature is often about mood, characters, relationships and the psychological. A strong plot is not necessarily a requirement for effective literature, and, therefore, there is not always the need for a true conclusion to a work of literature, particularly a short story.

Film is different. Film is much more plot-oriented, particularly stories of mystery and horror. Film therefore requires a climax to the tale, one that provides closure to the story.

The Birds is missing that dénouement. Since no explanation was ever provided for the cause of the birds' sudden assaults, a pragmatic response to those attacks was not possible. Given the scope of the attacks and the number of birds involved, a resolution involving seawater, freezing, bacteria, fire or the like was also not an option. The filmmakers wrote themselves into a hole; they were unable to devise a satisfactory conclusion to the film. Thus, as marvelous as *The Birds* truly is, many people are justifiably very disappointed with the film, because its inconclusive ending overshadows much that has gone before. But for many other people, including your author, *The Birds* is one of the greatest horror films of all time.

Chapter 29

"The Case of Charles Dexter Ward" by H.P. Lovecraft

Since many of the films that were purportedly based on a story or poem of Edgar Allan Poe's often took little, if anything, from any work of Poe's, it seems clear, as mentioned previously in this book, that many filmmakers viewed Poe's famous name as a marketing device only. Even producer-director Roger Corman, who made his name by adapting works of Poe's to the cinema for American-International Pictures in the 1960s, often used little of Poe's short stories in his films. And, with the release of *The Haunted Palace* in 1963, the jig was up. The film was based upon a novella by another famous American writer of horror fiction, H.P. Lovecraft, but because the name of Lovecraft was not as marketable as Poe, the film was given the title of a poem of Poe's and was marketed as a Poe film, even though there is truly nothing of Poe in the storyline of the film.

Background

Howard Phillips Lovecraft was born in 1890 in Providence, Rhode Island. While Lovecraft wrote some fiction in his younger days, it was around 1917, at the encouragement of several friends, that Lovecraft began writing fiction on a regular basis. By the late 1920s, Lovecraft's works in the category of horror were frequently published in the genre magazines of the day. "The Case of Charles Dexter Ward" was written by Lovecraft in 1927 but the short novel was not published until four years after Lovecraft's death, in the May and July 1941 issues of *Weird Tales*, a pulp magazine. Lovecraft passed away in 1937, at the age of 46.

The Tomb of Ligeia (1965), starring Elizabeth Shepherd in dual roles, is another film purportedly based upon a work of Edgar Allan Poe's, in this case, the short story "Ligeia," but actually an original work.

The Literature

"The Case of Charles Dexter Ward" begins at its end, with Charles Dexter Ward, a 26-year-old man who appears to be substantially older, having just escaped from a mental institution near Providence, Rhode Island. The short novel then turns to the events leading up to Ward's mysterious disappearance, which involve an ancestor of Ward's, Joseph Curwen, a practitioner of black magic, who was killed by a group of New England townspeople around 1771. In the present day, Ward brought Curwen back to life and Curwen and Ward then resumed Curwen's original experiments of bringing the most knowledgeable people of all time back to life in order to gain their immense wisdom, hopefully leading the two to immense power. In the surprise ending of the tale, it was actually Curwen, a close lookalike of Ward's, who disappeared from the mental institution at the beginning of the story and died, Curwen's second death in his multiple existences.

Much of the story line of "The Case of Charles Dexter Ward," particularly the sections on Joseph Curwen, are based on letters, diaries, newspaper stories and other historical documents that were discovered by either Ward or Dr. Willett, Ward's doctor from birth, although unlike *Dracula* by Bram Stoker, the text of the story does not consist of a collection of documents. Lovecraft writes the short novel in the style of an historical research paper, from time to time citing to the appropriate documents and sometimes quoting from them, to support his conclusions about Curwen and Ward. That style of writing, unfortunately, does mute some of the horror of the tale, as it can be difficult to find the terror hidden in a research paper. Additionally, and to be consistent with the style of the story, many of the original documents are set forth in the dialectic writing of some old variation on English, making them very difficult to read. It may be assumed that many readers, such as your author, glaze over several of those sections of the text, gaining little of substance from them.

Despite the style, there is considerable horror in the tale, with the best section being Dr. Willett's solo investigation of the tunnels underneath the Ward bungalow. The scene is set mainly in the dark with Willett, as he makes his way through the catacombs, smelling a horrible odor and hearing a dismal moaning, like a sort of slippery thumping. As Willett looks down into a cylindrical well, he sees an outline or entity, not really a man or creature, leaping clumsily up and down the bottom of the shaft, apparently one of the unfinished beings that Ward had called up with his experiments and incantations. Willett flees from the site, temporarily "as stark raving mad as any inmate of Dr. Waite's asylum" (Chapter V, "A Nightmare and a Cataclysm"). Lovecraft's imagery in this scene is unforgettable, aided by Lovecraft's use of many senses, such as the howling of the various beasts of the catacombs and the smells from Ward's bungalow that provides the entrance to the catacombs. Sound and smell are important components of Lovecraft's writing throughout the novella.

Among the clever horror motifs that Lovecraft employs in the story is the painting of Joseph Curwen, with a visage that is almost an exact replica of Ward's. When it is hung in Ward's house, it is an ominous and foreboding presence. Its unexplained destruction, "with what must have been malignly silent suddenness" (Chapter III, "A Search and an Evocation") is puzzling, as the painting seems to have peeled away from the wood, curled and then crumbled into small bits which lay scattered on the floor in a fine blue-grey dust. Lovecraft cleverly ties that imagery of the destroyed painting into the later destruction of Curwen/Ward, when all that is left of the figure in the prison cell is a fine bluish-grey dust.

"The Case of Charles Dexter Ward" has a surprise ending. Most readers will think that Joseph Curwen and Charles Ward have melded together into one. Instead it is Joseph Curwen who has been revitalized into the body of a Dr. Allen, which Willett discovers partially as a result of clues one might find in a detective story—a fake beard and glasses. Willett also has an informant, in the ancient spirit that writes that Willett must kill Curwen. When Willett discovers Ward's remains, he is convinced that it is Curwen in the asylum, not Ward. Thus, a story of great horror has ended as a detective story, with Dr. Willet an exceptional investigator.

Lovecraft writes in an old-fashioned style, with the novella being far longer than it should have been. Nevertheless, there is a strong, even horrific plot hidden within, which had the potential for a good horror film. In 1963, an adaptation of Lovecraft's novella was made for the cinema, although the title of the film had nothing to do with Lovecraft.

The Film

The Haunted Palace (1963)

The credits to *The Haunted Palace* characterize the title of the film as "Edgar Allan Poe's The Haunted Palace," with the source material being listed as follows: "From the poem by Edgar Allan Poe and a story by H.P. Lovecraft." The poem "The Haunted Palace," written by Edgar Allan Poe, was first published in the April 1839 issue of the *American Museum* magazine, a literary magazine circulated in Baltimore, Maryland. The poem is quoted verbatim in Poe's story "The Fall of the House of Usher."

"The Haunted Palace" concerns a king in ancient times who ruled his dominion in glory until the forces of evil brought his reign to the ground. In order to justify the reference to Poe in the title of the movie, Vincent Price, in voiceover, reads four lines from the last stanza of the poem as the film segues from the prologue about Joseph Curwen to the main storyline of Charles Dexter Ward. Additionally, once the the action of the film concludes, the last four lines of that same stanza are read by Vincent Price, in a voiceover, as the words scroll down the screen.

That is all there is of the poem in the film that takes its name. However, while the subject matter of the poem and the language quoted is irrelevant to the film, the title is appropriate. Most of the story is set in a large mansion (referred to in the film as a palace, to match the film's title) outside the village of Arkham which is haunted by the ghost of Joseph Curwen.

While the plot of the film owes much to H.P. Lovecraft, the film is, essentially, an original work. In the prologue, Joseph Curwen, believed to be a warlock, is tied to a tree and burned to death by the villagers of Arkham. Curwen's chief sin seems to be luring young and beautiful females to his palace and then doing something to them unknown. As Curwen dies, he exclaims a curse against the villagers and all of their descendants.

In the main part of the story, set 110 years after the prologue, the great-great grandson of Curwen, Charles Dexter Ward, along with his wife, Ann, comes to the village of Arkham to inspect the palace which he has inherited, There he is possessed by the ghost of Joseph Curwen, by way of the painting of Curwen hanging in the palace. While Curwen speaks of some horrific experiments about bringing evil gods back into the world, his primary energies are spent in resurrecting his mistress of a century ago and taking his revenge on the descendants of the villagers who destroyed him. At the conclusion of the movie, the villagers attack and set fire to the palace. Dr. Willett rescues Ward at the last instance, but is it Ward or Curwen whom he rescues?

There is no doubt that *The Haunted Palace* is inspired by "The Case of Charles Dexter Ward." The painting of Joseph Curwen is a key component of the story as it is in the film, as is the return of Joseph Curwen from the dead, although in the story he appears in his own body and in the film he appears in Ward's body. The creatures in the catacombs, or at least one of them, appears in the laboratory in the cellar of the palace at the end of the film, although it is not quite clear what it is doing there. The film's story of the possession of Ward by Curwen arguably comes from the novella, as it may be the influence of Curwen from beyond the grave that causes Ward to acquire his single-minded interest in Curwin in the novella and to bring Curwen back to life. Similarly, the ending of the film is probably inspired by the short story because in each, it is not quite clear which person is inhabiting the body that looks like that of Charles Dexter Ward. However, the primary story line of the film of Curwen cursing the villagers, trying to bring his mistress back to life, possessing the body of Ward and wreaking his revenge on the villagers is all original to the film.

There are essentially no female characters in Lovecraft's novella. That deficiency is remedied in the film, as it almost always is when a story without female characters is adapted to the cinema. Here, the character of Curwen's mistress, Hilda, is added to the prologue (and she re-appears at the end) and Ward's wife, Ann, is a new character in the movie. Both are played by attractive actresses, Cathy Merchant and Debra Paget, respectively, so that is a positive for the movie.

Perhaps the main disappointment in the adaptation of the story to film is that while "The Case of Charles Dexter Ward" concerns fantastic ideas of bringing exceptional people back from the dead to steal their knowledge and hideous creatures trapped in the catacombs beneath Curwen's house, *The Haunted Palace* concerns the fairly mundane idea of the ghost of a dead person possessing the

Joseph Curwin/Charles Dexter Ward (Vincent Price) holds the head of the body of his beloved Hester, who died around a century before, with the hope of bringing her back to life, as Curwin's assistant, Simon Orne (Lon Chaney, Jr.), looks on, in *The Haunted Palace* (1963).

body of a live person. It is true that in the conclusion of the film, Curwen may be trying to mate Ann Ward with the thing in the basement, to create a race of super creatures, but the storyline is so confusing at that point that it is not really clear what is going on. In any event, that plot point is a minor element of the film. In the story, H.P. Lovecraft shoots high with his themes. The film, on the other hand, aims for nothing special.

The production of the film, as always with Roger Corman's "Poe" adaptations for American-International, is first class. It has an excellent cast, is shot in color with magnificent sets and contains some good special effects in the fire at the palace. Unfortunately, the long shots of the outside of the magnificent palace will not convince anyone, a common flaw in these Corman productions. There are a number of well-known character actors in the film, including Elisha Cook, Jr. as one of the villagers, Milton Parsons as one of Curwen's associates and Lon Chaney, Jr., now relegated to character roles, playing Simon Orne, the caretaker of the palace and Curwen's other associate. What fantastic faces these three actors have!

This is the only film in which Lon Chaney, Jr., and Vincent Price appeared together, unless one counts *Abbott and Costello Meet Frankenstein* (1948). Vincent Price is the star of the film and he gives one of his best performances ever, playing two characters, Ward and Curwen, and convincingly going back and forth from one to the other using only his tone of voice, expression on his face and the way he stands. Chaney, with his craggy face, large nose and large head, aided by a little makeup, has a more frightening look in *The Haunted Palace* than in most of his starring roles in other horror films.

For those who have read Lovecraft's novella, *The Haunted Palace* is a film of missed opportunities. The movie fails to recreate the essence of the horror of Lovecraft's writing because the second half of the film diverts so much from the story of the novella. Indeed, the film seems intended to fit into the style and pattern of the Roger Corman-Poe adaptations of the era rather than intended to treat the different subject matters in Lovecraft's writings in a different manner. Nevertheless, for those who have not read the novella and are not prejudiced by what-could-have-been, *The Haunted Palace*, standing on its own, is quite interesting. People who enjoy it may be surprised to find that it is not based on a work of Edgar Allan Poe's.

Chapter 30

The Haunting of Hill House by Shirley Jackson

Shirley Jackson was interested in the supernatural throughout her life and, according to literary critic Lenemaja Friedman, after reading a book about 19th century psychic researchers who rented a supposedly haunted house in order to study it, Jackson decided to write a ghost story. She searched through newspapers, magazines and books for pictures of suitably haunted-looking houses and found one in California that actually had been built by an ancestor of Jackson's. She also did extensive research about ghosts, including reading many true ghost stories. The result was *The Haunting of Hill House*, a well-received novel published in 1959 and *The Haunting* (1963), one of the best ghost movies of all time.

Background

Shirley Jackson was born in San Francisco, California, on December 14, 1916. Beginning in college, she wrote both short stories and poetry and after graduation, began writing novels. Jackson became both famous and notorious when her short story "The Lottery" was printed in *The New Yorker* in 1948. That story is still read today, as is *The Haunting of Hill House*. Shirley Jackson passed away on August 8, 1965; she was only 48 years old.

The Literature

The Haunting of Hill House is the story of John Montague, a doctor of philosophy whose primary academic interest is the analysis of manifestations of the supernatural, and the three individuals who come to an abandoned old mansion at Montague's request to assist in his investigation of the causes and effects of psychic disturbances in supposedly haunted houses. One of the guests is Luke Sanderson, the nephew of the owner of the house, who was forced upon Montague by his aunt as a condition of renting the house. Montague selected the other two invitees because of their prior experiences with psychic phenomena. Montague chose the vivacious Theodora because she had once shown some extrasensory perception by identifying a high percentage of the cards held up by a laboratory assistant out of her sight and hearing. The other guest is Eleanor Vance, who was chosen by Montague because at the age of twelve, about a month after her father died, a shower of stones fell on her house for three days, for no apparent reason.

During the course of their short stay at Hill House, the four protagonists of the novel experience the presence of spirits that reside in the edifice, a presence that cannot be explained away by either imagination or logic. Montague's scientific exploration then ends in tragedy, with the death of one of his invitees.

The Haunting of Hill House is not, however, the story of just these four persons. There is the overriding presence of a fifth personality in the novel— Hill House itself. Hill House was built about 80 years before by a man named Hugh Crain, as a country home for his children and grandchildren. Its history was marked with several tragedies, including the death of his young wife when her carriage overturned in the driveway before she ever entered the house, the deaths at an early age of his two subsequent wives and the suicide of a companion to a family member. Since the time of the companion's death, no one has been able to live in Hill House for more than a few days. In the nearby village, Hill House is believed to be haunted.

Shirley Jackson employs many clever techniques to create an aura of horror in the novel. One of Jackson's methods is her personification of Hill House. Jackson first describes the edifice from the outside, as follows: "Hill House seemed awake, with a watchfulness from the blank windows and a touch of glee in the eyebrow of a cornice.... [A] house arrogant and hating, never off guard, can only be evil" (Chapter 2, Part 1). When Eleanor first enters the house, she thinks, "I am like a small creature swallowed whole by a monster ... and the monster feels my tiny little movements inside" (Chapter 2, Part 2). This characterization of the mansion continues throughout the book, as if Eleanor and the others are not just fighting the ghosts within the house but, also, Hill House itself.

Another technique employed by Jackson may be called gradualism, to coin a term when it comes to horror stories. The horror of the novel starts slowly, building gradually to a crescendo of shock at the climax of the tale. The first anomaly noticed by the visitors at Hill House is that no matter how hard they try to keep them open, all of the interior doors of the house close on their own. Obviously, that does not create any sense of horror in either the occupants or the reader. It is just an early manifestation that there may be something wrong with Hill House. Next comes the cold spot outside the nursery door, another mild indicator of habitation by the spirits. From there, however, matters truly escalate. There is the loud knocking and banging on the bedroom doors, the writing in chalk on the hallway walls, the blood on Theodora's clothes and the writing in blood on Theodora's wall. By the time all of those events have occurred, there is no question that Hill House is haunted, the only uncertainty being the effect the haunting will have on its four inhabitants.

Another successful technique of Jackson's is that she always keeps her ghosts off-screen, so to speak, at least when they are operating within the house. They are heard, with the loud banging and knocking and the sound of the winds through the house. They are felt, in the cold spot by the nursery and in the moment when a frightened Eleanor, believing that she has been holding Theodora's hand, discovers that it was the hand of something unknown. They may even be smelled, in the musty odor of the library that Eleanor senses. They are never seen, however, except in the manifestations of their actions, such as the doors bending in or the writings discovered on the walls. Less is often more in these types of stories and the unknown face of the enemy adds to the suspense of the novel.

Shirley Jackson was writing more than a ghost story in *The Haunting of Hill House*. She was also addressing themes of maternal love, guilt, family, lesbianism and loneliness. This is accomplished by the emphasis on Eleanor Vance, somewhat to the exclusion of the other characters. The novel is told from the point of view of Eleanor and, except for a brief moment at the beginning of the novel, she is the only character whose inner thoughts are conveyed to the reader. Eleanor is running away from a life in which she cared for her invalid mother for many years and now lives with a sister whom she hates. She has no friends or home of her own; she is clearly the most vulnerable of the visitors to Hill House. Thus, the ghosts of the manor target their wrath on Eleanor, with the writing on the wall, HELP ELEANOR COME HOME ELEANOR, and the sometimes child-like nature of the ghost, all designed to prey on Eleanor's susceptible mind. When both Luke and Theodora reject Eleanor in the real world, Eleanor finally snaps.

It is at this point that *The Haunting of Hill House* starts to falter in its horror elements. The novel has been building gradually to its ghostly climax but then the climax is not what the reader expects. The ending of the novel is not a litany of ghostly horrors but rather, is Eleanor going mad. As Eleanor goes crazy, she becomes one of the ghosts of the house, banging on the doors of the others and running away, and also darting quickly in and out among the labyrinth of the house with which she is suddenly quite familiar. She then climbs the stairs of the tower, perhaps to commit suicide, the same as once happened on those stairs with a prior occupant of the house. Eleanor's inner thoughts are crazed, as she thinks of her mother and starts to believe that Hill House can become her home. For the only time in the novel, the ghosts can be seen as the imaginings of an unstable woman, weakening some of the horror that has gone before.

To be fair, the ending of *The Haunting of Hill House* is consistent with what has gone on previously, with the spirits focusing on the weakest of the guests, Eleanor, and causing her to go crazy. Thus, Eleanor's mental instability, while not caused by the ghosts, is exacerbated by them. Eleanor's actions, including her subsequent suicide (if it was suicide), rid the house of all of its occupants, the goal of the spirits, as the other three guests soon leave to return to their regular lives, and after they leave, Hill House, as Jackson writes, "not sane, stood against its hills, holding darkness within; it has stood so for eighty years and might stand for eighty more" (Chapter 9, Part 4). Jackson then ties her ghost story all together because if Eleanor committed suicide so that she could come home to Hill House and join the spirits that are there, her idea did not work. As Jackson writes, in the concluding phrase of the novel, after the guests left Hill House, "whatever walked there, walked alone" (Chapter 9, Part 4). Thus, the ghosts are triumphant once again.

The final language of the novel is a restatement of a portion of the opening paragraph of the book. Thus, Montague's habitation of the house has been irrelevant to the ghost or ghosts that walk the manor. Nothing has changed at all, and nothing may change for another eighty years.

The Haunting of Hill House is cinematic in several ways, particularly in the gradualism of the horror and the technique of never showing the ghosts, somewhat similar to the concept behind the Val Lewton horror films from RKO in the 1940s. And, just a few years after its publication, Shirley Jackson's novel of the spirit world made it to the screen, with the film bearing the simple title, *The Haunting*.

The Film

The Haunting (1963)

Although *The Haunting* is a fairy close adaptation of Shirley Jackson's novel, a number of changes, large and small, were made in the story when it was adapted to the screen. Most of those changes were designed to add to the horror element of the tale, making the film a truly frightening experience.

Dr. John Markway, an anthropologist with an interest in psychic phenomena, rents Hill House for research in ghostly occurrences. He brings with him Luke Sanderson, a young playboy who will inherit the house some day, Theodora, a young woman with extrasensory perception, and Eleanor Lance, a timid woman who was been living with her sister and brother-in-law after the death of her invalid mother for whom she was caregiver for many years. It is unknown why two of the character names were changed slightly from the novel or why Hill House is now 90 years old instead of 80 years of age as described in the book, but those changes seem of little significance.

The Haunting opens with a voice-over narration from Markway describing the house, by quoting some of the well-known language from the opening paragraph of the novel. He states, "Hill House had stood for ninety years and might stand for ninety more. Silence lay steadily against the wood and stone of Hill House, and whatever walked there, walked alone."

However, once Eleanor, or Nell as she is usually called, arrives at the mansion, all of the voice-overs are from the inner thoughts of Nell's, as she undertakes her adventure in Hill House. Thus, the screenwriters have recognized that much of the strength of the novel comes from telling the story from the point of view of Nell's and that her inner thoughts are crucial to the story development. Unfortunately, the difference between literature and film is most apparent here, as the dictates of time and the sometimes unwieldiness of using voiceover narration limit the scope of the thoughts of Nell's that can be used in the film. Thus, the viewer never becomes as well acquainted with Nell in the film as the reader does in the book, making Nell's actions at the end of the movie somewhat less understandable than they are in the book.

The personification of Hill House is carried over into the film. In addition to some of the language of the book being incorporated into the film, the house is described by Markway as being "born bad," the nursery is called the heart of the house, the doors at times seem to be breathing in and out, and at the end of the film, Nell states that the house is "alive, watching, waiting, waiting for me." The dialogue is supplemented throughout the film by silent, montage shots of both the outside and inside of the house, as the edifice appears to be watching and hovering over the occupants, waiting for its chance to destroy them.

In terms of gradualism, the film falls surprisingly short. While the first indication of spirits in Hill House is the closing of the doors, the next is the banging and attacking at the door behind which Nell and Theo are hiding, to be followed by the much milder discovery of the cold spot outside the nursery. Big events rotate with smaller ones, thereby causing the rhythm of the film to be somewhat off. There is not a slow but inexorable build to the climax but rather, an oscillating cycle of horror as the plot advances. Surprisingly, the attack on Theo's room and clothes and the writing on Theo's wall about Eleanor coming home, high fright moments of the book, are skipped in their entirety in the movie.

Nevertheless, most of the changes in the story are for the better, at least in terms of the horror element. While the nuances of *The Haunting of Hill House* are eliminated, the fright factor is increased. Mrs. Dudley, the house cook, is a figure of comic relief in the novel as the characters make fun of her throughout the tale. In the film, she is more of a Mrs. Danvers character, adding to the evil that seems inherent in Hill House. She introduces the house to the guests, intoning, "There won't be anyone around if you need help. We couldn't hear you, in the night. No one could. No one lives any nearer than town. No one will come any nearer than that." (The speech is from the novel, Chapter 2, Part 1.) Even when Mrs. Dudley smiles, it appears to be a smile of evil and foreboding, not of humor.

Unlike the novel, the Theo of the film displays several instances of extrasensory perception, knowing in advance, for example, that Nell wants to change her hair style, or, more importantly, that she is not sorry about her mother's death. Theo's sudden bursts of advance knowledge upset the balance of the house, as does her subtle manifestations of lesbianism. (In the book, Theo displays no ESP abilities and her lesbianism is muted.) The minor adjustments in Theo's characterization for the film add to the unease both in the house and in the viewer. Similarly, in the novel, Nell displays some interest in Luke but in the film, she starts to have feelings about Dr. Markway. There is dramatic irony here, as the viewer knows that Markway is married, while Nell does not. Again, this minor element of the story adds to the unease in the film. With the viewer experiencing some disquiet from these secondary aspects of the movie, the horror elements have a greater opportunity for effect.

The Haunting was directed by Robert Wise, well-known to movie fans for directing famous big budget films such as *West Side Story* (1961), *The Sand Pebbles* (1966) and *Star Trek: The Motion Picture* (1979). Horror film fans, however, remember him best for two horror films he directed for producer Val Lewton, namely, *The Curse of the Cat People* (1944) and *The Body Snatcher* (1945), both, to some degree, ghost stories. As noted above, in the novel *The Haunting of Hill House*, the horror is generally kept off screen, so it was natural for Wise, an alumnus of the Val Lewton horror films, to do the same in the movie adaptation. And, much of the strength of the film lies in Wise's direction.

In the moments when the ghosts seem to attack, Wise keeps his camera within the same room as the occupants, so that the viewer has much the same experience as the characters. The viewer hears the banging, the running and the wind, and suffers through the silence in between the knocking. The viewer sees the doors bending in and the doorknobs turning slowly. Much like the characters, the viewer does not know what the unknown beyond the doors is. Wise adds to the terror by employing askew angles for his camera, very high and very low shots, montage cuts to inanimate objects, varied lenses to mirror the distortion in Nell's mind, and off center shots of the characters. The horror is never seen but it surely is there.

The Haunting uses a clever parallel structure to its story, which does not completely derive from Shirley Jackson's novel. In the film, the back-story of Hill House is that it was inherited by Abigail Crain who lived in the nursery of the house from a young age until she died. In her later years, when she was bedridden, Abigail brought a young girl from the village into the house as a companion to care for her. One night, when the companion was entertaining a farmhand on the veranda, she did not hear Abigail pounding for help. Abigail died. Similarly, Nell worries that she did not respond to her mother's cries on the night her mother died, leading to the mother's death. The companion and Nell are mirror images of each other.

The companion committed suicide by hanging herself from the top of the circular staircase in the library. Near the end of the film, Nell also climbs the staircase, with the apparent intent to kill herself, reinforcing the doppelganger that the two are. Nell actually dies when her car crashes into a tree on the house's winding driveway. The wife of Hugh Crain, the man who built Hill House, died at that same tree when her carriage overturned. Thus, the first and most recent deaths associated with Hill House occur at the same location.

Early in the film, the characters are often seen in reflection, whether in the polished floor or in a mirror, to create an unreality to the situation. (Again, this ties to Nell not being a real person, but a reflection of the ghost of the companion that walks the hallways.) At the end, when Nell is running through the house in a crazy manner, she abruptly sees her reflection in the mirror on two occasions, tying into the parallel structure of the film. Nell, in a lighter moment in the film, pretends to dance with the statue of Hugh Crain, but in her final runs through the house, she stops at one point to, for her, actually dance with Hugh Crain. This parallel structure adds to the myth-like character of the haunting of Hill House.

The ending of the film is different than the novel. Just as in the book, Mrs. Markway (Grace) makes a surprise appearance at Hill House, but in the film she is not a figure of comic relief, as she was in the novel. Grace is a skeptic who is willing to sleep in the nursery of the mansion, the epicenter of the haunting. Grace disappears when Nell starts her ramblings, making a surprise appearance

After her near death on a circular staircase, Eleanor "Nell" Lance (Julie Harris) begs Luke Sanderson (Russ Tamblyn) to allow her to stay in Hill House, in *The Haunting* (1963).

in the trapdoor at the top of the circular staircase, a truly alarming moment for the viewer. Grace also appears, wraith-like, at the end, before Nell's car crash, perhaps contributing to the crash, but again creating a shocking moment for the viewer. While Robert Wise never shows his ghosts on screen, the images of Grace are a living substitute therefor.

Nevertheless, the use of Grace to provide shocks to the viewer, and also to substitute for whatever ghosts there may be in the house, is manipulative on the part of the filmmakers. Grace has no reason to be in the movie, other than to provide jolts to the viewer. Also, even if some of Grace's unusual actions can be blamed on the ghosts of the house, they are still inexplicable. However, the manipulation does work, increasing the fright sensation and shocks at the end of the movie.

Nell's demise at the end of *The Haunting* is handled differently than in Jackson's novel. In the book, it appears that Nell has committed suicide, so that she can come home to Hill House and walk the hallways as a spirit, but there is room for disagreement on that interpretation. For example, just before the car hurled into the tree, "she thought clearly, *Why* am I doing this? Why am I doing this? Why don't they stop me?" (Chapter 9, Part 3). Thus, the ghost of the manor may have possessed Nell, causing the crash. The ending of the novel is ambiguous.

In the film, there is no ambiguity. Nell cannot control the steering wheel; the ghosts seem to have taken over the wheel. The crash is not suicide but results from the haunting. Again, the film went with a more frightening but less nuanced ending for the story. The ghosts of the cinema have truly claimed a victim for Hill House and *The Haunting* is a rare horror film, for its time, in which the horror elements are triumphant.

The last voice-over in the film modifies the parallel structure of the feature. Markway narrated the opening of the film; Nell narrates its ending. And, the change in the final language of the film is in stark contrast to that of the book. Nell concludes the film by stating, "Hill House has stood for ninety years and might stand for ninety more.... Silence lies steadily against the wood and stone of Hill House, and we who walk here, walk alone." Thus, Eleanor has become another ghost of the mansion and Hill House has what it wants, for a while.

Other Adaptations

The Haunting was remade in 1999, with a script that was substantially based on Shirley Jackson's novel, but with several modern modifications. Although the new film was a mild box office success, it was far from a critical success.

Chapter 31

"The Family of the Vourdalak" by Aleksei Tolstoy

"Vourdalaks," according to Aleksei Tolstoy's story, is the Slavic term for vampires. Much like traditional vampires, vourdalaks rise from the grave to suck the blood of their victims. However, vourdalaks have one characteristic that makes them even more terrifying than other vampires. Vourdalaks prefer to suck the blood of their closest relatives or most intimate friends in order to turn them into vourdalaks also.

Background

Aleksei Konstantinovich Tolstoy, a second cousin of Leo Tolstoy's, was born in St. Petersburg in 1817, the son of a government worker. In 1841, Aleksei's first published work, *The Vampire*, was released. It was not well-received and although Tolstoy wrote three other tales of the supernatural, only one of those was published in his lifetime. For example, "The Family of the Vourdalak" was written in in 1839 but it was not published until 1884, nine years after Tolstoy's death. Tolstoy is better known today for his poetry, satirical works and historical novels. Tolstoy died in 1875 at the age of 58.

The Literature

The narrator of "The Family of the Vourdalak" is an elderly gentleman named the Marquis d'Urfé who, sitting in Vienna in 1815, tells a terrifying tale that took place in 1759, when he was sent on a diplomatic mission to Moldavia.

During the Marquis' stay at a house in a small village in Moldavia, he encountered several vourdalaks—Gorcha, the father of a family who set out to the mountains to hunt down a Turkish bandit but came back completely changed; the grandson of Gorcha who was killed by Gorcha but later returned from his grave as a vourdelak; and Sdenka, Gorcha's beautiful daughter, with whom the Marquis fell in love. In the terrifying and then exciting conclusion to the story, the Marquis returned to the village to see Sdenka again and barely escaped with his life after being attacked by a horde of blood-seeking vampires, including Sdenka.

"The Family of the Vourdalak" is an excellent tale of 19th century Gothic horror, similar to but in many ways different from the other vampire literature of the era. Tolstoy, by emphasizing the relationship between the Marquis and Sdenka near the end of the story, imbues his tale with a sensuality that is inherent in both *Carmilla* and *Dracula*. The first time they meet, the Marquis tries to seduce Sdenka, believing she is sweet and innocent. When the Marquis returns for his second visit, Sdenka, now a vampire, turns the tables on him. The Marquis finds Sdenka to be even more beautiful than he remembered her, but also more mature, passionate, sensual and ravishing. With her "strange wantonness of manner," she fills the Marquis' whole being with a "strange, almost sensual feeling, part fear, part excitement." The Marquis almost succumbs to Sdenka's advances, saved only by the cross he is wearing.

On the other hand, unlike the beautiful Carmilla or the stately Dracula, the vampires in "The Family of the Vourdalak" are common folk, struck down by the curse of the undead. As the title implies, Tolstoy's story is about a family, not just about one vampire, making it easier for the reader to relate to and understand the horror of vampires. The vampirism in the story spreads like a disease through Gorcha's family, particularly because it is understandably hard for any son to want to kill the patriarch of his family (in this case, Gorcha's son having to kill his father, recognizing that Gorcha has become a vourdelak) or for a mother to leave her child out in the cold (in this case, the grandson's mother allowing the child back into the family house, even though she knows the young boy was dead and had been recently buried). "The Family of the Vourdalak" is more horrifying that most tales of vampires, because it is about real people, with real emotions, not just aristocratic examples of the undead.

Tolstoy does not forget the horror elements in "The Family of the Vourdalak." For example, at the end of the story, as the Marquis is about to fall in love with Sdenka again, the stab of pain from a crucifix the Marquis is wearing shocks the Marquis out of his daze, providing an instant realization of the true being that Sdenka has become. As the Marquis tells his listeners, "Looking up at Sdenka I saw for the first time that her features, though beautiful, were those of a corpse; that her eyes did not see; and that her smile was the distorted grimace of a decaying skull. At the same time, I sensed in that room the putrid smell of the charnel-house."

"The Family of the Vourdalak" is not well-known today. In fact, if it were not for the short film version by Mario Bava which is included in *Black Sabbath* (1963), Tolstoy's story would probably be completely forgotten, which is a shame because Tolstoy's story, with its interesting perspective on vampires, its sensual aspects and exciting conclusion, is a very effective piece of horror literature.

The Films

Black Sabbath/I tre volti della paura (1963)

In 1963, Mario Bava directed an Italian horror film titled *I tre volti della paura*, which translates, in English, to *The Three Faces of Fear*. The film was comprised of three unrelated horror stories. When the film was released in America in 1964, it was re-titled *Black Sabbath* and several changes were made, including the order of the stories, the musical score and even some significant plot points. For this chapter of *Classic Horror Films and the Literature That Inspired Them*, the Italian version of the film will be discussed.

The middle and longest segment of *Black Sabbath* is titled "The Wurdalak." It is based substantially upon the Tolstoy short story, "The Family of the Vourdalak." Thus, young Count Vladimir d'Urfe, during a trip through rural Russia, decides to stay one night at the home of a man named Gorca who is away on a hunt after a Turkish bandit. At Gorca's house, Vladimir falls in love with Gorca's beautiful daughter, Sdenka, and also watches as the entire family becomes, one by one, a family of vourdalaks including, perhaps, Sdenka.

While the end of "The Wurdalak" strays from the plot of Tolstoy's short story, the remainder of the film is a close adaptation. Thus, Vladimir learns that Gorca has warned his family that if he returns longer than five days after leaving on his hunt after Ali Bek (an inexplicable change from the ten days of the short story), Gorca is to be knifed in the heart because he will have become a vourdalak. When Gorca finally returns, he has the head of Ali Bek packed in his bag, his dog howls at him and has to be shot, and Gorca is no longer interested in eating. Gorca's first victim is his young grandson, whom he takes outside after locking Vladimir in his room. Readers of the short story will recognize all of those plot points.

"The Wurdalak" also incorporates several particularly clever moments from Tolstoy's story. The five day period for Gorca's return is supposed to end at the stroke of midnight in the film, but since Gorca returns while the clock is still chiming, has he arrived in time or not? When the grandson, Ivan, returns from the dead, his plaintive cries of "I'm cold. Let me in" are very convincing, making it understandable that his mother, Maria, lets him back into the house. The shot from behind of Ivan kneeling at the door of the house, his hands high against the door as if he is beseeching the heavens, as the camera slowly moves in, is one of the most memorable shots in all of horror films, remaining in the viewer's memory long after many other horror films have been watched. The moment also reinforces the theme of both the short story and the film, i.e., that the narrative is about a family as much as it is about some vampires. This idea can also be seen earlier in the film, when the entire family, significantly without Vladimir, gathers just outside the house on Gorca's return and late in the film, when the entire remaining adult family members gather around Sdenka to initiate her into the world of the vourdalaks.

As noted several times in this book, film is different than literature and so, even though the source material is only a short story, there is some clever tightening of Tolstoy's plot for the film. For example, there is no introductory narrative to the film segment. Almost immediately after the opening credits, Vladimir, while travelling on his horse, accidentally discovers Ali Bek's headless body with Gorca's knife in its heart, leading Vladimir to stop at Gorca's house and then stay the night. On the first night of his return, Gorca kills his grandson. In the short story, the attacks on the grandson take place over a two-night period.

Black Sabbath goes for some shocks that are not contained in the short story. When Maria opens the door for her vampire-son, Ivan, it is Gorca who is suddenly standing there. The young boy is gone. That is a true shock to Maria and also to the viewer. Pietro, the brother who is supposed to watch over Gorca the first night, appears to have fallen asleep on the job. However, when his body is turned over, he has the marks of the vampire on his neck, another shock to the viewer.

"The Family of the Vourdalak" has one of the most exciting conclusions of any vampire story, as the Marquis barely escapes on horseback as a swarm of vourdalaks chase after him. It would be interesting to see that ending filmed sometime. "The Wurdalak," however, goes for a less exciting but possibly more memorable ending. Vladimir has convinced Sdenka to run away from the evil her family has become. After a long ride on horseback, they decide to spend the night in the ruins of an old convent. However, the vourdalaks are on to them and while Vladimir is sleeping, they surround Sdenka, who begs for mercy, arguing that Vladimir loves her. In striking language, Gorca responds, "Sdenka, no one can love you more than we do."

When Vladimir wakes up, Sdenka is gone. He travels back to the family homestead and finds her there. Much like the short story, Sdenka is particularly seductive and attractive at this point, and Vladimir succumbs to her overwhelming beauty and the power of her eyes. Since Sdenka loves Vladimir just as much as Sdenka's family loves Sdenka, she must turn Vladimir into her victim. She is successful. Thus, for the first time in the cinema of the vampires, the vampire is not destroyed at the end of the film but instead, continues to live on and multiply, presumably ravaging the countryside even more.

Mario Bava beautifully directs "The Wurdalak," both in his mix of shots employed and in his use of color photography. He is particularly clever in the use of sounds to set scenes, such as the howl of the wind or a door slamming, or to tell his story, such as the noise of the dog being killed on the demand of Gorca and Sdenka's cry after being attacked by her family, both scenes not shown on-screen but the sounds being heard off-screen. (Bava's clever use of sound is even more apparent in the other two segments of *Black Sabbath*.) Bava cleverly eschews much of vampire lore for his film. Vampires appear to be able to come out during the day, do not sleep in their coffins at night and cannot change into various animals, such as bats. "The Wurdalak," however, has much to answer for in allowing the vampires to survive at the end of the film. That soon became the standard finish for vampire films of the era, such as *Count Yorga, Vampire* (1970) and *House of Dark Shadows* (1970).

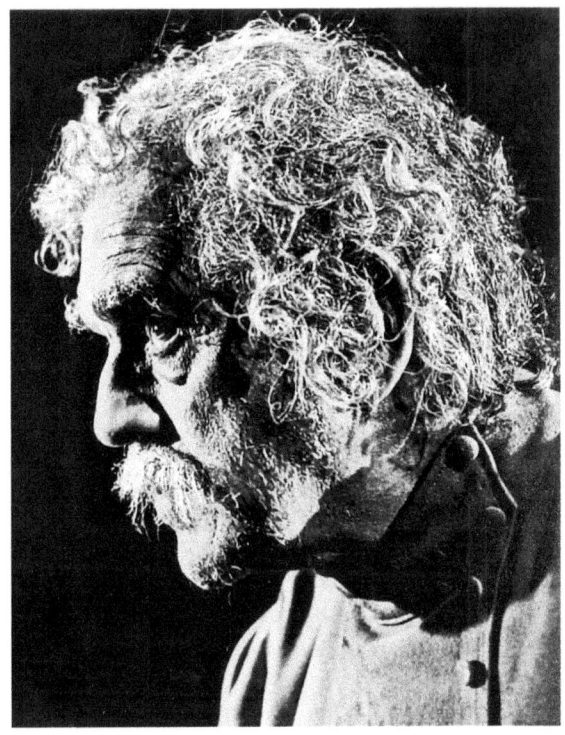

Boris Karloff usually looks different in each of his film appearances. He is shown here in his makeup for the patriarchal vampire, Gorca, in *Black Sabbath* (1964).

In the 1960s, multi-part horror films became common, including *Tales of Terror* (1962), *Twice-Told Tales* (1963) and *Spirits of the Dead* (1968). Each included adaptations of, or purported adaptations of, short written works of horror. However, out of all of the short horror adaptations of the 1960s, the most successful is "The Wurdalak." Indeed, this middle segment of *Black Sabbath* is one of the most effective tales of vampires in the entire cinema of horror.

The Night of the Devils/La notte dei diavoli (1972)

"The Wurdalak" segment of *Black Sabbath* (1963) and *The Night of the Devils* have much in common. Both are adaptations of Tolstoy's "The Family of the Vourdalak." Both films were made in Italy, with Italian Mario Bava directing the original and Italian Giorgio Ferroni directing the remake. There is less than a decade between the release dates of the two films. Bava's version is, by far, the better known, probably because it received a wide release in America as a result of its being distributed by American-International Pictures, and also because it played on television for many years, at a time when many local stations still had their regular weekend horror hosts. *The Night of the Devils*, with its more risqué storyline and bloody sequences, was less appropriate for television viewing and it came out at a time when local stations started to schedule fewer movies, including horror films. Few have heard of *The Night of the Devils*, which is unfortunate because it can hold its own against its more famous predecessor.

The Night of the Devils follows the basic plot of the Tolstoy story, although in a modern setting, as a man named Nicola (the Marquis character from the story) is involved in a minor automobile accident, disabling his vehicle. Seeking assistance with his car, Nicola walks through the woods until he sees a house. There he meets Gorca and his family just after Gorca's brother was killed by Jovan, Gorca's son, because the brother had become a vampire. Gorca believes that a witch who has been terrorizing the countryside has caused the curse of the vourdalak in Gorca's family. Gorca finally decides to set out to destroy the witch that forces the family to stay in their cottage at night, with doors and windows barred. Jovan approves of that action but tells Gorca that if Gorca is not back by 6:00 p.m. (sunset), Jovan will have to kill him. Gorca returns, having killed the witch, but it is not clear if Gorca has returned by the deadline. Nevertheless, Jovan is loath to kill his father, and his hesitation results in the family, one after the other, turning into vourdalaks. When Nicola returns to Gorca's house to rescue Sdenka, Gorca's beautiful daughter with whom he has fallen in love, it is unclear whether Sdenka has turned into a vampire also.

The obvious difference between Tolstoy's story and *The Night of the Devils* is that the film is set in contemporary times, with Nicola using a car, Sdenka taking a taxi in the city and the setting of the modern hospital where Nicola is treated after his experiences with the vampires. In some cases in which a classic horror story is updated and set it in modern times, the plot and the contemporary setting often seem discordant, deleteriously affecting the storyline. Fortunately, that does not occur in *The Night of the Devils*. Once the story moves to Gorca's house, there are no manifestations of modernity. The house does not have a television or telephone, a horse does most of the heavy lifting and pulling and the family wears old-fashioned clothing. The edifice is located far away from any large village making it isolated from the rest of mankind, thus becoming a common horror film setting. While Nicola and Sdenka wear modern clothing and Sdenka has a modern hairstyle, the film seems to be set back in time, when vampires and witches may have believably roamed the countryside.

That is not to say that *The Night of the Devils* ever becomes an old-fashioned horror film. The tone is set early in the film, when Nicola has hallucinations in the hospital, which involve shots of naked women and the pulling of a bloody, beating heart out of the body. These moments of sex and gore seem gratuitous but they do establish, early on, that *The Night of the Devils* is a different kind of horror film. Later, there is more sex, as Nicola and Sdenka couple, and then more gore, as blood percolates out of bodies when stakes are driven through their hearts and bites on the neck result in streams of blood. These later moments of sex and gore are not gratuitous to the plot; they move the story forward. However, they are a reflection of filmmaking in the 1970s, gratuitous in the sense that the film would probably have been shot in a different manner in later decades.

The Night of the Devils is a bright and colorful film, not just in the scenes in the city but also in the main part of the film, as the plague of vampirism strikes Gorca's family. There is, of course, that very red blood that flows from victims' bodies, but there are also colorful flowers and toys that appear in the film. The inside of Gorca's house is well-lit. Even the woods in which much of the action takes place seem open and sunny. Most filmmakers shoot horror films in shadows or in the dark. Director Giorgio Ferroni went in the opposite direction for this film and it works, perhaps because the technique is so unusual. Indeed, because of its unexpected atmosphere, emphasis on sex and blatant gore, the viewer can never become complacent watching the film, adding to the tension the movie creates.

Two of the best scenes in *The Night of the Devils* come from Tolstoy's short story. Interestingly, they are handled differently in *The Night of the Devils* from the way they were handled in *Black Sabbath*. One is the return of Gorca's grandchild after she has become a vourdalak. This comes just after Gorca's killing and the decomposition of Gorca's face has shocked the viewer. First, there is a shot of the legs of the missing Irina walking back to the cottage with her favorite doll. Next, her mother comes out to greet her, they embrace and then there is a quick attack by Irina, leaving the mother's face and body as a bloody mess. While perhaps not as effective as the similar scene in *Black Sabbath*, it is closer to the version described in Tolstoy's short story. It is very compelling.

The other is Nicola's escape from the vourdalaks, after he believes that Sdenka has become a vampire. He rushes to his car, the motor hesitates for a few tries and then he takes off. His car then dies down the road. Accompanied by the laughter of the two vampire-children, Nicola is under assault by three of the vourdalaks, all from Gorca's family. He is able to fend them off with an axe but when he finally gets his car going, two jump onto the outside of the vehicle. He is just able to knock them off by the speed and turning of the car, allowing him to escape to the city. This is a terrifying section of the movie, with Nicola barely escaping. This scene, with the vourdalaks chasing after Nicola in his car and leaping onto it, is a modern equivalent of the moment in the short story wherein the vourdalaks jump on the Marquis' horse as he tries to make his escape. That scene was a highlight of the short story, just as it is a highlight of the film. In these two regards, *The Night of the Devils,* modern tale though it may be, is closer to the plot of the Tolstoy story than *Black Sabbath*.

Much like Tolstoy's short story, Nicola tells the core story of *The Night of the Devils* in retrospect, although in the film, these are the recollections of Nicola as he is lying in a straightjacket at a city hospital. It is not a simple narration. This structure delays the commencement of the primary story of the film for many minutes and because the opening seems just to be a device to show sex, blood and gore, and the virtuosity of the director, it takes too long for the viewer to become involved in the travails of Gorca's family. The film would have been better if the core storyline started immediately.

Of course, the primary plot purpose of the opening at the hospital is to set up the surprise ending, when Sdenka comes to Nicola's hospital room and Nicola kills her, believing she is a vourdalak. Because her face does not decompose upon death, Nicola realizes he has made an awful mistake. This is a clever ending for the film, different from the ending of the story or of *Black Sabbath*. Most viewers will catch onto the plot twist just a few seconds before it happens, which is somewhat surprising because it is a cheat ending. In the film, when Nicola goes back to Gorca's house to rescue Sdenka, Sdenka had clearly changed. Instead of being somewhat shy and demure, she has transformed, as the Sdenka of the story did, into a coquettish and sexier person. Also, Nicola observes that Sdenka's body is cold and she has blood on her neck. Those are clear indications that she had become a vampire. Also, after Sdenka comes to the hospital, she disappears. No one knows where she has gone. If Sdenka is not in the hospital for nefarious reasons, why does she vanish in such a suspicious manner? These inconsistent plot points tarnish the surprise ending of the movie.

The twist at the end of the film relies on an interesting phenomenon that happens to a vourdalak when it is killed in *The Night of the Devils*. Parts of their faces cave in, the skin peels away and the visage decomposes. At the end of the slow metamorphosis, the head becomes skull-like. This happens several times in the film and the special effects are outstanding, a bit of movie magic that reaches the level of the ending of *Horror of Dracula* (1958), which set the standard for this type of vampire effect. It is characteristic of the high production values and the overall quality of *The Night of the Devils*, a film that, while it is not quite the equal of the Wurdalak segment of *Black Sabbath*, is an outstanding horror film in its own right.

Chapter 32

"The Masque of the Red Death" by Edgar Allan Poe

While Roger Corman's 1964 film *The Masque of the Red Death* was the first full-length adaptation of Edgar Allan Poe's famous short story of the same name, it was not the first appearance of the Red Death in a feature-length film. In *The Phantom of the Opera* (1925), at the annual masked ball at the Opera House, the revelers are interrupted by a spectral figure, robed in red, who identifies himself as the Red Death. Although the appearance of the figure in the 1925 silent film does not match Poe's description of the character, they have much in common. This Red Death of the cinema appears at a masquerade ball attended by the wealthy, wears a mask and in both, he is described as a "spectral" figure. Clearly, Gaston Leroux, the author of *The Phantom of the Opera*, and the screenwriters of the 1925 film were familiar with their Edgar Allan Poe.

The Literature

As "The Masque of the Red Death" begins, the countryside has been devastated by a vicious plague known as the Red Death. Even though the disease has depopulated about half of his dominions, the wealthy Prince Prospero is unconcerned about those people. Instead, he invites a thousand of his friends from among the knights and dames of his court to retire to the deep seclusion of one of his abbeys, which has been amply provisioned with food, drink and entertainment. There, the wealthy expect to survive the plague by locking out the Red Death.

After about five or six months of this seclusion, at a time when the pestilence rages most furiously on the outside, the Prince decides to hold a magnificent masquerade ball on the inside of his castle. In the midst of this revelry, however, the crowd suddenly realizes that a new masked presence has appeared among them. The figure of the stranger is tall and gaunt, is "shrouded from head to foot in the habiliments of the grave" and has assumed the visage of the Red Death. Prince Prospero is outraged at the presence of the uninvited figure and its blasphemous mockery. He rushes at the stranger with a drawn dagger but once he draws near, the dagger drops from his hand and the Prince falls to the floor, dead. The other revelers seize the masked figure, which stands tall and erect, and they are shocked to find that there is no tangible form under the garments or the mask. Each of the revelers in turn then drops to the floor dead, just as those on the outside of the abbey are dying, having finally been consumed by the Red Death.

In terms of style, "The Masque of the Red Death" is an unusual story of Edgar Allan Poe's. It is written in the third person and contains only one character of significance (if any). Unlike most of the other tales by Poe, "The Masque of the Red Death" is an allegory hidden within a horror story. On a simplified basis, the story is about the rich receiving their final comeuppance for their superior attitude and detachment toward the troubles of those around them. The story is better seen, however, as an allegory about death, i.e., that no matter how wealthy one is, death can only be delayed but never defeated. The Red Death is, in this case, the great equalizer.

Nevertheless, most readers probably enjoy "The Masque of the Red Death" as a horror story only, and in that regard, it is outstanding. Poe brilliantly creates an atmosphere of dread in the strange abbey of Prospero's, while the pestilence of the Red Death is raging on the outside. The abbey has seven unusual rooms, built in irregular locations and each with a different color throughout, including the stained glass windows, except for the last one, which has a black carpet and is shrouded with black velvet tapestries, but with window panes the color of a deep blood scarlet. The firelight in the black-red room that streams through the blood-tinted windows produces such "gaudy and fantastic appearances" that few in the company are even willing to enter the space. A gigantic clock of ebony is also in the room and when the clock strikes the hour, it gives a loud and deep sound that is so peculiar in note and emphasis that the orchestra stops playing and the dancers stop dancing. It is as if the ebony clock is counting down the time until each reveler's death. The appearance of the Red Death occurs at the most spooky time possible, at midnight, after twelve chimes of the disquieting clock ring throughout the abbey bringing all movement in the abbey to a stop.

Poe cleverly personifies the plague, or death itself, in the form of the masked figure. As Poe writes, "He had come like a thief in the night," causing each of the revelers to die "in the blood-bedewed halls of their revel." The story ends with a patented Poe shocker, as the Red Death is not a corporeal figure but a phantasm, ghost-like under a cloak and mask, a metaphor for death. So, and as demonstrated in its final paragraphs, "The Masque of the Red Death" surely is an allegory, but one with a horrifying atmosphere, unforgettable imagery and a surprise ending.

The Film

The Masque of the Red Death (1964)

The Masque of the Red Death is broadly based on the Poe short story of the same name, as a deadly disease ravages the villagers on the outside of Prospero's castle while Prospero fills the edifice with the aristocratic and the wealthy. To expand Poe's short story, which has the slightest of plots, the screenwriters have added a village girl named Francesca, whom Prospero brings with him to his castle after capturing her father and lover with the intent to kill at least one of them; Prospero's mistress Juliana, who joins him in devil worship; and some scenes of self-indulgence and debauchery among the invitees of the castle.

One short sequence of the film is based on "Hop-Frog," a story by Edgar Allan Poe that was first published in 1849 in *The Flag of Our Union*, a Boston newspaper. In that story, a court jester named Hop-Frog, who is described as a dwarf and a cripple, wreaks his revenge on a king and his seven councilors for their general evilness but in particular, for the king pushing a female dancer, another dwarf, and throwing a goblet of wine in her face. At a masquerade ball, Hop-Frog talks the king and his aides into dressing as orangutans, with Hop-Frog pretending to be the keeper who has chained them together. At the masque, Hop-Frog manages to tie his victims to a low hanging chandelier, pull them off their feet and then burn them to death.

Similarly, in *The Masque of the Red Death*, a dwarf named Hop-Toad seeks revenge on an aristocrat named Alfredo for his ill-treatment of Hop-Toad's dancing partner, Esmeralda, also a little person, by convincing him to attend the masque dressed as an ape. There, Hop-Toad ties Alfredo to a chandelier, pours brandy on him and burns him to death. Since Poe's "The Masque of the Red Death" is very brief, additional scenes and story arcs had to be added to the cinematic version of the story. It is nice that the screenwriters did so, in part, by incorporating another work by Poe.

The Masque of the Red Death has a reputation as the best of the Poe adaptations by Roger Corman, a reputation that is well-deserved. As expected from a Corman production from the era, the film has magnificent sets, extravagant

Gino (David Weston), unmasked, at right, has just won his first sword fight ever (note the cut on his forehead) to the chagrin of Prospero (Vincent Price), standing next to Gino, as his fiancé, Francesca (Jane Asher), looks on in *The Masque of the Red Death* (1964).

period costumes and lush color photography. What is unexpected, based on the prior films in the series, is that the scenes are fully populated, with numerous extras in both the early moments in the village but, more importantly, in the scenes in Prospero's castle. To be most effective, the storyline required numerous performers portraying the wealthy in those scenes, to properly show them as decadent, insipid and cruel. The number of extras also contributes to the awe created at the end of the film, in the massive death sequence, aided by shots of the falling and dead bodies taken from high above, confirming the enormity of the casualties.

The Masque of the Red Death contains what is probably Corman's best directorial effort, with many shots displaying the virtuosity of the filmmaker while also contributing to the effectiveness of the film. As an example, when Prospero's mistress Juliana believes she has become betrothed to the devil (and after an ineffective and superfluous dream sequence, an unfortunate Corman trademark), the film comes alive as Juliana walks back to the main room of the castle. Her walk takes her through three of the single-colored rooms of the mansion, shown without a cut as the camera slides around the walls of the room and stops when she does in each room, until she emerges into the main hall of the edifice. At that point, the camera is stationary and almost at floor level, with Juliana on the far side of the vast room. As the pendulum of the clock swings to and fro in front of the camera, Juliana walks closer to the pendulum and the stationary camera, again without a cut, until there is a quick cut and then numerous quick cuts, with the sudden appearance of a large crow, slashing Juliana to death. The entire sequence is a highlight of the film.

The set direction for the film is also admirable. The use of the single-colored rooms comes from the Poe short story and although the rooms are never mentioned in the film, they provide an amazing and original setting for some of the scenes of the feature. The one black room, with a red-tinted window, recreating Poe's best setting in the story, is used as the location for Prospero's first meeting with the Red Death and later, as the location of Prospero's death. Another well-staged moment occurs when the Red Death touches the revelers in the great hall of Prospero's castle, causing them to perform their dances of death with exaggerated deliberateness. As the dancers move unusually slowly in the background, Prospero has his final talk or negotiations with the Red Death, a very eerie scene, indeed.

The Masque of the Red Death seems to contain the two themes from Poe's short story, but upon further review, that is not necessarily the case. Edgar Allan Poe's short stories were usually very brief and while Poe was a master of creating atmosphere and employing just the right word in just the right place, he was not much on characterization. Prince Prospero barely appears in "The Masque of the Red Death" and his sins seem to be more of obliviousness than cruelty. The Prospero of the short story is not necessarily someone who needed to be punished. Since both the poor on the outside and the wealthy on the inside die, the story is primarily about the certainty of death, a certainty that does not respect wealth or class boundaries.

In the film version of the story, as the Red Death states, he killed many—"the peasant and prince, the worthy and the dishonored"—but allowed six to live. Although one is an old man in the village who has not previously been mentioned in the film, the others are characters of good repute, such as Francesca, a religious person, and Gino, her brave lover. In the film, Prospero is characterized as completely evil, evidenced by his destruction of the village by fire, killing anyone who stands up to him and delighting in the death or humiliation of others. Thus, in the film, the death of Prospero and all in his ensemble seems to be a punishment for their evil, a final comeuppance for the wealthy, as it were. Death is not inevitable in the film. Only those the Red Death chooses must die.

In the story, the Red Death is a phantom that walks, does not talk and turns out to be ghost-like in substance. The film handles the character differently, as the Red Death talks to several people, including Prospero, and in the film's surprise, the unmasked figure has the face of Prospero, already afflicted with the Red Death. While the surprise ending of Poe's story is stunning, it would not have translated well to a feature length film and the modification of the presentation of the Red Death for the movie is undoubtedly for the better. Indeed, at the end of the film, it is revealed that there are seven figures of Death stalking the countryside, all dressed in different colors. (The colors approximate the colors of the seven rooms in the Poe short story.) This results is one of the most haunting images in all of horror films, as the many figures of Death end the film, walking single file through the ravaged countryside, presumably on a mission to bring the touch of Death to more people.

A negative of the production is its cheesy special effects (an unfortunate characteristic of other Corman productions), such as the camera focusing in on the red clothing of the Red Death and the obvious jump cuts before the skin of the aristocrats is shown as having turned red. Where, as Poe wrote, is the blood bleeding profusely from the pores of the victims? Given the right special effects, this could have been a truly gory moment. Also, some of the storyline contains obvious padding, such as the character of Juliana and her interest in Satan and the killing of Alfredo by Hop-Toad.

As was often the case in these Corman productions, there is a quote from the Poe story shown on-screen after the action of the film has ended. In this case, it is the last line of the story, "And Darkness and Decay and the Red Death held illimitable dominion over all." And, as was often the case in these Corman productions, the use of that sentence is inappropriate. With the seven figures of Death closing out the film, it is Death that holds dominion over the countryside, not just the Red Death.

These are minor matters, at best. The positives of the film far outweigh its negatives. Roger Corman has finally brought a Poe tale to the cinema that is faithful to both the storyline and atmosphere of the short story that inspired it. *The Masque of the Red Death* is highly recommended.

CHAPTER 33

"The Viy" by Nikolai Gogol

Black Sunday/La maschera del demonio (1960), an Italian film directed by Mario Bava, is usually considered to be the most famous adaptation of Nikolai Gogol's "The Viy." However, although the credits to the film refer to a story by Nikolai Gogol and all sources cite "The Viy" as the source material for the film, it is difficult to discern many similarities between the two works, other than that they are both set in Russia and both may involve a witch. Thus, it was not until 1967 that a true adaptation of "The Viy" finally reached the cinema.

Background

Nikolai Vasillevich Gogol was born in 1809 in Sorochyntsy, Russia, an area that is now part of the Ukraine. His father was a writer who died when Gogol was only 15. At the age of 18, Gogol moved to St. Petersburg, where he eventually became a professor of history at the University of St. Petersburg. By 1831, Gogol was publishing collections of his short stories, some of which are still read today, such as "The Overcoat," which like "The Viy," has a ghostly element to it. "The Viy" was first published in 1835. Gogol passed away in 1852.

The Literature

"The Viy" tells the story of Homa, known as the philosopher, who, along with two other young students at the Bratsky Monastery in Kiev, Russia, gets

Barbara Steele stars in *Black Sunday/La maschera del demonio* (1960), purportedly based on "The Viy," by Nikolai Gogol, but, in fact, an original work.

lost on his way home on his summer vacation and thus becomes involved with an old woman who turns out to be a beautiful young witch. After being ridden like a horse by the witch, Homa escapes from the witch's clutches by grabbing a piece of wood and whacking the old woman with all of his might. Several days later, Homa is dragged back to the scene of his encounter with the witch and is locked into a church with the woman's body for three frightening nights. On the first two nights, Homa protects himself from the witch by staying within a hand-drawn circle on the floor of the church but on the third night, the situation comes to a deadly end. Homa is attacked by the witch, "a countless multitude of monstrous beings" and "a squat, thick-set bandy-legged figure" with a face made of iron known as Viy. As soon as the Viy finds Homa, all the fiends attack the philosopher. Homa falls to the ground dead, his soul fleeing from his body in terror.

At the beginning, "The Viy" does not appear to be a horror story at all, as it is written in a light manner. By contrast, the ending of the story, with Homa spending three nights locked in a church with a witch, is truly frightening. As one reads the story, it is not quite clear when the narrative changes from a lighthearted tale to one of terror. The metamorphosis truly sneaks up on the reader, making the horror elements at the end even more frightening than they would otherwise be. In addition, the ending of the story creates an almost mythological setting that is hard to forget. Because the monsters in the church miss the first cock's crow after their final attack on Homa, they must remain in the church forever, stuck in the doors and windows. Over time, the edifice becomes overgrown with forest trees and rough grass, and no one is able to locate the former house of worship, now an abandoned church filled with monsters.

In addition to devising a strong plot, Nikolai Gogol keeps the tale interesting by the structure of the story and its imagery. Gogol subtlety incorporates sexual imagery into the story, in the moments in which the witch rides Homa like a horse and vice versa, causing Homa to become "aware of a fiendishly voluptuous feeling, he felt a stabbing, exhaustingly terrible delight." Gogol also makes good use of contrasting elements—the old woman changes into the young witch; the witch rides the philosopher and then the philosopher rides the witch; and a house of worship, the church, becomes the permanent home of some very monstrous creatures.

The one disappointment in the story is the appearance of the title monster. The Viy is described as squat and bandy-legged, covered all over with black earth, with arms and legs like strong sinewy roots and long eyelids which hang down to the very ground. In the author's note to his story, Gogol writes, "The 'Viy' is a monstrous creation of popular fancy. It is the name which the inhabitants of Little Russia give to the king of the gnomes, whose eyelashes reach to the ground." Nevertheless, while the Viy has a strange appearance, its small stature makes the creature somewhat less than intimidating. His only frightening aspect is his face made of iron.

After the conclusion of the main story, Homa's former companions learn about the demise of Homa and one comments, "[I]t was because he was afraid; if he had not been afraid the witch could not have done anything to him." Perhaps that line creates a little bit of a theme to the story, that the ability of the supposed supernatural comes more from the fright of its victims than from any actual powers the supernatural may have. In support of that theme, it may be that Homa dies from fright on that third night in the church, particularly because the spirits cannot seem to reach him inside his hand-drawn circle on the first two nights in the church. However, "The Viy" is better read as a horror story only, a tale of a witch who, along with some very powerful demons, may still be alive in the doors and windows of that forgotten church, and, if ever found, could scare just about anyone to death, not just a philosopher.

The Film

Viy (1967)

The first true film adaptation of "The Viy" was produced in Russia, the country of the story's origin. Of course, since the release of the movie was in 1967, the country of the film's production is more properly referred to as the Soviet Union. *Viy* is one of the closest adaptations of a horror story ever filmed, bringing to mind the 1916 silent film, *The Queen of Spades*, another close adaptation of a Russian short horror story, also made in Russia.

While *Viy* does not have the reputation of *Black Sunday*, it is a very good film in its own right. The filmmakers were keen enough to stick closely to Gogol's original storyline because unlike the stories of Edgar Allan Poe, for example, "The Viy" has a strong plot, making it easy to adapt to the cinema. Of course, some changes were made, as they always are in the transition from literature to film, but most seem to be more of emphasis rather than significance. An interesting change between story and film involves the incident with the old witch on Khoma's first night at the farmhouse. When the witch's ride on Khoma's back ends in the movie, Khoma beats the witch, almost to her death. Khoma does not ride the witch back to the farmhouse. Thus, the film removes most of the sexual imagery from the story, perhaps a reflection of Soviet society in 1967.

In addition to hewing closely to Gogol's main storyline, the filmmakers incorporate small moments from Gogol's story into the film, such as a tear coming down the witch's face in the church before she rises from the dead and Khoma's hair turning gray after the second night in the church. These moments add some nice horror touches to the film.

The special effects in *Viy* are outstanding, starting with the ride by the witch on Khoma's back. It starts out with Khoma walking with her on his back. As the fog fills the background, Khoma seems to be walking in slow motion. Then he gradually lifts into the sky, with his feet still moving, and the witch on his back. Eventually they seem to be flying as high above the ground as an airplane. Throughout, nothing seems phony about the special effects, even as the two fall rapidly to the ground.

The highlight of the film is the final night in the church. This is set up by his first two nights in the church that, while scary, only involve the young girl coming back to life and her coffin flying through the air, trying to break down the invisible shield around Khoma's circle. On the third night, however, after Khoma starts his chanting, the witch suddenly rises again, but this time she conjures up the demons. A skeleton walks and clatters along the floor, large hands come out of the walls, and strange animal and human-like creatures appear. The witch calls for the vampires and the werewolves and even more strange beings of all shapes and sizes arrive, some crawling down the wall on their rear ends, other with big ears and multiple eyes and noses, and some without mouths. The witch then summons Viy and a creature arrives, larger than expected but matching Gogol's description of the monster in most respects. And, unlike the Viy in Gogol's short story, the Viy of the Cinema, with his size, deep voice, huge head and large eyes, is quite scary. No one, including your author, would ever refer to the movie Viy as "less than intimidating."

This scene in the church on the third night is aided by the excellent musical score, the witch's laughter in the background, some quick cutting between the several participants, the fabulous makeup and the flawless special effects. The filmmakers have managed, through their own movie magic, to put on the screen what Gogol described in his story as "a countless multitude of monstrous beings" trooping into the church. The edifice is filled with more monsters than possibly in any other horror film. It is a stunning moment.

A comparison of *The Queen of Spades* (1916) and *Viy* is instructive, since both are faithfully based on famous short horror stories written by Russians. While *Viy* is surprisingly effective, *The Queen of Spades* is disappointingly boring. The difference seems to be that *The Queen of Spades* just plods along, faithfully telling the short story's plot, but using very little of the cinema's storytelling tools, in the hopes that a good story alone is enough to carry the film. Those filmmakers learned, presumably to their dismay, that while a good story alone may suffice for literature, it is not enough for the cinema. By contrast, the creators of *Viy* used the underlying Gogol story as a springboard for incorporating the strengths of the cinema, particularly its special effects, shot selection, musical score and other sounds, to relate key incidents in the story, turning them into an incredible fantasy of the cinema. Movies really are different than literature.

Viy misses becoming the classic that it could have been because the protagonist, Khoma, is not very likable in his own right. Khoma seems to be more of a drunk and a coward than anything else. He is somewhat heretical about his religion, surprising because he is a student at the Kiev monastery. As a result, it is hard for the audience to share in Khoma's fright and predicament on a personal level. The audience always views the story from afar, never becoming emotionally attached to Khoma, substantially diminishing the effectiveness of the film. *Viy* is also hurt somewhat by the non-horrific brightness and open-air quality of many of the scenes outside the church, dissipating some of the horror of the tale. In that regard, more of the dark style and mood of *Black Sunday* would have been helpful for the film.

Nevertheless, *Viy* is an excellent horror film, perhaps the best one ever to come from Russia. If the film could escape from the shadow of *Black Sunday*, a well-respected horror film with which it truly has no relationship, and become readily available for viewing, viewers who love their horror films would surely delight in *Viy*.

Chapter 34

Rosemary's Baby by Ira Levin

Probably as a consequence of the Motion Picture Production Code of the early 1930s, the American horror cinema historically tended to shy away from the subject of the occult and Satanism. Although the Code did not specifically ban those subjects, the Code had, at its core, a religious view of art and film. *Rosemary's Baby* (1968) changed all of that. The film, which delivered a serious depiction of witches and Satanism, was a critical and financial success. Thus, it was not unexpected that films on the same or similar subjects would soon be produced in Hollywood. *Rosemary's Baby* opened the doors for *The Exorcist* (1973), *The Omen* (1976) and many, many other films about witches, the occult and the Devil.

Background

Ira Levin was born in 1929 in New York City, the setting for *Rosemary's Baby*. His early writings included scripts for military training films and television and later, he wrote several Broadway plays, the most famous one being *Deathtrap*, a mystery that premiered in 1978. His first novel was a mystery, *A Kiss Before Dying*, which won the Edgar Award for Best First Novel in 1954. His other well-known works in the mystery and science fiction genres are *The Stepford Wives*, published in 1972, and *The Boys from Brazil*, published in 1976. All of those films were made into motion pictures, as was his most famous novel, *Rosemary's Baby*, first published in 1967.

The Literature

Rosemary's Baby opens with Rosemary and Guy Woodhouse renting an apartment in a building known as the Bramford in New York City, even after they learn that the building has a sketchy past involving witchcraft. Shortly after moving in, Rosemary and Guy meet Roman and Minnie Castevet, a couple with an apartment on the same floor as Rosemary and Guy. As events unfold, it turns out that the Castevets are devil worshippers. In exchange for some supernatural assistance in furthering his career, Guy joins their cult and then becomes involved in a conspiracy to impregnate Rosemary with the seed of the devil. Rosemary eventually discovers the plot against her but it is too late. The baby is born and when Rosemary sees the baby, the son of Satan and not of Guy, her maternal instincts come forth. As the novel ends, Rosemary has decided to care for the baby as though nothing unusual has happened.

It must be far different reading *Rosemary's Baby* today than it was upon the book's original publication. The 1968 film version is so famous that even those who have yet to see the movie undoubtedly know that the novel is about witchcraft and Satanism. Thus, when Guy gets his part in a play after an actor named Baumgart goes blind and when Minnie suggests that Rosemary use Dr. Saperstein as her obstetrician instead of Dr. Hill, who was Rosemary's first choice, the modern reader knows that those are not innocent matters but rather, part of a broad plot against Rosemary's baby. This is not dissimilar to reading a whodunit while knowing in advance who the killer is. Those who read the book back in 1967 would come to those same revelations only in retrospect.

Yet for all of that special knowledge, the book remains an engrossing read today. The primary reason is, of course, the novel's strong plot, with its unique subject matter and its twists and turns along the way. Another reason is that the story is always told from the viewpoint of Rosemary's. The reader is always cognizant of Rosemary's thoughts and feelings, becoming happy, sad or apprehensive whenever she is. The reader is with Rosemary as she unravels the plot against her and her unborn child, understanding her thought processes. The reader is always involved in the travails of Rosemary's and since she is a likable character, the reader empathizes with her situation.

Another factor is that the novel goes against type. A story of this nature, with witches and the supernatural, would usually have been set in the distant past or in an old dark house. By contrast, *Rosemary's Baby* is set in the very contemporary 1960s, with references to the Kennedys, a newspaper strike and a visit by the Pope to New York City. It is a tale of horror in the middle of a real city, amidst the goings on of everyday life including, for Rosemary, finding an apartment, entertaining friends and making a marriage work. The horror of

Satanism within a common and realistic setting of a large city is one of the factors that makes the novel stand out from the horror novels of the past.

Levin builds on that theme late in the novel when Rosemary discovers the evil that is directed against her. She escapes from her apartment and tries to find someone who can help her. Rosemary cannot contact any of her friends; they all seem to be out-of-town or busy. The obvious choice for Rosemary is to contact Dr. Hill, her first obstetrician, but he turns his back on her. As large as New York City is, Rosemary is all alone, with scary things happening to her. It is as if the entire city has turned into a fright house for Rosemary.

Unexpectedly, in a book about witches and devil worshipers, the most evil person is not one of the Satanists. It is Rosemary's husband Guy, who allows his wife to be drugged and then violated; allows his wife to suffer great pain during her pregnancy without providing her with any relief; and has no problem conspiring with the evildoers to kill Hutch, a friend of his who has discovered the Castevets' secret, all for a boost for Guy's acting career. This is actually another selling-one's-soul-to-the-devil story but this is one of the most brutal of them all. There is no humor in *Rosemary's Baby*.

The novel has several surprises throughout but the two stunning ones occur near the end. Rosemary believes the Satanists want to sacrifice her baby to the Devil, but instead, Rosemary learns to her dismay that she is actually giving birth to the son of the Devil. Even more surprising, the Satanists get away with it and with Rosemary's help. As of 1968, it was a rare horror novel in which the villains got away with it at the end. The practice became more common after the success of *Rosemary's Baby*.

With *Rosemary's Baby*, Ira Levin has written a relatively short novel, in a clean and lean writing style, with few detailed descriptions. There are some specifics of the clothes people are wearing, short descriptions of a few of the characters, a few details given of Rosemary's and Guy's apartment and not much else. Ira Levin is not writing a gothic novel; he does not try to establish mood and atmosphere for his tale of witchcraft. The novel is substantially plot-oriented and, as a result, it almost reads more like a script for a movie than a novel of horror. It is therefore not surprising that *Rosemary's Baby* was adapted into a very successful movie in 1968, just a year after the book's publication.

The Film

Rosemary's Baby (1968)

Since the novel *Rosemary's Baby* is so plot-oriented that it reads almost like a movie script, it is not surprising that the 1968 film is a faithful adaptation of the original story. The film moves along very quickly, making it seem much shorter than its actual length of 137 minutes. The sense of brevity is aided by the fact that the story line is not interrupted by stylistic camerawork or obtrusive cutting by the director, and there is no padding, such as the insertion of some humor to lighten the effect of the story. The movie is just as humorless as the novel. Film is usually more plot-oriented than literature; the film version of *Rosemary's Baby* emphasizes that attribute, to its benefit.

Much like the book, all of the events of the film are seen through the lens of Rosemary's understanding and feelings. Rosemary is in every scene in the film. The viewer is shown nothing that Rosemary does not also see. For example, when Dr. Hill decides to turn Rosemary over to her husband and Dr. Saperstein, the viewer learns about that turn of events at the same moment Rosemary does. There is no shot of Hill calling Saperstein outside of Rosemary's presence. Presumably, Guy has been spending a lot of time with the Castevets, outside Rosemary's presence, hatching their plot against Rosemary. The viewer has no special knowledge of that. All the viewer sees is what Rosemary sees—Guy finding an excuse to leave the apartment every time some obstacle appears to Guy's and the Satanists' plans.

As a result, and just like in the book, the reader is with Rosemary when she begins to realize that there is a conspiracy against her and her unborn child. The viewer is shocked along with Rosemary when it turns out that Guy, and later, Dr. Saperstein are involved in the plot. The audience is always invested in Rosemary's story, the highs, the lows and the scary parts. With the audience so invested in Rosemary, the horror of her situation is much more real.

Another style point taken from the book is its use of setting. New York City is seen in aerial shots over the opening credits and Rosemary takes several trips into Manhattan during the course of the film. While the film is not quite as successful as the book in incorporating the big city into its story, the film still has the anomaly of the horror of a coven of Satanists operating in the very real world, as contrasted with practicing their craft in an isolated house or hundreds of years ago. Just like the novel, *Rosemary's Baby* is not a gothic tale of witches. Almost every set in the movie is bright, including the Woodhouses' apartment, and most of the performers wear bright clothing. These contradictions between story and setting, which come from the novel, were unique to this type of film at the time. Indeed, Polanski seems to have deliberately gone against horror film conventions, as Levin did in the book, making *Rosemary's Baby* into a special viewing experience.

With Mia Farrow in every scene in the movie, the film would not have worked without an excellent performance from the young actress, and she does not disappoint. She is good early in he movie as a young woman in love with

A pregnant Rosemary (Mia Farrow) desperately tries to escape from her husband and Dr. Saperstein in *Rosemary's Baby* (1968).

her husband and then convincing as she struggles through her first pregnancy. She excels, however, once she discovers the plot against her and her baby. Rosemary becomes focused on her investigation but also become a little hysterical and unhinged. Because of the subtle and gradually changing performance by Mia Farrow in the last part of the film, Dr. Hill's decision to turn on Rosemary in the film is believable, even though it was not that believable in the novel.

The rest of the featured players are good. Ruth Gordon won an Academy Award for Best Supporting Actress for her role as Minnie Castevet. The standout supporting performance, however, is by Sidney Blackmer, as the always dapperly dressed Roman Castevet. By contrast with Ruth Gordon's broad performance, Blackmer's performance is understated, yet displaying a quiet wickedness. The big disappointment among the actors is John Cassavetes, who is never convincing as Guy Woodhouse. Cassavetes always seems to be without emotion, even when emotional events are occurring. Cassavetes gives the only unimpressive performance of the movie although, to be fair, that may be because the role is not well written, as Guy turns from a genuinely loving husband to a completely evil character almost overnight and with very little motivation.

Director Roman Polanski shoots the film in the lean and clean style of the novel, never letting his camerawork become obtrusive. This may be the best compliment that can be given to a director. There are, however, a few impressive stylistic moments in the film, used to move the plot forward, not to display the virtuosity of the director. One occurs in the most important scene in the early part of the film, Rosemary's dream during her real-life rape. There is cutting between the real-life rape and the dream Rosemary is having, with unusual images being inserted, such as the face of the ship's young captain turning into an image of Hutch, a typhoon knocking the ship around, Rosemary's prone body being raised on a board in a chapel with freakish paintings on the ceilings, and a ghoulish hand stroking Rosemary's skin. Sounds are also important, with a clock ticking, a fire sizzling and the chanting of the Satanists in the background during different parts of the dream. Unlike most dream sequences in films, Polanski almost always keeps his images distinct and clear, a technique used to great effect by Alfred Hitchcock in the dream sequences in *Spellbound* (1945).

The book is better than the movie at conveying the emotions of Rosemary's, the motivations of Guy's in falling in with the Satanists and the subtle and gradual build up of the scheme against Rosemary's baby. The film excels at its climax, as Rosemary enters the Castevets' apartment through the fake door in the closet, knife in hand. For the first time in the film, much of the sequence is shot in the semi-dark, as Rosemary makes her solitary and secretive walk into the unknown of the Castevets' apartment. Even in the brighter moments in the sequence, the light seems to come from the fixtures in the apartment. Polanski continues to show events from the perspective of Rosemary, except that the viewer never sees the baby. In that one instance, all the viewer sees is Rosemary's horrified reaction to the face of her son. The scene then segues into the exaltations of an international coven of Satanists, claiming that God is dead but the son of Satan has been born, one of the most frightening endings of any horror film. But there is still one more twist left.

If there was any doubt that the Motion Picture Production Code was impotent by 1968, *Rosemary's Baby* ended the argument. With a tale of Devil worshipers, some partial nudity in the rape dream sequence, and some disparaging comments about God and the Pope, the rules of the Code were broken. None of those, however, equal the amazing moment at the end of the film when a group of Satanists get away with their evildoings. Rosemary has decided to protect, nurture and raise the son of the Devil. The Satanists are never punished for their conspiracy; the Devil reigns supreme. By 1968, the Motion Picture Production Code was gone, never to be resurrected.

Chapter 35

The Devil Rides Out by Dennis Wheatley

Hammer Studios turned to Dennis Wheatley, a British novelist who wrote a number of books about the occult, for the inspiration for its 1968 horror film, *The Devil's Bride*, known in England by the title of the book on which it was based, *The Devil Rides Out*. In addition to fitting squarely within the Hammer Films tradition of adapting horror novels to the screen, *The Devil's Bride* was also part of a trend of the era toward producing horror films about the devil and Satanic practices, perhaps best exemplified by the American horror films, *Rosemary's Baby* (1968) and *The Exorcist* (1973).

Background

Dennis Wheatley was born in London, England in January 1897. Wheatley was a prolific writer, authoring short stories, historical and biographical works and over 50 novels, including 11 novels about Duke De Richleau, an English adventurer similar to Bulldog Drummond (although De Richleau is actually a French exile living in England). The De Richleau novels were usually tales of adventure, including some of which were also about the occult. The second book in the series, *The Devil Rides Out*, published in 1934, is a tale of devil worship. Rex Van Ryn and Simon Aron, characters in the first novel, join De Richleau in the new adventure and throughout the second novel, there are references to the trio's prior adventure in Russia. Wheatley died on November 10, 1977, at the age of 80.

The Literature

The Devil Rides Out is a story of witchcraft, the occult and devil worship, pitting the Duke De Richleau and his allies against Mocata, a practitioner of black magic who is seeking the lost Talisman of Set, the most potent of all charms, whose possessor can bring calamity upon the world, causing either another world war or Armageddon. In order to accomplish his purpose, Mocata uses Tanith, a beautiful young woman who is a perfect medium for Mocata's activities, and Simon Aron, who was born when certain stars were in conjunction and is therefore useful to Mocata in his rituals. By the end of the novel, De Richleau has broken up a black mass, rescued Tanith and others from the hands of Mocata and has killed Mocata.

Three scenes in *The Devil Rides Out* are worthy of particular mention. The first is the Sabbat conducted by Mocata. On a throne of stones, a dark figure slowly materializes, changes into a greyish shape and then forms into the Goat of Mendes, a monstrous creature with a bearded head of a giant goat, two great cloven hoofs, long pointed ears and four enormous curved horns. In the middle of the orgiastic ritual seemingly led by the goat, De Richleau and Van Ryn manage to rescue Aron by driving their car with the headlights burning bright into the crowd and toward the goat, grabbing Aron at the last moment. This is an horrific yet exciting portion of the novel.

Perhaps the high point of the novel is Mocata's attack on De Richleau and his friends in the library of house of Richard and Marie Lou Eaton. De Richleau has secured everyone within a pentacle drawn on the floor. Everyone is told to stay within its boundaries. Mocata attacks Richard Eaton first, unconsciously convincing him that De Richleau is crazy and there is no reason to remain within the pentacle. When that does not work, Simon suddenly feels thirsty and wants to leave the pentacle; the parties hear Rex, who had gone away with Tanith, at the door of the library entreating them to let him in; the library is plunged into darkness and becomes cold; and then a beast-like horse viciously attacks the pentacle, without success. This is the most frightening section of the book.

Although the scene within the pentacle seems, in many ways, to be the climax of the book, the gang still has to rescue Fleur, the daughter of the Eatons, and prevent Mocata from obtaining the Talisman of Set. After crossing many barriers, Mocata seems to have trapped them in the underground of a ruined church in France. As Mocata raises a knife and prepares to strike it into Fleur's body, Marie Lou speaks some ancient words. Instantaneously, the whole chamber rocks as if struck by an earthquake. The Talisman bounces down the steps of the tomb to De Richleau, Mocata stumbles back, the Goat of

Mendes is thrown to the floor and dies and Fleur appears to change, her body gradually forming itself into the Lord of Light. The figure announces that the forces of evil have been driven back into the dark and will never trouble them again.

The last scene is particularly noteworthy because it is a female character, Marie Lou Eaton, who actually rids the earth of the evil that is Mocata. As the Lord of Light states, nothing De Richleau could have done would have mattered "had it not been for She who is the Mother. The Preserver harkens ever to the prayer which goes forth innocent of all self-desire" (Chapter 33, "Death of a Man Unknown, From Natural Causes"). Prior to recent decades, it was very unusual for a horror film or book to have a woman as the slayer of the monster.

The most significant problem with *The Devil Rides Out* is that it is, quite frankly, boring, caused by the fact that the novel sometimes seems, as others have described it, like a "knowledge dump." The book is full of long sections where De Richleau tells allegedly true stories about the occult, witchcraft and the devil, usually in order to convince other characters in the novel that his concerns about Mocata are real. These sections, however, read like boring college lectures with De Richleau going on for page after page describing allegedly true occult events and incorporating strange names and places. Most of De Richleau's lectures are irrelevant to the main story line of the book. If Wheatley had significantly tightened his text, the otherwise strong plot of the book would have been much more effective.

In the Author's Note to *The Devil Rides Out*, Dennis Wheatley wrote that prior to writing the book, he did considerable research into occultism and black magic to secure the accuracy of the details in his account. While that surely provides some credibility for the novel, there was no reason to regurgitate all of that information for the reader. No work of fiction is going to convince readers of the validity of black magic, so the only practical effect of this style of writing is to make the book less effective. For *The Devil Rides Out*, that is a shame because parts of the book are very well written, more than adequately displaying the horror of Mocata and his devil worshippers.

Even though Dennis Wheatley is practically forgotten today, his work lives on in a few films that were adapted by his writings, the most famous of which is *The Devil's Bride*. Since the boring lectures would obviously be dropped in the film version and the strong plot of the novel would therefore have a chance to come through, *The Devil Rides Out* would seem to be a good choice for adaptation to the cinema and, of course, Hammer Films did just that.

The Film

The Devil's Bride/The Devil Rides Out (1968)

The Devil's Bride is a surprisingly faithful adaptation of Dennis Wheatley's novel, *The Devil Rides Out*. The film cuts the irrelevancies of the novel and focuses on its strong core plot. In addition to cutting the knowledge dumps set forth in the book, the movie makes cuts in other aspects of Wheatley's book, with the movie essentially overlooking the romance between Tanith and Rex, eliminating the backstory of Tanith and foregoing the reasons why Tanith and Simon became a part of the cult. The film also moves the final Black Mass to England, near the Eaton home, thereby eliminating the book's chase into Paris and the obstacles thrown at De Richleau before he gets to the final ceremony run by Mocata.

The climax of *The Devil's Bride* provides an interesting variation on the ending of the novel. Once again, it is Marie Eaton who saves her child, but instead of first stating some magic words to Mocata, she starts to break up the ritual by announcing, "Only they who love without desire shall have power granted them in the darkest hour." Marie's speech is a clever re-working of the language the Lord of Light speaks in the book after the death of Mocata. Marie then repeats the magic words that De Richleau had said earlier in the film, leading to the destruction of the temple.

The obvious place where *The Devil's Bride* is inferior to the Wheatley novel is in its special effects. Novelists are never constrained by budgetary considerations or difficulties of creating special effects or makeup. Novelists are only bound by the limits of their imaginations. On the other hand, budgetary considerations are obviously an important consideration in any film production and also, special effects can only do so much. Thus, *The Devil's Bride* is lacking in just those sections where the book is very strong. As two examples only, when the Goat of Mendes appears at the Sabbat in the novel, he is a huge, monstrous and scary figure. In the film, he is an actor made-up to look like a man-goat, small in stature, with the goat-like features seeming to be a mask. Also, in the film attack on De Richleau at the Eaton home where De Richleau and his allies are protected within the magic circle (the pentacle in the book), a foot high spider attacks the group. This spider, which is the only attack on the protective circle that does not come from the book, is totally unconvincing and hardly scary. It looks as if the special effect is one of the discarded items from the prop room of *Tarantula* (1955). In these moments, there is simply no comparison between book and film. The book is far superior in creating a feeling of horror in the reader.

A lobby card for *The Devil's Bride* (1968) portrays some of the ritualistic aspects of the film.

The obvious place where *The Devil's Bride* is superior to the Wheatley novel is, as expected, the lack of knowledge dumps in the film. Of course, De Richleau still has to educate the characters and the audience on the bona fides of black magic and devil worship and, of course, De Richleau has to pepper his talk with strange names and strange places. However, for the most part, De Richleau's talks in the film are perfunctory and when he gives his speech to the

Eatons, as he must for plot purposes, that speech is cleverly done off camera, thereby slowing down the film not even a whit. Screenwriter Richard Matheson clearly recognized that the lectures in the novel slowed down the novel and in a film, those types of speeches would have brought the movie to a complete stand still. Film, by its very nature, has to trim the fat when it is adapting a written work for the cinema and in this case, the trimming adds to the effectiveness of the film.

For those who believe that books are always better than the movies they inspire, *The Devil Rides Out* is an example of one type of book for which that almost never occurs, i.e., books with strong plots that are weighted down by filler material or by detours from the main storyline. Even though the film version of *The Devil Rides Out* does not display the imagination of the novel, it is the far better work. Most people who view the film will never have read the book. Not knowing what they are missing, they will probably be quite impressed with the imagination of the film.

While the special effects of *The Devil's Bride* are disappointing in many ways, including the fact that they often seem like special effects, they are quite good in some instances. The attack of the Angel of Death on the black steed against the protective circle in which De Richleau and his allies have found protection is well done, as is the destruction of the temple during the final Black Mass. In terms of budget, there are plenty of extras taking part in the mass rituals, including the orgiastic ritual in the countryside, and there are numerous other scenes outside in the country, including a car chase along narrow roads. *The Devil's Bride* is a first-class production.

In terms of acting, it is refreshing to see Christopher Lee playing the hero of a horror film, in this case Duke De Richleau. Lee is good, as always, in the movie, but hero or not, there still seems to be an aura of evil about him. De Richleau is quite arrogant. He also seems to know many secrets of the occult. One has to wonder where he acquired that knowledge. De Richleau is the hero of the film but in the person of Christopher Lee, some viewers might just have a little bit of doubt.

Charles Gray is outstanding as Mocata. In the book, Mocata is described as a pot-bellied, bald-headed man of about 60 years of age, with an unattractive lisp. Charles Gray is just the opposite. Gray is the epitome of the upper class English gentleman, with his gray hair, handsome face and cultured voice. The scene in which Mocata almost hypnotizes Marie Eaton, with dialogue taken directly from the novel, is Charles Gray at his best. Even when Mocata is wearing the silly robes of his ritual, he is an evil figure, in the person of Charles Gray.

The Devil's Bride has some perplexing aspects to it. In the book, Mocata was after the powerful Talisman of Set, a worthy goal of any Satanist. In the film, Mocata simply wants to baptize Simon and Tanith into his cult. It is never made clear what the significance of that act could be. Indeed, Mocata's underlying motive is never explained in the film. He seems to be a person who wants to do evil just for evil's sake, which, come to think of it, is a pretty good definition of Satan and his Satanists. The movie also fails to provide a coda to the climactic scene at the Black Mass, announcing afterwards only that Tanith is alive and therefore Mocata must be dead. Mocata's body is never shown. In the book, Mocata's body is found on the stone steps of the Eaton house.

The Devil's Bride was released the same year as *Rosemary's Baby*. The two films are substantially different in their time periods, the underlying motive of the devil worshippers, their setting and their tone. In the latter regard, *The Devil's Bride* is a louder, special effects version of Satanism; *Rosemary's Baby* is the softer version with its Satanists being quietly malevolent although very effective. Both films are highly recommended but *Rosemary's Baby* is the better of the two films.

Chapter 36

"Don't Look Now" by Daphne Du Maurier

Daphne du Maurier enjoyed going on vacation in the off-season, as her biographer Martyn Shallcross wrote, so that du Maurier could enjoy the atmosphere of the locations and use the insights she gained there in her writing. One of those off-season trips was to Venice, Italy with her son, Christian. There she may have received the inspiration for "Don't Look Now," as a mysterious and dark, out-of-season Venice provides the locale for the story, the second most famous short story du Maurier ever wrote.

The Literature

"Don't Look Now" is a mild tale of the supernatural, involving premonition and extra sensory perception, rather than monsters, witches or devil worshippers. The story concerns a married couple, John and Laura, who are vacationing in Venice to try to get their lives back on track after the recent and sudden death of their young daughter, Christine. While dining in a restaurant, John and Laura spot two sisters at a table across the room. One of the sisters is blind and professes to be a psychic. The blind sister then has a vision, seeing Christine in the restaurant, sitting between John and Laura and laughing. Later, the blind sister prophesizes that if John and Laura remain in Venice, they will be in trouble. Laura leaves Venice but before John can leave, he sees Laura on a ferry, in the company of the sisters. There is a look of distress on Laura's face. When John remains in Venice to search for Laura, the prophecy comes true, as John is brutally murdered by a serial killer.

On first reading, "Don't Look Now" appears to be a slight tale, with not much happening in the story. On a second read, du Maurier's cleverness becomes apparent. Most of "Don't Look Now" is a study in subtlety, with the story having only two strange incidents before its conclusion—the blind sister seeing Christine sitting between John and Laura in the restaurant and John seeing Laura in the company of the sisters on the ferry when Laura is actually in England. "Don't Look Now" then ends in the surprise murder of John. A tale of subtlety resolves itself by a sudden burst of violence and blood. The ending would never have been so effective if the remainder of the story had been filled with moments of horror.

Another effective element of the story is that it is told solely from John's perspective. Much of the tension in the story is created by John's bewilderment, his unstated feeling that he is losing touch with his wife, his feeling of being lost in a foreign country and later, actually being lost in the streets of Venice. The reader is with John in his predicament, his final realization of the significance of seeing Laura in Venice when she was actually in England and his death.

This approach to point-of-view actually provides some "monsters" for the story because from John's viewpoint the two sisters are monsters, seemingly stealing his wife from him. When John first sees the sisters across the room, the blind one (who John does not then know is blind) is staring at him, not with an idle glance "but something deeper, more intent, the prominent, light blue eyes oddly penetrating, giving him a sudden feeling of discomfort." As the blind sister reappears throughout the story, John usually describes her in terms that are evocative of a fiend. In fact, however, John is wrong. The blind sister is a good person with good intentions.

At the end of the story, there is a real fiend—the little girl who turns out to be a "little thick-set woman dwarf, about three feet high, with a great square adult head too big for her body." The "little girl" had appeared previously in the story, but her sudden transformation into a killer makes her the true monster of the story.

The effectiveness of "Don't Look Now" is aided by du Maurier's use of doubling and opposites. The two sisters are twins, but one can see and one is blind. Laura reacts emotionally to the death of her daughter while John reacts in a more rational manner. Laura leaves Venice while John remains. John does not believe in psychics but he is one himself. The little girl John sees in Venice is actually a dwarf.

It may take the reader some time to realize that the blind sister's premonition, that if John and Laura stay in Venice they will be in trouble, does not relate to the illness of their son, the reason Laura actually returned to England, but rather to John remaining in Venice after Laura leaves. If John had left with Laura or shortly thereafter, as originally intended, John's death would not have occurred. Therefore, while John's vision of Laura with the sisters on the ferry is a premonition of John's death, it is that same vision of Laura that keeps John in Venice, resulting in his death. In other words, the vision foretells John's death but also causes the death.

"Don't Look Now" is an excellent short story but because the cinema is much more interested in bursts of horror than moments of subtlety, the story would not seem to be a good candidate for a screen adaptation. Yet surprisingly, the film version of "Don't Look Now" was released just a few years after its publication, so director Nicolas Roeg apparently saw nothing difficult about adapting a tale of subtle horror to the cinema.

The Film

Don't Look Now (1973)

Don't Look Now (1973), the film version of Daphne du Maurier's short story of the same name, retains much of the story's atmosphere of understated uneasiness and potential terror. The film is a close adaptation of the short story but, of course, changes were made.

The first change from story to film is that in the story, Christine died from fatal meningitis. In the film Christine drowns in a stream and the incident is shown in the film, not revealed in retrospect. The change is important to the film for several reasons. While John is working in the house, he suddenly has a premonition that his daughter is in trouble and he rushes out to try to save her. This moment sets up John's psychic abilities, which are a key to the storyline of the film. Also, the raincoat that Christine is wearing in the scene is important. It gives a reason for John chasing after the "little girl" at the end of the film, also a significant element of the film's plot. In du Maurier's story, John's chase after the little girl near the end of the tale is inexplicable.

The other reason for the change is more for style than substance. While director Nicholas Roeg does not completely eschew the main motif of the story, the doubling and opposites of characters and incidents, he creates additional motifs for the film that arise from its opening scenes. The red of Christine's outfit in the opening sequence is seen in the red of the girl John chases in Venice, the red in the photograph of the church John is restoring and the red of the blood that flows from John's body after his knifing. Red is shown in clothes and other objects throughout the film. The water in which Christine drowns is repeated in the water of the Venice canals, the murder victims who are found in the waters and John fishing a little girl's doll out of the water. The glass which breaks and puts holes in Johnnie's bike tires as he chases after his sister, Christine, appears again when a wood beam breaks the glass on the high plank on which

John is standing in the church in Venice and in the glass John kicks out in his final death throes in the film. These and several other motifs are cleverly used in the film to tie all of the sequences together.

Other changes in the plot are employed to make the film more cinematic than the story. While the story and the film have the same ending, the film's version is more dramatic. In both versions, when the blind sister starts to have a fit and go into trance, John leaves the sisters' hotel room and gets lost in the streets of Venice. In the story, that is the last the reader learns about the sisters. In the film version, the blind sister screams in terror that they must fetch John back. Thus, the sister's original premonition of danger for John if he stays in Venice has now turned into a premonition of a clear and present danger. While the other sister goes out to chase John, Laura has just returned to Venice and she is out looking for John also. Laura continues to chase after John, while John is oblivious to the danger. Thus, the film version has heightened excitement in its ending that does not in any way lessen the surprise and shock of the female dwarf knifing John. Here is another example where literature and film are different. The ending of the story works very well in that format; the ending of the film is just right for a cinematic version of the same tale.

The film is beautifully directed, with Nikolas Roeg making good use of Venice for the story, never letting Venice seem like a tourist attraction. Rather, Venice always seems like a cold and dreary place, in keeping with the tone of the story. Although the location of Venice comes from the du Maurier story, Roeg uses the cold, dark waters of the city to great effect, tying them to the drowning death of Christine that opens the film.

As entertaining as *Don't Look Now* is, once the film is over, one gets the feeling that while it may not have been all cinematic smoke and mirrors, there is a lack of substance to the film. Much like the short story, not much really happens in the movie. In addition, there are several moments of obvious padding in the film. One is the gratuitous sex scene between John and Laura, which was apparently notorious at the time of the film's release. While one could argue that the scene displays that Laura is back to normal once she hears about the blind sister seeing Christine in the restaurant, it really seems more like padding and padding that panders to the film style of its era. Interestingly, in the short story, a similar moment occurs but John and Laura decide that it is not the right moment to make love.

Then there is the moment when the high scaffold that John is standing on in the church falls, with John perilously close to taking a drop to the hard surface of the church below. He is barely rescued before he would have fallen to his death. One can argue here that the scene is used as a red herring, to show that the blind sister's prophecy about the danger of John staying in Venice was cor-

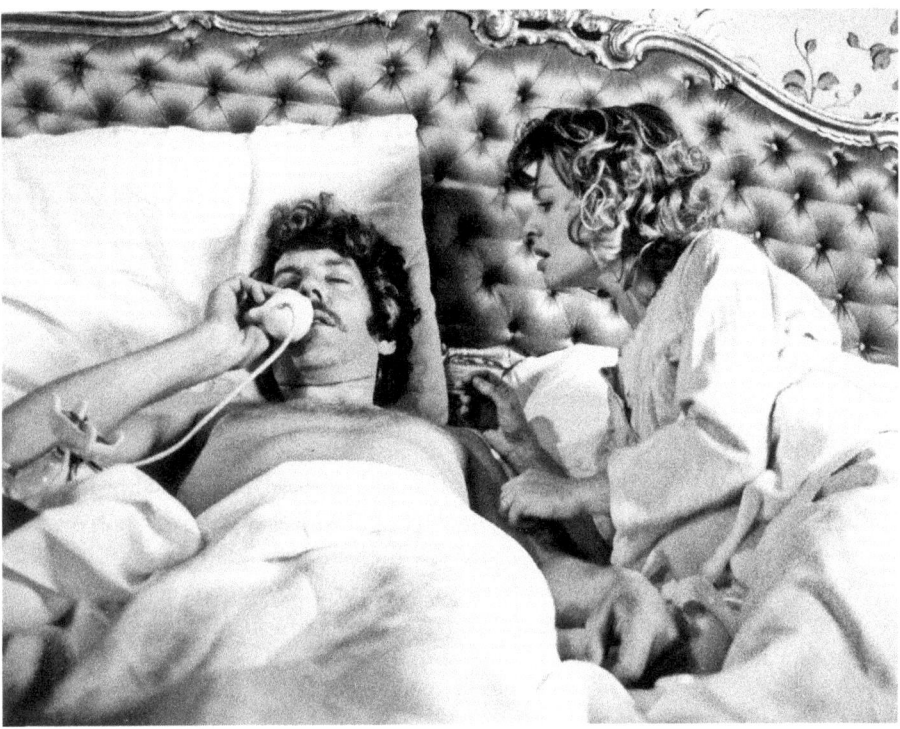

In *Don't Look Now* (1973), John (Donald Sutherland) and Laura (Julie Christie) receive a call from England, informing them that their son Johnnie is ill.

rect, but instead, it once again seems like padding, an attempt to create an exciting moment in the middle of a slow moving film.

There is an enigmatic character in the movie, the bishop for whom John is working, but in the end, he has nothing of significance to do with the film. There is also a superfluous scene in a church where Laura lights some candles. While the film does streamline John's search for Laura in Venice, which goes on for far too long in the story, there are still some extra scenes of a policeman following John and the owners of the sisters' hotel being unable to understand John in English (even though before that moment, John seemed to have no trouble conversing in Italian).

Don't Look Now would have been better if about 10 to 20 minutes had been excised from its running time of approximately 110 minutes. Nevertheless, *Don't Look Now* received great critical reviews and commentary at the time of its release, and it is still well-regarded to this day. *Don't Look Now* is different that most every other horror film that has ever been made. Flaws and all, the film is well worth a view.

Chapter 37

The Exorcist by William Peter Blatty

An exorcism is the act or ritual of driving a demon or the devil out of people, places or things that are possessed. Although the practice was not historically limited to Christians, today it is most associated with the Catholic Church and today, to the extent there are any exorcisms, the exorcist is a cleric of the Catholic Church. While exorcisms are officially religious rituals, in pop culture they are only two things—the climaxes to a novel written by William Peter Blatty and its film adaptation.

Background

William Peter Blatty was born in New York City in 1928. Blatty attended a Jesuit preparatory school in Brooklyn and went to college at a Jesuit school, Georgetown University in Washington, D.C., the locale for *The Exorcist*. After exiting the Air Force in the 1950s, Blatty turned to a career in writing, publishing articles and some humorous books. In the 1960s, Blatty worked on Hollywood screenplays, including the adaptation of his novel, *John Goldfarb, Please Come Home*, and *A Shot in the Dark* (1964) and *Gunn* (1967).

While a junior at Georgetown University, Blatty read the newspaper coverage of a 14-year-old boy in Maryland who was purportedly possessed. Blatty thus became interested in exorcisms and conducted research into supposed real exorcisms and historical cases dating back to the Bible. In 1971, Blatty finally published his fictional version of an exorcism, in a book that became a best seller.

The Literature

Although *The Exorcist* is a modern novel of horror, it relies on the storytelling techniques of classic horror novels from long ago. Before getting to the primary story, author William Peter Blatty lets the reader become familiar with the two characters who will suffer the most at the hands of the monster, painting them as likable people, seducing the reader into becoming invested in their well-being. Chris MacNeil, a famous actress shooting a film in Washington, D.C., has just moved to the Georgetown section of the city with her 11-year-old daughter, Regan, or Rags, as her mother sometimes calls her. Chris is very likable, smoothly questioning some of the motivations in her current movie's script, gently handling the bellicose and often drunk director, Burke Dennings, and deftly balancing her professional career with her love for her daughter. Regan seems delightful. Early on in the novel she makes her mother the sculpture of a bird as a present and enjoys a Shirley Temple movie and dinner out with her mother.

Much like *The Haunting of Hill House* by Shirley Jackson and similar tales, the manifestations of the horror that are about to afflict Regan start with small incidents, which gradually escalate into the serious. At first there are merely noises in the ceilings, personal items of Regan's seem to go missing and then the heavy bureau in Regan's room seems out of place as if someone had moved it. Regan acquires an imaginary friend named Captain Howdy, who communicates with Regan through a Ouija board.

Matters soon begin to intensify. When a doctor examines Regan, she levels a stream of obscenities at the doctor. A foul, unpleasant smell starts to permeate Regan's bedroom. At a dinner party of Chris's, Regan comes downstairs, urinates on a rug and tells an astronaut who is a guest at the party that he is going to die in space. Regan's bed then starts shaking and even rises several feet from the floor.

Finally, the full-fledged demon appears in Regan's body. It spews obscenities at anyone in its sight, vomits on people, creates a sickening odor in the room, speaks other languages, sometimes appears as other people such as the recently deceased Burke Dennings or harasses the priest, Damien Karras, by turning into his recently deceased mother and trying to lay a guilt trip on him over his lack of care for her when she became ill. In the most famous image from the book, the devil in Regan's body can turn her head around in a 360° turn. The monster of *The Exorcist* will not disappoint any reader.

Hearkening back to older horror novels, *The Exorcist* is told in the style of a mystery or, in this case, two mysteries. One is a medical mystery—what is causing the disease or whatever it is that manifests itself in Regan's suffering? All of the medical doctors and psychiatrists cannot find the cause of Regan's illness. The other mystery is a more conventional mystery—was Burke Dennings murdered and, if so, by whom? William Kinderman, a detective with the Washington police force, suspects foul play in the death of Dennings, whose body was discovered down a steep flight of steps near the MacNeil house, with his head turned completely around and facing backwards. Kinderman pieces all of the clues together and determines that Regan must be the killer, although he cannot figure out how an 11-year-old girl could have accomplished the misdeed.

In addition to employing all of these storytelling techniques of the horror genre, author William Peter Blatty does not forget the most important part of the story, a stunning climax. The entire novel builds slowly to the main event, which is the actual exorcism. It is conducted by the two priests and takes several days until it reaches its conclusion. All the time, the demon in Regan is spewing insults and obscenities and threatening to kill Regan, while challenging his long time nemesis, Father Merrin. The exorcism ends with surprises, in the death of one person and a recreation of the death of Burke Dennings in the murder of another. The climax, which is sad and then happy, is dramatic and stunning.

The Exorcist is an excellent novel but it has its weaknesses. Much like many horror novels before it, *The Exorcist* spends too much time trying to find a rational explanation for Regan's malady, as she goes from doctor to doctor and test to test. Even when Chris brings in Damian Karras for a potential exorcism, Damien takes too long, for fictional purposes, to gather evidence to convince the Catholic Church that he should be permitted to conduct an exorcism. Damien's delays are the most aggravating, since Church officials quickly agree to the exorcism after only a cursory review of Damien's research.

A false note in the story is Kinderman, the police detective. Kinderman is incredibly sharp; he is an excellent detective. Nevertheless, in his investigation, Kinderman attempts to convince the others that he is a bumbler, talking about irrelevant matters and never getting directly to the point of the investigation. Once an interview seems to be over, he comes back with another set of questions, apologizing all the time for his bumbling. He appears at unexpected moments, as if he is harassing people. He carries an overcoat with him.

Viewers of television detective shows of the 1960s and 1970s will easily recognize that Kinderman is based on the well-known television detective, Columbo, who was played by Peter Falk in a television series titled *Columbo* that originally ran on NBC from 1968 to 1978. Columbo acted much like Kinderman, never getting to the point, coming back with new questions after the interview seemed to be over, often harassing the subjects and also being an excellent detective. Kinderman's overcoat is based on Columbo's raincoat.

It may be that enough time has passed that the *Columbo* television show is long forgotten or younger readers may have no knowledge of the program at all. For those who remember the series, however, the character of Kinderman is a disconcerting, jarring element in *The Exorcist*.

For a novel that has the title *The Exorcist*, with all of the religious connotations that come from that word, religious issues are, surprisingly, not an important part of the book. Of course, the heroes of the novel are priests, Father Damien Karras and Father Lankester Merrin. Father Merrin is an important but minor character. He does not appear until the last 50 pages of the book (except for the puzzling prologue) and little is actually learned about him by the reader. Father Karras is a much more important character in the novel and the reader does learn much about him, particularly concerning his guilt over his mother and his growing self-doubts about his faith. The exorcism itself is filled with religious symbolism, including the reading of several rituals and the use of holy water and the crucifix. The exorcism depicts the core Christian battle between God and Satan. On the surface, therefore, *The Exorcist* is a religious novel, as well as a horror novel.

That is, however, a surface impression only as religion is actually an insignificant aspect of the novel. An exorcism is out of line with every day religious beliefs and practices, even of the Catholic Church, thereby making the exorcism a non-religious event in the novel. In a strange paradox, it is psychiatrists who recommend the exorcism; the Church is reluctant to conduct one, even though it is the Church's ritual. The ceremony is done for the benefit of Chris MacNeil and Regan, non–Catholics and perhaps atheists, so for them the ceremony is non-religious, just a means to rid the monster. It is much like the use of a crucifix to scare away a vampire.

As a result, the exorcism, although admittedly much longer and much more intense, is not much different than killing a vampire with a stake through the heart or shooting a werewolf with a silver bullet. Thus, modern horror story though it may be, *The Exorcist*, in the structure of its plot and in the demise of its monster, owes much to the classic novels of horror. And, perhaps it is for that reason, at least in part, that *The Exorcist* is such a fine novel.

The Film

The Exorcist (1973)

Used in some of the advertising for *The Exorcist*, it is one of the most famous stills in Hollywood horror film history. Father Merrin (Max von Sydow) first arrives at the MacNeil house to perform his strange ritual. The priest is dressed in black. He is carrying a small satchel and wearing a black hat. The lighting for the scene comes primarily from a large, round streetlight and from a light beaming from an upstairs bedroom of the house. The scene is shot from across the street and behind the exorcist, causing him and some of the other objects in the scene to appear as if in silhouette. It is a striking introduction to this personage of wonder and apprehension.

The famous publicity photograph for *The Exorcist* (1973) in which Father Merrin (Max von Sydow) first arrives at the MacNeil residence to perform the exorcism.

It is somewhat unusual for a shot in a film to be based on the description contained in the source material but that is what occurs in this scene in *The Exorcist*. In the same moment in the novel, Chris MacNeil looks out of the window of her house and sees "a tall old man in a threadbare black raincoat and black felt hat, his head bowed patiently in the rain as at his side he was gripping a black valise. For an instant, a silvery buckle gleamed in streetlamp glow as the bag shifted tightly in his grip" (Part IV, Chapter One). Except for the point of view from behind Father Merrin, the shot of the exorcist in the photograph is almost identical to the description in the book.

This is one of many indications that the movie, *The Exorcist*, is an incredibly faithful adaption of the novel, even beginning with a variation on the puzzling prologue to the novel, except that in the film the prologue is even longer and more puzzling. The screenplay for the film was written by William Peter Blatty and his name appears above the title, so it is not surprising that the film is a faithful adaptation of Blatty's novel.

There are, of course, some changes between novel and film. One involves Lieutenant Kinderman. The character's Columbo-type characteristics are essentially eliminated from the movie. Part of the reason for this may have been that a Columbo character actually on the screen would have caused most viewers to be distracted from the story, wondering why Peter Falk is not in the film. Another reason is probably that the part of Kinderman is substantially reduced for the film, thereby providing little time for the development of his character.

With the reduction of the importance of the part of Kinderman, the core mystery of the novel has essentially been eliminated. Kinderman does very little investigating in the film. Although he picks up the head of the bird sculpture that Regan made, near the body of Burke Dennings, Kinderman never ties that clue into Dennings' murder. The sub-plot of Karl, the housekeeper, potentially being Dennings' killer is completely gone. The only reason that Kinderman is still in the film is to provoke the realization in Chris MacNeil that her daughter killed Burke Dennings. The character of Kinderman could have been eliminated from the film without deleterious effect.

There are some new moments in the film, many of which relate to Damien's relationship with his mother. There is a scene with the mother after she has been brought to an old age facility and Damien has a disturbing dream about her after her death. This ties into the ending of the film, when it is the demon in Regan imitating Damien's mother that is one of the reasons that causes Damien to become angry and challenge the demon to enter his body, although it is the death of Merrin that is still the core reason. Also during the exorcism, an image of the statue of a monster that Father Merrin observed in Iraq during the prologue to the film appears in Regan's room, thereby tying the prologue to the main story of the film, at least a little bit.

As is often the case when a novel is adapted into a film, the story is streamlined. As a result, the film is relatively poor on character development. The viewer learns little about Chris and Regan before their troubles begin and once they start, all the viewer learns is that Chris is a caring mother. On the other hand, the streamlining of the story eliminates the boring sections of the novel. The doctors' investigations into Regan's malady and Father Karras' inquiries into the requisites for an exorcism are tightened for the film. Those sections no longer become dull after a while. This also provides more time for the exorcism, the climax of the film, to take place, a decided plus for the movie.

The film excels in the scenes in which Regan is possessed by the devil and in the ritual of the exorcism itself. There are no pretensions here of working in the Val Lewton style. The manifestations of the demon in Regan's body are manifest and striking. There is the vomit oozing from Regan's mouth and the projectile vomiting onto people in her room, the incredible cold in the room (shown by the visible breath of the occupants in the room), the foul language and the rocking of the bed. There is the voice coming out of Regan's mouth, clearly not that of Regan's and sounding like something that could be the devil's. Later, there are the voices of different people coming from Regan's mouth, such as the voice of Damien's mother. There is the crucifix masturbation scene. There is Regan's face, white with cheeks built up and covered with red scars, eyes sometimes completely white in the sockets and other times with strikingly bright pupils and the very long tongue. And, of course, there is the signature moment in the film, when Regan's head turns around and faces backwards, with a crunching sound, all the while yelling expletives. It is a believable special effect and years after one sees the film, it is the one moment that is always remembered. The 1970s were a time when the horror was right there, up on the screen, and not implied. *The Exorcist* fits that description exactly and, in fact, is one of the films that led the cinema in the next several decades into showing explicit horror on the screen.

The exorcism itself seems more like a religious ceremony in the film than the novel, with reading of rituals jointly by the priests, use of the crucifix and holy water, and multiple invocations of Christ in order to combat the devil. In addition to being a fine actor, Max von Sydow looks the part of Father Merrin, weary and wise, more than a match for Regan's demon. His very presence in the film provides the exorcism with a religious overtone.

While the screenplay could have been tightened even more, such as eliminating the prologue and the Kinderman character, its screenplay fits very well into its running time of two hours. *The Exorcist* is an excellent horror film, one of the best of the 1970s.

CHAPTER 38

Ritual
by David Pinner

In 1973, after director Robin Hardy completed his editing of *The Wicker Man*, the studio thought so little of the film that it cut the movie by many minutes and then released it in England on the bottom half of a double bill with *Don't Look Now* and only on *Don't Look Now*'s showings in England's secondary theaters. Neither film was considered anything special at the time of their respective releases but both are now considered cult horror classics. Thus, many unsuspecting British horror film fans may have had a special treat when they went to see the double bill in 1973, unexpectedly viewing two horror film classics for the price of one.

Background

David Pinner was born in Peterborough, England, in 1940. He trained as an actor at the Royal Academy of Dramatic Art and thereafter appeared on stage and in television on many occasions. While appearing in the West End in Agatha Christie's famous mystery play, *The Mousetrap*, Pinner wrote his first novel, *Ritual*, a mystery story with supernatural overtones. It was first published in 1967. Although Pinner wrote two other novels, most of his writing has been for the stage. A few of those plays are genre works, such as *Fangborn* (1966), about a lesbian vampire, and *All Hallows' Eve* (2002), a ghost story.

The Literature

It is difficult to summarize the plot of *Ritual*, because it is seldom clear what is real and what is imagined in the novel, whether some of the events that happen are mere performances put on for the benefit of the main character, David Hanlin, a police officer, or whether Hanlin is recalling events from the distant past of his life. Suffice it to say, the novel opens with the discovery of a body of an eight-year-old girl, Dian Spark, at the base of an old oak tree in the Cornish village of Thorn. A monkey's head and three garlic flowers are fastened to the trunk of the tree with a hat pin, and Dian is clutching a spray of garlic in her dead hand. Inspector David Hanlin arrives to investigate, believing more on a hunch than anything else that witchcraft was involved in the death of Dian. Hanlin's investigation does not go particularly well and after several other deaths in the village, all apparent murders, the killer is finally discovered but not by Inspector Hanlin.

Ritual is known today primarily for the horror film that it inspired, *The Wicker Man* (1973), and not surprisingly, *Ritual* has aspects of the unworldly in it. Mrs. Spark, a supposed witch, conducts a séance in an attempt to contact Dian and later hypnotizes Gilly Rowbottom, the young girl who discovered Dian's body, to determine if Dian's death was murder. Mrs. Spark has the ability to get inside David Hanlin's brain, conjuring up internal images and memories, many about his sexual inadequacies and career failures, thereby expecting Hanlin, who is "not strong enough to withstand fear," to go mad from his "imaginative battering" (Chapter 22). Lawrence Cready, a villager who used to be an actor, appears to be able to read Hanlin's mind, and quite accurately at that.

The title of the novel refers to an annual ritual of the village of Thorn, which occurs on Midsummer's Eve, a day that is commemorated in many countries around the date of the summer solstice in June of each year. Many cultures celebrate the occasion with eating, drinking, merrymaking, dancing, parades and the lighting of bonfires. The village of Thorn celebrates the occasion in a substantially different manner. Mrs. Spark, the village witch, leads dancing villagers from the town through the cornfields and onto the beach, with the moon high in the sky. There the villagers, including the children, imbibe a mixture of crude spirit and homemade wine. Most of the village children and the adults wear costumes of animals but, in addition, two adults are made up as transvestites.

A large sack is opened at the beach, revealing a white horse. The goat figure jumps onto the horse's back and forces the horse to charge into swords brandished by the witch and her daughter. The swords gouge the horse's throat and the animal dies in agony. The head of the horse is axed from its body and put on a raft to float to the sea. The rest of the horse is cooked in a large fire and then eaten by the villagers, "flesh, blood, hair and all ... simply vomited straight to their bowels" (Chapter 17). Then several of the villagers fornicate with people other than their spouses, as everyone looks on.

The ritual of Midsummer's Eve in the village of Thorn is one of the highlights of the novel, explicit in its bestiality, its violence, its seduction of the young and the carnal knowledge of the adults. It is representative of David Pinner's depiction of the sickness and decay of the Cornish countryside throughout the novel. Clearly, *Ritual* is not Thornton Wilder's *Our Town*. But for all of its depravity, the ritual of Pinner's novel does not embody the occult. There are no devil worshippers; there is no human sacrifice. Clearly, *Ritual* is also not *The Devil's Own*, by Norah Lofts, or *The Devil Rides Out*, by Dennis Wheatley.

Rather, *Ritual* is an evocation of a strange society, the village of Thorn, where people have so little in their personal lives that they must resort to the occult or something similar to survive. None of the children have any hope, so they follow a young leader, Fat Billy, who has nothing to offer them. Mr. Spark seems to be little concerned about the death of his youngest daughter. Anna Spark, the sister of Dian's, is only interested in sex. The Reverend White, the local church pastor who waters the graves of the dead at night with a watering can that has no bottom, has no influence on the villagers. The village of Thorn is a dysfunctional society. Witchcraft and the ritual are not the causes of the dysfunction; they are the manifestations of it.

If *Ritual* is not exactly a horror story, perhaps it is a detective novel. On its face, it follows the pattern of classic detective stories. In the opening chapter, a body is discovered. A police inspector then arrives in town to investigate the death. He interviews many of the suspects and searches for clues. Before the true killer can be found, there are several other murders. In the end the killer is revealed.

That scenario has the structure of many good mystery novels, including those of Agatha Christie's and, indeed, the revelation of the killer in *Ritual* has some similarity to the ending of Christie's famous play, *The Mousetrap*, in which David Pinner was appearing at the time he wrote his novel. However, unlike the classic detectives of literature, Inspector Hanlin is incredibly poor at his job. His investigation is not well thought out. Most of his interrogations do little in advancing the ball toward a solution of the crimes. He does not handle the physical evidence well, leaving his fingerprints on a potential murder weapon. He falsely accuses just about everyone in the village of committing the crimes. He is badgered and intimidated by the villagers, not the other way around. Perhaps most importantly, Hanlin does not discover the murderer; that is left to someone else.

While it may be hard to determine the genre in which *Ritual* falls, the strengths of the novel are readily apparent. Pinner laces his book with sarcastic humor about the characters, such as when Hanlin tells Cready that he can smell incest in the village, Cready is surprised to find that incest has a different odor than other kinds of fornication. Pinner is also a master of description, particularly when he is describing the unusual. Inspector Hanlin has an eye disease, requiring him to wear sunglasses much of the time. When he takes them off in the dark of the church, Pinner describes Hanlin's eyes as glimmering "opaque and pale as the flag-stones ... with a smokey unreal colour ... [throbbing] like perch eyes in translucent water" (Chapter 3). Anna, the young nymphomaniac, is succinctly introduced as "twenty-three, sexual, and loving it" (Chapter 1). Cready's live-in manservant is described as "good-looking in the Hollywood format," his smile "all gums, pink gums" and his teeth "like a four year old's, very tiny and eager to bite anything" (Chapter 10).

The novel leaves many unanswered questions. Was the death of Dian Spark just an accident? Is Mrs. Spark truly a witch? Is there any meaning to the ritual of the slaying of the horse? How could an entire village be involved with witchcraft and the occult? Why did the killer do what he did? In the end, the greatest strength of *Ritual* is that it remains an enigma, a tantalizing enigma, but an enigma nonetheless.

The Film

The Wicker Man (1973)

The Wicker Man involves Sergeant Howie, a Scottish policeman, who receives an anonymous letter that Rowan Morrison, a 12-year-old girl on Summerisle Island, has been missing for quite some time. Howie proceeds to the island by way of seaplane to investigate the disappearance, but when he questions the islanders, none admit to ever knowing a Rowan Morrison and none profess to recognize the picture of the girl that Sergeant Howie has. The sergeant is not deterred in his search for the missing girl, and during his investigation, learns that the island is run by Lord Summerisle, the largest landowner in the area, and that the islanders are all pagans, believing in strange rituals such as the need for a human sacrifice to ensure a good harvest. Howie, a Christian, is horrified by the islanders' behavior, but his horror turns quickly to terror when he learns that he was drawn to the island, by a ruse, so that he could be the requisite human sacrifice. As the film concludes, Howie is burned inside a tall figure of a man, made out of wicker.

While the film has a different story line than *Ritual*, the influence of the novel on the film is patent. Both works involve an outsider, a policeman, coming alone to an insulated society to investigate a crime against a young girl. Despite being officers of the law, the policemen do not receive any respect from the

In *The Wicker Man* (1973) Lord Summerisle (Christopher Lee) along with Willow, the landlord's daughter (Britt Ekland), welcome the missing Rowan Morrison (Geraldine Cowper) after she has just tricked Sergeant Howie into voluntarily coming to his own sacrifice.

townspeople. They are treated in a demeaning manner by most everyone they meet. In both works, the locals turn out to be pagans, worshipping strange gods in bizarre annual rituals.

Indeed, the May Day ritual from *The Wicker Man* is substantially based on the Midsummer's Eve celebration in *Ritual*. In the film, the islanders wear animal cowls to disguise themselves, march from the town to the beach with all of the islanders involved, including the children, and then make a sacrifice to the sea, in this case, barrels of ale rolled into the waters. Lord Summerisle dresses as a woman, similar to the transvestite garb described in the novel. A living sacrifice is then given to the gods although in the film, it is a human sacrifice, not the sacrifice of a horse.

Another shared characteristic of *The Wicker Man* and *Ritual* is that the island of Summerisle is every bit as strange and enigmatic as the village of Thorn. In Summerisle, both adults and children sing songs about sex, the may pole is openly discussed as a phallic symbol, there are nude fertility dances and beliefs in reproduction without sexual union, and a young girl is treated for a sore throat by putting a live toad in her mouth. While the Thorn of the novel was also a very strange town, little of Thorn's weirdness came from sexual matters so in that regard, the two works diverge.

One of the best-remembered scenes from *The Wicker Man* is inspired by a scene from Pinner's novel. In the novel, Inspector Hanlin stays in a room in Anna Spark's house and Anna, a budding nymphomaniac, tries to seduce Hanlin through the walls. Hanlin is tempted but in the end, Anna is unsuccessful. In the film, Sergeant Howie is staying in a room above the bar with the landlord's beautiful daughter, Willow, staying in the room next door. Willow attempts to seduce Howie through the walls, by singing a song, tapping on the walls and dancing in the nude. Howie, a good Christian, is tempted but he does not succumb. However, much like Inspector Hanlin in the book, it is clear that during some moments in Willow's seduction, if Sergeant Howie "had had the ability to climb directly through the wall and mount her, he would have done so" (Chapter 9).

The Wicker Man is structured as a detective story, but no one would confuse Sergeant Howie with the incompetent Inspector Hanlin. Howie truly handles the investigation of the missing Rowan Morrison in a professional manner. He shows Rowan's picture around the island, checks the school's register to see if she was ever a student there, checks the island's register of births and deaths and even opens a grave to see if Rowan's body has been deposited there. Howie is observant, noticing an empty desk in the schoolroom and a missing picture on the wall of the local tavern, which could be clues to Rowan's disappearance. In a slightly extra-legal foray (but one common to detective stories), Howie breaks into a photographer's studio to locate the missing picture. Of course, at the end, the viewer comes to realize that all of the clues Howie finds are a set-up, to get Howie, a virgin, a representative of the King and a fool, to the local May Day festival on a voluntary basis. Howie misses the ruse that has been played on him, resulting in his own death, but it is worth noting that if Inspector Hanlin were the detective in the film, he would probably not have been astute enough to follow the clues, possibly resulting in his life being spared.

In addition to the obvious differences in the plots, there are two other matters that distinguish *The Wicker Man* from *Ritual*. First, *The Wicker Man* raises significant questions about religion in modern society. Sergeant Howie represents the Christian faith, the dominant religion outside of Summerisle. Lord Summerisle and the islanders represent paganism, the only "religion" on Summerisle. Sergeant Howie believes in the resurrection; the people of Summerisle believe in reincarnation. Both sides on the issue believe very strongly in their own religion and their dispute on the merits, if there are any merits to a dispute about faith, are never resolved. The viewer never learns, for example, whether or not the harvest on Summerisle was abundant later that year as a result of the human sacrifice. The only conclusion the film reaches is that the dominant religion rules the day on Summerisle, just as other dominant religions dictate the rules in other areas of the world.

The other important difference between the two works is that *The Wicker Man* ends in a human sacrifice, the islanders' offering to the gods, in the hope of once again having a good harvest on the island. In *Ritual*, the actual ceremony on the beach, whether the reader considers it intriguing or disgusting, does no actual damage to anyone. Except for the horse that is slaughtered, the Midsummer's Eve event is simply a festive celebration for the villagers, at least from their perspective. In *The Wicker Man*, the May Day ritual results in the murder of Sergeant Howie, making *The Wicker Man* a much darker story than *Ritual*.

The Wicker Man is excellently acted, with Christopher Lee, as Lord Summerisle, and Edward Woodward, as Sergeant Howie, doing battle as Professor Moriarty and Sherlock Holmes once did before, although in this case, the Professor Moriarty character is the winner. The location shooting in Scotland adds immensely to the contradiction of the film, that a pagan religion can thrive in the modern day world. The music of the film, in the songs that the islanders sing with the liveliest of melodies (with those amazing sexual lyrics), gives the film an ambience seldom seen in other films of its kind. Are there any other horror films with so many songs?

Oddly enough, for most of its length, *The Wicker Man* is actually nothing special, as the strange goings-on in Summerisle never seem to meld into a significant whole. Because of that and much like *Ritual*, *The Wicker Man* can be hard to characterize, arguably a mystery, a horror film or an allegory about religion in modern day life. However, once the plot twist is revealed at the end and the islanders' intentions about Sergeant Howie are made known, the film takes on a different dimension. The lingering image of the film is the vision of an incredibly tall figure of a man, built of twigs and reed, burning to the ground with Sergeant Howie inside. At that point, all of the scenes of the film make sense and it is easy to characterize *The Wicker Man*. It is, at its core, a horror film and one of the most unusual ones of the 1970s.

Other Adaptations

The Wicker Man was remade in 2006, in a film with the same title, starring Nicholas Cage as the policeman who investigates the disappearance of a young girl on an island off the Pacific Coast in America. The film received poor reviews.

Chapter 39

Carrie
by Stephen King

In many ways, *Carrie* (1976) was a groundbreaking horror film. It was the first adaptation of a Stephen King novel to the cinema. The fiend is a teenager, rare in horror films once the teenage monsters of the 1950s were dispatched. It was also the first horror film with a monster that was a monster because it possessed the power of telekinesis, the ability to move objects by one's mind alone.

Background

It is not surprising that Maine is the setting for *Carrie*. Stephen King was born on September 21, 1947, in Portland, Maine. After attending college in Maine, King started contributing stories to magazines, until he obtained a full time teaching position at a high school in Maine. While there, he continued to write stories for magazines, while also developing ideas for novels.

Carrie was King's first novel to be published. Oddly, King became discouraged at the progress of an earlier draft of *Carrie* and threw the manuscript away. His wife retrieved it and encouraged him to finish it. The rest, as they say, is publishing history. (Perhaps that is why King dedicates the novel to her.) King has written many successful novels in the realm of horror, several of which have been adapted into films and television programs, including *The Shining*, which is discussed in the next chapter of this book.

The Literature

Carrie is a story of high school and horror, subjects that in the minds of many people go together, but never quite like Stephen King imagined it. Carrie, the central figure of the novel, is a lonely, unpopular high school senior at Ewen High School in Chamberlain, Maine. After gym class one day, Carrie has her first menstrual period ever, bleeding so profusely down her legs that she believes she is dying. Her fellow classmates mercilessly taunt her over the incident, even throwing tampons and sanitary napkins at her. As a result of her involvement in the incident, pretty Chris Hargensen, one of the most popular students in the school, is prohibited from going to the senior prom and another student, Sue Snell, is so upset about her own involvement in the incident that she convinces her boyfriend, popular Tommy Ross, to ask Carrie to the ball in Sue's place.

At the prom, Carrie and Tommy are voted King and Queen but once they get onto the stage, Chris and her boyfriend, Billy Nolan, dump pig blood onto Carrie and Tommy from two buckets that they had previously hung in the rafters of the gym. This humiliation sets Carrie off and she uses her powers of telekinesis to wreak havoc in the school and throughout the town, eventually killing many people, including her mother, before Carrie also succumbs.

Carrie is tension-filled throughout, caused primarily by its central figure, a warped young woman who has the frightening power of telekinesis, but also by Stephen King's unusual storytelling technique. Most horror stories do not disclose or even foreshadow the ending of the story, but in *Carrie*, Stephen King goes against common wisdom and practice by revealing to the reader on several occasions, in advance of the conclusion of the novel, that on the night of the prom, there were over two hundred deaths and the destruction of a town. Thus, the death and destruction at the end of the novel is not a surprise to the careful reader.

Although King's style prematurely discloses part of the ending of *Carrie*, King uses this technique to create suspense for the reader because the reader still does not know when and how the death and destruction will occur. To add to the suspense, King discloses the time of the evening as events occur during prom night, as if there were a ticking clock in the background and matters were moving inexorably to the calamity. Then, even with all of the foreshadowing, the ending does come as a shock to the reader. The scope of Carrie's telekinetic powers is vast and her path of destruction through the town causes fires, explosions, people electrocuted by open wires and a death toll of over 400 people. Carrie, still a young girl but with vast telekinetic powers, has caused more death and destruction than all of the monsters of horror that have come before her.

King ties his tale together with his use of the motif of blood, excellent imagery for any horror story. The triggering event to the entire story of the Chamberlain catastrophe occurs when Carrie has her first menstrual period in the shower after one of her gym classes. There is so much blood in the opening scene of the novel that a handprint in Carrie's blood ends up on the gym teacher's shorts. Blood is often a part of the religious diatribes that Carrie's mother, Margaret White, speaks to Carrie. Billy and his friends kill two pigs at old man Henty's farm, filling a pail and a half with the blood. At the prom, after they are crowned King and Queen, two buckets of blood are spilled on Carrie and Tommy. Carrie is covered in pig blood and later her own blood as she carves a path of destruction through the town. At the end of the novel, as Sue runs away from the dead body of Carrie, she emits a howling, cheated scream and she feels, in the last line of the main part of the novel, "the slow course of menstrual blood down her thighs."

While *Carrie* is a tale of horror, it is also a tale of high school and the petty cruelties that often exist in that academic setting. Carrie White is a typical outcast of society and the school system. Her fellow students took an instant dislike to her in grade school because of her unusual religious beliefs, figuratively beaten into her by her mother. Even in high school, Carrie dresses differently than the other kids in school because of her mother's beliefs. Carrie is treated cruelly by the other students in school, and she has no friends outside of school. Carrie has grown bitter and insecure in high school, a difficult environment for any student who is just a little bit different. She is humiliated by the incident in the shower room and she is worried that Tommy's invite to the prom is a practical joke.

Carrie's psyche has been so damaged by her mother and the other students at the school that she loses it all when the blood is spilled on her head at the prom. A close reading of the novel, however, discloses that it is not really the blood that drives her crazy. Rather, it is the laughter from the students at the prom. From Carrie's perspective after the blood spills, "Someone began to laugh, a solitary, affrighted hyena sound.... A second voice joined the first, and was followed by a third—girl's soprano giggle—a fourth, a fifth, six, a dozen, all of them, all laughing." The humiliation from grade school through twelfth grade wells up in Carrie, setting her off on her path of destruction.

Carrie may be a monster but she is driven to it by others. Readers of the novel will obtain some satisfaction in the comeuppance of the snobbish high school students, including the death of the two perpetrators, Chris and Billy. Unfortunately, *Carrie* is a novel of horror, not a coming of age novel, and therefore the revenge of the creature is horrible, vast and deadly to many innocent folk. Thus, any sympathy for Carrie is tempered by the great losses she causes.

The plot of *Carrie* is told in the third person but through the perspective of different characters, including Carrie, Sue Snell and Chris Hargenson. Interspersed through these parts of the novel are alleged real documents, most written after the main events of the story and supposedly factual reminiscences or scientific research papers into what happened in Chamberlain on the night of the high school prom. These secondary sources include newspaper and wire stories, scientific journals and books, magazines, an autobiography by Sue Snell and testimony before a state investigatory committee. Interestingly, all of these secondary sources could be removed from the novel and the book could still be read straight through, with a complete understanding of the plot and with the horror elements intact. These documents can therefore be viewed as superfluous.

That, however, is not the case. These secondary materials, while not essential to the story line, are essential to the effectiveness of the novel. Because there is a documentary trail of the story of Carrie, the story is placed in the real world, not just in the imagination of the author.

In the end, King uses these documents, their real word significance and the conflicting scientific theories expressed in them, to provide a surprise ending for his novel. The last document in the book is a letter from 1988, a decade after the Carrie incident, in which a new character in the novel, Amelia Jenks, is writing to Sandra Jenks about Sandra's niece, Annie, who is only two years old. On one occasion, Amelia saw Annie playing with marbles and the marbles were moving up and down and around on their own, with Annie giggling. Thus, *Carrie* ends with an open question: is there another Carrie on the horizon?

The Film

Carrie (1976)

With the exception of the insertion of entries from magazines, scientific journals, books and the like, Stephen King's novel is a lean and focused work, with little extraneous material. It has a remarkable protagonist and a spectacular conclusion. The book is a perfect fit for the cinema and it is therefore not surprising that the 1976 screen adaptation of *Carrie* is largely based upon the book, until the destruction of the high school by Carrie. At that point, Carrie returns home to seek the comfort of her mother, not to kill her. The mother has other ideas and after she stabs Carrie with a huge knife, Carrie responds with a knife attack of her own, causing sharp kitchen implements to rise through the air, pin the mother to the wall and kill her. It is a stunning moment in the film.

After the mother's death, the house starts to slowly disintegrate and cave in on its own, killing Carrie and burying her with her mother's body in their own personal cemetery in the ground. The last shock of the film occurs several days later when Sue Snell walks slowly to the pit of the destroyed house to put flowers on the eerie burial ground. Suddenly, a hand reaches out from beneath the ground and grabs her. It is a chilling moment for the viewer.

These shock moments at the end of *Carrie* are original to the film. Prior to the calamity of the prom, the movie follows the plot of the book very closely, except for the characterizations of some of the players. The film does do a good job with the portrayal of Sue Snell and Tommy Ross, with their good intentions that somehow go awry. The role of the gym teacher, Miss Desjardin, is expanded in the film and renamed Miss Collins. Her caring nature is an important part of the plot of the movie and her death at the hands of Carrie at the prom is all the more shocking. However, Margaret White, Carrie's mother, while still a religious fanatic and evil person in the film as she was in the novel, does not seem as wicked as the character in the book. Stephen King was able to provide a long history of Carrie's relationship with her mother in the novel, while the film only shows contemporaneous events. Thus, the depth of Margaret's religious malevolence does not come through in the movie.

For a similar reason, the Chris and Billy of the film are never as malicious as the two characters of the novel. Billy is barely in the film and Chris seems petulant, at worst. The viewer is never privy to the thoughts of those characters, as the reader is, and the viewer therefore never gets to really know them and understand how vile the two are. One could argue that the tempering of the natures of Margaret, Chris and Billy is only a mild loss for the film, but, in fact, it does undercut the satisfying portion of the ending of the book when Carrie's tormentors receive their comeuppance in death. In the film, the ending is less satisfying because the evil of the villains is not quite that great.

In a similar vein, the film's story of high school and the callousness of the students to someone who is a little different, while obviously a part of the film, is somewhat downplayed in the movie. Once again, because the film only shows contemporaneous events, Carrie's long history of trouble in school, starting from grade school, is not conveyed to the viewer. In the events shown onscreen, the girls seem silly and vacuous rather than wicked. The boys seem immature and clueless. One could almost have more sympathy for them than Carrie and therefore their ultimate destruction in the film is not as satisfying as it was in the novel.

As noted above in the discussion of the novel, Stephen King foreshadows the ending of *Carrie* in several places by mentioning the death and destruction that will occur on the night of the prom. In the film version, there is almost no foreshadowing. Of course, viewers have to expect that something will go wrong for Carrie at the prom, or why make the movie. However, those viewers cannot predict exactly what will happen at the ball, particularly because Carrie's telekinetic powers are downplayed in the film prior to the prom. However, the knowledge that Chris and Billy have put buckets of pig blood in the rafters of the gym and that Carrie has some telekinetic powers, plus the characterization of Carrie and the anomaly of Tommy Ross taking her to the prom, are enough for the movie audience to continue figuratively turning the pages of the movie until the end of the film.

Much like the novel, blood is a recurring motif in the film, in Carrie's menstrual period in the gym, her mother's diatribes and the pig blood spilled from the beams of the gym. Carrie is covered in blood when she leaves the prom. The motif of blood provides good imagery for the film, although it does not carry the storyline as well as it does in the novel because the film is somewhat circumspect in its blood imagery.

Carrie (Sissy Spacek), after being drenched in pig blood, walks home from the prom, in *Carrie* (1976).

The above discussion highlights once again the problems with reading a novel before and close to viewing its film adaptation. It is too easy to compare the novel to the film and perceive weaknesses in the film that may not actually be there. The novel *Carrie* must stand on its own and the film *Carrie* must be enjoyed and evaluated on its own, without reference to the source material. As a horror film and not as a screen adaptation of a horror novel, *Carrie* is terrific.

There are good performances in the supporting roles, particularly Piper Laurie as Margaret White and William Katt as Tommy. Laurie received an Oscar nomination for Best Supporting Actress for her role. The film would never have worked, however, without the fine performance by Sissy Spacek in the title role. Spacek is believable when Carrie is mousy and submissive, then when she is assertive to her mother, later when she beams at the prom and in the conclusion when she is a true monster. Carrie is a genuine chameleon. It took an excellent and versatile actress to perform the role, and Spacek met the challenge. She received a well-deserved Oscar nomination for Best Actress for her role as Carrie.

The scene at the prom starts out as a slice of Americana, just like the picnic scene in *Picnic* (1955). Its theme is "Love Among the Stars." The gym is brightly and colorfully decorated, with flashing metallic stars, crepe paper and globes hanging from the ceiling. There is a good band on stage. The boys look uncomfortable in their rented tuxedos. All of the students seem to be in good spirits. Tommy Ross is the perfect date for Carrie. He talks to her, gives her confidence and even kisses her. It is the last place one would expect a calamity to occur.

Matters turn a little strange, however, when Tommy finally convinces Carrie to dance. The scene of them dancing on the gym floor is somewhat surreal. The camera is below them shooting toward the ceiling, as if there are no other dancers on the floor. Without a cut, Tommy and Carrie spin and spin to the music, faster and faster, with the camera doing 360° turns in the opposite direction as if Tommy and Carrie are in their own personal land of make-believe. (Here, there is some foreshadowing of the next section of the film because the prom is a land of make-believe for Carrie and reality is soon to set in.) Carrie becomes happier and happier at the prom and when she and Tommy are announced as the king and queen, the smile on Carrie's face is wide and captivating. The viewer can see that this is the happiest moment in Carrie's life. It may be the only time she has ever smiled in her life.

The prom sequence is so beautifully set up by director Brian de Palma that when the pig blood is spilled on Carrie, her subsequent actions seem almost justified. Carrie's blowup does not occur because of the laughter of the people at the prom (which she only imagines) or her frustration at years of scorn from society. Rather, it is the destruction of Carrie's one great moment of happiness that causes her to explode. This is different than the novel but perhaps more effective. Then, with her eyes wide open and seemingly blank, Carrie becomes a monster, killing all who are in the gym, including those who befriended her such as Miss Collins and Tommy. She is a creature gone amok, unable to distinguish between those she destroys.

The catastrophe at the prom is beautifully staged. While there is music in the background, there is no dialogue and only a little background noise, such as clapping and whistling. The scene is shot in slow motion, until the buckets drop. Then de Palma uses many of the tools of the cinema to show what happens, including a kaleidoscopic view of the audience laughing (only in Carrie's imagination), split screens of Carrie and the manifestations of her telekinetic powers, tinted shots, a fire hose that moves on its own and then some very brutal deaths, including an electrocution and the falling basketball backboard ramming into Miss Collins, when she is pinned against the wall. The scene ends in a spectacular fire.

While Carrie's scope and path of destruction are different in the novel and the film, the film version is stunning, aided by the manner in which the scene is shot. The prom sequence in *Carrie* is unforgettable, both before and after the spilling of the blood. Add the several original and unexpected shock scenes at the end of the film and *Carrie*, though different than the novel, is at least its equal. *Carrie* was the first adaptation of a Stephen King novel to the cinema and for many horror film fans, it is still the best one.

Other Adaptations

For a book that was written in 1974 and had its first film adaptation in 1976, it is somewhat surprising that there have already been two remakes of *Carrie*. In 2002, there was a made-for-television movie also named *Carrie*. It starred Angela Bettis as Carrie and first aired on NBC on November 4, 2002. The story returned to the cinema in 2013, once again titled *Carrie*, with Chloë Grace Moretz playing the title role.

Chapter 40

The Shining
by Stephen King

Stephen King has called *The Haunting of Hill House* by Shirley Jackson one of the finest horror novels of all time. Thus, it is not surprising that in his first ghost novel, *The Shining*, King makes a reference to *The Haunting of Hill House*. There is a moment in the tale when Jack Torrance, the new caretaker of an isolated hotel named the Overlook, believes that the Overlook "was having one hell of a good time" terrorizing the occupants, perhaps causing them to "end up flitting through the Overlook's halls like insubstantial shades in a Shirley Jackson novel, whatever walked in Hill House walked alone" (Chapter 33, "The Snowmobile"). For those who have read Shirley Jackson's novel, it is gratifying to read this homage from Stephen King to another great horror novel and novelist.

The Literature

The Shining involves Jack Torrance, an unemployed alcoholic and frustrated writer with a wife named Wendy and a son named Danny, who takes a job as the winter caretaker at the Overlook, an isolated resort located high in the Rocky Mountains in Colorado. Once there, Jack and his family are haunted by the ghosts of visitors and victims from many different decades of the hotel's existence. Matters come to a head on December 2, when a masquerade party that actually took place in 1945 now fills the ballroom of the resort. The spirits of the hotel manifest themselves throughout the edifice and completely take over Jack's mind, encouraging him to kill his wife and severely punish his son. Jack sets out to do just that, convinced in his mind that his actions are justified, but in the end, Jack dies when the resort is blown to bits by its untended boiler. Wendy and Danny, with the help of Hallorann, the tall black cook from the hotel who is mentally called back to the resort by Danny, survive.

The title of *The Shining* comes from a moment in the story when the Torrances have arrived at the Overlook and the last guests and all of the staff are about to depart. Hallorann has a talk with Danny just before Hallorann leaves for the winter. He recognizes that Danny has a special power, the same as Hallorann. Hallorann says, "What you got, son, I call it shinin on, the Bible calls it having visions, and there's scientists that call it precognition.... They all mean seeing the future" (Chapter 11, "The Shining"). Actually, Danny's power involves more than precognition. Danny has the ability to read his parents' minds and, to a lesser degree, the minds of others.

The Shining deals with many themes, including isolation, mortality, creativity and the nature of reality, but the overriding non-supernatural theme of the novel is familial relationships. Wendy must still deal with thoughts of her mother, who is always critical of her and does not seem to love her. Jack must deal with memories of his father who was physically abusive, particularly toward his mother. Jack's fall from success and his alcoholism have frayed his relationship with Wendy, who has considered divorce on several occasions. Both Jack and Wendy are trying to raise Danny in an appropriate manner, but Danny's ability to shine and his parents' problems make that difficult to accomplish.

The Overlook is hardly the right place to deal with those difficult personal issues, particularly since the ghosts of the hotel focus on personal weaknesses to further their destructive purposes. Yet through all its difficulties, the family still loves each other, as shown by Danny still going to Jack after Jack once broke Danny's arm and Danny recognizing that the figure attacking him at the hotel, while it looks like his father, is not really the man he adores. Perhaps more than any other horror story, *The Shining* cleverly entwines a personal story into the horror.

The highlight of *The Shining* is its ending, when the ghosts of the resort finally attack, not directly, but through Jack. The ghosts have created their own monster in Jack, using his disappointments, anger and perceived slights to turn his mind against his family. This scenario demonstrates another connection to *The Haunting of Hill House*, where the ghosts pick on Eleanor Vance, the most insecure and weakest member of the Hill House occupants, to cause the most damage.

In addition to *The Haunting of Hill House*, Stephen King makes several references to "The Masque of the Red Death" by Edgar Allan Poe. There is a long quote from the Poe short story in the epigraph to the novel. While *The Shining* and "The Masque of the Red Death" involve different types of story, the former being about ghosts and the latter about the plague, there are similarities in the setting and motifs of the works, particularly in their references to masks. The climaxes of each occur at a masked ball, Poe's Red Death is masked and Danny perceives that when his father attacks, his face is really just a mask.

While there is much that is clever about the novel and the climax is quite engrossing, *The Shining* is overlong and, in many respects, boring. Jack Torrance is not a likable character even before he reaches the Overlook, and there is therefore little sympathy for him in the novel. The explosion at the hotel at the climax is a convenient way to end the story, although it is not a very satisfactory one, partially because it leaves many questions unanswered. Why is the resort haunted? How is Danny's ability to shine involved in the spirits' interest in the Torrances? Because of the sudden ending, none of the issues of the Overlook have been resolved by the end of the novel.

Nevertheless, *The Shining*, although somewhat unfocused, has a strong plot. It therefore had the potential to make a terrific movie and just a few years after it was published, a movie was made from the novel, which was directed by one of the most celebrated filmmakers of the era.

The Film

The Shining (1980)

The director of *The Shining* is Stanley Kubrick, well-known at the time for his groundbreaking films, *Lolita* (1962) and *Dr. Strangelove or: How Learned to Stop Worrying and Love the Bomb* (1964) as well as two films in the science fiction genre, *A Clockwork Orange* (1971) and the classic *2001: A Space Odyssey* (1968). Kubrick's skills as a director are apparent in *The Shining*, with helicopter shots outside the facility, steadicam shots of the characters moving inside the hotel including Danny riding his tricycle throughout the hotel, the use of mirrors to enhance the ghost effects and the famous framing shot of Jack Nicholson in the broken bathroom door of the Overlook, shouting, "Here-ere-ere's Johnny." However, Kubrick was also one of the writers for the film and it is in the screenplay where Kubrick and the movie fail. The script is overlong and unfocused, much like the novel. However, the film, unlike the novel, also makes very little sense.

A strength of the novel is Danny's ability to shine but in the film that power is essentially overlooked, calling into question the title of the movie. When the Torrances arrive at the Overlook on the last day of the season, they meet Dick Halloran, the resort's cook, who has a private meeting with Danny. He explains to Danny that they both have a power to shine. Yet, other than

Danny knowing in advance that his father had obtained the job at the Overlook and perhaps reading Hallorann's mind about Room 237, Danny displays few elements of precognition. From time to time he sees the ghosts of two girls at the hotel but his parents see ghosts also. Hallorann never tells Danny to call him if he gets into trouble, so when Hallorann mentally hears Danny's call late in the film from a long distance away, that is just as easily explained by Hallorann's shining, not Danny's. In fact, it is not really clear that Danny has the power to shine in the movie.

Another strength of the novel relates to its subplot of the personal problems of the Torrance family playing out against the backdrop of the spirit world. Unfortunately, the relationships of Jack and Wendy with their parents are not even mentioned in the movie. In fact, the viewer never really gets to learn much about Jack, Wendy and Danny before the ghosts commence their rampage. Thus, because the Torrances' personal problems are not an undercurrent of the film, an important theme and nuance of the novel are missing from the film.

Similarly, there is almost no background provided for the history of the Overlook resort. The hotel's manager, Stuart Ullman, tells Jack a little about the backstory of the hotel, including the fact that four presidents and lots of movie stars have stayed there. Almost reluctantly, Ullman also mentions that the winter caretaker from several years before, Delbert Grady, went mad and killed his two daughters and his wife with an axe before committing suicide by putting a shotgun in his mouth and pulling the trigger. Jack laughs off the story. Dick Hallorann tells Danny never to go into Room 237, but he never explains what is wrong with the room.

Other than that, the background of the Overlook is undisclosed to the viewer. Apparently, there is no history of crime, gangsters or killings or, for that matter, any hauntings at the facility. Thus, from the viewer's perspective, the ghosts manifest themselves without any reason to do so. Arguably, in the novel, the spirits are interested in Danny because of his special power, although that is not as clear in the text as many find it to be. In the film, Danny is the most minor of characters, hardly the focal point of the Overlook's ghosts. As another example, the novel sets the foundation for a gala masked ball that was held in 1945, and masks are an important motif of the story so that when the masked ball suddenly comes to life in the ballroom many years after it originally occurred, the reader understands the significance of the event. In the film, the similar occasion is a night of dining and dancing in the gold ballroom in 1921, but that event has no relevance for the viewer. There are clearly ghosts haunting the Overlook, but who they are and why they are there is left unexplained. *The Shining* is a film of ghosts for ghosts' sake.

Then there are the strange matters incorporated into the film for little reason.

Why does Danny become possessed by his friend Tony during the climactic ending of the film? Danny speaks in a strange voice at this time, as if he is believes he is performing in *The Exorcist*. In fact, the use of his finger as the personification of Tony makes Danny seem like he is possessed by a ventriloquist, not a spirit. Ullman mentions that the Overlook was built over an Indian burial ground, which is the only posited reason for the hotel being haunted. However, it is not clear why Indian burial grounds have more ghosts than Caucasian burial grounds and in any event, Indians were probably smart enough not to bury their dead so high in the mountains that they could not reach the area for six months out of every year. Also, why does that blood keep coming out of the elevator door, filling the foyer? That is as inexplicable as Danny seeing the ghosts of Delbert Grady's daughters several times early in the film and then the ghosts never reappearing during the remainder of the movie.

Jack Nicholson's performance as Jack Torrance in *The Shining* is a matter of taste. Viewers either like it or hate it; there are no opinions in between those extremes. For those who dislike his performance, such as your author, Nicholson overacts outrageously in the role. While that may be justified late in the film, when Jack Torrance is legitimately crazy, Nicholson, with his wild-eyed expression and strange smile, actually overacts in the first scene of the film, continuing through his early days at the Overlook. As a result, Jack Torrance seems crazy from the very beginning of the movie. One can imagine Jack, disappointed by his writing problems, going crazy within the isolation of the Overlook on his own. Who needs any ghosts? The novel, by contrast, builds Jack's segue into insanity very deliberately, making it more effective and believable.

Also, Shelley Duvall is not very convincing playing Wendy Torrance. She is unable to persuade the audience that her character ever had any relationship with Jack prior to the beginning of the film, also undercutting Jack's turn to insanity. Her sudden pivot into a strong woman at the end of the movie is also not credible, because no foundation is laid for the transformation and Duvall is unable to carry the personality change on her own. Nevertheless, Duvall has the ability to display one of the most expressive faces of terror in horror film history, which she uses on many occasions near the end of the movie. If Fay Wray is noted for her screaming in horror films, Duvall should have some repute for her faces of terror.

The best performances in the film come from the supporting players. Scatman Crothers, playing Dick Hallorann, the only sympathetic character in the movie, seems sincere and caring. Joe Turkel, as the bartender, has an aura of evil about him even though he only serves drinks to Jack. Philip Stone, as Delbert Grady, the only truly evil person in the film, frightens the audience even though he gives an understated performance.

Wendy Torrance (Shelley Duvall) hides in the bathroom of the family apartment at the Overlook Hotel, preparing to defend herself with a kitchen knife, as her husband, Jack Torrance (Jack Nicholson), uses an axe to break into the room, in *The Shining* (1980).

One nice touch in the film is that the Overlook is not an old haunted house, filled with shadows and dark areas. Stanley Kubrick has deliberately made the facility large and open, with Danny riding his bike down long halls, Jack writing his book in the open lobby and Wendy cooking in a very large kitchen. Most rooms are brightly lit with vivid colors throughout. This change of setting and therefore mood for a horror film is a welcome change from the usual mise-en-scène of most horror films. Another strong point of the film is the memorable scene in Room 237, with a young lady appearing out of the shower, advancing to Jack, kissing him and then turning into a blotched-filled hag. The novel is much more circumspect about what happens in its Room 217. Also, in the film version, when Hallorann flies from Florida, treks through a Colorado snowstorm and comes back to the Overlook to rescue Danny, Hallorann is immediately dispatched by Jack with a hatchet to the chest. It is a true surprise, particularly for those who have previously read the novel.

The revised ending to the film is also a distinct positive. In the novel, since Stephen King had no other good ending, he simply allowed the hotel to blow up, killing Jack and apparently all of the spirits. In the film, Jack freezes to death in the hotel's maze, after being knifed by Wendy and after chasing Danny through the labyrinth. Danny actually tricks his father, by walking back in his own footprints, so that Jack cannot follow him. The ending of the film works, because it is Wendy and Danny who kill the monster, not fate. Also, since the Overlook is a snowbound hotel high in the Rockies, a death by freezing is consistent with the setting of the film, making the hotel's environment an even more important part of the plot.

Despite these positives, *The Shining* is a disappointing film. It is padded, unfocused and not very believable. A ghost story can be plausible if it is internally consistent, provides a reason for the existence of the ghosts and does not take frolics and detours from the main storyline. Stephen King's novel had the potential to be adapted into a good film but the 1980 film version does not meet expectations.

Other Adaptations

In 1997, *The Shining* was adapted into a three-part television mini-series that was broadcast on ABC. The show starred Steven Weber as Jack Torrance and Rebecca de Mornay as Wendy Torrance. Stephen King wrote the script for this adaptation of his novel.

Bibliography

Auchard, John. Introduction to *The Portable Henry James*. New York: Penguin, 2004.
Belford, Barbara. *Bram Stoker: A Biography of the Author of Dracula*. New York: Alfred A. Knopf, 1996.
Bell, Ian. *Robert Louis Stevenson: Dreams of Exile*. Edinburgh: Mainstream, 1992.
Binyon, T.J. *Pushkin A Biography*. New York: Alfred A. Knopf, 2003.
Bleiler, Richard. *Science Fiction Writers: Critical Studies of the Major Authors from the Early Nineteenth Century to the Present Day*, 2d ed. New York: Charles Scribner's Sons, 1999.
Clarens, Carlos. *An Illustrated History of the Horror Film*. Toronto: Longman's Canada Limited, 1967.
Davidson, Edward J. *Poe: A Critical Study*. Cambridge: Belknap Press of Harvard University Press, 1957.
Ellman, Richard. *Oscar Wilde*. New York: Alfred A. Knopf, 1988.
Evans, Arthur B. "The Fantastic Science Fiction of Maurice Renard." *Science Fiction Studies* 64 (November 1994). http://www.depauw.edu/sfs/backissues/64/evans.htm.
Everson, William K. *Classics of the Horror Film*. Secaucus, N.J.: Citadel Press, 1974.
_____. *More Classics of the Horror Film*. Secaucus, N.J.: Citadel Press, 1990.
Friedman, Lenemaja. *Shirley Jackson*. Boston: Twayne, 1975.
Guffey, Robert. "Charles Darwin and the Suppressed Science of Dr. Mirakle." *Video Watchdog* 166 (January/February 2012).
Joslin, Lyndon W. *Count Dracula Goes to the Movies, Stoker's Novel Adapted, 1922–2003*. Jefferson, N.C.: McFarland, 2006.
Loban, Lelia. "The Many Masks of the Opera Ghost." *Scarlet: The Film Magazine* 7 (Spring 2011).
Mast, Gerald. *A Short History of the Movies*. New York: Bobbs-Merrill, 1971.
McLynn, Frank. *Robert Louis Stevenson: A Biography*. London: Hutchison, 1993.
Oppenheimer, Judy. *Private Demons: The Life of Shirley Jackson*. New York: G.P. Putnam's Sons, 1988.
Pederson, Jay P. *St. James Guide to Science-Fiction Writers*, 4th ed. Detroit: St. James Press, 1996.
Perry, George. *The Complete Phantom of the Opera*. New York: Henry Holt, 1988.
Pringle, David. *St. James Guide to Horror, Ghost and Gothic Writers*. Detroit: St. James Press, 1998.
Quinn, Arthur Hobson. *Edgar Allan Poe: A Critical Biography*. Baltimore: Johns Hopkins University Press, 1941.

Rhodes, Gary D. "The Curious Undead Life of Tod Browning's *Dracula*." *Monsters from the Vault* (Summer 2011).

_____. *White Zombie Anatomy of a Horror Film*. Jefferson, N.C.: McFarland, 2001.

Rosner, Lisa. *The Anatomy Murders*. Philadelphia: University of Pennsylvania Press, 2010.

Seymour, Miranda. *Mary Shelley*. New York: Grove Press, 2000.

Shallcross, Martyn. *The Private World of Daphne du Maurier*. New York: St. Martin's Press, 1992.

Weaver, Tom, Michael Brunas and John Brunas. *Universal Horrors*, 2d ed. Jefferson, N.C.: McFarland, 2007.

Wells, H.G. *The Complete Science Fiction Treasury of H.G. Wells*. With a preface by the author. Originally published as *Seven Famous Novels*, New York: Alfred A. Knopf, 1934. Reprint: New York: Avenel Books, 1978.

Index

Numbers in ***bold italics*** indicate pages with photographs.

Abbott and Costello Meet Dr. Jekyll and Mr. Hyde (1953 film) 61
Abbott and Costello Meet Frankenstein (1948 film) 88, 277
The Adventures of Robin Hood (1938 film) 96
All Hallows' Eve (play) 333
All That Money Can Buy (1941 film) 186, 188–191, ***190***
American-International Pictures 109, 271, 292
American Museum (periodical) 274
Angel, Heather ***204***
Anna Karenina (1935 film) 58
"Annabel Lee" (poem) 29, 31, 151
Asher, Jane ***299***
Astaire, Fred 97
Ates, Roscoe ***123***
Auric, Georges 42, 256
The Avenging Conscience (1914 film) 27, 29–32, 33

Balderston, John L. 73
Barnett, Ivan 114, 115
Barrymore, John 46, ***47***, 49, 53, 55, 61
Barrymore, Lionel ***180***
Bastedo, Alexandra 239
Battleship Potemkin (1925 film) 38
Bava, Mario 289, 291, 292, 302
Before I Hang (1940 film) 192
"The Bells" (poem) 31
Benét, Stephen Vincent 186–189, 191
Bentley's Standard Novels 3
Beranger, Clara S. 46, 48
Bergman, Ingrid 54, 55, 56

Bettis, Angela 347
Beyond Tomorrow (1940 film) 207
The Birds (1963 film) 266–270, ***267***
"The Birds" (story) 263–265
Birth of a Nation (1915 film) 27
The Black Cat (1934 film) 75, 149–151, ***150***, 163, 164, 165, 166
The Black Cat (1941 film) 155
"The Black Cat" (story) 31, 145, 146–147, 153, 154
Black Friday (1940 film) 61
Black Moon (1934 film) 156, 159–161
Black Moon (novel) 156–158
Black Sabbath (1963 film) 289–292, ***291***, 293, 294, 295
Black Sunday (1960 film) 302, ***303***, 305, 306, 307
Blackmer, Sidney 312
Blair, Janet 261, ***262***
Blatty, William Peter 326–328, 331
Blood and Roses (1960 film) 237–240, ***238***
The Blood Splattered Bride (1972 film) 243
The Body Snatcher (1945 film) 75, 216–220, ***218***, 283
"The Body Snatcher" (story) 214–216
Brahm, John 204, 206
Bram Stoker's Dracula (1992 film) 83–87, ***86***
Branagh, Kenneth 24
Brando, Marlon 136
Bride of Frankenstein (1935 film) 6, 7, 12, 13–***18***, ***14***, 76, 105, 108
Brides of Dracula (1960 film) 64
Browning, Tod 73, 84, 120, 122, 123
Bucket of Blood (1934 film) 35
Burgess, Dorothy 160

357

Burke, Kathleen 131, *132*
Burn, Witch, Burn (1962 film) 259–*262*
Burn Witch Burn! (novel) 1, 176–178, 179, 182, 183, 185
Burroughs, Edgar Rice 121
Byron, Lord 3, 13, 15

The Cabinet of Dr. Caligari (1920 film) 31
Cage, Nicholas 339
The Caine Mutiny (novel) 29
Calhoun, John C. 187
Campbell, Bill *86*
Carmilla (novella) 62, 234–237, 240, 243, 288
Carrel, Dr. Alexis 170
Carrera, Barbara 133, 134
Carrie (1976 film) 340, 343–347, *345*
Carrie (2013 film) 347
Carrie (novel) 340–343
Carrie (2002 television movie) 347
Cartwright, Veronica *267*
Casablanca (1942 film) 96
"The Case of Charles Dexter Ward" (story) 271–274, 275
"The Cask of Amontillado" (story) 153–154, 166
Cassavetes, John 312
Cat People (1942) 105, 115, 189, 221, 233
Chandler, Helen *74*, 75
Chaney, Lon 69, 92, 94, *95*, 96, 99, 102
Chaney, Lon, Jr. *276*, 277
Christie, Agatha 333, 335
Christie, Julie *325*
La Chute de la Maison Usher (1928 film) 111–113
Citizen Kane (1941 film) 174
Clancy of the Mounted (1933 serial) 162
Clive, Colin *9*, *18*, 24
A Clockwork Orange (1971 film) 350
Columbia Pictures 156, 192, 195
Columbo (television series) 328
Conan Doyle, Arthur 31
Conjure Wife (novel) 257–259, 260, 261, 262
Connell, Richard 158
Conrad, Joseph 253
Cook, Elisha, Jr. 276
Coppola, Francis Ford 84, 85
Corman, Roger 32, 109, 118, 151, 152, 167, 271, 276, 277, 296, 298, 299, 301
Corri, Adrienne 32, *34*
Count Yorga, Vampire (1970 film) 64, 291
Cowper, Geraldine *337*
Craig, James 189
Creep, Shadow! (novel) 176
Crisp, Donald 57, 213
Crosby, Bing 97

Crothers, Scatman 352
Crypt of the Vampire (1964 film) 243
The Curse of Frankenstein (1957) 18–22, *20*, 23, 25, 83, 250
The Curse of the Cat People (1944 film) 213, 283
The Curse of the Doll People (1961 film) 182–185, *183*
The Curse of the Werewolf (1961 film) 247–250, *248*
Cushing, Peter *20*, 66, 242

Daisy Miller (novella) 251
Damon, Mark *116*, 117
Daniell, Henry *218*, 219
The Dark Blue (periodical) 234
Dark Enchantment (1953 film) 207
Dark Shadows (television series) 64
Darwell, Jane 189
Daughter of Dr. Jekyll (1957 film) 61
Daughter of Time (novel) 201
Dead of Night (1945 film) 34, 40, 113
Deane, Hamilton 73
Deathtrap (play) 308
DeNiro, Robert 23
The Devil and Daniel Webster (1941 film) 186, 188–191
"The Devil and Daniel Webster" (story) 186–188
The Devil Commands (1941 film) 192, 196–199, *198*
The Devil-Doll (1936 film) 169, 178–182, *180*, 184, 244
The Devil Rides Out (novel) 314–316, 317, 319, 335
A Devil with Women (1930 film) 156
Dieterle, William 191
Dione, Rose *123*
Dmytryk, Edward 197
Dr. Cyclops (1940 film) 184
Dr. Jekyll and Mr. Hyde (1920 film) 46–50, *47*, 108
Dr. Jekyll and Mr. Hyde (1932 film) 50–54, *52*, 150, 169
Dr. Jekyll and Mr. Hyde (1941 film) 54–58, *57*
Dr. Jekyll and Mr. Hyde (novella) 1, 43–46, 223
Dr. Strangelove (1964 film) 350
Don't Look Now (1973 film) 323–*325*, 333
"Don't Look Now" (story) 321–323
Dracula (1931 film) 8, 18, 43, 71–76, *74*, 78, 84, 120, 169
Dracula (1931 Spanish film) 87
Dracula (novel) 1, 7, 62–67, 68, 82, 221, 235, 288

Dracula: Dead and Loving It (1995 film) 88
Dracula's Daughter (1936 film) 76–78, 234
Dracula's Guest" (story) 67–68
du Maurier, Daphne 263–264, 321, 324
Duvall, Shelley 352, 353

Earles, Daisy *123*
Eck, Johnny *123*
The Edge of Running Water (novel) 1, 192–196
Eisenstein, Sergei 38
Ekland, Britt *337*
Eleonora" (story) 151
Ellerbe, Harry 117
Ellison, James *204*
Elwes, Carey *86*
Endore, Guy 244–246, 250
Eugene Onegin (novel) 36
The Evening Mirror (newspaper) 27
The Exorcist (1973 film) 308, 314, 329–332, *330*
The Exorcist (novel) 326–329
Eyssen, John Van *79*

"Facts in the Case of M. Valdemar" (story) 148, 154
Fahey, Myrna *116*, 117, 118
The Fall of the House of Usher (1928 film) 111–113
The Fall of the House of Usher (1949 film) 113–116
"The Fall of the House of Usher" (story) 35, 106–11, 113, 115, 147, 274
"Family of the Vourdelak" (story) 287–289, 290, 292
Farrow, Mia 311, *312*
Ferrer, Mel 175, *238*
Ferroni, Giorgio 292–293
Fisher, Terrence 24, 84
The Flag of Our Union (newspaper) 298
Fleming, Victor 54, 57
Fletcher, Bramwell *204*
42nd Street (1933 film) 98
Foster, Susanna 99
The Four Horsemen of the Apocalypse (1921 film) 106
Frankenheimer, John 136
Frankenstein (1910 short) 7–8
Frankenstein (1931 film) 8–13, *9*, *12*, 15, 18, 20, 21, 23, 25, 69, 83, 87, 93, 105, 108, 120, 130, 133, 169
Frankenstein (novel) 1, 3–7, 10, 43, 67, 92, 131, 221
Frankenstein Created Woman (1967 film) 25
Frankenstein Meets the Wolf Man (1943 film) 25

Franklin, Pamela *255*, 256
Freaks (1932 film) 120, 122–125, *123*, 133, 169
Freund, Karl 173, 174
Frid, Jonathan 85
Friedlander, Lewis 166
Frye, Dwight *9*, 175
Fulton, John P. 143

Garland, Judy 97
Gaunt, Valerie *79*, *80*, 81
Gay, Ramón *183*
Gerard, Emily 63
The Ghost of Frankenstein (1942 film) 17, 25
The Godfather (1972 film) 85
Gogol, Nikolai 302–304, 305, 306
Gold Is Where You Find It (1938 film) 156
Gone with the Wind (1939 film) 54
The Good Earth (1937 film) 58
Gordon, Ruth 312
Gough, Michael 100
Grant, Richard E. *86*
Gray, Charles 319
Griffith, D.W. 27, 30, 32
Grindé, Nick 192
Grunwald, Anatole de 40
Gunga Din (1939 film) 162
Gunn (1967 film) 326
Gwynne, Fred 25–26

Hammer Studios 18, 20, 21, 25, 43, 60, 88, 100, 102, 107, 240, 242, 244, 250, 314, 316
Hands of a Stranger (1962 film) 175
The Hands of Orlac (1924 film) 172
The Hands of Orlac (1960 film) 175
The Hands of Orlac (novel) 169–172
Hardy, Robin 333
Hatfield, Hurd 226
Hatton, Rondo 120
The Haunted Palace (1963 film) 271, 274–277, *276*
"The Haunted Palace" (poem) 274
The Haunting (1963 film) 209, 231, 281–286, *285*
The Haunting (1999 film) 286
The Haunting of Hill House (novel) 1, 195, 209, 223, 278–281, 283, 327, 248, 349
Hedren, Tippy *267*
Here Comes Mr. Jordan (1941 film) 96
Herrmann, Bernard 191
Hilton, Daisy *123*
Hilton, Violet *123*
Hinds, Samuel S. *164*
Hitchcock, Alfred 99, 227, 239, 263, 266, *267*, 268, 269, 313
Hollywood Inn (1942 film) 97

Holt, Jack 160
"Hop-Frog" (story) 298
Hopkins, Anthony 66, 85, *86*
Hopkins, Miriam 55
Horror of Dracula (1958 film) 61, 78–83, *79*, *80*, 100, 250, 295
House of Dark Shadows (1970 film) 291
House of Dracula (1945 film) 201
House of Fright (1960) 58–60, *59*
House of Usher (1960) *116*–118
The Hunchback of Notre Dame (1939 film) 257
Hussey, Ruth *211*
Huston, Walter 189

In a Glass Darkly (book) 234
Ingram, Rex 106, 107, 108
The Innocents (1961 film) 251, 253–256, *255*
Intolerance (1916 film) 27
The Invisible Man (1933 film) 96, 105, 108, 140–144, *141*
The Invisible Man (novel) 126, 137–140, 144
The Irish Republic (book) 207
The Island of Dr. Moreau (1977 film) 132–136
The Island of Dr. Moreau (1996 film) 136
The Island of Dr. Moreau (novel) 126–129, 130, 137
Island of Lost Souls (1932 film) 129–133, *132*, 133, 135, 136

Jackson, Shirley 1, 195, 209, 278–281, 284, 327, 348
James, Henry 251–253
James, M.R. 228–230
Jameson, Joyce *153*
Jekyll and Hyde (musical) 61
John Goldfarb, Please Come Home (novel) 326
Johnston, Margaret 261
Joyce, James 251

Karloff, Boris 10, 12, 18, 20, 21, 69, 143, 150, 151, 163, 164, 166, 192, 195, 196, 197, 198, 218, 219, 220, 291
Katt, William 346
Kenton, Erle C. 132
Kerr, Deborah 254, *255*, 256
Kerruish, Jessie Douglas 200–203, 206
Kidnapped (novel) 43
King, Stephen 340–343, 344, 347, 348–350, 354
King Kong (1933 film) 129
Kipling, Rudyard 162
A Kiss Before Dying (novel) 308

Lady Frederick (play) 103

Lady in the Lake (1947 film) 51, 266
Lancaster, Burt 133, 136
Lanchester, Elsa 13, 15, *18*
Lansberry, Angela 226
The Last Laugh (1924 film) 68
Laughton, Charles 131, *132*, 136, 143
Laurie, Piper 346
Lee, Christopher 20, 32, 58, *80*, 85, 175, 243, 319, *337*, 339
Le Fanu, Sheridan 62, 234–237, 240, 242, 243
Leiber, Fritz 257–259, 261, 262
Leiber, Fritz, Sr. 257
The Leopard Man (1943 film) 115
Leroux, Gaston 87, 89–92, 93, 94, 96, 97, 98, 100, 101, 102, 171, 296
Levin, Ira 259, 308, 310, 311
Lewin, Albert 226
Lewton, Val 115, 161, 213, 218, 230, 233, 261, 281, 283, 332
"Ligeia" (story) 147
Lippincott's Monthly Magazine (periodical) 221
Liza of Lambeth (novel) 103
Lofts, Norah 335
Lolita (1962 film) 350
Lom, Herbert 100, 101, 102
Lorre, Peter *153*, 154, 168, 170, *174*, 175
The Lost Weekend (1945 film) 213
"The Lottery" (story) 278
Lovecraft, H.P. 271–274, 275, 276, 277
The Loving Spirit (novel) 263
Lugosi, Bela 69, 71, 72, 73, *74*, 75, 78, 85, *130*, 131, *150*, 151, 156, 163, *164*, 165, 166, 167, *218*, 219

Macardle, Dorothy 207, 210
MacDonald, Kenneth 197
Mad Love (1935 film) *170*, 172–175, *174*
The Magician (1926 film) 106–108
The Magician (novel) 103–105
Mala, Norma *59*
Malyon, Eily *204*
Mamoulian, Rouben 51
The Man They Could Not Hang (1939 film) 192
The Man with Nine Lives (1940 film) 192
Mansfield, Martha *47*, 48
March, Fredric 46, 51, *52*, 53, 55, 61
March, Joseph Moncure 162
Mare Nostrum (1926 film) 106
Mark of the Vampire (1935 film) 169
Martin, John *211*
Martinelli, Elsa *238*
Mary Shelley's Frankenstein (1994 film) 22–25
Masque of the Red Death (1964 film) 298–301, *299*

"Masque of the Red Death" (story) 296–298, 349
Massie, Paul 58, *59*
Matheson, Richard 151, 261, 319
Matthews, Lester *167*
Maugham, W. Somerset 103–105, 106, 107, 108
Meet Me in St. Louis (1944 film) 97
Melford, George 73, 87
Melville, Herman 251
Merchant, Cathy 275
Merritt, Abraham 1, 176–178, 179, 182, 184, 185
"Metzengerstein" (story) 147
MGM 54, 58, 120, 169, 179, 221, 224
Milland, Ray *211*, 213
Milton, John 161
Mr. Smith Goes to Washington (1939 film) 96
Mondragón, Jorge *183*
Moore, Douglas 186
Moreland, Mantan 160
"Morella" (story) 147–148, 151–152
Moretz, Chloë Grace 347
"Most Dangerous Game" (story) 158
Motion Picture Production Code 77, 308, 313
The Mousetrap (play) 333
The Mummy (1932 film) 85
The Munsters (television series) 25
Murders in the Rue Morgue (1932 film) 129, *130*, 150, 165
Murnau, F.W. 68, 69, 71, 84
Muse, Clarence 160
Mysterious Martin (novel) 121

Naldi, Nita 48
The Narrative of Arthur Gordon Pym (novel) 145
Nicholson, Jack 350, 357
The Night of the Devils (1972 film) 292–295
Night of the Eagle (1962 film) 259–*262*
Nobel Prize 170
Nosferatu (1922 film) 68–71, 84
The Nutty Professor (1963 film) 61

O'Connor, Una *141*, 143
Ogle, Charles 8
Oldman, Gary 85
Olivier, Laurence 66
The Omen (1976 film) 308
Orlacs Hände (1924 film) 172
Our Town (play) 335
"The Oval Portrait" (poem) 112
"The Overcoat" (story) 302

Paget, Debra 155, 275

Pall Mall Gazette (periodical) 214
Paradise Lost (poem) 16
Paramount Pictures 213
Parsons, Milton 276
Payne, Laurence *34*
Penney, Ralph *198*
The Phantom of the Opera (1925 film) 69, 92–96, *95*, 296
Phantom of the Opera (1943 film) 96–100, *97*, *99*, 102, 169
The Phantom of the Opera (1962 film) 100–102
The Phantom of the Opera (musical) 102
The Phantom of the Opera (novel) 87, 89–92, 171
Philbin, Mary *95*, 96
Picnic (1955 film) 346
The Picture of Dorian Gray (1945 film) 144, 169, 221, 224–227
The Picture of Dorian Gray (novel) 1, 48, 111, 186, 221–224
Pierce, Jack 10
Pikovaya dama (1916 film) 38–40
Pikovaya dama (opera) 42
Pinner, David 333–336, 338
"The Pit and the Pendulum" (story) 166
Pitt, Ingrid 239, 240, *241*
Plutarch's Lives (book) 16
Poe, Edgar Allan 27–29, 31, 105, 109–111, 117, 119, 145–148, 149, 150, 151, 152, 154, 155, 162–163, 164, 165, 166, 167, 271, 274, 296–298, 300, 305, 349
Polanski, Roman 311, 313
Polidori, John 3, 62
The Portrait of a Lady (novel) 251
"The Premature Burial" (story)
Price, Vincent 32, 109, *116*, 117, 118, 151, *153*, 274, *276*, 277, *299*
Pride and Prejudice (1940 film) 58
Psycho (1960 film) 227, 269
"The Purloined Letter" (story) 3, 62
Pushkin, Alexander 1, 36–38, 39, 40, 41, 42

The Queen of Spades (1916 film) 38–40, 305, 306
The Queen of Spades (1949 film) 39, 40–42
"The Queen of Spades" (story) 1, 36–38, 42
Quintana, Elvira *183*

Rains, Claude 96, *97*, *99*, 101, 102, *141*, 143, 144
Rathbone, Basil 54, 155
The Raven (1935 film) 163–*167*, *164*
The Raven (1963 film) 167
"The Raven" (poem) 27, 151, 162–163, 165, 166

Rebecca (book) 264
Rebecca (1940 film) 197, 239
Reed, Oliver **248**
Reeves, Keeanu **86**
Renard, Maurice 169–172, 173, 175
Renoir, Claude 239
Renoir, Jean 239
Revere, Anne 197, **198**
Ripley, Clements 156, 158
Ritual (novel) 333–336, 337, 338, 339
RKO 281
Robbins, Tod 120–122, 123
Robinson, Pete **123**
Roeg, Nicholas 323, 324
Rosemary's Baby (1968 film) 308, 310–313, **312**, 314, 320
Rosemary's Baby (novel) 259, 305–310
Rosito, Angelo **123**
Russell, Gail **211**
Ryder, Winona 85, **86**
Rymer, James Malcolm 62

The Sand Pebbles (1966 film) 283
Sanders, George 226
Sangster, Jimmy 19
Saturday Evening Post (periodical) 186
Schlitz **123**
Schreck, Max 69
Scott, John **211**
The Sea Hawk (1940 film) 257
Sears, Heather 100
Service, Robert W. 162
The Set-Up (1949 film) 162
Shelley, Mary 1, 3–7, 8–10, 12–13, 15–26, 67, 87, 105, 131
Shelley, Percy Bysshe 3, 15
Shephard, Elizabeth **272**
Sherriff, R.C. 143
The Shining (1980 film) 351–354
The Shining (1997 television mini-series) 354
The Shining (novel) 340, 348–350, **353**
Shirley, Anne 189, **190**
Simon, Simone 189, **190**
Sloan, Edward Van 11, 66, 75
Sloane, William 192–196, 197
The Son of Dr. Jekyll (1951 film) 61
Son of Dracula (1943 film) 76
Son of Frankenstein (1939 film) 18, 25, 75
Spacek, Sissy **345**, 346
Spellbound (1945 film) 313
"Spurs" (story) 121–122, 124
Star Trek: The Motion Picture (1979 film) 283
Stensgaard, Yutte 239
The Stepford Wives (1972) 308

Stephens, Martin **253**, 256
Stevenson, Margaret Balfour 43
Stevenson, Robert Louis 1, 43–46, 47–56, 58–61, 87, 105, 214–216, 219, 220
Stevenson, Thomas 43
Stoker, Bram 1, 7, 62–68, 69–73, 75–78, 82–85, 87–88, 105, 234, 235, 273
Stone, Philip 352
The Story of G.I. Joe (1945 film) 244
The Strange Case of Dr. Jekyll and Mr. Hyde (novella) 43–46, 53, 55, 223
Stuart, Gloria 142
Student of Prague (1913 film) 107
Sunrise (1927 film) 68
Sutherland, Donald **325**
Sydow, Max von 329, **330**, 332

Tales of Terror (1962 film) 151–155, **153**, 291
Tamblyn, Russ **285**
Tamerlane and Other Poems (book) 27
Tandy, Jessica **267**
Tarantula (1955 film) 317
Taylor, Rod **267**
Tchaikovsky, Peter Ilyich 42, 98, 99
The Telltale Heart (1928 film) 34
The Tell-Tale Heart (1934 film) 35
The Tell-Tale Heart (1960 film) 32–34
"The Tell-Tale Heart" (story) 27–29, 30–33
Terry, Alice 107
Tey, Josephine 201
Thesiger, Ernst **18**
The Time Machine (novel) 137
"To Helen" (poem) 151
"To One in Paradise" (poem) 31
Toland, Gregg 174
Tolstoy, Aleksei 287–289, 290, 293, 294
Tolstoy, Leo 287
The Tomb of Ligeia (1965 film) **272**
Topper (1937 film) 207
Tracy, Spencer 43, 46, 54, 56, **57**, 61
Transylvania Superstitions" (essay) 63
Treasure Island (novel) 43
Turkel, Joe 352
The Turn of the Screw (novella) 251–253, 254–256
Turner, Lana 54, 55, 56
Twice-Told Tales (1963 film) 291
The Twilight Zone (television series) 36, 201, 261
The Two Faces of Dr. Jekyll (1960 film) 58–60, **59**
2001: A Space Odyssey (1968 film) 350

The Undying Monster (1942 film) 203–205, **204**
Uneasy Freehold (novel) 200–203

The Unforeseen (novel) 207
The Uninvited (1944 film) 207, 209, 210–213, *211*
Universal Studios 8, 10, 16, 18, 20, 21, 25, 26, 31, 76, 77, 88, 96, 97, 108, 120, 132, 151, 155, 163, 169, 182, 206, 235, 244, 246
Unknown Worlds (periodical) 257
Updike, John 259
Urquhart, Robert *20*

Vadim, Annette *238*, 239
The Vampire Lovers (1970 film) 240–242, *241*
"The Vampyre" (story) 3, 62
Varney the Vampire (novel) 62
Veidt, Conrad 172
Viy (1967 film) 305–307
"The Viy" (story) 302–304, 305
Vlad the Impaler 83

Wait Until Dark (1967 film) 135
Walpurgis Night 67, 68
The War of the Worlds (novel) 137
Ware, Irene *167*
Webber, Andrew Lloyd *102*
Wegener, Paul 107, 108
Wells, H.G. 126–129, 131, 133, 135, 136, 337–140, 142

Werewolf of London (1935 film)
The Werewolf of Paris (novel) 244–246
West Side Story (1961 film) 283
Weston, David *299*
Whale, James 13, 24, 108, 133, 142, 143
Wheatley, Dennis 314–316, 317, 318, 335
White Zombie (1932 film) 156
The Wicker Man (1973 film) 333, 336–339, *337*
The Wicker Man (2006 film) 339
Wiene, Robert 172
Wilde, Oscar 1, 48, 111, 221–224
Wilder, Thornton 335
"William Wilson" (story) 147
Wise, Robert 218, 219, 283, 285
The Witches of Eastwick (novel) 259
Witness for the Prosecution (1957 film) 143
Wodehouse, P.G. 121
The Wolf Man (1941 film) 75, 97, 221, 250
Woodward, Edward 339
Woolf, Virginia 251
Wouk, Herman 29
Wray, Fay 161, 352
Wyngarde, Peter 261, *262*

Young Frankenstein (1974 film) 25

www.ingramcontent.com/pod-product-compliance
Ingram Content Group UK Ltd.
Pitfield, Milton Keynes, MK11 3LW, UK
UKHW021843140426
5217IPUK00022B/1565